DRUGS AND
DEMOCRACY IN
LATIN AMERICA

Published in association with the
Washington Office on Latin America (WOLA)

DRUGS AND DEMOCRACY IN LATIN AMERICA

The Impact of U.S. Policy

edited by

Coletta A. Youngers
Eileen Rosin

LYNNE
RIENNER
PUBLISHERS

BOULDER
LONDON

Published in the United States of America in 2005 by
Lynne Rienner Publishers, Inc.
1800 30th Street, Boulder, Colorado 80301
www.rienner.com

and in the United Kingdom by
Lynne Rienner Publishers, Inc.
3 Henrietta Street, Covent Garden, London WC2E 8LU

Library of Congress Cataloging-in-Publication Data
Drugs and democracy in Latin America : the impact of U.S. policy /
Coletta A. Youngers and Eileen Rosin, editors.
  Includes bibliographical references and index.
  ISBN 1-58826-278-2 (hardcover: alk. paper)
  ISBN 1-58826-254-5 (pbk.: alk. paper)
  1. Narcotics, Control of—Latin America—International cooperation. 2. Narcotics, Control
of—Caribbean Area—International cooperation. 3. Narcotics, Control of—United
States—International cooperation. 4. Human rights—Latin America. 5.Human rights
Caribbean Area. I. Youngers, Coletta. II. Rosin, Eileen, 1954–

HV5840.L3D777 2004
363.45'098—dc22   2004014978

British Cataloguing in Publication Data
A Cataloguing in Publication record for this book
is available from the British Library.

Printed and bound in the United States of America

The paper used in this publication meets the requirements
of the American National Standard for Permanence of
Paper for Printed Library Materials Z39.48-1992.

5 4 3 2 1

Contents

Illustrations

Acknowledgments

T his volume is the result of the three-year Drugs, Democracy, and Human Rights Project carried out by the Washington Office on Latin America (WOLA), a nonprofit policy, research, and advocacy organization working to advance democracy, human rights, and social justice in Latin America and the Caribbean. Founded in 1974, WOLA plays a leading role in Washington policy debates about Latin America. WOLA facilitates dialogue among governmental and nongovernmental actors, monitors the impact of policies and programs of governments and international organizations, and promotes alternatives through reporting, education, and advocacy. Since 1989, WOLA has documented and analyzed the impact of U.S. international drug control policy across the region, resulting in numerous publications and conferences and ongoing dialogue with policymakers.

We want to express our deep appreciation to the contributors to this volume, who dedicated their time and energy to this research project. In addition to those listed in the contributors section on page 397, we particularly want to acknowledge the work of Rut Diamint, who carried out the research on the Southern Cone, and Rick Rockwell, who coordinated the research on Central America. Ana Carolina Alpírez also provided significant information on Guatemala. Though not included in this volume, their analyses are fundamental to the project's purpose and conclusions and can be accessed via our website (www.wola.org).

In addition, two WOLA consultants—Sandra Edwards in Ecuador and Kathryn Ledebur in Bolivia—produced regular memos that were released as part of this project. Our colleagues Martin Jelsma and Pien Metaal of the Transnational Institute in Amsterdam guided us through the workings of the United Nations drug control apparatus. Lora Lumpe and Joy Olson provided research and documentation on U.S. police assistance programs vital to our understanding of their role in U.S. international drug policy. One of the chapter contributors, Adam Isacson, deserves special recognition for his unwavering willingness to provide information and to review chapters.

We are grateful for the funding provided by the Open Society Institute, which made this project possible, and the consistent support provided by Aryeh Neier and George Vickers. Additional support was provided by the Ford Foundation, the John Merck Fund, and the General Service Foundation.

The Drugs, Democracy, and Human Rights Project was initiated by former WOLA executive director George Vickers and former deputy and executive director Bill Spencer. Numerous former and present WOLA staff members have also contributed to the project, including: Gina Amantangelo, Rachel Farley, Jason Hagen, Tina Hodges, Gabi Kruks-Wisner, Katie Malouf, Rachel Neild, Eric Olson, Kimberly Stanton, Geoff Thale, and John Walsh. Special merit goes to executive director Joy Olson and associate Laurie Freeman, both of whom dedicated significant time and energy to the production of this volume. WOLA financial manager Nadia Malley helped keep our budget in order. The following WOLA interns also provided assistance: Margaret Hughart, Annise Maguire, Mira Mendoza, Diana Ramírez, Andrea Rogoff, Eleni Wolfe-Roubatis, and Aaron Zeichner.

JoAnn Kawell and Cathy Sunshine provided invaluable assistance in editing and preparing this volume for presentation to the publisher. Book chapters originally in Spanish were translated by Lucien Chauvin. Juan Luis Guillén and Enrique Bossio translated chapters from English into Spanish for publication in Latin America.

We are also grateful to the many individuals who took the time to review and comment on earlier drafts. Among those who deserve mention are: Robert Albro, Jo-Marie Burt, Chuck Call, Roderic Ai Camp, Jim Cason, Gillian Clissold, Jennifer N. Collins, Kevin Healy, Carlos Indacochea, William LeoGrande, Robert Perito, Ted Piccone, John Lindsey-Poland, Ken Sharpe, Michael Shifter, Francisco Thoumi, and Bill Walker. WOLA board members Dick Erstad, Louis Goodman, William LeoGrande, Cynthia McClintock, and Lars Shoultz provided inestimable guidance as well. Initial advice was also given by Carol Bergman, Tom Cardamone, Lisa Haugaard, Amit Pandya, and Sanho Tree. Winifred Tate provided significant guidance to us on Colombia. Jeremy Bigwood provided important documentation through his never-ending quest to obtain official information via Freedom of Information Act requests. The National Security Archive's Peru Documentation Project, headed by Tamara Feinstein, was the source of significant information for the chapter on Peru. Margaret Popkin answered innumerable questions on Latin American legal systems and terminology.

Each chapter author would also like to thank a list of individuals and organizations that contributed to his or her research and writing efforts and/or who gave of their time in interviews. Though they are too numerous to include here, we wish to acknowledge the input of all of those across the region who participated, in some way, in this project.

Finally, we wish to thank Lynne Rienner for having the faith and confidence in WOLA to support the publication of this volume and for her patience with our extended deadlines.

While the views expressed in this volume are those of the authors and the editors alone, the insights provided by the colleagues referred to above greatly strengthened the chapters presented here. The editors and the Washington Office on Latin America are responsible for the content of the introduction and conclusion (Chapters 1 and 10, respectively).

This volume is the culmination of many years of research and analysis on U.S. international drug control policy. The most important acknowledgment of our work will come from increased public and policymaker debate on drug policy issues and, ultimately, a shift toward alternative policies that are both more effective and more humane.

C.A.Y.
E.R.

DRUGS AND
DEMOCRACY IN
LATIN AMERICA

1

The U.S. "War on Drugs":
Its Impact in Latin America
and the Caribbean

Coletta A. Youngers and Eileen Rosin

T he extensive illicit drug trade and U.S. policies designed to reduce it have stimulated significant academic research both in the United States and elsewhere in the Western Hemisphere. Much of that literature concurs that these policies have failed to realize their objectives to reduce significantly the production and availability of illicit drugs. There is also much research on the impact of drug production and consumption as well as on drug control policies themselves. This volume, in contrast, is about a relatively little-researched topic: the collateral damage of the U.S. "war on drugs." It is the first systematic study of U.S. drug policy that identifies key policy components and analyzes policy impacts and tendencies regionwide.

The project examined what the war on drugs means for institutions and policy arenas central to the future of democracy and human rights, including the military, the police, and the judicial and legal systems. Our report begins with two detailed studies, on U.S. military and police counterdrug assistance programs, that together provide a comprehensive picture of U.S. international drug control policy. It then presents six case studies, covering five countries considered central to international drug control efforts—Bolivia, Colombia, Ecuador, Mexico, and Peru—as well as the Caribbean, considered by the United States to be a key transit zone for illicit drugs. (Not all parts of Latin America have felt the impacts of U.S. drug control policy as directly as the countries covered in the case studies. Consequently, although Central America and the Southern Cone were part of our larger investigation, they are not included in this volume.[1]) The results of the study clearly show the very real costs of what has become an unwinnable war. We hope it will serve to make the drug war's collateral damage a significant part of the debate on drug policy in both the United States and Latin America.

• The U.S. "War on Drugs"

In the mid-1980s, the explosion of crack cocaine and its related violence in the United States set in motion many of the hard-line U.S. drug control

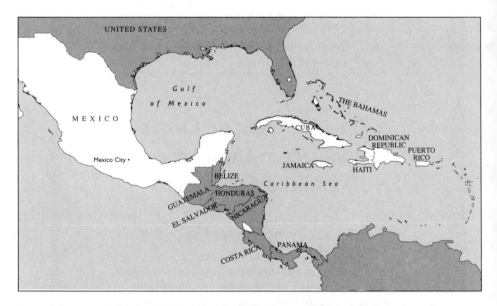

policies still in effect today. In 1986, President Ronald Reagan first declared illicit drugs a national security threat. Three years later, President George H. W. Bush launched the Andean Initiative as part of his strategy for an intensified drug war. Within the United States, rigid legislation, enhanced law enforcement, and elevated rates of incarceration are the government's preferred tools against the manufacture, dealing, and consumption of illicit drugs. Overseas, U.S. policy has sought to reduce the supply of drugs—especially cocaine and heroin—by curbing drug production in the so-called source countries and by seizing shipments en route. Latin America and the Caribbean are the primary theaters for these efforts.

The source-country approach has focused primarily on the coca leaf, a traditional crop among Andean peasant communities that is also used to make cocaine, and to a lesser extent on the opium poppy used for heroin production as well as on marijuana. The presumption is that reducing supply will make the illicit drug trade more dangerous and costly. This in turn is assumed to drive down production, drive up prices, and ultimately discourage U.S. citizens from buying and using illicit drugs.

This reasoning continues to dictate policy today. The U.S. State Department's *International Narcotics Control Strategy Report* for 2003 sets forth the rationale:

> Our international counternarcotics programs target the first three links of the grower-to-user chain: cultivation, processing, and transit. The closer we can attack to the source, the greater the likelihood of halting the flow of drugs altogether. Crop control is by far the most cost-effective means of cutting supply. If we destroy crops or force them to remain unharvested, no drugs will enter the system.[2]

The centerpiece of the Andean Initiative was to empower Latin American military and police forces to carry out counterdrug initiatives, and significant U.S. training and support was provided to those forces willing to collaborate. With the end of the Cold War at the end of the 1980s, and with Central America's internal conflicts winding down, the Andean region quickly replaced Central America as the primary recipient of U.S. security assistance. At the same time, the U.S. Congress designated the Defense Department as the "single lead agency" for the detection and monitoring of illicit drug shipments into the United States. Congress backed its directive with dollars, providing millions for U.S. troops and for aid to local security forces. For those on the front lines—primarily in the Andean countries of Bolivia, Colombia, and Peru—the metaphorical "war on drugs" became all too real a battlefield.

The narrow focus of U.S. efforts has promoted what is widely referred to among those knowledgeable about the region as "militarization." This refers to the expanding role of both Latin American and U.S. military forces in counterdrug efforts, to the training of civilian police forces in military operations and strategies, and to the trend for U.S. military and police assistance to take priority over aid for socioeconomic goals or democratic institutions. It also characterizes the way in which the U.S. government has seen the drug problem through the lens of national security policy. Drugs are seen as a threat to the United States coming from outside its borders, an enemy against which a war must be waged. In contrast, many governments in the region focus on the structural roots of the problem in social and economic realities. They point to the voracious demand for drugs in the United States and Europe as motivating the drug trade. The industry to supply this demand, they note, has found room to flourish in their countries because of extreme poverty and because of the inability of weak civilian institutions to solve societal problems.

Standard drug war terminology makes use of a powerful metaphor. As a guide to policy, however, it is fraught with problems. The presumed "enemy" is not an organized army that can be identified and defeated but rather a set of social and economic forces that sustain the trade. The drug war mentality ensures that U.S. drug control resources are skewed toward interdiction and law enforcement efforts. But such policies, which fail to take into account the complex social and economic roots of both illicit drug production and consumption, tend to shift the pattern of players in the drug trade without significantly reducing the trade itself.

In fact, since the Andean Initiative was launched in 1989, the global and regional scope of the drug trade has expanded significantly. Notably,

---

Terminology Used in This Volume

- We have tried to avoid using the phrase "drug war" except when referring specifically to those policies and actions that are characterized by the "drug war" approach to drug control.
- The frequently heard term "counternarcotics" is not precise: cocaine is not technically a narcotic drug, nor are marijuana, ecstasy, methamphetamines, or many of the other drugs that are targets of drug control efforts. "Counterdrug" and "antidrug" are more appropriate terms.
- The term "security forces" refers in this chapter to both military and police bodies. When referring to armies, navies, and air forces but excluding police, this study employs the terms "military" or "armed forces." Likewise, "security assistance" is shorthand for "military and police assistance."

the distinction between producer and consumer countries has blurred. When the United States first declared illicit drugs to be a national security threat, drug production was based almost exclusively in what were considered to be source regions—Latin America for cocaine, Asia for heroin. Drug consumers were largely found in Western countries, primarily the United States. Now, both production and consumption of illicit drugs take place across the globe. Marijuana, once imported from Latin America, now also flourishes at production sites in the United States, and methamphetamine laboratories have turned up all over the country. As cocaine is smuggled out of countries like Peru, ecstasy produced in the Netherlands is smuggled in. Illicit drug consumption, once highly uncommon in most Latin American and Caribbean countries, has increased exponentially across the region. Cocaine use has exploded in Brazil, Argentina, and Chile since the late 1990s, particularly among young people.[3]

As a result of the so-called war on drugs, U.S. military and police aid to Latin America has risen significantly to rival economic and social aid (Figure 1.1).[4] Yet the effectiveness of the military and police aid is unproven, and its negative consequences are largely unexamined.

U.S. government funding for economic development is still substantial, and some funding is also provided for democracy-building initiatives such as judicial reform and the strengthening of civil society. While socioeconomic and democracy-building efforts are referenced throughout the text—and often put forward as potential alternatives—it is beyond the scope of this study to undertake a thorough evaluation of the impact of such programs to date. Moreover, the positive effects of such programs may well be undermined by the unexamined consequences of U.S. military and police assistance. This study focuses on that collateral damage, exposing the urgent need for greater public debate and congressional oversight of these security assistance programs.

• Fundamental Flaws in the Supply-Side Approach

A significant gap exists in U.S. drug control programs between expansive goals and limited achievements. U.S. officials routinely assert that international counterdrug programs are successful. Short-term tactical successes are indeed evident—coca crops are eradicated, traffickers are arrested, and shipments are intercepted. Nonetheless, total coca production has remained remarkably steady (Figure 1.2). There is no evidence demonstrating a significant reduction in the supply of illicit drugs on U.S. city streets. To the contrary, the stability of price and purity levels of drugs points to their continued accessibility. Winning the drug war is as elusive today as it was when the effort was first launched.

The drug trade, it seems, is more like a balloon than a battlefield. When one part of a balloon is squeezed, its contents are displaced to anoth-

Figure 1.1   U.S. Aid to Latin America and the Caribbean, 1997–2005

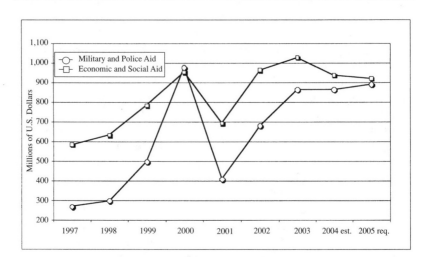

Source: U.S. State Department, *International Narcotics Control Strategy Report*, various years. Adapted by Adam Isacson for the Washington Office on Latin America (WOLA).

Note: This chart represents U.S. aid for Argentina, the Bahamas, Belize, Bolivia, Brazil, Chile, Colombia, Costa Rica, the Dominican Republic, the Eastern Caribbean (Antigua and Barbuda, Barbados, Dominica, Grenada, St. Kitts and Nevis, St. Lucia, St. Vincent, and the Grenadines), Ecuador, El Salvador, Guatemala, Guyana, Haiti, Honduras, Jamaica, Mexico, Nicaragua, Panama, Paraguay, Peru, Suriname, Trinidad and Tobago, Uruguay, and Venezuela, plus regional programs. The figures do not include the Bush administration's HIV/AIDS initiative, begun in 2004, which has yet to allocate aid by country. Some data for some years are not available; actual amounts may be significantly higher.

er. Similarly, when coca production is suppressed in one area, it quickly pops up somewhere else, disregarding national borders. Arrested drug lords are quickly replaced by others who move up the ranks; dismantled cartels are replaced by smaller, leaner operations that are harder to detect and deter. When drug-trafficking routes are disrupted by intensive interdiction campaigns, they are simply shifted elsewhere.[5]

Andean coca cultivation, as depicted by the State Department's own annual estimates, is remarkable for its stability at around 200,000 hectares per year. While the division among coca-producing countries has fluctuated, the total land area under cultivation each year has not varied dramatically.[6] Moreover, according to U.S. government statistics, the average yield of coca leaves per hectare has risen over time, so that even apparent declines in cultivated land area may not translate into less coca available for processing into cocaine.[7]

In announcing the U.S. government figures for 2003 coca production,

Figure 1.2   Coca Cultivation in the Andes, 1988–2003

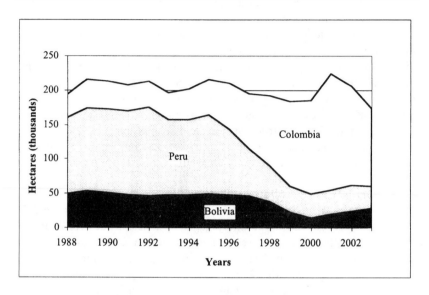

Source: U.S. State Department, *International Narcotics Control Strategy Report 2003*, "Policy and Program Developments," table, pp. 22–23.

U.S. officials all but declared victory. A sharp drop in Andean region coca cultivation, from 223,700 hectares in 2001 to 173,450 hectares in 2003, was attributed to a significant reduction of Colombia's coca crop and a smaller reduction in Peru.⁸ While U.S. officials took the drop as a sign of success, the reduction represents only a 5 percent decrease, if measured from 1999 instead of the 2001 high point.[9] And evidence is already mounting of a shift in coca production within Colombia to new areas, as farmers flee massive fumigation campaigns. Furthermore, recent experience in Bolivia shows that such successes can be short-lived. In 2000, the Bolivian government announced that it had reached its goal of "zero coca." Since then, however, widespread replanting of coca in new areas has led to new increases in production. For 2003, the U.S. State Department reported a 17 percent increase in Bolivian coca cultivation to more than 18,000 hectares, with production shifting from the Chapare to the Yungas region.[10]

A similar phenomenon happens with arrests of traffickers. Removing one set of international drug dealers has often simply cleared the way for rivals and new entrants to the drug trade, rather than reducing the size of the drug market. Smashing the large Mexican and Colombian cartels led to the formation of groups that are smaller and harder to detect. Larger and more frequent drug seizures, often offered as evidence of policy success, are in fact inherently ambiguous indicators. They may instead reflect increased drug production and trafficking, as traffickers seek to compensate for their anticipated losses.

The U.S. strategy focuses on wiping out drugs at their source or seizing them in transit. The objective, however, is to decrease their availability in the United States by causing drug prices to rise and thus discouraging some percentage of potential buyers. Official U.S. figures, however, show that cocaine's retail price dropped fairly steadily during the 1980s and early 1990s. The price never rebounded, even as purity rose and then stabilized. The same patterns hold true for heroin. The low and stable prices for cocaine and heroin that have prevailed since that time show that, despite U.S. efforts, the supply of drugs continues to be robust.

• The Drug Trade's Collateral Damage

The research presented in this volume reflects the awareness that the drug trade itself has produced profoundly negative consequences for countries across the Western Hemisphere. Increased drug abuse is just one of the harms caused by the drug trade—in Latin America and the Caribbean, international drug trafficking breeds criminality and exacerbates political violence, greatly increasing problems of citizen security and tearing at the social fabric of communities and neighborhoods. It has corrupted and further weakened local governments, judiciaries, and police forces. The cocaine production process can be extremely damaging to local environments, polluting rivers and streams and depleting soils.

In short, the physical and moral damage to individuals, communities, and societies from the illicit drug trade is creating new challenges for local governments already struggling to overcome endemic poverty and injustice. Likewise, as the world's largest consumer of illicit drugs, the United States also confronts a multitude of problems stemming from illicit drug abuse and related violence. In both cases—Latin America as well as the United States—drug abuse puts increasing demands on government resources, requiring increased expenditures on police, courts, treatment and education programs, and public health programs.

The vast quantities of money generated by the drug trade can have a devastating impact as well. Drug trafficking–related corruption has influenced the actions of politicians across the political spectrum. The drug trade undermines efforts to reform and improve the efficacy of police forces and the justice system. It fuels political violence, as so vividly illustrated in the case of Colombia, where both left-wing insurgents and right-wing paramilitary groups thrive on the funds provided by the illicit drug trade. The large profit margin created by the illegal nature of the enterprise also allows traffickers to amass significant weapons and firepower. In some cases, they are better armed and have more sophisticated technology than local police forces.

In sum, illicit drug production, trafficking, and consumption are taking an immense toll on the people and governments of the hemisphere. Controlling these illegal activities is imperative for the social, economic, and political well-being of all. However, the U.S. model of international drug control policy implemented over the last fifteen years has had little, if any, success against the drug trade. Instead, it has added a new layer of widespread and serious negative consequences.

• The Drug War's Collateral Damage

The impact of U.S. drug control policy on human rights, civil liberties, and democratic practices in the United States has generated significant collateral damage, and many of the problems documented throughout this study are just as relevant and real in the United States as abroad. Some policies—such as mandatory minimum sentencing—were first implemented in the United States and then incorporated into Latin American drug control despite the concerns raised in the United States regarding fairness and due process.[11]

This volume, however, provides a thorough examination of the drug war's collateral damage in Latin America and the Caribbean. Careful research is particularly needed because distinguishing between the damage caused by the drug trade and that caused by the policies designed to confront the trade can be difficult, and the identification of direct causality is often elusive. Because Latin American and Caribbean countries have long histories of military rule, weak democratic processes and institutions, and great inequalities in the distribution of wealth and power, drug policy may seem to be just one more factor affecting efforts across the region to consolidate and deepen democratic processes.

Each of the countries studied has its unique character and history, and the implementation and impacts on the ground of U.S. drug control policies vary widely from one to the other. In order to allow for cross-country comparisons and to address the causality issue, researchers in each case study were asked to follow similar guidelines and to look at a common set of themes. The following were the principal issues explored in the research presented in this volume:

Civil-military relations and the role of the military. The role of the military forces in the drug war is analyzed with attention to changes in military missions. In particular, researchers considered whether the military's role has expanded in the areas of public order and/or domestic law enforcement functions; the existence and efficacy of mechanisms for military accountability for human rights violations, corruption, and crimes committed in the context of counterdrug operations; the nature of civil-military relations; and whether civilian control and oversight over military forces have been enhanced or weakened as a result of drug control policies.

The role of local police forces. The role of police forces is explored with a focus on the appropriateness of the counterdrug roles assigned and the U.S. training and assistance provided; how relations with both the military and civilian government institutions are affected by drug control efforts; the potential tradeoff between short-term tactical gains and long-term institutional reforms; and whether or not mechanisms for effective civilian oversight, transparency, and accountability have been put in place.

Human rights. The fundamental questions here are if forces with poor human rights records have received U.S. assistance prior to having gone through meaningful reform; whether or not human rights violations have occurred directly or indirectly as a result of U.S.-backed drug control activities; and if such cases do exist, whether those responsible have been held accountable. Another question is the extent to which current drug control policies foster social conflict, political instability, and violence, particularly in regions where forced coca eradication policies are being carried out.

The rule of law and civil liberties. Sweeping antidrug laws, largely modeled after U.S. legislation, are now in force in almost every country studied. The researchers looked into whether this legislation complies with internationally accepted due process standards. They also investigated whether sentences in drug-related cases are commensurate with the gravity of the crime committed and whether defendants are provided adequate legal defense. In general, they have tried to determine whether civil liberties and the right to a fair trial are respected in drug trafficking–related cases. A related question is whether or not drug control policies are carried out in accordance with the country's constitution.

Civilian oversight, transparency, and accountability. The case studies explore the extent to which there is legislative oversight of drug policy, how local drug policies are formulated and who participates in that process, the extent of public debate, access to relevant information, and the ability of civil society organizations to monitor and evaluate counterdrug policies.

Fostering democratic processes. Researchers also considered the common complaint heard across the region: that U.S. drug policy is imposed by Washington, using either the "carrot" or the "stick," with little consideration for socioeconomic and political impacts, and that local policymakers have had limited room to try their own alternative approaches to policy or program design. The weight given to multilateral processes is also examined.

Finally, special attention is paid to the complex and often explosive dynamics in coca-growing regions where forced eradication, or in the case of Colombia, aerial spraying, is being carried out. These are the areas where a "militarized" approach can be most dangerous, pitting local security forces against the local population and creating a high potential for violence and human rights abuses. These are also the areas where the strategy may be targeting the wrong population, as the impact of coercive drug control efforts falls disproportionately on poor, subsistence-level farmers.

Because coca cultivation for the illicit drug industry is far more extensive than opium poppy production, coca and cocaine play a much greater role in the study than do poppies and heroin or marijuana. The U.S. policy approach varies depending on the country—marijuana eradication, for example, is important in Jamaica and Mexico—but in general, U.S. drug control policy places greater emphasis on stemming coca and cocaine production.

• Access to Information and Fostering Public Debate

The ability of citizens and civil society organizations to monitor and to evaluate U.S. programs abroad is fundamental for democratic governance. Effective oversight is needed to ensure the proper use of taxpayer dollars as well as effective implementation of U.S. foreign policy objectives. Security assistance programs—including those related to counterdrug efforts—are inherently risky. "They involve strengthening institutions that have a monopoly of legitimate violence over states with rule of law deficiencies and histories of social conflict," notes one researcher. "Citizens, the media and Congress must have access to the information necessary to judge whether a particular military aid effort is congruent with standards of human rights and good governance."[12]

The experience of this study shows both the potential and the difficulties in gaining such information. On the U.S. policy side, we were able to build on an earlier research project—*Just the Facts*—jointly carried out by the Latin America Working Group (LAWG) and the Center for International Policy (CIP). Frustrated by the gaps in their own understanding of U.S. military programs, these two organizations sought to gather all of the publicly available information on U.S. military programs in the Western Hemisphere. While most congressional and other analysts have considered only military assistance programs supervised by the State Department, the LAWG and CIP also studied Defense Department programs, including those related to drug control. Soliciting information on these programs through congressional channels, they constructed a database "that offers the most comprehensive information publicly available on U.S. defense and security assistance programs in Latin America and the Caribbean: arms transfers and sales, training programs, bases, exercises, and the laws that govern them."[13]

Additional research was needed to obtain the same level of information on U.S. police assistance programs. Washington Office on Latin America (WOLA) staff filed various Freedom of Information Act requests with the Drug Enforcement Administration (DEA), the Federal Bureau of Investigation (FBI), and other agencies providing police assistance, and information was sought through congressional offices monitoring overseas drug control programs. Some valuable information was gained; for example, we now have a "mapping" of DEA assistance and its presence in the region, described in Chapter 3, that was previously unavailable. Yet it is still true that the U.S. government does not make sufficient data available to allow for a comprehensive picture of the multiple police assistance programs currently in place.

Researchers found it particularly difficult to obtain information from U.S. embassies on the details of local drug control operations. While U.S.-based researchers are usually provided access to the appropriate embassy officials, requests by our locally based researchers for interviews or information were routinely routed instead to the public affairs office, where they received only limited information already available on the Internet.

Despite the progress made through the *Just the Facts* project, gaining access to current information about U.S. military programs remains difficult and requires continual pressure from Congress and nongovernmental organizations. The Defense Department considers much congressionally mandated reporting to be burdensome. In 2002, Congress dropped the requirement that the Defense Department report publicly on its drug control spending. Information on certain kinds of training—such as that provided by U.S. Special Forces—is now most often classified.

The results of this study show significant collateral damage from current drug control policies. Across the hemisphere, those most directly affected—civil society groups, community organizations, local governments, and common citizens—should be encouraged to participate in debate on these policies and how they could be made more effective and less harmful. This requires greater access to information and transparency in U.S. drug control policy. The information and analysis presented in the following chapters is intended to help foster such transparency as well as to contribute to this much-needed debate.

• Notes

WOLA associate Laurie Freeman contributed to the writing of this chapter.

1. Please see the website of the Washington Office on Latin America (WOLA), www.wola.org, for additional materials on the Southern Cone and Central America.

2. U.S. State Department, Bureau for International Narcotics Control and Law Enforcement (INL), *International Narcotics Control Strategy Report (INCSR) 2003*, "Policy and Program Developments," March 2004. The INCSR for all years can be accessed from www.state.gov/g/inl/rls/nrcrpt/.

3. GTZ, *Drugs and Poverty: The Contribution of Development-Oriented Drug Control to Poverty Reduction*, a cooperative study of the Drugs and Development Programme (ADE) and the Poverty Reduction Project of GTZ (Deutsche Gesellschaft für Technische Zusammenarbeit), June 2003, p. 10.

4. Please see the WOLA website (www.wola.org) for the data for this and all other charts or graphs in this volume.

5. Numerous sources discuss these phenomena, among them: Eva Bertram et al., *Drug War Politics: The Price of Denial* (Berkeley: University of California Press, 1996); Bruce M. Bagley and William O. Walker III, eds., *Drug Trafficking in the Americas* (Coral Gables, Fla.: University of Miami, North-South Center; New Brunswick, N.J.: Distributed by Transaction Publishers, 1994); UN Development Programme, Colombia, *El Conflicto, Callejón con Salida*, Human Development Report for Colombia, 2003 (Bogota: September 2003), especially chapter 13.

6. It is worth noting that the surveillance methods for estimating illicit crop production do not necessarily produce accurate statistics, and disputes often arise as to crop production levels. In general, while drug policy statistics may be useful for comparative purposes, they should be viewed with some skepticism. See WOLA's website for more information.

7. *INCSR 2001*, "South America."

8. Center for International Policy, "The State Department's data on drug crop cultivation," memo, 22 March 2004, p. 3.

9. See *INCSR 1999*.

10. *INCSR 2003,* "South America."

11. See, for example, Human Rights Watch, *United States—Punishment and Prejudice: Racial Disparities in the War on Drugs,* report, May 2000; and The Sentencing Project, *Drug Policy and the Criminal Justice System* (Washington, D.C.: 2001).

12. Communication from Adam Isacson, Center for International Policy, 10 November 2003.

13. Please see *Just the Facts* on the Center for International Policy website, www.ciponline.org/facts/.

2

The U.S. Military in the War on Drugs

Adam Isacson

F ew dispute that the United States has a troubled history of relations with the Western Hemisphere's armed forces. Examples abound of support for military dictatorships, training of personnel in abusive techniques, and relationships forged with unsavory or criminal officers.

While the most dramatic of these examples took place during the Cold War's darkest days, some of the same patterns in U.S.–Latin American military relations continue today. U.S. policymakers continue to see the region more as a source of potential threats than as a zone with potential for greater cooperation, sustained democratization, and shared prosperity. The search for threats leads Washington to turn to the region's militaries to solve problems such as violence, insecurity, drug trafficking, and other criminality, even though these problems have complex social and economic causes. U.S. aid and doctrine then encourage militaries to increase their internal roles, with negative consequences for human rights and political space, civil-military relations, democracy, and regional security.

The Cold War drew to a close about 1990, ushering in a period of peace and reform that brought hope for a break with these patterns. But that break never came. Instead, the "war on drugs" quickly filled the vacuum. Military aid levels were maintained and even increased, though often this was done through new funding channels.

By militarizing its war on drugs, Washington intensified some of the worst aspects of its Cold War approach to Latin America. Fighting drug trafficking provided a new rationale for military operations against an "internal enemy," and counterdrug aid came with little incentive for institutional reform. This has hampered promising efforts throughout the region to consolidate democracy, improve civil-military relations, move toward cooperative security, and end impunity for corrupt or abusive security force personnel.

Overemphasizing the drug war's military dimension has caused the United States to repeat another Cold War error. U.S. policy is once again neglecting the historical and structural factors—poverty and inequality, corruption and impunity, the lack of basic citizen security guarantees—that foster perceived threats to U.S. interests. This all-stick-and-no-carrot approach has too often blinded U.S. policymakers to the political realities their allies face. A notable example was the George W. Bush administration's failure to respond to Bolivian president Gonzalo Sánchez de Lozada's pleas in 2003 for economic support in the face of growing opposition fueled by that country's continuing economic crisis. This approach has also had the unintended consequence of building a power base for populist leaders and movements that have made opposition to U.S. policy a key focus of their rallying cries—as did the movement that overturned President Sánchez.

The drug war has also aggravated some disturbing distortions in the U.S. foreign policy making process. With the antidrug budget spread across a bewildering array of agencies and programs, the desire to maintain operating funds and influence within the executive branch becomes a strong motivation for many officials. Bureaucratic inertia prevents badly needed reforms to a strategy that has failed, whether measured in illicit crop acreage or in prices for illegal drugs.

Antidrug assistance programs have also contributed to a broader militarization of U.S. foreign policy decisionmaking. Congress has given the Defense Department control over significant amounts of counterdrug military and police aid, while the Pentagon has increased its interactions with regional counterparts during a period of budget cuts and retrenchment for the diplomatic corps. The result is more than just a bureaucratic adjustment. It increases the likelihood that military and security priorities will take precedence in the formation of U.S. policies toward the region.

Today, as the "war on drugs" merges with a new open-ended "war on terror," we face the depressing likelihood that Washington will repeat many mistakes of the past.

• Before the Drug War

Unlike the militaries of North America and Europe, nearly all Latin American and Caribbean armed forces have historically been oriented more toward internal "enemies" than toward external threats. Prolonged conflicts between states have been remarkably rare. In the region with the world's worst income disparities, most violence has occurred within, not across, borders.

The region's armies have nonetheless proven mostly inept at fighting the many guerrilla movements that have arisen over the years. For "success" against guerrillas, they have had to depend on large-scale U.S. assistance or horrific "dirty wars"—or, too often, both. Military force has been frighteningly effective, however, against those seeking reform through nonviolent means, such as trade unionists, land reform advocates, whistleblowers who denounce corruption, human rights defenders, independent journalists, and opposition political figures. The resulting closure of political space has hampered the development of transparent, participatory democracies and worsened divisions in already polarized societies. Militarization—that is, overinvolvement of the armed forces in aspects of governance other than external defense—has been an all-too-frequent phenomenon.

The United States has strengthened these tendencies through transfers of weapons and equipment, training in lethal skills, intelligence sharing, joint exercises, and a whole gamut of "engagement" activities in which nontraditional military roles are encouraged. Many of the region's armed forces in fact owe their very existence to U.S. government sponsorship of security structures and constabularies in the decades before World War II.

During the Cold War, billions of dollars from Washington allowed militaries throughout the Western Hemisphere to balloon in size. U.S. advisers encouraged their Latin counterparts to adopt counterinsurgency doctrines, which emphasized irregular military and paramilitary operations alongside the general population—from combat to military-led development efforts—to weaken and root out a perceived communist threat. In promoting its National Security Doctrine,[1] the United States reinforced the inclination of military leaders to see their main enemy as within the civilian population. The tragic consequences are well known: coups, military dictatorships, death squads, and disappearances between the 1950s and the 1980s.

The Legal Framework

During the same period, Congress set up procedures intended to monitor U.S. military aid and place restrictions on its use. The Foreign Assistance Act of 1961 (FAA) put most Defense Department spending on foreign military aid under the supervision of the State Department (see Appendix 1). The FAA also gave Congress greater ability to place limits on military assistance by making such assistance part of the annual budget authorization and appropriations process. Current law, for instance, prohibits aid to governments that came to power through military coups, commit gross and consistent human rights violations, support international terrorism, or are "controlled by the international communist conspiracy."[2] Foreign aid law also requires significant transparency with regard to military assistance. The FAA and annual foreign aid appropriations bills require the executive branch to submit public documents every year on everything from arms sales to trainees to the use of private contractors in Colombia.

After the Vietnam War and revelations of U.S.-sponsored military coups in Latin America and elsewhere, Congress added broad restrictions designed to prevent U.S. assistance from strengthening abusive security forces. Two of the best-known mid-1970s restrictions are Section 502B of the FAA, which sought to ban aid to abusive militaries, and Section 660, which banned all aid to foreign police forces. However, over the years both vague definitions (such as "gross" violations of human rights) and numerous exceptions to the law (such as allowing police training for drug control activities) have been used to mask the lack of political will to enforce the restrictions. These practices have rendered the 1970s reforms virtually toothless.

Programs

For most of the Cold War years, the U.S. government funded foreign military assistance chiefly under two or three aid programs authorized by the FAA and a corollary law governing U.S. State Department–managed foreign aid and sales, the Arms Export Control Act of 1968. The Military Assistance Program (MAP) provided the bulk of aid for decades. In 1976, Congress separated out military training by funding it through a new program, International Military Education and Training (IMET). MAP then consisted of grants of cash and weapons until it was phased out in the late 1980s. Subsequently, more weapons transfers were channeled through the Foreign Military Financing (FMF) program, which funds transfers of equipment, services, and some training for foreign governments.

MAP, IMET, and FMF—all part of the annual foreign aid budget—made up the vast bulk of Washington's Cold War military transfers, including the Ronald Reagan administration's large military outlays for Central America in the 1980s. They also paid the "tuition" of nearly all students attending the U.S. Army's controversial School of the Americas in Panama (moved to Fort Benning, Georgia, in 1984). Much other Cold War counterinsurgency training was the work of U.S. military training teams, including the Army Special Forces (Green Berets), who fanned out through the region in the 1960s in the wake of the Cuban revolution to help local militaries stem further rebel outbreaks. Between 1980 and 1991, MAP and FMF contributed more than U.S.$2 billion to the Western Hemisphere's security forces; IMET added another U.S.$110 million.[3]

Agencies

The State Department historically served as the principal agency for U.S. involvement in drug control overseas. But the Justice Department and the Defense Department also had early roles that later served as the basis for growing involvement as the war on drugs gained momentum.

The State Department's Bureau for International Narcotics Matters (INM), founded in 1979 and now known as the Bureau for International Narcotics and Law Enforcement Affairs (INL), was small and marginal during most of the Cold War; an assignment to this so-called drugs-and-thugs section was generally not sought after. Counterdrug aid programs began during the 1970s, but during the Cold War they were dwarfed by counterinsurgency security assistance.

The main drug control program, International Narcotics Control (INC), was managed by the INM. The INC program provided U.S.$500 million to the region between 1980 and 1991, with U.S.$340 million of it during the last five years of that period (1987–1991). A significant portion of these monies (between one-fourth and one-half) supported crop substitution, judicial/prosecutorial functions, and other nonmilitary efforts.[4] In comparison, El Salvador's counterinsurgency effort received U.S.$192 million in one year alone (1984) from nondrug military aid channels.[5]

The Drug Enforcement Administration (DEA), housed in the Justice Department, was also involved at this stage. It was created in 1973 under the administration of President Richard Nixon, who coined the term "war on drugs" during the 1968 presidential campaign. During most of the 1970s its focus was overwhelmingly domestic. Nevertheless, intelligence sharing and joint operations with law enforcement agencies, mostly police, increased in many countries where illicit drugs were produced or transshipped (see Appendix 1 and Chapter 3, this volume).

Congress chose not to lump counterdrug military and police aid together with standard aid programs, instead creating a "firewall" to ensure that recipient militaries would not divert counterdrug aid toward other missions. Thus the State Department's INL bureau produces annual end-use monitoring reports to make certain that INC-provided aid is being used for its intended purpose. As a result of this distinction, some legal conditions applied to military aid under FMF and IMET—such as mandatory cutoffs for countries decertified for failure to combat drugs, or for countries that fail to exempt U.S. military personnel from International Criminal Court jurisdiction—do not affect the flow of INC aid.

Military aid during the Cold War period was ultimately overseen by the State Department. In coordination with the White House's National Security Council, the State Department provided policy guidance and, with input from the Pentagon, determined annual aid requests submitted to Congress. Much of this guidance came from the department's Bureau for Inter-American Affairs (now known as the Bureau for Western Hemisphere Affairs). Ambassadors and senior diplomats often had significant influence over the day-to-day management of the military assistance programs. This arrangement remains largely in place today. The Defense Department, however, in part because of drug war arrangements, has measurably increased its ability to act autonomously.

Even in the previous period, the Pentagon had much latitude in the design and operation of military aid programs. A regional command structure incorporating all the armed services coalesced after World War II and was solidified with the 1986 passage of defense reform legislation. U.S.

Southern Command (Southcom), which has most of Latin America and the Caribbean as its area of responsibility, is currently one of five powerful regional commands coordinating U.S. military activities throughout the world.[6] Southcom became a central actor and an important presence in the constellation of bureaucracies carrying out U.S. foreign policy in Latin America during the Cold War.

Southcom is the smallest of the military commands, but its staff of about 1,100 makes it a significant presence in regional affairs. According to journalist Dana Priest, "More people work there dealing with Latin American matters than at the departments of State, Commerce, Treasury and Agriculture, the Pentagon's Joint Staff, and the office of the secretary of defense combined."[7] The command draws upon a significant operating budget and posts military personnel in every country. Some of these personnel operate at U.S. bases in the region (Cuba, Honduras, Puerto Rico, Panama until 1999). Both in the Cold War period and today, Southcom has been the most significant U.S. agency in the regional military-to-military relationship.

Nominally managed by the secretary of defense, the Joint Chiefs of Staff, and the deputy assistant secretary of defense for Western Hemisphere affairs, Southcom enjoys a high degree of autonomy and responsibility for the development of military assistance policies. Its chief role is to guard against possible threats to U.S. national security. When such threats are not imminent, as has largely been the case in Latin America, the command seeks to "shape the security environment" by cultivating contacts and developing relationships and channels of communication with officers of all of the region's friendly militaries.

Based in Quarry Heights, Panama, until a 1999 move to Miami, Southcom has been responsible for U.S. security and military operations in all of the Western Hemisphere except Mexico and Cuba. Southcom incorporates units from all branches of the armed services (Army, Navy, Air Force, Marines), with a separate subcommand for Special Operations Forces. It manages military advisory and assistance groups, known as Milgroups, in U.S. embassies throughout the region. Some of the Milgroups also maintain offices within host-country defense ministries. The Milgroups, generally consisting of four to six persons, are charged with carrying out aid programs and arms sales. They also choose students for U.S. military training, encourage their counterparts to buy U.S. weapons, and organize military exercises, among other duties.

Many of the Defense Department's requests for specific military aid initiatives originate with Southcom, which usually develops them after close consultation with recipient-country defense and military leaders. Because of its presumed awareness of potential threats and its relationship with the region's militaries, Southcom often gets its way in internal debates over security and foreign policy toward the region.

Another key set of agencies carrying out Cold War policy, of course, were those of the intelligence community—the Central Intelligence Agency (CIA), the Defense Intelligence Agency (DIA), and the National Security Agency (NSA) in particular. The DIA maintains defense attaché offices in U.S. embassies (not to be confused with Milgroups) to gather information, and the NSA listens in on signals communications. The Cold War exploits of the CIA in Latin America are well known and need not be repeated here. The agency—certainly a key channel for military assistance, though information about the amount of this aid has not been made public—acted with very little accountability to Congress until the 1970s. In that decade revelations of failed assassination attempts in Cuba, as well as support for coups in Chile and Guatemala (among others), forced legislators to institute reforms. There has been somewhat more oversight of the intelligence community since then, though most has occurred in secret, closed-door sessions of the congressional intelligence oversight committees.

End of the Cold War

In the wake of the controversial U.S. involvement in Vietnam, the Cold War consensus favoring unfettered military assistance to developing countries began to fall apart. The pro–human rights policy of the Jimmy Carter administration (1977–1981), the mid-1970s reforms to the FAA, and the worldwide emergence of nongovernmental human rights organizations all helped increase awareness about the moral consequences—and long-term risks to U.S. interests—of aiding abusive foreign militaries. The debate during Ronald Reagan's administration (1981–1989) about sponsorship of wars in Central America was emotional and bitter and left its own legacy of skepticism about U.S. military involvement overseas.

The late 1980s and early 1990s saw a post–Cold War period of democratic opening in Latin America and the Caribbean, with an accompanying decline in the number of threats U.S. policymakers perceived in the region. Successful peace processes were concluded in Central America. In Colombia, there were settlements with the M-19 and smaller guerrilla groups, though not with the Revolutionary Armed Forces of Colombia (FARC). Transitions from dictatorship to elected rule—if not full-fledged democracy—occurred nearly everywhere.

Fledgling democracies made tentative assertions of civilian control. They appointed civilian defense ministers, moved police forces outside military command structures, and even attempted to roll back military impunity and budget autonomy. With neither external nor internal threats to justify large security forces, many of the region's militaries began to shrink. As political space began to open for nonviolent reformers, several countries witnessed an unprecedented emergence of "civil society." Analysts and activists seeking a replacement for the old National Security Doctrine promoted the notion of "human security," that is, employing the state's resources to guarantee the satisfaction of basic human needs.[8]

The collapse of the Soviet bloc left few compelling missions or pretexts to justify either large militaries in the region or large military aid programs in Washington. The U.S. government, which had spent the better part of a century cultivating close and costly military-to-military relationships, was faced with a stark choice: Southcom, and other U.S. bureaucracies responsible for security in Latin America, would have to adapt by finding new justifications for current budget levels—or undergo a deep reduction in size and influence.

• The Militarization of Drug Control

A new mission began to reveal itself even as the Cold War was drawing to a close. During the second half of the 1980s—as crack cocaine appeared, with devastating consequences for depressed U.S. urban areas—Reagan administration officials revived the phrase "war on drugs." Illicit drugs were presented as the new primary threat to U.S. national security.

That approach quickly gained bipartisan support. "It's time to declare an all-out war, to mobilize our forces—public and private, national and local—in a total coordinated assault upon this menace which is draining our economy of some two hundred and thirty billion dollars," House Speaker Jim Wright (D-Texas) declared.[9] In 1986 and 1988, Congress passed bipartisan legislation to toughen U.S. drug policy both domestically and overseas. The legislation also required the U.S. government to "certify" foreign countries' cooperation in antidrug efforts. Governments that failed to meet these certification standards faced sanctions that included a cutoff of most forms of U.S. aid and trade benefits and, within multilateral lending institutions, an automatic "no" vote by the influential U.S. representative on loan requests from the offending nation. The certification process— a unilateral mechanism emphasizing punishment for noncompliance with U.S. expectations—has understandably been unpopular in a region highly sensitive to bullying by the power to the north.

The late-1980s drug war legislation brought moderate increases in antidrug military and police assistance to Latin America. In 1987, State Department INC funds for the hemisphere's security forces surpassed U.S.$30 million for the first time. Most of this amount supported police forces' efforts to interdict drug shipments and to seek the arrest of kingpins masterminding the illegal trade.[10]

The Andean Strategy

It was Reagan's successor, George H. W. Bush (1989–1993), who pushed through the first major increase in counterdrug foreign military assistance. This was in 1989, arguably the year in which Colombia's Medellín drug cartel was at the apex of its power. President Bush and William Bennett, the first "drug czar," developed the so-called Andean strategy, a policy shift that focused on cocaine production in the coca source countries of Colombia, Peru, and Bolivia.

The center of this strategy was the Andean Initiative—a five-year package of aid, the majority for the security forces of Colombia, Peru, and Bolivia—which the administration designed and moved through Congress in 1989. The Andean Initiative's intention was to front-load military and police aid. The plan was that such aid would be the largest part of the regional package in 1990 and 1991, then would slip to less than half of the total in 1992–1994, as levels of cocaine production presumably decreased and alternative-development efforts took root. In 1990, Andean Initiative funds totaled U.S.$231.6 million, of which all but U.S.$48.6 million were military and police assistance. The administration's intention was to increase the share of economic aid, so that by 1992 it would be U.S.$283.9 million out of a total of U.S.$497.7 million.[11] This did not happen, however. Cocaine production failed to decrease. Moreover, Bill Clinton's administration, which took office in January 1993, did not continue its predecessor's plans. During its first term, the Clinton administration in fact allowed a moderate decrease in both military and economic aid.

Most military aid through the Andean Initiative was channeled through Foreign Military Financing (FMF). This program had been used heavily in Central America only a few years before but was declining everywhere except the Andes by the early 1990s. Including FMF, military and police assistance for Colombia jumped from U.S.$18 million in 1989 to U.S.$93 million in 1990. That year, Colombia surpassed El Salvador, with U.S.$81 million, as the Western Hemisphere's number-one regional recipient of security assistance—a position it has maintained to this day.[12]

In addition to FMF, the small INC program was also growing. With increases to the Andes and to the Caribbean, INC assistance hemisphere-wide jumped to U.S.$72 million in 1990 from U.S.$55 million the year before. By 1991, the regional total rose to U.S.$88 million.[13]

Within the context of the Andean strategy, U.S. officials encouraged Latin American armies to fight drugs by taking on internal roles that would be unthinkable for the U.S. military at home. With U.S. training, equipment, and diplomatic backing, Latin American militaries on counterdrug missions began to mount roadblocks, perform internal surveillance (including wiretaps), execute searches and seizures, force down suspicious aircraft, eradicate crops (or support police eradication efforts), patrol rivers, and, in some cases, arrest and interrogate civilians. Currently, Bolivian military personnel participate in the 1,600-member Joint Task Force cutting down coca in the Chapare and Yungas regions.[14] The Dominican navy and Jamaican Defense Force patrol territorial waters, pursuing and boarding suspicious vessels, while the Peruvian navy does the same on rivers.[15] Mexico's military has led efforts to arrest drug kingpins. Ecuador's army monitors civilians' movements near its northern border. Across the border in Colombia, a U.S.-created army counterdrug battalion stages roadblocks and clears areas for herbicide fumigation.

For the most part, the region's states were initially reluctant to increase the military's internal counterdrug role, especially at a time of tentative democratic reform. Civilian leaders viewed drugs as a law enforcement problem, not a security threat. Some, particularly activists in civil society, argued that the root of the problem lay in the failure to reduce U.S. addicts' demand for illegal substances. In 1990, the ambassadors of all three Andean countries "asked the United States not to provide this level of military assistance"; they instead called for greater access to U.S. markets in order to provide economic alternatives.[16]

For their part, the region's armed forces did not adopt the new mission with great enthusiasm. While the drug war offered a means to sustain budgets and military-to-military contacts with the United States, few saw any possibility of a quick victory (however defined), much less the promise of medals or rapid promotions as rewards for successes. Many also feared the extreme temptation that traffickers' bribes would present to low-paid officers and soldiers.

Nonetheless, Washington throughout the late 1980s and 1990s encouraged Latin American and Caribbean nations to militarize their counterdrug efforts. Much of this encouragement was in the form of economic incentives, since fighting drugs meant more military assistance through the Andean Initiative and new Defense Department programs. But there was also heavy public diplomatic pressure. The demands to meet targets for the annual certification process, and critical language appearing in official U.S. reports, encouraged countries to increase the military's internal role in order to be seen as cooperating with the United States.

Even in countries without significant drug production or transit problems, U.S. diplomats pressed for increases in military involvement. For example, in countries such as Argentina and Chile, a key message that U.S. diplomats and Milgroup personnel transmitted in meetings with host-country officials was the need to increase the military's drug interdiction role.[17]

Police forces, U.S. officials often argued, were too corrupt and inefficient or too underfunded and overwhelmed to take on wealthy, well-organized drug-trafficking organizations. Another reason given was the convenience of military ties. The mid-1970s ban on police assistance (Section 660 of the FAA) left U.S. security assistance personnel with few contacts or relationships with police counterparts, while military-to-military relations remained close after years of Cold War programs. Officials also argued that the military was the only institution capable of policing remote zones where drugs most frequently transit. According to Southcom chief General James Hill:

> In Chile, only the military has the assets to protect Chilean borders and land in northern Chile from drug trafficking. In Paraguay, only the military can counteract the continuous violations of Paraguayan airspace as drugs enter and exit the country. In Brazil, only the military can prevent the country's rivers from becoming highways for precursor chemicals and go-fast boats.[18]

Though aid often goes to military units with other, nondrug responsibilities, it has also been common to encourage the creation of specialized counterdrug units that become the U.S. military's principal partners in each country. The budgets for the "Devils" task forces in Bolivia, the Air-Mobile Special Forces Groups in Mexico, and the Colombian army's counterdrug brigades, for example, have relied almost completely on funds from Washington. Such units have worked—often awkwardly—in support of police forces. In a number of countries, the United States also helped to create counterdrug units within the police (see Table 2.1).

U.S. Agencies and Drug Control

While redefining drugs as a national security threat increased outlays to many Latin American security forces, it also led Washington to beef up counterdrug agencies with foreign policy responsibilities, both civilian and military. Within the State Department, drug control gained much higher prominence in Washington and within U.S. embassies in target countries. In addition, U.S. defense and intelligence agencies assumed vastly greater

Table 2.1   Examples of Counterdrug Military and Police Units Created with U.S. Support

Military	Police
• Bolivia: Army Green Devils and Black Devils Task Forces; Navy Blue Devils Task Force; Air Force Red Devils Task Force • Colombia: First Army Counternarcotics Brigade; Navy Riverine Brigade • Mexico: Air-Mobile Special Forces Groups (GAFEs); Amphibious Special Forces Groups (GANFEs)	• Bolivia: Special Drug Police Force • Colombia: Anti-Narcotics Division (DIRAN) • Dominican Republic: National Directorate for Drug Control (DNCD) • Ecuador: National Anti-Narcotics Directorate (DNA) • Guatemala: Department of Anti-Narcotics Operations (DOAN), now Antinarcotic Analysis and Information Service (SAIA) • Jamaica: Constabulary Force Narcotics Division • Paraguay: Anti-Narcotics Secretariat (SENAD) • Peru: Peruvian National Police Narcotics Directorate (Dinandro)

counterdrug roles, at a time when they were facing declining post–Cold War budgets and uncertainty about their future missions.

State Department International Narcotics Control. Bill Clinton's first presidential term (1993–1997) saw a steady post–Cold War decrease in total military and economic aid to Latin America and the Caribbean. The decline would have been much steeper if not for the sharp rise in counterdrug assistance through the State Department's INC program. This began in Clinton's first term and accelerated at dizzying speed during his second term.

In contrast, economic and social aid has not recovered Cold War levels. Largely because of aid to Colombia, total military and police assistance to the hemisphere exceeded economic and social aid in 2000. In 2003 and 2004, the regional totals for military and police were nearly equal to the totals for economic and social programs. This is a new phenomenon; even at the height of the Cold War, economic aid far exceeded military aid.

The INC program's worldwide budget grew from U.S.$113 million in 1990 to U.S.$517 million in 1999. It benefited not only from the political prominence of the drug war but also from the aggressive leadership and bureaucratic persistence of long-serving assistant secretaries of state for INL such as Robert Gelbard (1993–1997) and Rand Beers (1998–2002).[19] INC aid also had particularly strong support from the White House after the 1996 appointment of General Barry McCaffrey, a former commander of Southcom, as drug czar—head of the president's Office of National Drug Control Policy. The program's budget also had support from key leaders of the Republican majority in both houses of Congress after the 1994 elections.

The growth in budget and bureaucratic prominence helped make the INL Narcotics Affairs Sections (NAS) at U.S. embassies quite powerful organizations throughout the region. The trend was reinforced by a mid-1990s shift in emphasis from interdiction to crop eradication, the two main forms of overseas drug supply reduction. Interdiction requires deployment of U.S. assets at bases and in international waters, and close cooperation with security forces, to find drug production facilities and to stop shipments of drugs by air, land, sea, and rivers. Crop eradication—which U.S. officials argue is easier because the crops themselves are out in the open and do not move—involves the forcible (or, rarely, voluntary) destruction of crops either by security forces on the ground or, in the case of Colombia, by aerial fumigation.

The shift was formalized in late 1993, when President Clinton signed Presidential Decision Directive (PDD) 14. This directive specified that while interdiction would be the goal of the U.S. military's own operations, the majority of assistance to the region's security forces would go toward eradication. This "source zone" strategy resulted in a leveling-off of aid to most countries where drugs are smuggled but not produced. For the main drug-producing countries, however, it led to sharp increases. These included Bolivia, Peru, and especially Colombia, where cooperation between several U.S. agencies and the Colombian police had brought the death or arrest of most major cartel leaders by the mid-1990s.

INL funds and supports police and military units in Peru and Bolivia that carry out forcible eradication of coca and poppy crops. These missions usually involve security forces personnel, ferried in on U.S.-supplied planes, helicopters, or vehicles, invading coca fields and uprooting the plants manually.

In Colombia, home to roughly two-thirds of South American coca and three armed groups that depend on drug revenue, U.S. officials decided that security considerations would not allow them to follow the Peru-Bolivia manual eradication model. In 1994, the scandal-weakened government of Ernesto Samper was persuaded to allow the INL to expand its aerial herbicide spraying to eradicate coca and poppy in Colombia. Fumigation grew rapidly from 5,600 hectares sprayed in 1996 to 127,000 hectares in 2003.

Colombia is the only country in the Americas that allows aerial spraying of herbicides. In Peru and Bolivia it is still prohibited because of social and environmental concerns. Though affected populations have issued thousands of complaints of indiscriminate spraying, health and environmental damage, and destruction of alternative-development projects, the spraying continues to expand in Colombia.[20]

Because of the unrest they often inspire, campaigns have depended on U.S.-funded military units to keep order in coca-growing zones. The results of placing the military in such a direct, adversarial relationship with the civilian population have often been disastrous. Abuses have been frequent, and institutional damage has been compounded by the impunity that members of the U.S.-funded units enjoy.

The rise in counterdrug military aid to Latin America, a region with a troubled human rights history, soon provoked concern among activists and key members of Congress. In 1996, Congress added an amendment to the 1997 foreign aid appropriations bill intended to control the risks of financing an ambitious new role for the military. This measure, known as the Leahy Amendment after its chief sponsor, Senator Patrick Leahy (D-Vermont), prohibited INC aid to any foreign military or police unit that included members credibly alleged to have committed gross human rights violations with impunity. The Leahy Amendment has appeared in appropriations bills for every subsequent year. After 1998 it was broadened to include not only INC but also all other security assistance programs financed by the FAA.

The Leahy Amendment has been used occasionally to cut off assistance to particular brigades of the Colombian army and air force. In general, however, the State Department has not aggressively enforced the Leahy Amendment in the region. The United States has not even used the threat of aid cutoffs, for instance, in response to repeated naming by nongovernmental organizations of military units in Mexico and Bolivia whose members have violated human rights with impunity. The quality of databases that U.S. embassies maintain to review the backgrounds of potential aid recipients varies greatly across the region. Leaving the definition of "unit" up to the State Department has kept the Leahy Amendment from being applied to training; individual trainees themselves are considered units, with the result that "clean" individuals routinely receive U.S. training and return to abusive brigades or battalions.

The Pentagon's role as lead agency. While the INC program came to dominate military aid to the hemisphere funded through the FAA, the drug war brought even more sweeping change for the U.S. military in Latin America. Counterdrug activities became Southcom's main mission during the 1990s. With the Cold War's end, and with its 1999 exit from the Panama Canal Zone looming, the regional military command had no other threats to justify its activities. Put simply, Southcom needed more reason to exist than defending the canal from hypothetical invaders, preparing for natural disasters, fending off waves of migrants, building schools and bridges, and engaging partner militaries. In the words of former Southcom commander-in-chief General Maxwell Thurman, the drug war was "the only war we've got."[21]

The radical mission switch quickly acquired a firm legal basis. In 1988, Congress added a new section to title 10, the portion of the U.S. Code governing defense and the military. Section 124 made the Pentagon the "single lead agency" for detecting and monitoring illegal drugs transiting to the United States by air or sea. Under this authority, the Defense Department may use its enormous budget to pay for such drug interdiction operations as radar sites, surveillance flights, naval and Coast Guard maritime patrols, and intelligence gathering throughout Latin America and the Caribbean. Section 124 also authorizes the presence of U.S. military personnel on counterdrug missions in the region.

Southcom's early missions as it assumed this lead agency designation included Operation Blast Furnace in Bolivia in 1986 as well as operations Coronet Oak and Coronet Nighthawk, based in Panama, which sought to interdict suspected drug-smuggling aircraft. Operation Green Clover and its successor, Operation Laser Strike, coordinated U.S. efforts to interdict drugs being shipped by air, river, or sea. Operation Centra Spike helped, through signals intercepts, to locate fugitive Medellín drug boss Pablo Escobar.[22]

By the 1990s, the drug war had become the principal mission of

Southcom personnel stationed at bases in Panama and Puerto Rico and, to a slightly lesser extent, those in Cuba (Guantánamo) and Honduras. A Relocatable Over-the-Horizon Radar (ROTHR) system in Puerto Rico, in coordination with seven radars in Colombia and Peru, watched the skies for suspicious flights, aided by regular flights of radar-equipped planes. Joint Inter-Agency Task Force (JIATF) East, a facility in Key West, Florida, coordinates and processes the information gathered by radars, flights, and signals intercepts. It shares information with U.S. aircraft based in the region, primarily at counterdrug forward operating locations (FOLs). These FOLs (recently renamed cooperative security locations, or CSLs), shown in Figure 2.1, are located in Ecuador (Manta), El Salvador (Comalapa), and Aruba and Curaçao (Hato and Reina Beatrix international airports) and are used to visually identify suspicious flights. Finally, information is passed to host-country air forces or navies (or U.S. vessels with a foreign shiprider aboard), which attempt to interdict suspected traffickers or force them to land.

The FOLs—the newest long-term U.S. military presence in the region—were developed after the 1999 closure of U.S. bases in the Panama Canal Zone. The United States reached a ten-year agreement with Ecuador for the use of Manta in November 1999. The site, focused on the southern

Figure 2.1   Forward Operating Locations/Cooperative Security Locations

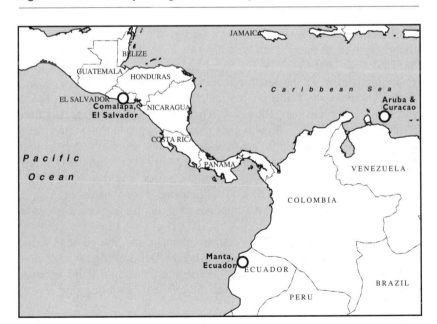

Colombia source zone, is operated by the Defense Department, primarily the U.S. Air Force. A ten-year agreement with the Netherlands for Aruba and Curaçao was signed in 2000. The Curaçao site is operated by the Defense Department, primarily the Air Force, while the Customs Service operates Aruba. Both sites focus on northern South America and the Caribbean. The same year, the U.S. also reached a ten-year agreement with El Salvador for the Comalapa facility. The U.S. Navy operates this site with a focus on eastern Pacific maritime trafficking routes. The Defense Department spent U.S.$137 million on improvements to these airfields, nearly half of that at Manta alone. The Netherlands Antilles and Ecuador sites were fully functional by late 2002 and the Salvador site by late 2003.[23]

The ten-year agreements governing the FOLs provide unrestricted airfield access twenty-four hours a day—but only to U.S. aircraft on counterdrug detection and monitoring operations. Each FOL normally hosts from a few dozen U.S. personnel to a few hundred at peak periods. These include pilots, controllers, maintenance workers, and support personnel from the U.S. Air Force, Navy, Coast Guard, Customs, intelligence agencies, and private contractors. Opposition political leaders and civil society groups have expressed concerns about violations of sovereignty and about the possibility that their countries will be dragged into U.S. counterterror campaigns. However, the facilities have yet to establish a record for good or ill, as they have just barely come online. In fact, many of Southcom's most valuable aircraft have been moved out of the region to take part in Middle Eastern missions.

Southcom seeks to stop the flow of drugs at sea using radar and overflights, as well as naval and Coast Guard patrols. In international waters, the U.S. Navy and Coast Guard board and search vessels believed to be smuggling drugs. In the territorial waters of countries that have signed bilateral agreements, Southcom has only limited authority to pursue, board, and search suspected smuggling craft. These bilateral agreements vary from restrictive arrangements allowing hot pursuit only to shiprider agreements that permit U.S. personnel to board and search in territorial waters as long as a representative of the host-nation security forces is aboard the U.S. vessel. Shiprider agreements raise sovereignty issues, and they have been a source of domestic political friction. In Ecuador, owners of fishing vessels have taken legal action against Southcom, charging frequent harassment by counterdrug maritime patrols.

In the Andes, Southcom is also involved in the source-zone aerial interdiction operation known as the Airbridge Denial Program (or, more colloquially, the "shootdown policy"), aimed at breaking the link between Bolivian and Peruvian coca fields and the criminal-run processing centers

El Salvador's FOL: Expanded Military-to-Military Contact

In 2000, the Salvadoran government signed a ten-year agreement with the United States for the establishment of a forward operating location (FOL) at the existing Comalapa airbase. With the Manta and Aruba/Curaçao FOLs in progress, the U.S. still needed one to monitor flights over the Eastern Pacific. When extensive negotiations with Costa Rica failed, the United States turned to its longtime ally, El Salvador. Agreement was quickly reached, and El Salvador's Legislative Assembly ratified it four months later, in July 2000.

Approval of the FOL did not escape debate in El Salvador. During the war years of the 1980s, the Salvadoran military had been extensively involved in domestic civilian affairs. A key component of the Salvadoran peace accord signed in 1992 was the explicit removal of the military from civilian policing functions. Legislative Assembly members from the Frente Farabundo Martí para la Liberación Nacional (FMLN), the political party of the former guerrilla groups, opposed ratification on a number of grounds, including that it violated the peace accord, placed foreign troops in El Salvador, and violated the law governing the National Civilian Police. The FMLN's challenge to the treaty was rejected in the courts.

The establishment of the FOL also opened the possibility for increased engagement between U.S. and Salvadoran forces. As General Charles Wilhelm, then commander-in-chief of Southern Command, stated to the Salvadoran chief of staff, General Álvaro Antonio Calderón Hurtado: "We realize, in a diplomatic sense, this plan is for counterdrug only. As a practical matter, all of us know this agreement will give us a superb opportunity to increase the contact with all our armed forces in a variety of ways. ... I hope to further exploit this opportunity to provide modest support to you and your modernization efforts."*

Increased engagement did indeed take place. In 2001, the U.S. provided military training to 1,082 Salvadorans, ranking El Salvador second in forces trained that year, outpaced only by Colombia.**

* Dana Priest, *The Mission: Waging War and Keeping Peace with America's Military* (New York: W.W. Norton & Co., 2003), p. 206.
** See the Center for International Policy website, *Just the Facts*, "Foreign Military Training Report," www.ciponline.org/facts/fmtr.htm.

of Colombia. It was begun in 1994 after a period of internal debate about how shooting down civilian aircraft could be reconciled with international law. A May 1994 State Department internal memorandum expressed concern that "a shootdown leading to the death of innocent persons would likely be a serious diplomatic embarrassment for the United States, [and] subject the [U.S. government] to intense criticism before the International Civil Aviation Organization."[24] Indeed, the program, which involved an awkward mix of agencies and contractors, was suspended in Peru after the Peruvian air force, acting on U.S. intelligence, accidentally shot down a small plane carrying a family of U.S. missionaries in April 2001, killing a mother and her baby daughter.

Efforts to reinstate the program have been slowed by delays in establishing new procedures and training personnel, as well as by an ongoing debate within the executive branch about the program's effectiveness. During the years the shootdown policy was in effect, the total illicit-crop area for all of South America continued to grow as new plantings increased exponentially in Colombia. Meanwhile, traffickers easily adapted by shifting to river and maritime routes. Nonetheless, in August 2003 Defense Secretary Donald Rumsfeld announced the Airbridge Denial Program's reinstatement in Colombia. As of mid-2004, the program remained suspended in Peru.

Southcom has nowhere near the capacity to cover the entire airspace and sea between drug-producing areas and the U.S. border. The command readily admits, "Our detection, monitoring and tracking assets are only sufficient to cover 15 percent of the area, 15 percent of the time."[25] The situation worsens whenever the U.S. military shifts resources to another overseas commitment (Kosovo, Afghanistan, Iraq), as Southcom ends up losing its radar-equipped planes and other sophisticated assets to these higher-priority missions.[26]

Given these constraints, Southcom has chosen to focus its maritime interdiction efforts on periodic "surge" operations—concentrating assets in a specific zone for a fixed period of time—often in cooperation with regional navies that usually sail U.S.-provided vessels. Less frequently, Southcom collaborates with DEA and INL on joint eradication efforts, such as periodic campaigns to cut down marijuana in Jamaica and the Bahamas.

Southcom does not directly participate in drug eradication in Peru, Bolivia, and Colombia. U.S. troops are neither cutting down coca nor flying spray planes. It is the State Department's INL bureau that has chief responsibility for the eradication program's day-to-day operation, in cooperation with local forces. Eradication nonetheless depends heavily on Southcom support. The regional command has trained the military units responsible for guaranteeing the security of spray operations in Colombia, trained specialized units responsible for protecting and carrying out manual eradication in Peru and Bolivia, and participated in gathering intelligence for targeting crops to be eradicated.

A new regional military command, Northern Command, was formed after the September 11 terrorist attacks. Headquartered at Peterson Air Force Base in Colorado and responsible for the continental United States, Alaska, and immediate neighbors like Mexico, Canada, the Bahamas, and Cuba, Northcom is likely to play a significant antidrug role in the near future. What that role will look like, however—and how it will differ from Southcom's existing programs—remains to be established.

The Pentagon's lead agency role has also had an impact at home. While Section 124 specified that the Defense Department was to play its counterdrug role principally overseas, other legal provisions passed in the late 1980s and early 1990s increased the U.S. armed forces' domestic antidrug role as well. The military was authorized to carry out operations against drug transit on U.S. soil within twenty-five miles of borders with Mexico and Canada. This policy was questioned after U.S. Marines, part of the Joint Task Force 6 unit that has patrolled within the United States since 1989, killed a goat farmer in Redford, Texas, in 1997. Nevertheless, it continues in force today. Since 1991, U.S. troops have also provided training and other assistance to state and municipal police forces engaged in drug control activities.

The recent history of the United States includes few precedents for involving the military in an internal law enforcement mission. An 1878 law, the Posse Comitatus Act, prohibits the use of the armed forces in crime fighting and most other internal roles, particularly searches, seizures, and arrests. Episodic internal security roles in emergencies, such as natural disasters, riots, or the September 11 attacks, are considered to be exceptional. The rationale for this general prohibition is that the purpose of a military in nearly every successful democracy is limited to defense against violent threats to the state requiring the use of overwhelming force. Unless they are organized as an opposition army, a nation's own citizens never meet this definition and thus should not be subject to arrest or interrogation by soldiers. Because the military's unique training leads it to a bias in favor of using force, few democracies regularly call on it to play other roles—from building roads to meting out justice—that are more appropriate for civilians.

For this reason, many analysts view the U.S. military's expanded domestic drug war powers as a dangerous erosion of the Posse Comitatus principle—an erosion that has accelerated as the "war on terror" increases pressure to expand the military's internal role. "There comes a time when we've got to reexamine the old laws of the 1800s in light of this extraordinary series of challenges that we're faced with today," Senator John Warner (R-Virginia), the chairman of the Senate Armed Services Committee, said in late 2001.[27] Senator Joseph Biden (D-Delaware), the ranking minority member of the Senate Foreign Relations Committee, called in mid-2002 for greater military ability to carry out arrests, arguing that Posse Comitatus should be reexamined and "has to be amended." General Ralph Eberhardt, the commander of the new Northern Command, added: "We should always be reviewing things like Posse Comitatus and other laws if we think it ties our hands in protecting the American people."[28]

Counterdrug Military Aid

The complex pattern of U.S. military aid to Latin America includes aid under the counterdrug rubric and under other programs; aid administered by the State Department and by the Pentagon; and training as well as arms transfers and budgetary support. The largest programs are INC within the State Department and Section 1004, an obscure provision of the National Defense Authorization Act. With these programs in the lead, regional military and police aid has increased to levels as high as those seen at the height of the Cold War, adjusted for inflation. By the late 1990s, counterdrug programs accounted for more than 92 percent of all military and police assistance to the hemisphere (see Table 2.2). In 2000, even without the Plan Colombia aid package that multiplied it sixfold, the INC program provided U.S.$117 million in police and military aid to Latin America and the Caribbean.[29]

In contrast, the non-drug-related military aid programs that provided

Table 2.2   U.S. Military and Police Aid to Latin America and the Caribbean, 1997–2002

Program	Level of aid (millions of U.S. dollars)
Counterdrug Programs	More than 2,737 (92%)
International Narcotics Control	More than 1,769
Section 1004 (Defense Dept. Counternarcotics)	Approx. 705
Emergency Drawdowns	192
Section 1003 (Defense Dept. Counternarcotics)	61
Discretionary Funds from ONDCP	10
Nondrug Programs	More than 230 (8%)
Excess Defense Articles (EDA)	73
Foreign Military Financing (FMF)	71
International Military Education and Training (IMET)	62
Antiterrorism Assistance (ATA)	25
JCETs, exercises, intelligence agencies, etc.	Unknown

Source: Data compiled by Adam Isacson from numerous government reports, especially the Departments of State and Defense. See www.ciponline.org/facts/country.htm for a complete list of sources.

so much aid during the Cold War atrophied throughout the 1990s. The Foreign Military Financing program provided less than U.S.$4 million in 2000; the IMET program funded less than U.S.$10 million in nondrug training.[30] The symbol of Cold War military aid—the U.S. Army School of the Americas—accounted for only 652 of the 13,785 Latin American military and police personnel who received U.S. training in 1999. Even among those, twenty-six were in the school's counterdrug course.[31] These nondrug programs—as well as a robust exercise program and dozens of Joint Combined Exchange Training (JCET) deployments each year—served mainly to maintain close military-to-military relationships.

In all drug source zone countries, which have experienced a sharp rise in military assistance since the early 1990s, military aid has tended to arrive more expeditiously than has economic aid. The creation of new military and police units, the delivery of helicopters, and the expansion of eradication usually begin almost as soon as new aid is approved and become full-scale programs within a year or two.

Too often, though, economic and social aid has languished as bureaucracies and contractors take their time in allocating funds and responsibilities. The case of Colombia is illustrative. Since Plan Colombia's passage in 2000, more than U.S.$1.97 billion in military and police assistance has been delivered, and the planned expansion of aerial fumigation is nearly complete. Yet a great deal of alternative development funds remains unspent. As the House Appropriations Committee noted, more than half of the money appropriated two years earlier for judicial reform programs was still awaiting disbursement in September 2002.[32]

Defense Department counterdrug funding (Sections 1004 and 1033). Since the adoption of title 10, Section 124 of the U.S. Code in 1988, annual defense budget legislation has included a counterdrug line item, which reached U.S.$881.9 million in 2003.[33] The Defense Department's deputy assistant secretary for counternarcotics manages these funds through the counterdrug Central Transfer Account, which funds the U.S. military units (chiefly those under Southcom) and most private contractors on drug control missions. Since 1991 most of these funds have been administered as Section 1004 assistance.

Congressional and citizen oversight of this account has been difficult. While much of what it pays for is classified, it is also tiny in comparison to the entire defense budget—accounting for less than 25 cents of every $100 the Pentagon spends. (By comparison, the State Department–managed International Narcotics Control account makes up nearly $6 of every $100 in the annual foreign assistance budget.) Congressional oversight committees have surprisingly small staffs—the House Armed Services Committee, for instance, has a staff of forty-five people from both parties, including administrative staff, overseeing a U.S.$400 billion annual budget—and are unable to subject Defense Department counterdrug activities to much scrutiny.[34] Even the little transparency that currently exists has come under assault from the office of Defense Secretary Donald Rumsfeld, who has placed a priority on reducing the number of annual reports the Pentagon must provide to Congress.[35]

Section 124 does not allow U.S. military personnel to accompany host-nation forces on counterdrug operations or to "intentionally expose themselves to situations where hostilities are imminent." It does allow pursuit and boarding of vessels in international waters, close monitoring of air traffic in the region, and deployment of troops at bases (including the bases of host-country militaries) to gather and share intelligence.

It was not clear at first whether being charged with detecting and monitoring illicit drugs gave the Defense Department the right to use its budget to aid other countries' security forces for this purpose without the involvement of the State Department. Some in the defense establishment, however, viewed the Pentagon's new authority as justification for a parallel foreign aid program, outside the constraints of the Foreign Assistance Act. With almost no debate, Congress in 1990 clarified this ambiguity. The Defense Department was granted a limited ability to give out its own non-FAA military and police aid for counternarcotics. Section 1004, mentioned above, specified several types of assistance that could be paid for out of the Pentagon's Central Transfer Account (see Table 2.3).[36]

Section 1004 does not allow the Pentagon to give away weapons or most types of equipment; these transfers still must occur within the authority of the FAA. But its provisions do allow for extensive training of foreign security forces. It specifically allows U.S. military personnel to train foreign police forces, despite the dramatically different skill sets that distinguish police work from military missions. Congress did not include Section

---

Table 2.3   Types of Assistance Authorized by Section 1004

- Maintenance, repair, and upgrading of loaned Defense Department equipment
- Maintenance, repair, and upgrading of other equipment
- Transportation of personnel, supplies, and equipment within or outside the United States
- Establishment and operation of bases of operation or training facilities within or outside the United States
- Counterdrug training of law enforcement personnel, both foreign and domestic
- Detection and monitoring of drugs-related traffic coming into the United States
- Construction of roads and fences and installation of lighting to block drug smuggling across U.S. borders
- Establishment of command, control, communication, and computer networks for improved integration of law enforcement, active military, and National Guard activities
- Linguistics and intelligence
- Aerial and ground reconnaissance

1004 within permanent U.S. law; the provision was initially set to expire in 1995. However, it has repeatedly been renewed and currently extends through 2006.

Since 1997, Section 1004 aid to Latin America has grown significantly, and it is now one of the largest sources of military and police assistance to Latin America and the Caribbean. In 1997, Section 1004 aid totaled U.S.$142.8 million regionwide; by 2001, that had grown to U.S.$271.4 million (see Table 2.4). In 2003, Colombia alone was estimated to have received U.S.$136 million.[37]

Section 1004 funding is administered by the deputy assistant secretary of defense for counternarcotics and managed on the ground by Southcom. Within each U.S. embassy, however, the Narcotics Affairs Section, run by the State Department's INL bureau, takes the lead in coordinating expenditures. Thus at country level, INC and Section 1004 money often get intermingled to pay for the same counterdrug initiatives. The resulting overlap of budget authority and responsibilities between the INL and Southcom is a source of much programmatic inefficiency and bureaucratic turf battles.

At Southcom's behest, Congress approved a second, smaller antidrug military assistance program in the 1998 Defense Authorization Act. Section 1033 of that law established a five-year program to help the navies and police of Colombia and Peru to interdict drugs on rivers. Southcom argued that the program, authorized to provide more equipment than permitted under 1004, was necessary because efforts to stop drug smuggling by air were forcing traffickers to use the Amazon Basin's dense network of rivers, overwhelming local naval and police capacities.

The program became law despite questions, particularly from House

Table 2.4   Section 1004 Aid: Top Ten Recipients and Regional Total, 1997–2001 (thousands of U.S. dollars)

	1997	1998	1999	2000	2001	Totals
1. Colombia	10,321	11,775	35,887	68,710	150,042	276,735
2. Mexico	37,236	20,317	13,591	13,303	18,391	102,838
3. Peru	12,411	14,462	9,443	8,463	7,295	52,074
4. Ecuador	1,980	2,746	7,010	11,245	16,493	39,474
5. Bolivia	4,141	3,285	3,045	6,713	5,450	22,634
6. Venezuela	4,093	6,427	3,333	2,326	2,148	18,327
7. Brazil	2,888	3,436	1,313	534	1,257	9,428
8. Panama	2,384	2,591	638	645	1,054	7,312
9. Bahamas	507	549	608	1,765	1,851	5,280
10. Guatemala	743	869	787	1,087	1,166	4,652
Total Top 10	76,704	66,457	75,655	114,791	205,147	538,754
Other	66,051	66,888	58,450	76,547	66,288	334,224
Regional Total	142,755	133,345	134,105	191,338	271,435	872,978

Armed Services Committee members, about why Southcom sought to fund it through the defense budget and not the FAA. It provided up to U.S.$89 million in boats, equipment, and training to Colombia and Peru between 1998 and 2002, when the provision was set to expire.

Military aid programs rarely die out, however. In this case, the 2004 Defense Authorization bill passed by Congress in mid-2003 reincarnated Section 1033 within the context of the war on terror. The new law removed the word "riverine"—thus making it a catch-all counterdrug assistance program—and expanded the aid to eight countries worldwide, including Bolivia, Colombia, and Ecuador.

The State Department has no control over the Section 1004 or Section 1033 budgets, and because it is not part of the Foreign Assistance Act or annual foreign aid budget legislation, it is not subject to the same congressionally mandated human rights safeguards, reporting requirements, legislative branch scrutiny, or harmonization with larger policy goals. Although a weaker version of the Leahy Amendment has appeared in defense appropriations bills every year since 1999, the practice of channeling assistance flows through the defense budget evades the stronger safeguards that Congress has placed on military assistance since the 1970s. The more that Sections 1004 and 1033 and similar provisions are used as a source of military assistance, the more such legislative protections lose their relevance.

On two occasions, 2001 and 2002, the defense budget authorization law required a report on the amount of Section 1004 assistance that had been provided to every foreign country in the previous year. However, this requirement was dropped from the 2003 law. Thus, with the exception of two years, public reports do not allow for answers even to simple questions about the program such as "How much Section 1004 aid went to Guatemala last year?"

Indeed, so little information is provided about 1004 and 1033 that they are generally excluded from official estimates of assistance to foreign countries. After this author first heard the program mentioned offhandedly in interviews in 1997 with Defense Department and congressional armed services staff, it took months to verify its existence. State Department officials and staff of foreign aid appropriations committees, it turned out, knew little or nothing about what at the time was a six-year-old pot of money used to provide additional military aid.

Arms transfers. Most U.S. transfers of counterdrug weapons and equipment have taken place through the State Department's INC program, though several large items have been transferred through other mechanisms. The Defense Department programs (1004 and 1033) can provide some specific types of equipment, including patrol boats, upgrades, and specialized items but cannot legally transfer such lethal assistance as small arms and ammunition. In addition to grants, the United States sells, or licenses the sale of, more than U.S.$300 million in weapons and equipment to the region each year, sometimes well over that amount. Few sales involve equipment necessary for drug control, however, since grant aid programs already provide sufficiently large amounts.[38]

The most common U.S. strategy has been to help recipient countries create new military and police counterdrug units from scratch. Such units get almost all of their resources from U.S. aid programs, chiefly INC. Units like Colombia's Antinarcotics and Riverine Brigades use U.S.-funded weapons and ammunition, fly U.S.-funded helicopters or sail U.S.-funded boats, and in some cases even wear U.S.-funded uniforms, eat U.S.-funded rations, and sleep in barracks on bases built in part with U.S. funds.

Moving personnel around remote drug production and transit regions has proven to be a constant challenge. Means of transportation thus account for most of the costliest and highest-profile grants of weapons and equipment. Mexico, Peru, and especially Colombia have received the bulk of helicopters (counterdrug programs have provided Colombia eighty-four helicopters since 1999 alone, including twenty-two high-tech UH-60 Blackhawk utility helicopters). Cargo planes, particularly the workhorse C-130, have gone to the three main Andean drug source countries, Bolivia, Colombia, and Peru. Colombia, Mexico, Peru, and Venezuela have also received C-26 planes equipped with surveillance technology.

The United States has also provided numerous small boats for naval and coast guard riverine interdiction programs in Bolivia, Peru, and Colombia, as well as maritime interdiction programs in Central America and the Caribbean. Nearly all drug source and transit countries have received equipment to improve communications, surveillance, and signals intelligence gathering.

During the late 1990s, after several years of post–Cold War military downsizing, the Pentagon had a surfeit of excess or outdated equipment. Previously little-used FAA weapons recycling programs have thus been used to transfer equipment to drug war allies. The Excess Defense Articles (EDA) program (Section 516 of the FAA), for instance, allows the Defense Department to transfer weapons and equipment it has determined that it no longer needs. This has tended to benefit countries at the margins of the drug trade such as Argentina, the Dominican Republic, and Honduras.

Another mechanism that was used heavily from 1996 through 1999, but not more recently, is Section 506 of the FAA, which governs the practice of emergency drawdowns (see Table 2.5). This provision allows the president to transfer equipment and services to foreign countries for an emergency, including up to U.S.$75 million per year for "counternarcotics emergencies." Equipment that is drawn down is not considered excess;

Table 2.5   Drawdowns, 1996–1999 (millions of U.S. dollars)

Country	1996	1997	1998	1999	Total
Colombia	40.50	14.20	41.10	58.00	153.80
Mexico		37.00	1.10		38.10
Peru	13.75	2.30	5.30	4.00	25.35
Venezuela	12.25	1.00			13.25
Bolivia			12.00		12.00
Eastern Caribbean	8.50	1.50	1.50		11.50
Ecuador			1.80	4.00	5.80
Honduras			2.05		2.05
Brazil			2.00		2.00
Jamaica			1.00		1.00
Trinidad and Tobago			1.00		1.00
Guatemala			0.60		0.60
Dominican Republic			0.55		0.55
Panama				0.45	0.45
Total	75.00	56.00	70.00	66.45	267.45

Source: U.S. State Department, Office of Resources, Plans, and Policy, Congressional Presentation for Foreign Operations, Fiscal Years 2002, 2003, and 2004.

rather, it comes from the Defense Department's existing stocks. Like EDA, however, drawdowns do not require prior congressional approval or the appropriation of new funds. Four years of drawdowns during the 1990s paid for helicopters for Mexico and Colombia, cargo aircraft for Peru, patrol boats for Caribbean countries, and millions of dollars' worth of spare parts.

Training
Counterdrug programs are also the largest source of skills transfers in the region. In 2002, the United States offered training in skills ranging from marksmanship to human rights to 15,039 students from Latin America and the Caribbean (see Table 2.6). Colombia led the world in trainees in 2001 and 2002, with a total of 12,777.[39]

International Military Education and Training (IMET), the main FAA program that funds training, is not the principal support for U.S. training of Latin American military and police personnel. That distinction belongs to the Section 1004 program funded through the defense budget, which trained 7,112 people in the region in 2002, nearly half of all trainees. In Colombia, Section 1004 funded nearly three-quarters of the trainees. [40]

Little counterdrug training occurs in classrooms at military installations on U.S. soil. The vast majority is the work of small teams of U.S. military instructors sent overseas to train large numbers of students on or around foreign bases. Usually, these teams are Special Operations Forces—Army Green Berets, Navy SEALs, and Small Boat Units—or detachments of

Table 2.6   Top 10 Latin American Recipients of Training, 2002 (number of trainees, by funding source)

	Section 1004	IMET	JCETs and other Southern Command	FMF	Sales	INL	Others	Total
Colombia	4,845	544		655	31	339	63	6,477
Ecuador	984	104			156		23	1,267
Honduras	100	301	350	60	145		11	967
Bolivia	272	101	300	20	68		200	961
El Salvador		394	165	39			9	607
Mexico	348	114			30	96	12	600
Peru	264	90	83		45	5	20	507
Venezuela	103	78			243		21	445
Argentina		287			41		40	368
Dominican Republic	6	91	136	26	39	35	7	340
Top 10 Total	6,922	2,104	1,034	800	798	475	406	12,539
Regional Total	7,112	3,392	1,380	806	1,274	494	581	15,039

Source: U.S. State Department, Department of Defense, *Foreign Military Training in Fiscal Years 2002 and 2003* (Washington, D.C.: Department of State, May 2003).

Marines. With the exception of helicopter training and courses for mechanics and technicians, Southcom has found sending a handful of instructors to the region to be more cost-effective—and perhaps less subject to scrutiny—than bringing a classroom full of students to the United States.

The main exception was the Section 1004–funded training in the late 1990s of the Mexican army's Air-Mobile Special Forces Groups (GAFEs). Due to sensitivity about U.S. forces on Mexican soil, thousands of GAFE members traveled to Fort Bragg, North Carolina, for training in light infantry tactics and helicopter piloting and maintenance. The program, begun in 1996, was seen as part of an unprecedented turn toward partnership with Mexico's military for many internal counterdrug responsibilities. By 2000, the GAFE program had largely ended, and aid to Mexico had leveled off. Drug-trafficking patterns shifted toward maritime smuggling in the eastern Pacific Ocean. In response, much Section 1004–funded training for Mexico shifted to the Mexican navy's new Amphibious Special Forces Groups (GANFEs). Most of this training occurs at sea, on the soil of neither country.

Much nontechnical counterdrug training, particularly that provided by Special Forces teams on Section 1004–funded Counter-Drug Training Support (CDTS) deployments throughout the region, involves the transfer of skills that are equally applicable to counterinsurgency and surveillance of political opponents. These include light infantry and small unit tactics, intelligence gathering and analysis, marksmanship, and ambush techniques.

Critics of widespread counterdrug training have charged that much of it is Cold War–era counterinsurgency training in disguise and warned of the danger that lethal skills may be employed to abuse human rights or to weaken nonviolent political opposition.

Other U.S. Agencies

In addition to the State and Defense Departments, several other agencies and actors play important roles in drug control programs. For instance, since 1989 the White House's Office of National Drug Control Policy (ONDCP), whose chief is known colloquially as the drug czar, has been responsible for setting overall counterdrug policy, both foreign and domestic. At least in broad outlines, this office is also responsible for assigning resources for each aspect of the policy. The DEA, within the Justice Department, also has a large and secretive presence in nearly every country in the region. The DEA, Customs, and the Coast Guard split about U.S.$4.5 million annually, passed on to them from the INC program to fund counterdrug training of foreign law-enforcement personnel worldwide.[41]

Agencies of the U.S. government's intelligence community also increased their counterdrug role throughout the 1990s. In 1989, the CIA established the Counter-Narcotics Center and announced that it would commit one-fourth of its efforts in Latin America to antidrug efforts.[42] These efforts have included funding some training of foreign security forces and gathering intelligence about drug trafficking. CIA imaging and reconnaissance data have proven essential for estimating levels of illicit crop cultivation and drug production, as well as in locating suspected drug flights. Research into the precise counterdrug role of the CIA, NSA, and DIA is difficult, however, because of the extreme secrecy with which those agencies operate. (Even their combined annual budget has been classified in most years, with a court upholding this secrecy in 1999.[43])

Although very little unclassified information is available to verify the conclusion, it is still likely that the intelligence community, particularly the CIA's Directorate of Operations, is a source of significant amounts of antidrug military and police aid. CIA funding has probably not been employed for large-scale arms transfers: none of the region's security forces appears to have a fleet of CIA-supplied helicopters or patrol boats. CIA assistance has most likely included equipment and training related to intelligence gathering, surveillance (particularly of suspicious aircraft, boats, and vehicles), analysis, and maintenance of sources, as well as some sharing of sensitive information.

Much of what is known about the operational role of the intelligence agencies is learned after the fact, usually after a significant success or failure. The CIA played a large role in the 1992–1993 effort to capture and kill fugitive Medellín cartel boss Pablo Escobar in Colombia. It was for years quite close to disgraced former Peruvian intelligence chief Vladimiro Montesinos, who, while posing as an ally in the war on drugs, was also allegedly pocketing the proceeds of drug transactions and selling weapons to Colombian guerrillas. Moreover, the CIA and its contractor were, of all U.S. agencies involved in the aerial interdiction program, the most closely implicated in the accidental April 2001 shootdown over Peru.[44]

U.S. intelligence agency personnel offer another type of assistance that has significant effects yet is difficult to quantify—that is, sensitive intelligence about suspected illicit drug activity. CIA, DIA, and DEA agents share satellite and reconnaissance imagery, signals intercepts, and human intelligence related to drugs with their counterparts throughout the region. Section 1004 also authorizes the U.S. military to do the same.

Private Contractors

The war on drugs also relies heavily on outsourcing to private companies and, in fact, has to some extent pioneered this approach. Civilians—both U.S. and foreign citizens—serve as spray plane pilots, mechanics, logistics and supply personnel, search-and-rescue team members, air traffic controllers, radar site operators, helicopter copilots, intelligence gatherers and analyzers, and in other roles. Most have prior military experience, and some have only recently left military service. In February 2003, for example, the Bogotá daily *El Tiempo* reported that dozens of Colombian helicopter pilots had left the military shortly after completing training in the United States, only to be hired by private contractors to do the same work at a salary several times higher.[45]

Contractors often find themselves in greater proximity to Colombia's fighting than do active-duty U.S. military personnel. In Colombia in 2002, an April 2003 State Department report revealed, Defense and State had hired sixteen different U.S. companies to perform U.S.$150.4 million worth of services, some of them risky roles placing contractors very close to Colombia's conflict.[46] "Sooner or later, official Americans will be killed in Colombia carrying out their duties; when that happens, it will be big news," warned U.S. ambassador to Colombia Anne Patterson in October 2002.[47] This has not happened; however, eleven contractors died on the job in Colombia between 1998 and late 2003, with minimal media coverage.[48]

Contractors have been involved in several embarrassing or worrying incidents over the years. The April 2001 Peru shootdown is one such example. The CIA contractor involved, Aviation Development Corporation, was unable to halt the Peruvian air force's attack because its representatives spoke insufficient Spanish.[49] For 2000–2001, the Defense Department gave Military Personnel Resources International of Virginia a U.S.$4.3 million contract to offer management advice to the Colombian armed forces. After the contract expired, Colombia's defense minister told the press that the experience had been useless: "There was no empathy. ... In a country at war there isn't time to sit in committee meetings."[50] Several spray plane pilots working for INL contractor Dyncorp have died in crashes over southern Colombia, some shot down by guerrillas. Dyncorp search-and-rescue teams have had to face guerrilla fire to rescue crashed Colombian police helicopters in the southern Colombian department of Caquetá on two occasions, in 2001 and 2002.

In February 2003, a Cessna 208 plane carrying four employees of California Microwave Systems, a Defense Department contractor on an intelligence gathering mission, went down in Caquetá; FARC guerrillas killed one and took the other three hostage. A month later, three contractors on a mission to find the hostages, flying the same model single-engine plane, died when their aircraft crashed or was shot down.

Critics charge that using contractors is a means to avoid scrutiny and accountability. "Are we outsourcing in order to avoid public scrutiny, controversy or embarrassment?" asked Representative Jan Schakowsky (D-Illinois) in 2001. "Is it to hide body bags from the media and thus shield them from public opinion?"[51] It is also more difficult to get information about contractors' activities than about most other military assistance programs. Until the April 2003 report on Colombia, for example, it was impossible even to get a list of companies hired to carry out counterdrug efforts in that country. No such list is available for the entire region.

• Colombia, the Andes, and the Drugs–Terror Nexus

Colombia, considered in more detail in Chapter 4, is not only the region's largest recipient of U.S. funds and attention. It is also setting the context for how the United States understands the region, as well as the way in which the concepts of drug war, counterinsurgency, and antiterrorism are converging to define the broad framework for U.S. policy. In particular, the case of Colombia illustrates how the U.S. response to the September 11 attacks served to reinforce the already strong tendency to view the region largely in terms of security threats and to emphasize military initiatives over broader approaches to regional security.

Plan Colombia and the Andean Initiative

Colombia's decades-old conflict, as well as its status as a center for drug cultivation and trafficking, have made it by far the region's largest recipient of military and police assistance, both counterdrug and otherwise. In 2003, for instance, seven of every ten dollars in military or police aid to the entire hemisphere—a total of almost exactly U.S.$600 million—went to Colombia. On May 13, 2003, 358 U.S. military personnel and 308 U.S. citizen contractors (and dozens or hundreds of other noncitizens working for

U.S. contractors) were on Colombian soil carrying out counterdrug or counterterror missions.[52] Since 1999, Colombia has been the world's third-largest recipient of U.S. military and police assistance, and since at least 2001 it has had the largest numbers worldwide of military and police being trained under U.S. programs.

Colombia received lavish U.S. support for counterinsurgency in the 1960s and continued to receive moderate amounts of military aid throughout the Cold War. By 1990, however, only two guerrilla groups, the FARC and the National Liberation Army (Ejército de Liberación Nacional, or ELN), continued their insurgency. They were commonly viewed as virtual anachronisms. Most U.S. policymakers focused instead on what appeared to be a far greater threat: the powerful Medellín and Cali drug cartels. The corrupting influence of the cartels was destroying institutions, and their campaign of terror to prevent extradition to the United States was killing thousands.

The U.S.-supported effort to bring down the cartels took place almost completely without Colombia's military. The capture or killing of cartel leaders was the work of Colombia's National Police, supported by the CIA, the DEA, and—in the case of the search for Pablo Escobar—Centra Spike, a U.S. military signals intelligence-gathering operation. Journalist Mark Bowden, writing of the search for Escobar, recounts that "there were so many American spy planes over the city [Medellín], at one point 17 at once, that the Air Force had to assign an AWAC, an airborne command and control center, to keep track of them."[53]

The large cartels' disappearance altered the makeup of the drug trade but did not reduce the availability of drugs in the United States. At least 162 smaller so-called boutique cartels arose in place of the large criminal organizations.[54] These smaller organizations lacked the reach to continue the cartels' model of fostering coca cultivation in Peru and Bolivia and bringing the leaf or unrefined cocaine paste to Colombia for processing and transshipment. An alternative quickly emerged: coca itself rapidly became a mostly Colombian commodity. By 1998 Colombia accounted for the majority of South America's coca production, and by 2001 Colombia's share had increased to 76 percent (see Figure 1.2 in Chapter 1).[55]

The U.S. government also reacted quickly to the new pattern of drug production. Years of asking Colombia to allow a large-scale herbicide spraying program paid off when the government of President Ernesto Samper, weakened by a scandal involving a campaign donation from the Cali cartel, acceded to U.S. demands in 1994. The large-scale fumigation that followed destroyed crops, but coca production merely moved to new areas. The total amount of coca grown in the country continued to skyrocket. Both the FARC and paramilitary groups used their income from the drug trade to fund remarkable growth during the 1990s. By 1996, the guerrillas were able to launch destructive attacks on military bases in remote southern Colombia, devastating them and taking officers hostage. U.S. officials were concerned but still wanted to avoid direct U.S. involvement in counterinsurgency (see Chapter 4).

At the time, most U.S. security assistance to Colombia—some 90 percent in 1997—was going to the Colombian police. The military received little assistance because it was seen as corrupt and poorly run. Moreover, it faced numerous serious allegations of systematic human rights abuse, particularly collaboration with the murderous paramilitaries. The Clinton administration's initial response was to fund the creation of an elite, highly mobile counterdrug battalion within the Colombian army. The battalion was to "guarantee security conditions" for fumigation in areas where both guerrillas and coca were prevalent. In 2000, the administration greatly expanded this program as part of Plan Colombia, a U.S.$1.3 billion regional aid package.

Seventy-five percent of the U.S.$860 million Colombia received under the plan went to the security forces, with the largest share now going to the military. This funded two more counterdrug battalions and forty-five helicopters for the army's new Counternarcotics Brigade that would be used in the coca zones of southern Colombia. It also funded new aircraft and equipment for the Colombian police and air force, as well as an expansion of the navy's riverine program.

Under the plan, Colombia's neighbors also received U.S.$180 million for their own eradication and interdiction activities, as well as for efforts to counteract expected spillover of Colombia's violence and drug activity. Bolivia got both alternative development aid and security assistance to boost President Hugo Banzer's campaign to eradicate all illicit coca from the Chapare region. Peru got six KMAX helicopters, and Ecuador got a significant boost in aid to increase military and police presence along its northern border.[56]

After assuming office in 2001, the administration of George W. Bush continued the initiatives begun under Plan Colombia. Starting with its aid request for 2002, it repackaged INC military and economic aid for Colombia and six of its neighbors (Bolivia, Brazil, Ecuador, Panama, Peru, and Venezuela) as a regional effort called the Andean Regional Initiative (ARI). Seeking a combined U.S.$731 million for each year (though this amount suffered mild cutbacks in 2002 and 2003), the Bush administration used ARI funds to maintain existing efforts in Colombia and to pay for significant military and police aid increases for Colombia's neighbors. However, in the ARI's first year (2002), Colombia's neighbors saw smaller increases than originally anticipated, with the extra funds going to support efforts in Colombia (see Figure 2.2).

Figure 2.2   Military and Police Aid to Colombia and Its Neighbors

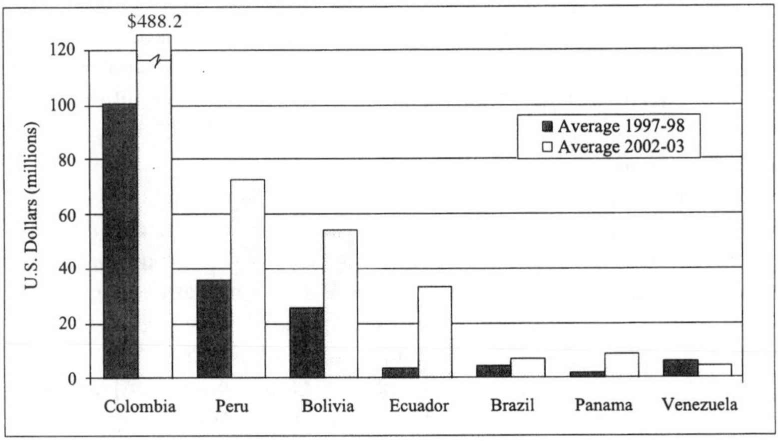

Source: U.S. State Department, *INCSR 2003.*

From Counterdrug to Counterterror in Colombia

Throughout the debate over Plan Colombia, and during the plan's initial implementation, mainstream opinion in Washington was still quite wary of finding the United States sucked into a costly, complicated counterinsurgency effort in Colombia. Faced with questions about slippery slopes, exit strategies, and even a new Vietnam, Clinton administration officials tried to assure skeptics that U.S. aid would continue to be restricted to antidrug activities. They pledged not to cross the invisible line between drug-fighting and counterinsurgency. "As a matter of Administration policy, the United States will not support Colombian counterinsurgency efforts," General McCaffrey said in November 2000.[57] Policy directives from the Clinton White House restricted even the sharing of intelligence to information having to do with the drug war. The forward operating location agreements with Ecuador, the Netherlands, and El Salvador limited U.S. assets at the bases to counterdrug missions only.

The George W. Bush administration was less reluctant to consider support for counterinsurgency in Colombia. As relevant diplomatic and defense positions were filled during the spring and summer of 2001, officials indicated that they were carrying out a "formal review" of the previous administration's drugs-only approach.[58] Defense and intelligence officials began to complain more vocally about their legal inability to warn the Colombian authorities about, for instance, imminent guerrilla attacks.[59] The RAND Corporation issued an influential report in June 2001 recommending support for the antiguerrilla fight, adding that "the U.S. program of military assistance to El Salvador during the Reagan administration could be a relevant model."[60]

The September 11 attacks on New York and Washington swept away any remaining Bush administration reluctance to support Colombia's larger war effort. In the aftermath of the attacks, Washington looked around the world for other potential terrorist enemies. In Colombia they found three organizations already on the State Department's list of foreign terrorist organizations: the FARC, the ELN, and the Autodefensas Unidas de Colombia (AUC, or the United Self-Defense Forces of Colombia) paramilitary umbrella group. Latin America has only one other group on the State Department's terror list: the remnant of Peru's Shining Path insurgents.

Executive and legislative officials immediately began drawing parallels between Colombia's armed groups—particularly the FARC—and Al-Qaeda. "There's no difficulty in identifying [Osama bin Laden] as a terrorist, and getting everybody to rally against him," said Secretary of State Colin Powell in October 2001. "Now, there are other organizations that probably meet a similar standard. The FARC in Colombia comes to mind, the Real IRA comes to mind, all of which, both of which are on our terrorist list down at the State Department."[61] Added CIA Director George Tenet the following February, "The terrorist threat also goes beyond Islamic extremists and the Muslim world. The Revolutionary Armed Forces of Colombia poses a serious threat to U.S. interests in Latin America because it associates us with the government it is fighting against."[62]

U.S. agencies with counterdrug responsibilities—including the drug czar's office, with a series of ads that premiered during the 2002 Super Bowl—worked to raise awareness of the link between drug money and terrorism. In early 2003 Southcom's General James Hill, speaking to Congress and to other groups, repeatedly asserted that "drugs are a weapon of mass destruction."[63] Officials now routinely refer to Colombia's armed groups as "narcoterrorists."

Momentum toward a larger military aid mission in Colombia increased after Colombians handed a first-round election victory to Álvaro Uribe, a candidate who pledged to put the country on a total war footing. In March 2002, the U.S. House of Representatives passed a nonbinding resolution calling on the administration "to assist the Government of Colombia to protect its democracy from United States–designated foreign terrorist organizations." In late March, the administration successfully asked Congress for more funds for the global war on terror. One sentence of this law had a dramatic effect on U.S. policy in Colombia: the Colombian military could use all past and current counterdrug aid for a "unified campaign" against drugs and against Colombia's armed groups. This allowed U.S. aid to pay for a host of new nondrug military and police initiatives in Colombia. In

November 2002, the Bush administration undid its predecessor's executive order banning the sharing of nondrug intelligence with Colombia's security forces.

In the context of the war on terror, the entire hemisphere is seeing a revival of Foreign Military Financing. The Bush administration's 2004 aid request calls for U.S.$143.1 million for Latin America and the Caribbean, including U.S.$33 million for countries other than Colombia—a sharp rise for a program that provided the region with only U.S.$5 million as recently as 2001. The new money will pay for efforts to improve military capacities in general, particularly the use of militaries to control empty zones with little state presence.

Regional Implications

Beyond Colombia—for now at least—FMF is the main funding channel for counterterror military aid, while INC and Section 1004 are still confined to support for counterdrug activities. Southcom's preference, as expressed in the Pentagon's suggested draft of the 2004 National Defense Authorization Act, would be to expand the purpose of Section 1004 for every country in the region to allow for "a unified campaign against activities by organizations in the Americas hemisphere actively engaged in, or designated as, terrorist organizations."[64] However, both congressional armed services committees removed this language from their versions of the bill.

The possibility of using counterdrug aid for counterterrorism raises the obvious question of what such aid would look like for the majority of the region's countries, which have no terrorist organizations within their borders. A partial answer can be found in the Defense Department's doctrine of effective sovereignty for the region's elected governments. Secretary of Defense Donald Rumsfeld defined this at a November 2002 meeting of the region's defense ministers as exercising control over lawless zones: "In this hemisphere, narco-terrorists, hostage takers and arms smugglers operate in ungoverned areas, using them as bases from which to destabilize democratic governments."[65] In the era of the war on terror, then, a move is afoot to view ungoverned areas—places like southern Colombia, Brazil's Amazon Basin, Panama's Darién Gap, or the triple border region between Argentina, Brazil, and Paraguay—as threats in themselves to the national security of the United States. Increasing state control of these areas is likely to become a central goal of Southcom operations and assistance in the region, as well as military aid programs like FMF. If the push for regionwide mission expansion continues and succeeds, INC and Section 1004 funds would also become available for such use.

Secretary Rumsfeld's November 2002 presentation also highlighted another proposal for regional counterterror military cooperation. Dubbed Operation Enduring Friendship, the Pentagon's plan would establish a semipermanent combined naval flotilla to patrol regional waters in search of traffickers of drugs or arms (or persons engaged in any other criminal activity).[66] Proponents argue that the operation would increase regional interoperability while making up for a post–September 11 pullback of U.S. maritime patrols for homeland defense. Critics view it as an expensive, unwieldy boondoggle likely to do little more than buy boats for the region's navies.

• The Risks of Continued Militarization

For many in Washington, the war on drugs and the war on terror are virtually indistinguishable in Latin America. The Bush administration and the Republican majority in Congress have blurred the distinction between counterdrug and counterterrorism and have criticized those who would maintain it as out of touch with a changed global reality. Assistant Secretary of Defense Peter Rodman even argued that expanding the purpose of military aid responds to a "moral impetus":

> As a practical matter, we cannot view Colombia as a country in which we either adhere to a counterdrug program or slide unwittingly into a Vietnam-style counterinsurgency. More realistically, we must pursue policies and fashion programs that permit Colombia to meet the challenge of the narco-terrorists so that U.S. forces are not called upon to do so. There is a strong moral and strategic impetus behind this support for one of the United States' oldest and most reliable hemispheric allies.[67]

Despite the claims of administration officials, however, the substantial risks of this policy direction are already apparent. Failure to take these risks into account, and to place security policy within a broader, nonmilitary context, is likely to lead to less rather than greater security for the United States.

Mission Creep

In the context of Colombia, perhaps Peru, and the Andean border zones, counterterrorism seems to be little different from old-school, Cold War–style counterinsurgency. Certainly, groups like the FARC, the ELN, and the paramilitaries in Colombia regularly launch terrorist attacks. But unlike the urban cells of Al-Qaeda and Hamas, the South American groups have hundreds or thousands of members organized in military structures, in control of vast yet remote territories.

According to reigning doctrine, a mainly military effort to weaken or defeat such groups would require paying for a significant buildup of existing security forces, with an emphasis on mobility, low-intensity operations, and close work with civilian populations to weaken illegal groups' support. It would require surveillance of civilian leaders in insurgent-controlled zones, reliance on informants, pursuit of an enemy hidden in remote areas, and a sustained military presence in far-flung territories. In other words, counterterrorism in the Andes means counterinsurgency or something very closely resembling it.

It is possible—though very unlikely—that increased military aid, with an expanded mission, could cause Colombia's insurgents to collapse like a house of cards. The more likely outcome, cited by those who see a potential Andean quagmire for the United States, is the Vietnam-like scenario of steadily increasing aid to prop up a corrupt elite, insufficient debate at home while key decisions are being made, and successive troop deployments until Washington finds itself inextricably stuck and suffering heavy losses. Others warn of the El Salvador scenario in which numbers of U.S. personnel are small but military aid reaches stratospheric levels while the armed forces carry out a dirty war and the spillover heightens instability and militaristic responses in neighboring countries. Colombia is more than fifty times larger than El Salvador.

Although either of these scenarios is plausible enough to be a source of major worry, as of late 2004 there was still little debate taking place in Washington about where the United States may be headed in Colombia. Some officials have mentioned the possibility of "Colombianization"—handing over more roles and budget responsibility to the Colombian state. But those who wish to stay the course, wherever that might lead, appear to have the upper hand. While attention focuses on the Middle East and more immediate terrorist threats overseas, the U.S. military commitment in Colombia continues to grow, quietly but rapidly.

Beyond the Andes and throughout the hemisphere, a vague definition of counterterrorism and the temptation to fight it with counterdrug programs could bring about a different kind of mission creep. Unless Congress is vigilant, programs like INL and Section 1004 may soon be pooled with FMF to help Latin American militaries prepare for a wide variety of threats. These would be only tangentially related, if at all, to drugs: migration, arms trafficking, organized and common crime, or perhaps even organized social protest. Given the vastness of the region's empty, ungoverned zones where terrorists or drug traffickers could hypothetically operate, the effective sovereignty doctrine could become a blank check for an enormous new military aid commitment in Latin America.

As the Bush administration links the war on drugs more closely with the war on terror, military aid programs may also creep from the foreign aid budget to the much larger, less transparent defense budget. Section 1004 already gave the Pentagon a foot in the door by granting the ability to provide its own assistance, free of diplomatic supervision, for a specific mission: counternarcotics. If this is used as a precedent for the war on terror, with the Department of Defense gaining control over the design, implementation, and destination of most U.S. military assistance, then one of the principal goals of the Foreign Assistance Act—the placement of military aid under State Department and congressional foreign relations committee control—will have been completely subverted.

Human Rights Abuses and Civil-Military Relations

The risks of counterdrug and counterterror military aid go beyond mission creep, however, as human rights advocates are quick to point out. Either mission requires historically repressive armed forces—whose training is oriented toward overwhelmingly defeating an enemy—to increase their internal role and their interaction with civilian populations. Worse, decades of counterdrug aid have continued the Cold War focus on an internal enemy, distracting governments from the tasks of reforming human rights practices and ensuring subordination to civilian justice systems.

Human rights defenders in Latin America, echoing debates over the civil liberties impact of the USA Patriot Act in the United States, highlight the potential dangers in giving governments such enormous latitude to define who is a terrorist. This inherently vague term, many rightly fear, may become a catch-all to describe any internal political opposition. The regional crusade against communists during the Cold War gives abundant precedent for concern. The war on terror—layered over the war on drugs—may similarly serve as a rationale for security forces to crack down on peaceful reformers and opponents of existing regimes. Labor and peasant leaders, human rights monitors, independent journalists, neighborhood activists, and members of opposition political parties may find themselves subject to surveillance, harassment, or worse from U.S.-funded, U.S.-trained security units. With disturbing frequency, regional leaders are already referring to their peaceful opponents—Bolivian coca growers, Colombian human rights groups, Honduran environmental activists—as terrorists or allies of terrorists.

Moreover, as in the drug war, U.S. counterterror assistance is likely to favor the military dimension over efforts to alleviate the corruption, impunity, poverty, and inequality that underlie much of the region's violence and illegal economy. Nor is U.S. aid likely to be accompanied by genuine efforts to end impunity or to make abusive officers face civilian justice for their crimes.

As Washington encourages governments to focus on a new security threat, attention to the finer points of civilian control of the military—such as determining doctrine, subordination to civilian justice, control over budgets, and ability to appoint or promote officers—is likely to lapse as the more compelling immediate goal takes precedence.

Most of the region's democracies are less than thirty years old. Even as they seek to consolidate civilian rule, military aid for increased internal roles is strengthening the one state institution that least needs strengthening. Moreover, cooperation and praise from U.S. diplomats and military officers gives a symbolic seal of approval to the region's militaries, thus increasing their political clout.

Even in the United States, the terror war has led some to question the wisdom of Posse Comitatus, the law that excludes the U.S. military from carrying out internal policing duties. If this principle is being eroded in Washington, the damage is likely to be far greater in the rest of the hemisphere.

Lost Opportunities

As noted above, regionwide military and police aid now nearly equals total economic and social aid. This is a new phenomenon; even during the Cold War, U.S. planners saw nonmilitary assistance as an important tool to create the prosperity and economic opportunity needed to discourage countries' citizens from going communist.

In the drug war and the war on terror, however, U.S. officials have placed far less emphasis on winning the hearts and minds of the population. U.S. aid to security forces has risen sharply, but that rise has not been matched by increased aid to strengthen rural development, local leadership, judicial sector capabilities, and other civilian governance needs. In fact, many Latin American states have seen their nonmilitary institutions weakened by years of internationally imposed austerity demands.

U.S. aid agencies have undergone a parallel shift. While Southcom and INL have seen their missions and budgets expand dramatically, the U.S. Agency for International Development (USAID) is a shadow of its former self. As economist Jeffrey Sachs notes:

> In its earlier days, USAID would have helped to lead a more sophisticated U.S. response [to Bolivia's October 2003 crisis], but in the past 20 years it has been shorn of its thinkers, strategists and development economists. Congressional pressures and presidential lack of interest have turned USAID into a service-delivery agency that undertakes specific projects in poor countries, such as food relief, rather than a strategic agency that analyzes complex development challenges and helps lead a suitable U.S. foreign policy response.[68]

The consequences of this disparity are already visible. Populations throughout the region have seen their incomes shrink during the same period in which their governments were moving toward democracy. The civilian sectors of their states have been drained of the ability to provide many basic services, and U.S. assistance has helped militaries to remain as strong as ever and to assume new internal roles. The result, verified by polling throughout the region, is that Latin Americans are increasingly disenchanted with democracy, admire the military's ability to get things done, and readily support populist leaders (some of them former military officers) who offer quick, personalistic solutions.[69]

Decisionmaking and Lack of Transparency in the United States

"Long before September 11, the U.S. government had grown increasingly dependent on its military to carry out its foreign affairs," notes Dana Priest. "The military simply filled a vacuum left by an indecisive White House, an atrophied State Department, and a distracted Congress."[70]

This state of affairs applies fully to the war on drugs, both before and after the advent of the war on terror. Foreign policy decisionmakers responsible for the big picture, as well as legislative oversight personnel, have largely abdicated the design of U.S. assistance to those with the greatest zeal for militarization. Southcom, INL, drug czars, and a coterie of drug war hawks in Congress set the direction for U.S. involvement in Latin America. Those charged with guaranteeing the full spectrum of U.S. interests in the region—such as the National Security Council, the State Department's Bureau of Western Hemisphere Affairs, and moderates on the congressional foreign relations committees—are consistent losers in bureaucratic battles—if they choose to fight at all.

Viewed from Latin America, the resulting policy often appears irrationally unbalanced, determined by the reigning obsession in Washington rather than by realities on the ground. Instead of finding the United States willing to discuss common goals of poverty alleviation, debt, trade, or even a regional security cooperation agenda, the region's leaders have had to deal first with a narcotized U.S. policy and now with a U.S. approach that views all aspects of regional relations, including counterdrug efforts, through the lens of terrorism.

There are several reasons for this pattern. As it is political poison for a U.S. candidate to appear soft on drugs, leaders of both branches of government rarely spend political capital on opposition to a tough antidrug policy—and few policies appear tougher than a military approach.

More generally, the U.S. defense establishment has seen its resources and foreign policy influence increase significantly since the end of the Cold War while diplomatic budgets and personnel have declined sharply. As a result, the assistant secretary of state for Western Hemisphere Affairs is far less visible in the region than the commander of Southcom, who visits most countries in his own plane on a regular basis. The assistant secretary has a host of U.S. interests to protect in Latin America beyond fighting drugs and terror: trade and investment, democratization, economic development, environmental protection, and cordial diplomatic relations, to name a few. By contrast, the commander's priorities are guided by just one overwhelming concern: protecting U.S. security. Yet he has a higher profile than the diplomat and more resources to dedicate to that single concern.

Militarization and hard-line policies also result when decisionmakers rely on partial information. Too often, U.S. officials maintain relationships only with their official counterparts in the region. Southcom interacts mainly with the region's militaries, counterdrug agencies speak mainly with their coequals, and diplomats mainly talk to host-country government officials. Most of these entities receive assistance from the United States and thus have a vested interest in sharing only information that reflects well on them.

There is a parallel dynamic of information filtering in Washington. Congressional oversight personnel—many of them overwhelmed and overworked due to limited legislative-branch staffing budgets—must weigh several versions of events in order to judge the efficacy of the programs they fund. Some versions come from nongovernmental organizations, left and right, some of them credible and others with ideological axes to grind. Most legislators, however, rarely question the official story, that is, the version provided by U.S. agencies—military and civilian—that have strong incentives to maintain and increase their budgets.

The persistence of this selective information dynamic, along with the lack of will or resources for thorough congressional oversight, places important responsibilities on citizens and the media. Journalists and nongovernmental organizations warn about risks or consequences of policies that the official versions often fail to mention. They also propose policy alternatives that fall beyond the often narrow range of possibilities presented by officials.

In order to play this important role, though, citizens must have access to information. They must be able to analyze not only a policy's effects but also its content and its design. Providing the public with information about foreign aid programs—whether through required reports to Congress, budget requests, hearings, comptroller's reports, press conferences, or other means—is crucial for proper oversight and democratic control over U.S. foreign policy. Access to information about military assistance needs to be expanded, not restricted.

• Conclusion

As the United States gears up for what threatens to be a new period of large-scale weapons transfers, training programs, and joint operations, the public needs to ask why Washington so often chooses to try to solve its problems in Latin America by going the military route.

Much of the answer has to do with U.S. political culture. Drug war strategy overseas is remarkably in step with the past few administrations' domestic policy choices. At home, the United States builds jails instead of treatment centers for those addicted to drugs. Telling people what really needs to be done—alleviating poverty, treating addicts, helping neighboring states create conditions for a legal economy to flourish—takes courageous leadership, something that has decidedly been missing from the drug war's political management. Instead, leaders have played on public fears, turning a public health issue into an all-out war on addictive substances and those who supply them.

A desire for shortcuts or quick solutions also reinforces expectations that military institutions can solve complex problems. In a region where civilian institutions are often weak and ineffective, the military appears to be an all-purpose tool—disciplined, cheap, and ready for deployment. Grants of hardware and a few Special Forces training deployments seem easier and cheaper than a comprehensive effort to build the capacities of elected officials and civilian institutions. Indeed, they *are* easier and cheaper. But the impact is short term. A military offensive can create order and reduce drug or terrorist activity in a particular area for a limited time. The occupying troops, however, eventually have to leave. If they leave behind the same stark inequalities and weak rule of law that existed beforehand, they will be condemned to launch similar offensives again and again.

The drug war is a bad precedent for the war on terror, not a foundation on which to build. Drugs are as available as ever on U.S. streets. Latin America's poor, neglected rural areas remain in deep crisis, making the drug trade an attractive employment option for many. More than a decade after the demise of the Cold War and its associated National Security Doctrine, human rights violations remain common, and poor civil-military relations continue. Resentment of the role of the United States in reinforcing these patterns is pervasive.

There is no simple military aid formula for managing the threat of drugs or the threat of terror. Success will be possible only if we choose to do it the hard way, taking on all of the factors—social, economic, institutional—that contribute to both drug trafficking and violence. While the war metaphor is compelling, by now it should be clear that few of the battles that matter most can be won with military force.

• Notes

1. This term emerged in the 1960s: "The NSD expanded greatly the concept of security, making it virtually synonymous with political, social, and economic development. ... This was essentially a call for a permanent and total war by the state against the enemies threatening *la patria* as well as a call for direct military involvement in the tasks of national development." Brian Loveman, *Por la Patria: Politics and the Armed Forces in Latin America* (Wilmington, Del.: Scholarly Resources, 1999), pp. 236–237.

2. Section 620, subsection (f) of the Foreign Assistance Act.

3. U.S. Agency for International Development (USAID), *U.S. Overseas*

Loans and Grants and Assistance from International Organizations (Washington, D.C.: USAID, 1981–1992).

4. Ibid.

5. Richard A. Haggarty, ed., *El Salvador: A Country Study*, Library of Congress, Federal Research Division, November 1988.

6. The others are European Command (covering Europe and most of Africa), Central Command (East Africa, the Middle East, and Central Asia), Pacific Command (East Asia and Australia), and Northern Command (North America, Mexico, Cuba, the Bahamas, and Puerto Rico). The latter was established after the September 11, 2001, attacks.

7. Dana Priest, *The Mission: Waging War and Keeping Peace with America's Military* (New York: W. W. Norton, 2003), p. 74.

8. See, for instance, United Nations Development Programme, *Human Development Report 1994: New Dimensions of Human Security* (New York: UNDP, 1994).

9. Andrew Liebman, *Frontline: Stopping Drugs, Part II* (WGBH/Public Broadcasting Service, 17 February 1987), www.pbs.org/wgbh/pages/frontline/shows/drugs/archive/stoppingdrugs2.html.

10. USAID, *U.S. Overseas Loans and Grants and Assistance from International Organizations* (Washington, D.C.: USAID, 1988–1992).

11. Washington Office on Latin America, *Clear and Present Dangers: The U.S. Military and the War on Drugs in the Andes* (Washington, D.C.: WOLA, October 1991), p. 10.

12. USAID, *U.S. Overseas Loans.*

13. Ibid.

14. U.S. State Department, *Fiscal Year 2004 International Narcotics and Law Enforcement (INL) Congressional Budget Justification (CBJ)*, June 2003.

15. Ibid.; INL, *International Narcotics Control Strategy Report (INCSR) 2002* (Washington, D.C.: U.S. Government Printing Office, 1 March 2003).

16. WOLA, *Clear and Present*, p. 12.

17. Author interviews with personnel at U.S. Embassy, Santiago, and U.S. Embassy, Buenos Aires, October 1998.

18. General James Hill, U.S. Southern Command, comments before the Council of the Americas, 9 January 2003, www.ciponline.org/colombia/03010901.pdf.

19. U.S. White House, Office of National Drug Control Policy (ONDCP), "An Overview of Federal Drug Control Programs on the Southwest Border" (ONDCP, 1997); INL, *FY2001 CBJ*, March 2000, p. 13.

20. U.S. State Department, *A Report to Congress on United States Policy Towards Colombia and Other Related Issues,* 3 December 2002, www.ciponline.org/colombia/02120302.htm.

21. WOLA, *Clear and Present*, p. 37.

22. A useful, though probably not comprehensive, list of U.S. military counterdrug operations is on the website of the Federation of American Scientists' Military Analysis Network.

23. U.S. General Accounting Office, Report 01-63BR, *Drug Control: International Counterdrug Sites Being Developed* (Washington, D.C.: GAO, December 2002).

24. U.S. State Department, "Action Memorandum, Use of Weapons Against Civil Aircraft" (Washington, D.C.: 10 May 1994), National Security Archive, electronic briefing book no. 44, "Shoot-Down in Peru," www.gwu.edu/~nsarchiv/NSAEBB/NSAEBB44/.

25. U.S. Southern Command, "Posture Statement of Gen. Charles E. Wilhelm," United States Marine Corps, Commander in Chief, United States Southern Command, before the Senate Armed Services Committee (Washington, D.C.: U.S. Senate, 13 March 1999).

26. See, for instance, Paul Richter, "Military Is Easing Its War on Drugs," *Los Angeles Times*, 20 October 2002.

27. Cited in *Time*, "Soldier on the Beat," 3 December 2001.

28. For both Biden and Eberhardt quotes see *Washington Times*, "Biden Backs Letting Soldiers Arrest Civilians," 22 July 2002.

29. INL, *FY2001 CBJ*, April 2000, p. 13.

30. U.S. State Department, Bureau of Resource Management, *FY2002 Congressional Presentation for Foreign Operations*, April 2001.

31. U.S. Defense Department, *Report on the U.S. Army School of the Americas,* prepared for the committees on appropriations, U.S. Congress, January 2000; and U.S. State Department, Bureau of Political-Military Affairs, *Foreign Military Training and DoD Engagement Activities of Interest in Fiscal Years (FMTR) 1999 and 2000: A Report to Congress*, joint report of the Defense and State Departments, March 2000, www.state.gov/t/pm/rls/rpt/fmtrpt/.

32. U.S. Congress, *House Appropriations Committee Report 107-663 on H.R. 5410*, 19 September 2002, p. 61.

33. U.S. Congress, Department of Defense Appropriations Act, 2003 (P.L. 107-248/H.R. 5010).

34. Author interview with House Armed Services Committee staff, 29 May 2003.

35. See, for instance, Donald H. Rumsfeld, "Defense for the 21st Century," *Washington Post*, 22 May 2003.

36. United States Congress, Public Law 101-510 (Washington, D.C.: Library of Congress).

37. H. Allen Holmes, coordinator for Drug Enforcement Policy and Support, U.S. Defense Department, letter in response to congressional inquiry, 23 January 1998; Ana Maria Salazar, Deputy Assistant Secretary of Defense for Drug Enforcement Policy and Support, U.S. Defense Department, letter in response to congressional inquiry, 19 March 1999; U.S. Defense Department, Office of the Deputy Assistant Secretary of Defense for Drug Enforcement Policy and Support, correspondence with authors, 21 September 2000; U.S. Defense Department, "Report on Department of Defense Expenditures To Support Foreign Counterdrug Activities," 29 December 2000; U.S. Congress, Conference Report 106-701 on H.R. 3908, 29 June 2000. On CIP website under Colombia; U.S. Defense Department, Assistant Secretary of Defense for Special Operations and Low Intensity Conflict, report required by the Floyd D. Spence National Defense Authorization Act for Fiscal Year 2001 (P.L. 106-398), 18 April 2002; U.S. Defense Department, "DoD Andean Initiative FY02 Colombia," Washington, document obtained 19 September 2001; and U.S. State Department, *A Report to Congress*, 3 December 2002, p. 14.

38. U.S. State Department, *FY2002, FY2003, FY2004 Congressional Presentation for Foreign Operations*, April 2001, February 2002, and February 2003, respectively.

39. U.S. State Department, Department of Defense, *Foreign Military Training in Fiscal Years 2002 and 2003* (Washington, D.C.: State Department, May 2003); U.S. State Department, Department of Defense, *Foreign Military Training and DoD Engagement Activities of Interest* (Washington, D.C.: State Department, March 2002).

40. Ibid.; U.S. State Department, Office of Resources, Plans, and Policy, *Congressional Presentation for Foreign Operations, Fiscal Year 2004* (Washington, D.C.: February 2003).

41. U.S. State Department, *Fiscal Year 2004 International Narcotics and Law Enforcement Budget Justification* (Washington, D.C.: June 2003).

42. WOLA, *Clear and Present*, pp. 29–30.

43. *Washington Post*, "Cloak Over the CIA Budget," editorial, 29 November 1999.

44. INL, *Peru Investigation Report*, 2 August 2001, www.state.gov/g/inl/rls/rpt/pir/.

45. *El Tiempo*, "Molestia de Estados Unidos por 'fuga' de pilotos colombianos entrenados para antinarcóticos," Bogotá, 18 February 2003.

46. U.S. State Department, "Report on Certain Counternarcotics Activities in Colombia," 14 April 2003, www.ciponline.org/colombia/03041401.htm.

47. U.S. State Department, U.S. Embassy, Bogotá, "Remarks by Ambassador Anne W. Patterson at the CSIS Conference," Washington, 8 October 2002, usembassy.state.gov/colombia/wwwsa034.shtml.

48. Representative Bob Barr, *The Barr Report on Plan Colombia and the War on Drugs* (Washington, D.C.: House Government Reform Committee, January 2003), p. 8; and Phil Stewart, "U.S. Contractors Pay Price of Drug War in Colombia," Reuters, Bogotá, 31 October 2003.

49. INL, "The April 20, 2001 Peruvian Shootdown Accident," under the *Peru Investigation Report*, 2 August 2001.

50. *Revista Semana,* Bogotá, 4 May 2001.

51. Representative Janice Schakowsky, "Schakowsky's Statement on Plan Colombia Before Subcommittee on Criminal Justice, Drug Policy and Human Resources," U.S. House of Representatives, 2 March 2001.

52. U.S. White House, presidential letter to U.S. Congress, 24 June 2002, www.whitehouse.gov/news/releases/2002/07/20020703-14.html.

53. Mark Bowden, "Killing Pablo," *Philadelphia Inquirer,* 20 November 2001.

54. Gabriel Marcella, *Working Paper 13: The United States and Colombia: The Journey from Ambiguity to Strategic Clarity* (Miami, Fla.: Dante B. Fascell North-South Center, University of Miami, March 2003), p. 7.

55. INL, *INCSR 1998, 1999, 2000, 2001, and 2002.*

56. U.S. State Department, Report to Congress, 27 July 2000, www.ciponline.org/colombia/080102.htm.

57. General Barry R. McCaffrey, Director, Office of National Drug Control Policy, "Remarks to the Atlantic Council of the United States," 28 November 2000, www.ciponline.org/colombia/112801.htm.

58. U.S. Defense Department, "Media Round Table with Peter Rodman, ASD ISA," 21 August 2001. Available at Defenselink.mil under News Archives.

59. *Washington Times*, "U.S. Law Bars Giving Colombians Data," 26 February 2002.

60. Angel Rabasa and Peter Chalk, *Colombian Labyrinth: The Synergy of Drugs and Insurgency and Its Implications for Regional Stability* (Santa Monica, Calif.: RAND Corporation, June 2001).

61. Jonathan Wright, "Powell Sees 'Gray Areas' in Defining Terrorism," *Reuters*, 25 October 2001.

62. George Tenet, Director of Central Intelligence, before the Senate Select Committee on Intelligence, "Testimony on the Worldwide Threat—Converging Dangers in a Post 9/11 World," 6 February 2002.

63. U.S. House of Representatives, House Armed Services Committee, General James T. Hill, commander, U.S. Southern Command, posture statement, 12 March 2003.

64. H.R. 1588, The National Defense Authorization Act for Fiscal Year 2004, as introduced in the House of Representatives, 3 April 2003.

65. Donald Rumsfeld, Secretary of Defense, statement at Defense Ministerial of the Americas, Santiago, 19 November 2002, www.defenselink.mil/speeches/2002/s20021119-secdef.html.

66. Ibid.

67. U.S. Senate, Western Hemisphere Subcommittee, testimony of Peter W. Rodman, Assistant Secretary for International Security Affairs, Department of Defense, 24 April 2002 (Washington, D.C.: April 24, 2002), usinfo.state.gov/regional/ar/colombia/02042402.htm.

68. Jeffrey Sachs, "Call It Our Bolivian Policy of Not-So-Benign Neglect," *Washington Post*, 26 October 2003.

69. See the annual polls of attitudes toward democracy by the nonprofit Corporación Latinobarómetro at www.latinobarometro.org.

70. Priest, *The Mission*, p. 14.

3

U.S. Police Assistance and Drug Control Policies

Rachel Neild

Two explicit agendas inform U.S. assistance and training for foreign police forces. The first is to combat transnational crime and is meant to produce impacts in the short term. The second is to support democratic institutional reforms that will create greater police accountability and effectiveness in the medium to long terms. Counterdrug assistance and training falls firmly in the first category. For the most part, however, these programs have not achieved their objectives of reducing the supply and purity of drugs on U.S. streets. Moreover, there is ample evidence that corrupt and unaccountable police forces are often incapable of mounting successful drug control operations. Nevertheless, U.S. drug war hawks have not studied and learned from the lessons of promising police reforms carried out in the Western Hemisphere since the end of the Cold War. They have not provided the necessary diplomatic backing, training, and assistance for professionalizing police forces and for increasing their accountability.

Until the late 1980s, most U.S. drug control assistance for Latin America was provided to the region's police forces. Both the U.S. and regional militaries were reluctant to engage in antidrug efforts, viewing them as a distraction from the real business of national security, which focused on anticommunism and counterinsurgency. However, U.S. antidrug efforts in Latin America were unable to find or create adequate policing capacities and partnerships in the region. This challenge, and the growing number of drug warriors on Capitol Hill, led to an enhanced role for both the U.S. and local militaries in U.S. drug control policy in Latin America.

U.S. pressure to involve regional militaries in the drug war and increasing U.S. military training of Latin American police run directly counter to numerous countries' efforts to civilianize and to professionalize these forces. The United States continues to work overwhelmingly with specially created police antidrug units despite their abysmal track record of abuse and corruption. Efforts to confront these problems have not focused on improving the overall accountability of entire police forces but rather on

creating small special investigative units that can be almost entirely isolated and controlled. U.S. coca eradication policies have also placed police at
the forefront of deeply conflictive and violent campaigns in which hundreds of poor farmers have been arrested and abused and significant numbers killed. The United States has supported, and in some cases even drafted, repressive drug laws whose application has served primarily to jail the
bit players: consumers, coca growers, and mules who transport small
amounts of drugs. This clogs the courts and aggravates already dire prison
conditions. But weak and corrupt judicial systems rarely prove capable of
detaining major drug traffickers.

U.S. drug control policies remain fundamentally at odds with attitudes
and priorities of partner nations, irritating international relations and
impeding program implementation. This disjuncture is reflected in the lack
of local support for and, therefore, lack of sustainability of many counterdrug strategies. An oft-repeated criticism of U.S. drug control strategies is
that they are designed to meet short-term operational goals rather than to be
workable over the long run. At times, U.S. personnel replace or substitute
for local law enforcement personnel who are judged inadequate to the task,
and there is little local capacity to fill the void once the operation is over
and the U.S. personnel have gone. State Department officials say they now
increasingly stress improvement of broader institutional capacity and
accountability. However, to date there is only uneven and fragmentary evidence that such programs are in operation.

Police reform is desperately needed across Latin America. As recent
studies of policing in the region make clear, practically every Latin
American police force is characterized by corrupt and abusive practices.[1]
Historically, the militarization of policing has been more profound in Latin
America than in any other region of the world.[2] Furthermore, police forces
that have served primarily to protect specific governments or political
regimes, and that have fought side-by-side with the military in brutal counterinsurgency campaigns, have proven to be unprofessional and ill-
equipped to conduct criminal investigations or implement crime prevention
strategies.[3]

Since the early 1990s, comprehensive and partial police reform efforts
have occurred across Latin America. The Central American peace processes
of the 1990s, which had significant international support, brought about the
broadest of these initiatives. Further police reforms have been undertaken,
with some successes but more failures, in Argentina, Brazil, Chile, and
Venezuela. Of the Andean countries, Colombia undertook an important
police reform in the mid-1990s, and Peru is in the midst of a reform process
that began in 2002. Following clashes between the military and police in
Bolivia in 2003, the issue is on the agenda in that country also.

The postwar police reforms in Central America focused mainly on the demilitarization of internal security, placing police under civilian ministries and bringing crimes committed by police under the jurisdiction of civilian rather than military courts. However, scholars note that demilitarization has not necessarily brought with it "fully accountable, non-partisan, participatory, and effective security systems."[4] Further efforts are needed to improve police skills, professionalism, and community relations. On the judicial side, countries across the region have undertaken major reforms seeking to increase judicial independence and increase the speed and transparency of the judicial process. However, these programs are still in their infancy and have received inadequate levels of support.

The key factor driving concern with police reform in Latin America today is the alarming rise in crime and social violence across the region.[5] Many factors feed this trend, including rapid urbanization, income inequality, availability of weapons, changing demographics, and the loosening of authoritarian social controls. What is more, Latin American governments that previously viewed drug production, trafficking, and consumption as fundamentally a U.S. problem are now starting to believe that their own rising domestic consumption is correlated with increasing local crime problems.[6] Along with police reform initiatives, crime prevention strategies are being undertaken across the region in response to these concerns, and international donors such as the Inter-American Development Bank are supporting these efforts. Less positively, many politicians find repressive policies and the rhetoric of zero tolerance deeply appealing, despite the limited capacity of their criminal justice systems and the high cost of repressive policies that stress incarceration, including for minor offenses.

There is a clear need for professional and accountable law enforcement and for national crime prevention policies that can guide resource allocation and coordinate multisectoral responses to factors underlying crime and social violence. There is also increasing demand from Latin American governments and civil society for models of police reform and assistance—both technical and financial—to support such reform processes. Many Latin American policymakers are open to constructive U.S. participation, such as the role of former New York Police Department commissioner Bill Bratton in advising the municipal police in Caracas, Venezuela, or Giuliani Associates' current contract with Mexico City authorities.[7]

U.S. counterdrug policies, however, appear to be sticking with the same failed strategies. For more than twenty years, assistance for counterdrug law enforcement has used expedient tactics in pursuit of short-term operational goals. But the prospects for success are constantly undermined by profound institutional and structural problems that will be fixed only through the strengthening of democracy and the creation of institutional accountability and the rule of law. Instead of fostering such reforms, U.S. counterdrug tactics too often run directly counter to measures that might enhance accountability and improve police-community relations and police services. Direct U.S. assistance for democratic reforms, moreover, is dwarfed by drug control programs seeking rapid results.

• U.S. Police Assistance in the Twentieth Century: From Cold War to Drug War

The United States has a long history of involvement in the development of police forces in Latin America and the Caribbean. During the early decades of the twentieth century, following U.S. invasions of Haiti, Cuba, the Dominican Republic, Panama, and Nicaragua, the U.S. created "constabulary-style police forces" in these countries.[8] These forces were military-police hybrids, and they produced a number of dictators, including Rafael Leónidas Trujillo in the Dominican Republic and Anastasio Somoza in Nicaragua.[9]

Post–World War II international assistance focused on the goal of containment. Under the Truman doctrine, developing countries were given a "subversive pressure ranking," and aid, including police assistance, was allocated according to this score. Dwight Eisenhower's administration (1953–1961) pressed for a reduction in military spending and launched a worldwide foreign police assistance program as preventive medicine against communism. During the 1950s, the State Department's International Cooperation Administration (predecessor to the U.S. Agency for International Development, or USAID) administered foreign police assistance. In the mid-1950s it created the Civil Police Administration (CPA) and later broadened the initiative to combine military and police assistance with assistance for judicial reform, calling it the Overseas Internal Security Program (OISP).

U.S. police assistance grew dramatically during the Cold War in Latin American countries considered friendly to U.S. interests. In 1962 the Interagency Committee for Police Assistance was formed under John F. Kennedy's administration with participation from the Central Intelligence Agency (CIA), the Federal Bureau of Investigation (FBI), USAID, the Treasury Department, and the Pentagon, with the aim of creating a centralized police program rather than having the CIA, Pentagon, and USAID running competitive and often conflicting programs. The Pentagon alone was interested in housing the new program, but others argued that smart counterinsurgency kept military and policing functions separate. The CIA reportedly feared that overt police assistance programs would undermine its covert missions and preferred to use the programs as cover for CIA agents rather than actually run the police assistance program themselves.[10]

Over the objections of USAID staff, who saw police assistance as unrelated to and possibly a problem for their development mission, USAID became the home of the ill-fated Office of Public Safety (OPS) in

November 1962. Byron Engle, former director of the CPA and a former CIA employee with some of their police programs, became the first director of OPS. USAID had little control over OPS, which was given autonomy in its budget, hiring, and logistics in order to avoid becoming marginalized, as the CPA had been. This autonomy also reduced congressional oversight of the new program.

The OPS's single largest program was in Vietnam, where OPS advisers trained Vietnamese police responsible for creating the infamous "tiger cages."[11] The other main area of OPS program implementation was Latin America. OPS provided weapons, equipment, and training in such areas as "criminal investigation, intelligence, patrolling, interrogation and counterinsurgency techniques, riot control, traffic control, weapon use and bomb disposal" to thousands of foreign police officers.[12] The primary focus of much of the training was to develop intelligence methods to combat the threat of communist subversion, although Engle tried to maintain a focus on institution-building for foreign police as well as on counterinsurgency.[13] Democratic policing or human rights compliance were never prerequisites for receiving police assistance from the OPS, nor was civilian control of police.

Increasing reports of human rights violations on the part of OPS-assisted police forces, coupled with accusations that the United States was training in torture methods and using the OPS as an intelligence apparatus, led to the imposition of broad limits on U.S. assistance to foreign police forces. In 1973 the U.S. Congress voted to end all police training conducted abroad. The following year, Congress passed Section 660 as an amendment to the Foreign Assistance Act (see Appendix 1), terminating USAID's OPS and cutting off funding "used to provide training or advice, or provide any financial support for police, prisons, or other law enforcement forces for any foreign government or any program of internal intelligence or surveillance on behalf of any foreign government within the United States or abroad."[14] During its thirteen years of operation, the program had trained more than one million police and sent approximately U.S.$325 million in equipment overseas.[15]

While often perceived as an overarching ban on U.S. police training and assistance, Section 660 applies only to activities funded through the annual foreign assistance budget passed by Congress. It never affected use of the separately authorized and appropriated budgets of the Departments of Justice, Defense, Treasury, or Transportation for training or otherwise assisting foreign law enforcement officials. An early exemption to Section 660 allowed the use of foreign aid monies for counterdrug activities.[16] In addition, a further series of amendments beginning in 1981 created a long list of exemptions, including a country-specific exemption for police training in Haiti during the regime of Jean-Claude Duvalier and a more general exemption for police training related to antiterrorism. The president was given the authority to provide assistance when necessary to ensure U.S. national security as well as in cases when it is "inadvisable to specify the nature of the use of such funds." Even before the most recent amendments to Section 660, in 1992, the U.S. General Accounting Office was able to identify 125 countries that received police training financed by U.S. taxpayers, despite the legislative "ban."[17]

After the collapse of the Berlin Wall and the end of the Cold War, peace processes in Central America included a central focus on reforming the security forces responsible for gross violations of human rights and the deaths of tens of thousands during the protracted—and U.S.-supported— civil wars of the region. El Salvador, where the United States and the United Nations helped to design and fund a major police reform, provided an initial success story and an indication of how valuable international assistance for police reforms could be. The United States and other donors have since gone on to build new police forces and practices in the former Yugoslavia, East Timor, and many other countries emerging from conflict.

In the process, a new norm of "democratic policing" has been emerging. One definition states that democratic policing is characterized by civilian control, nonpartisanship and nondiscrimination, and adherence to the general principles of human rights in the pursuit of police duties.[18] Noted police scholar David Bayley defines democratic policing in terms of adherence to three broad principles: *responsiveness* to the communities that police serve and not solely to the government; *accountability* through multiple mechanisms to multiple audiences; and *transparency*.[19] Other policing experts note the need for specialized oversight such as civilian review, accountability to the state through oversight by elected officials, the courts, and prosecutors, and accountability to local communities and civil society.[20]

The general prohibition of aid for police has, nevertheless, not hindered the evolution of a gamut of programs through what can be described as a "policy of exemptions" to Section 660. Rather than preventing police assistance as originally intended, the section's statutory authority has been hollowed out by a series of exemptions that have created multiple channels of funding for diverse programs through multiple agencies. This has, over time, created patches of agency turf and competition for programs and funds. The conduct of almost all police assistance programs as exemptions to Section 660 has made it impossible to have a national police assistance program or to develop policy guidelines and coordinated programs within the parameters of current law and funding. Congressional oversight of the diverse funding channels through which police assistance is provided is weak at best, and until recently few in Congress have shown any interest in addressing these structural issues.

The Washington debate about police assistance—or lack thereof—has changed for several reasons. First, there is increasing interest in providing better civilian police contingents (CivPol) to support humanitarian and postconflict interventions, and congressional advocacy and attention to the issues has increased with the new prominence of such interventions by the UN and other parties. Section 660 was recently amended to allow police assistance for rebuilding policing in postconflict settings and for certain training and assistance to build more professional management. Bill Clinton's administration issued a presidential directive that set out principles and guidelines for U.S. police to participate in peacekeeping missions. This was cancelled by President George W. Bush, however, and has not been replaced.

Second, the evident need for police reform brought the issue back onto USAID's agenda. The agency is currently supporting a program in Jamaica through a country-specific exemption to Section 660. A similar exemption now exists for El Salvador's ongoing International Criminal Investigative Training Assistance Program (ICITAP), as the postconflict exemption is considered to no longer apply a decade after that country's peace process. Nevertheless, USAID has been hampered in responding more broadly. In 2002 and 2003, it undertook an internal review process to discuss issues around starting new police assistance programs. Some in the agency argued that the experience of OPS should serve as a warning of the risks of undertaking police assistance again. Many others felt, however, that rule of law programs were needed to address the entire spectrum of criminal justice issues, including policing and crime prevention, in order to meet the threat that rising crime poses to poverty alleviation and democratic development.[21]

Finally, human rights advocates who previously saw only pernicious effects of police assistance now also see its importance in supporting democratic institutional reforms and greater police accountability outside of the United States. They remain concerned, however, about potential misuse and the need for transparency and accountability in all U.S. police aid programs, particularly in light of the new counterterror operational imperative.

The assorted pressures for a new police assistance policy resulted in congressional initiatives during 2003, including one that would have repealed Section 660 altogether and another that would have opened the door to more USAID police programming. Neither succeeded, in part due to strenuous opposition by the State Department's Bureau of International Narcotics Control and Law Enforcement (INL), which currently enjoys significant authority to conduct police assistance through the exemptions to Section 660. In early 2004, the administration again argued in congressional hearings for the repeal of Section 660.[22]

• Counterdrug Police Assistance

U.S. government assistance to foreign law enforcement agencies to curb drug trafficking began in 1949, when two Federal Bureau of Narcotics agents were sent to Turkey and France to try to stop the flow of heroin into the United States. By the 1960s and 1970s, federal drug law enforcement agents were conducting major international operations aimed at cutting marijuana and heroin importation across the Mexican border and at curbing heroin trafficking into the United States by the French mafia (the so-called French connection).

In the late 1970s, with increasing drug-related violence in South Florida, cocaine rose on the U.S. agenda. U.S. police aid and new USAID crop substitution programs focused on an effort to eliminate coca at the source. In Peru, Operation Verde Mar was launched in 1979 with 1,000 police flooding into the Huallaga Valley coca-growing region. They were supported by the Peruvian military and the imposition of a state of emergency giving security forces broad powers of search and seizure and detention. After the operation, U.S. officials pressed for a permanent police presence in the region to support ongoing eradication efforts funded by the State Department's Bureau of International Narcotics Matters (INM, the precursor to INL), to the tune of U.S.$17.5 million over five years. The Unidad Móvil de Patrullaje Rural (UMOPAR—Mobile Rural Patrol Unit) was created to provide a permanent police presence fighting drugs in the Huallaga.[23] A U.S.-funded UMOPAR unit was also created in the mid-1980s in Bolivia and took part in major eradication campaigns in the Chapare coca-growing region.

Along with growing drug problems came the development of the Washington drug control bureaucracy. President Richard Nixon (1969–1974) declared a "war on drugs" that led to the 1973 creation of the Drug Enforcement Administration (DEA) through the consolidation of the drug control functions of several existing offices and agencies.[24] However, U.S. Customs continued to conduct overseas enforcement operations and investigations. Meanwhile, the U.S. Coast Guard became involved in overseas antidrug enforcement and investigation; State Department–backed counterdrug assistance to foreign police agencies began in 1978; and FBI involvement in international drug control programs began in earnest in the 1980s.

A major turning point for U.S. counterdrug policy in Latin America came with the crack cocaine epidemic and the explosion of drug-related violence in U.S. inner cities in the mid-1980s. In September 1989, President George H. W. Bush (1989–1993) launched the Andean Initiative, which increased emphasis on source countries and led to a dramatic increase in levels of military assistance. These trends continued through the 1990s, with increasing military training of police in drug control programs.

The Pentagon and Police Training

Foreign police now receive U.S. training in a number of military institutions in the United States, including at the Western Hemisphere Institute for Security Cooperation (formerly School of the Americas), as well as in their home countries (see Chapter 2). This training is funded with International Narcotics Control (INC) monies channeled through the State Department's INL but also directly out of the Pentagon's own budget. Military training of police goes directly against efforts across the region during the 1980s and 1990s to bring police under civilian control and increase accountability.

While Section 660 governs police training funded through the foreign aid process, U.S. training of foreign police forces is also permitted by law directly through the Defense Department's budget. Section 1004 of the National Defense Authorization Act of 1991, described in greater detail in Chapter 2 and Appendix 1, allows the Defense Department to train foreign police forces for counterdrug purposes. Because it is not part of the Foreign Assistance Act, Section 1004 funding circumvents congressional scrutiny and human rights safeguards. According to the U.S. government's annual Foreign Military Training Report (FMTR) to Congress, the United States provided Section 1004 training to 674 police officers in Latin America in 2002.

A partial picture of military training of Latin American police can be obtained from the report covering fiscal year 2002. It shows that in Colombia Section 1004 funding was used to pay for "a variety of United States Marine Corps and Special Operations Forces (SOF) efforts, including aviation aircrew training, Colombian marine riverine training, and light infantry training of Colombian police and military." More than 4,800 Colombians were trained through Section 1004, including 100 Colombian police who received light infantry training. In Peru, according to the FMTR, there were 231 police officers out of a total of 237 security forces personnel trained with Pentagon funds under Section 1004. Training included aviation, counterdrug operations, search and rescue, and maritime interdiction, and 100 police officers received light infantry training. U.S. light infantry is described as "small unit tactics such as evasion, maneuver, and ambushing; marksmanship and proficiency with weapons; squad and platoon tactics; and combat in difficult terrains like jungles."[25]

While any U.S. military training of foreign police forces blurs the line between civilian and military roles, the implications of this training vary by country. In Costa Rica and Panama, which have no militaries, the police have taken on counterdrug roles fulfilled by militaries in other Latin American countries. But Section 1004 police training programs, such as the light infantry training given to Colombian and Peruvian police, are less appropriate and raise greater concerns. Similar training, also provided by Special Forces, was given to the Guatemalan police at a time when the U.S. Congress had suspended the Guatemalan military from receiving U.S.

training and when the Guatemalan counterdrug police were known for corruption.[26]

The training provided by the Pentagon to Latin American police forces, already troubling, is accompanied by broader U.S. policies that have encouraged extensive use of Latin American militaries in domestic counterdrug operations. This damages the effort to clearly distinguish between the military's duties in external defense and domestic policing. In the United States, by contrast, this distinction is enshrined in the principle of Posse Comitatus (see Appendix 1). Furthermore, the tactics and skills taught encourage the development of—or continued reliance on—skills that are profoundly antithetical to democratic policing standards. The logic of military action is the use of force to defeat an enemy in battle, and strict obedience to the command hierarchy is required. In policing, officers must protect and serve citizens by preventing crime and enforcing the law; the support and cooperation of citizens are essential to police effectiveness. In their daily work, democratic police use minimum force, relying on it only when necessary to protect against imminent danger. Patrol officers, typically working in pairs or small groups with little immediate supervision, use significant discretion in their contacts with citizens and need judgment and communication skills.

International Narcotics and Law Enforcement

The State Department's Bureau of International Narcotics and Law Enforcement is the hub of U.S. drug control efforts. It coordinates all U.S. overseas antidrug activities and manages the International Narcotics Control program, the main source of funding for the U.S. foreign drug control programs described here. International law enforcement training is managed and funded by the INL and carried out by a variety of U.S. law enforcement agencies including the DEA, the FBI, the Department of Justice, the Department of Homeland Security, and the U.S. Coast Guard.

The INL funds the law enforcement training given to police officers, judges, investigators, prosecutors, and customs and border officials on how to prevent, investigate, and prosecute drug-related crimes. In fiscal year 1999, this training involved 696 courses in more than ninety-five countries and was budgeted at more than U.S.$30 million. In FY2001, the INL sponsored training for more than 3,600 counterdrug law enforcement personnel worldwide.[27] Between FY1998 and FY2001, INL funding paid for training for approximately 10,000 foreign officials. Generally, training programs held in the United States are tailored to senior-level managers and policymakers, while programs offered in-country are reserved for operational personnel.[28] For FY2003, the INL's budget for Latin America and the Caribbean was U.S.$721.75 million, the vast majority of which was allocated to the Andean counterdrug initiative. Of its total budget worldwide,

37.4 percent was dedicated to law enforcement and another 18.2 percent to eradication.[29]

Police assistance is generally provided on a bilateral basis. According to one official, the INL encourages coordination in the recipient country rather than in Washington, D.C., among the various U.S. government agencies involved in a country program.[30] However, a 1992 U.S. General Accounting Office (GAO) report on police assistance abroad observed that "U.S. agencies may be duplicating efforts" in the provision of certain types of training, administrative work, and needs assessments. It noted that the Anti-Terrorism Assistance program, ICITAP, and the DEA all have interests in improving policing capabilities, yet "each agency conducts its own in-depth force capability and training needs assessment before commencing training." The 1992 GAO report cited lack of coordination and lack of policy guidance from Washington as two of the main problems with assistance programs:

> A former U.S. ambassador in Latin America said that because there is no U.S. policy guidance each agency pursues its own program agenda, which may not be in concert with long-term U.S. interests. Thus, he said, the U.S. government lacks a mechanism for considering how the various activities contribute to a strategy of fostering democratic institutions or to serving other national interests.[31]

This situation does not appear to have changed in any significant way, although INL and other State Department officials do say that there is increasing recognition of the need to confront police corruption and impunity in a more systematic fashion.[32] However, according to one State Department official, when key people from all the relevant agencies met in late 2001 or early 2002 to discuss a new assistance program to support police reform in Jamaica, this was the first time such strategic interagency coordination had taken place in the area of public security assistance.[33]

The Drug Enforcement Administration

The DEA, which like the FBI operates under the authority of the U.S. attorney general, is the only U.S. government agency that concentrates solely on drug control. About 10 percent of the DEA's operations are international (see Figure 3.1 for DEA funding in Latin America only); it is the principal agency coordinating drug enforcement intelligence overseas and conducting drug law enforcement operations. It shares jurisdiction in certain areas with the FBI and/or the CIA. Since its inception in the 1970s, the DEA has massively increased its budget and also its presence in Latin America. As of 2002, the DEA had thirty-eight offices located in twenty-four countries in Latin America and the Caribbean.[34] Following the September 11 terror attacks in 2001, the DEA shifted some of its emphasis toward narcoterrorism (see Appendix 1).[35]

Figure 3.1   DEA Funding, 1998–2004

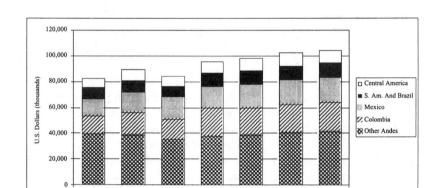

Source: DEA response to questions from Ranking Member José Serrano (D-New York), July 2003. On file at WOLA.

DEA functions and organization. Most DEA foreign drug control programs are run through the Office of International Operations, which includes the Special Operations Division and the Office of Aviation Operations. The Special Operations Division targets the communication systems of Mexico- and Colombia-based trafficking groups that transport and distribute drugs into the United States—the so-called kingpin strategy, which first evolved in 1992. The Office of Aviation Operations, with duty posts in Peru, Colombia, Bolivia, Mexico, Puerto Rico, and the Bahamas, carries out air-to-ground surveillance, overflights, photographic reconnaissance, and rapid deployment of personnel and equipment.[36] The DEA has 680 intelligence analysts worldwide gathering drug-related intelligence (Figure 3.2 shows DEA agents and other personnel stationed in Latin America).[37] It also provides equipment and training to Joint Information Coordination Centers in more than twenty countries, primarily in Central and South America and the Caribbean.[38] These centers are modeled after and linked to the DEA's own El Paso Intelligence Center.

The DEA cannot legally conduct investigations or make arrests abroad and must work with local partners that have the legal standing to do so. During bilateral investigations, DEA agents work closely with local counterparts—developing sources of information, interviewing witnesses, working undercover, assisting in surveillance efforts, and providing forensic analysis. The aim is to produce indictments and prosecutions in either the host country, the United States, or a third nation.[39] Revelations during the

Figure 3.2   DEA Staffing in Latin America (Agents and Other Personnel)

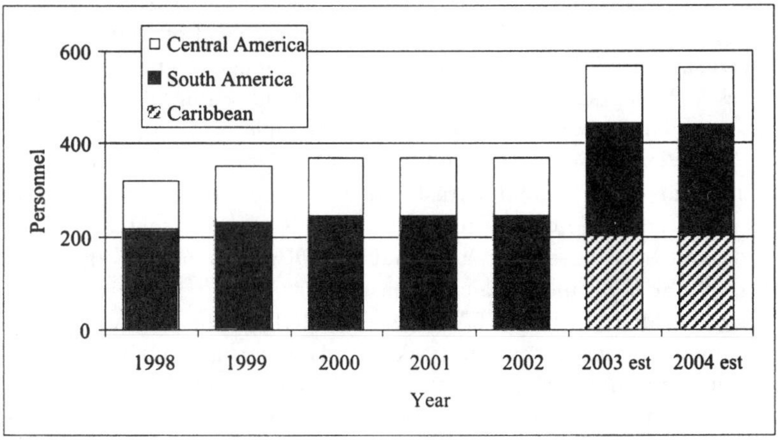

Source: DEA response to questions from Ranking Member José Serrano (D-New York), July 2003. On file at WOLA.

1970s that traffickers were arrested and tortured in foreign countries at the behest of DEA agents, and sometimes with DEA agents present and even involved in interrogations, led the U.S. Congress in 1976 to pass the Mansfield Amendment.[40] This amendment prohibits DEA agents from taking part in arrests, conducting electronic surveillance, or being present during foreign police enforcement operations unless they have a waiver from the ambassador.

DEA agents' official role is to advise and to offer real-time intelligence to host-nation personnel on the front lines of an operation. In practice, however, when it comes time to make an arrest or a seizure, DEA agents—or, occasionally, U.S. Special Forces members under the authority of Southcom—also participate in what are known as endgame operations alongside host-nation police forces and sometimes military forces as well. Various off-the-record conversations indicate that, in part because of mistrust of the host-nation forces' ability to do the job without endangering all involved, DEA agents are usually themselves in the front line, "kicking in doors."[41] This reality, and DEA agents' efforts to force operations to produce results even on the most unfertile ground, have earned them the reputation, in many Latin American countries, of being cowboys barely under control.

Police training is a key tool to improve the capabilities of the DEA's local partners. The DEA provides extensive training through its International

Training Section in Quantico, Virginia, and through teams of instructors who provide training on site in foreign countries. In 2001, the DEA trained 965 police in 192 in-country programs.[42] Between the DEA and its predecessor agencies, more than 40,000 foreign officers and officials have been trained since 1969.[43] The curriculum features a range of enforcement techniques including surveillance methods, drug field-testing, intelligence collection, and law enforcement management principles and skills.

While U.S. training can build skills and relationships, it has not proven an adequate tool to deal with local police corruption. Within Latin American police forces, drug control squads—many created with U.S. funds and training—have a dismal record of corruption and abuse. Mexico's FEADS, the Jamaican Constabulary Force's narcotics division, Bolivia's UMOPAR and FELCN, Peru's UMOPAR and DINANDRO, and Colombia's DIRAN all present track records of corruption, abuse of power and authority, human rights violations, and politicization.

Guatemala is another case in point. The United States funded the creation of the Department of Anti-Narcotics Operations (DOAN), developed its "investigative and operational capacity," and provided training, equipment, and infrastructure.[44] Nevertheless, it was shut down after a few years because of human rights abuses and pervasive corruption, including the theft of more than two tons of cocaine that had been confiscated from traffickers. By late 2002, DOAN was disbanded and replaced by the Anti-Narcotic Analysis and Information Service (SAIA, by its Spanish acronym). SAIA is funded and trained by the U.S. embassy's antidrug unit, the Narcotics Affairs Section (NAS). The State Department has expressed both hope and concern for the new unit, saying that the vetting procedures might help produce an effective antidrug force but that the Guatemalan government would have to "protect the SAIA from the tremendous corruption that led to the disbanding of the DOAN."[45]

Corruption and the SIUs. In the mid-1990s, in response to corruption and leaks of sensitive information during operations, the DEA began to screen and train special foreign police units known as Sensitive Investigative Units (SIUs). These are specialized units within antidrug units that mainly carry out intelligence and special investigations. The creation of an SIU allows intensive training to be focused on a specific group that can then receive separate, privileged treatment and, in theory, be protected from the vices of the broader police institution.

The vetted unit program initially began in Mexico in May 1996. After the government of Mexico approved the concept, twenty-one Mexican police were screened and then trained by the DEA.[46] In 1996 Congress approved U.S.$20 million for FY1997 to expand and support the program.[47] Since then, U.S.$20 million has been included annually in the DEA budget for what is now called the Sensitive Investigative Unit Program, which includes a five-week specialized training course at Quantico. In Latin America, the DEA has now established vetted units of antidrug law enforcement officers in Mexico, Colombia (with four units), Ecuador, Peru, Bolivia, Brazil, and the Dominican Republic (see Table 3.1).[48] The DEA claims important successes for the program, including successful investigations in 2002 by SIUs in Colombia, Mexico, and Peru that resulted in arrests of major traffickers and significant seizures.[49]

In the Andes, SIUs and drug control units frequently report to the U.S. embassy's NAS before they report to national political authorities. In some cases, senior national political authorities say that they have minimal contact with the units, which function in an opaque fashion. This direct infringement of national sovereignty is tolerated because noncooperation brings rapid and serious reprisals from the United States. In the words of one official, "As long as the gringos are happy, we don't have any problems. Anti-narcotics is their top issue, so any problems can affect the entire government."[50] But by undermining local control and the chain of command, the U.S. strategy reduces the support and real cooperation of local authorities, who have no say in policymaking or implementation. This lack of local official engagement in turn means that these units are often neglected or disbanded once U.S. support is reduced or ends, with the result that the U.S.-created counterdrug police capabilities and operations are rapidly lost.

According to DEA officials, however, SIU units are providing a model that Mexican authorities are taking up more broadly, by implementing polygraph tests (integrity screening) for all personnel assigned to the federal attorney general's office, which has authority over the federal police.[51] In

Table 3.1   Sensitive Investigative Units in Latin America and the Caribbean

Country	Operational funding (thousands of dollars)			Number of SIU members
	FY 2000	FY 2001	FY 2002	FY 2002/3
Mexico	940	340	2,255	126
Dominican Republic	N/A	497	485	30
Colombia	2,190	3,640	2,955	161
Ecuador	1,232	875	780	46
Peru	1,867	2,550	1,750	133
Brazil	170	444	935	80
Bolivia	2,500	2,650	1,235	150
Total	8,899	10,996	10,395	726

Source: DEA response to questions from Ranking Member José Serrano (D-New York) July 2003. On file at WOLA.

Peru, the DEA has not shared polygraph training or equipment with the Peruvian police. It has insisted on conducting the entire process unilaterally, even when this provoked a crisis that was resolved only by removing both the head of the Dinandro antidrug police and the DEA country representative.[52]

The DEA and eradication programs. The DEA also coordinates and cooperates with foreign governments in other programs, such as crop eradication and substitution, designed to reduce the availability of illicit drugs.[53] Coca eradication campaigns have been among the most provocative aspects of U.S. counterdrug operations in the Andean source countries as they target poor farmers and have failed to offer adequate or viable alternative development programs. This has been particularly problematic in Peru and Bolivia, countries where coca has historically been grown and used by the local population. U.S.-backed policies that make coca cultivation illegal in these countries and demand eradication are a classic manifestation of the phenomenon of "overcriminalization."[54]

Overcriminalization occurs when laws punish activities—in this case growing coca beyond the restricted amount allowed for traditional noncocaine uses—that a large percentage of the population does not consider to be crimes. It is a particular problem when significant numbers of people are regularly engaged in these activities or depend on them for their livelihood, as in parts of Bolivia, Peru, and Colombia. Implementing such laws places the police and other officials charged with eradication into confrontation with local population. It also encourages corruption as police are tempted to become "regulators" of the illegal market, and thus benefit from its proceeds, rather than enforcing the very unpopular laws.

In the Andes, the United States has insisted on compliance with eradication targets. It has threatened countries with curtailment of aid and trade benefits if they fail to comply, even though eradication operations have frequently produced social upheaval and violent clashes between the police or military and local coca growers. Such clashes have resulted in deaths, serious injuries, and massive detentions. Eradication efforts are widely cited by U.S. and Bolivian analysts as a key factor in the October 2003 forced resignation of Bolivian president Gonzalo Sánchez de Lozada. In March 2003, Peruvian president Alejandro Toledo called a halt to eradication after massive rallies against it threatened to destabilize his government. Eradication was reinitiated in August when U.S. officials informed the Peruvian government that failure to do so would prevent Peru from benefiting from the Andean Trade Preference and Drug Enforcement Act.

Oversight of the DEA. External oversight of the DEA has been strikingly weak. The secretary of state and the U.S. ambassador to the country in question are supposed to be responsible for oversight of the DEA's work with and support for foreign police. No single congressional committee has jurisdiction over the DEA (see Appendix 1). More important, U.S. politicians of both parties are reluctant to risk appearing soft on drugs by raising troubling questions about the way the DEA does its business. The DEA is one of the few agencies that has ever received more money from Congress than was requested.[55] A July 1999 hearing was the first oversight hearing on the DEA's overall operations held in a decade by either congressional judiciary committee.[56] Congressional hearings have often focused on antidrug activities within specific countries or regions, and the DEA's role has sometimes been discussed as part of those examinations. But since the mid-1980s, none of the committees, subcommittees, or task forces with jurisdiction to examine the DEA has conducted thorough hearings on the international aspects of DEA operations.[57]

Assessments of the DEA's strategies are hampered by the agency's apparent disinclination to learn from its own operational experience. For years, the DEA had no system of "after-action analysis." A GAO audit of DEA operations in Mexico found that agents kept no records of operations deemed to be failures.[58] An Office of Management and Budget report on the DEA found that the agency was unable to demonstrate progress in reducing the availability of illegal drugs in the United States. DEA performance measures are not correlated with drug availability, and DEA managers are not held accountable for achieving results.[59]

Questions about the agency's performance have arisen, however, as more resources are sought for the war on terrorism. While increasing funds for other law enforcement agencies, the proposed White House budget for FY2004 contained no significant increase over the previous year for the DEA—a harsh reality check for an agency that had seen its budget more than double since 1995.[60]

In the wake of September 11, the DEA has moved to climb on the counterterrorism bandwagon in the hopes that linking drug use to the threat of terrorism would help it preserve its budget and influence. Former DEA administrator Asa Hutchinson was quick to point out that "while the DEA does not specifically target terrorists, we will target and track down drug traffickers and drug-trafficking organizations involved in terrorist acts."[61] The distinction between terrorists and drug traffickers operating in Colombia and other places has been effectively obliterated. U.S. Attorney General John Ashcroft declared, "Terrorism and drugs go together like rats and the bubonic plague. They thrive in the same conditions, support each other and feed off each other."[62]

Federal Bureau of Investigation

The FBI has had an overseas presence for more than sixty years. Its legal attachés (LEGATs) in U.S. embassies facilitate investigative communications between the United States and the host country. Because of its responsibility for fighting organized crime, the FBI has staked out a role in drug-trafficking investigations and works closely with the DEA.[63] FBI involvement in drug-related cases mushroomed in the 1980s and 1990s. The 1990s saw a major increase in LEGAT posts, with expansion in Latin America increasingly focused on drug control missions. In Latin America and the Caribbean, LEGATs are based in Argentina, Barbados, Brazil, Chile, Colombia, the Dominican Republic, Mexico, Panama, and Venezuela.

The FBI developed and apparently maintains an active role in training foreign police and paramilitary forces abroad. Although few details are available about specific Latin American training programs, a former FBI director testified in 1991 that FBI special agents were "working with U.S. military and Panamanian officials to restructure the Panamanian police force, and FBI laboratory, polygraph and investigative assistance was provided to El Salvador following the killing of six Jesuit priests [in 1989]."[64] Significant numbers of foreign police are trained at the FBI Academy in Quantico, but there is no comprehensive annual report on FBI training. Information received through the Freedom of Information Act (through a request from a member of the House Judiciary Committee) shows that in Latin America, Mexican and Colombian police receive the most FBI training, with 6,053 Mexican police trained between FY1995 and FY2002 and at least 756 Colombians trained between FY1998 and FY2003.[65]

The FBI has also worked closely with the DEA in creating the Sensitive Investigative Units. Together, the FBI and DEA vetted three kinds of units in the Mexican attorney general's office: the office of the counter-drug special prosecutor (Fiscalía Especial para Atención a Delitos contra la Salud, FEADS), the organized crime unit, and the U.S.-Mexican bilateral task forces. As of 1999, they had vetted hundreds of agents (see Chapter 8). Yet that year the DEA admitted that U.S. law enforcement agencies were no longer sharing sensitive information with FEADS because of corruption, and in January 2003 the FEADS was disbanded entirely.

To fight trafficking and other facets of the illegal trade in drugs, such as money laundering and the provision of precursor chemicals, specialized skills and capabilities are required. Organized drug crime is notoriously difficult to fight without the use of wiretaps and undercover and sting operations, given the ability of traffickers to bribe or retaliate violently against potential investigators and witnesses. The FBI and DEA have pressed for legislation to allow wiretaps and other undercover tactics, which are viewed as running counter to legal restrictions in some Latin American countries. Yet without strong controls and accountability mechanisms, such tactics are highly vulnerable to abuse. This is reflected in successive political espionage scandals in the region, notably in Alberto Fujimori's Peru and in Mexico, where the Mexican ruling party engages in constant and extensive wiretapping of political opponents.

The political dynamics shaping the FBI's counterdrug work changed after September 11 as the bureau came under criticism for failing to act on intelligence that might have provided prior warning. In May 2002, the FBI announced reorganization plans that would divert more than 400 agents currently assigned to drug-related investigations to counterterrorism activities. FBI director Robert Mueller testified in June 2002 that as a result of the reassignments the FBI would "be more deliberate in opening cases involving drug cartels and drug-trafficking organizations, making sure our efforts do not overlap or duplicate those of the DEA."[66] Still, the FBI continues to focus on drug investigations in Mexico, the border region of the U.S. Southwest, and the Eastern Caribbean.

As in the case of the DEA, congressional oversight over FBI programs has been weak. Within Congress, the House and Senate committees on the judiciary bear primary responsibility for oversight of both domestic and international FBI programs. The House International Relations Committee and the Senate Foreign Relations Committee have responsibility for traditional U.S. military and police foreign assistance programs. In this context, they have placed some effective legislative restrictions on FBI overseas police/paramilitary training and assistance programs in Northern Ireland (motivated by concerns that the FBI had trained forces that committed or condoned the murder of several defense attorneys there). Despite repeated congressional mandates to expand the FBI's international role, however, none of these committees has held extensive hearings on the international antidrug role played by the FBI. This is not likely to change as current congressional and FBI concerns focus overwhelmingly on counterterror activities.

U.S. Customs Service

Now part of the Department of Homeland Security, the U.S. Customs Service is the nation's oldest law enforcement arm, founded in 1789. It has jurisdiction over any commodity, vessel, or person that crosses the U.S. border. As of March 2002, Customs had 1,475 agents authorized by the DEA to conduct drug investigations. This number did not diminish following September 11, despite a subsequent presidential directive that Customs make defense against terrorism its highest priority. Commissioner Robert Bonner stated that he had no intention of pulling back from drug investigation and interdiction efforts.[67]

U.S. Customs conducts joint training with the DEA and the Internal Revenue Service on drug control enforcement policies, port security issues, counterterrorism programs, and intelligence operations.[68] Most Customs

Service antidrug training takes place in host countries. In 2001, more than 2,300 people received drug-related training from Customs, with funds provided by the State Department through the INL.

Congress established the Customs Service Air Program in 1969 in response to an increase in drug smuggling via light private aircraft. In 1999 the program had 114 aircraft deployed throughout the drug source and transit zones, including advanced early warning (AEW) aircraft providing radar coverage over the jungles and mountainous regions of Central and South America.[69] They also patrol the vast U.S.-Mexico border and international shipping lanes and air routes. Following the mistaken downing in April 2001 of a civilian plane in Peru, which killed a U.S. missionary and one of her children, all U.S. agency flights operating in the Andean region, including Customs AEW flights, were suspended until 2003. After September 11, these planes were largely redirected toward monitoring U.S. airspace and borders.[70]

Bureau of Alcohol, Tobacco, and Firearms

In 1968 the Treasury Department's Bureau of Alcohol, Tobacco, and Firearms (ATF) was mandated to enforce federal statutes involving illegal arms trafficking into and out of the United States. In 1974, after it became apparent that firearms originating in the United States were frequently used by international drug traffickers and terrorists, ATF launched the International Traffic in Arms (ITAR) initiative.[71] With the INL, ATF works to support the Interamerican Drug Abuse Control Commission of the Organization of American States, which includes among its priorities the curbing of the illicit arms trafficking that supports drug trafficking.

Since 1974, the ITAR program has worked closely with foreign governments to enforce U.S. federal firearms laws, to gather intelligence regarding the dynamics of international firearm trafficking, and to offer assistance to foreign law enforcement regarding illegal trafficking of weapons of U.S. origin. ATF established country offices in Mexico City in 1992 and in Bogotá in 1990 to assist in identifying the sources of illegally trafficked firearms and to train local law enforcement personnel working to trace illicit firearms. In February 1993, ATF conducted a firearms-trafficking workshop in Honduras for senior law enforcement officers and military personnel from thirteen Central American countries. In July of that year, it helped to establish the Jamaican National Firearms and Drug Intelligence Center.[72]

ATF declined to provide any data in response to a Freedom of Information Act request made in 2003 for information on its other activities in Latin America. Given the increase in armed crime and violence throughout the region, and the close association between drugs and weapons trafficking, this is an area where focusing greater attention and resources could bring real benefits both to U.S. law enforcement and to national authorities and law enforcement in Latin America.

U.S. Coast Guard

The U.S. Coast Guard is the lead federal agency for maritime drug interdiction and shares lead responsibility for air interdiction of maritime routes with the U.S. Customs Service.[73] The Coast Guard's counterdrug mission is to reduce the supply of drugs from the source by denying smugglers the use of air and maritime routes in what it calls the Transit Zone. This is a six-million-square-mile area that includes the Caribbean, Gulf of Mexico, and eastern Pacific. In meeting the challenge of patrolling this vast area, the Coast Guard coordinates closely with other federal agencies and countries within the region.[74] The Coast Guard conducts frequent combined operations with military and law enforcement organizations from many of the countries in the Caribbean. In addition, the Coast Guard assists in the development of local maritime law enforcement, such as the development of the Haitian Coast Guard (with the Canadian Coast Guard), and a long-term training effort to strengthen the Panamanian National Maritime Service.[75] With funding from the INL, the U.S. Coast Guard trained more than 300 foreign law enforcement agents in maritime law enforcement in 2001.[76]

International Law Enforcement Academies

The most recent development in U.S. training of foreign police is a network of international law enforcement academies (ILEAs) funded largely through the INL budget. ILEAs have already been established in the United States, Hungary, Thailand, and Botswana. Negotiations on the creation of an ILEA for Latin America (ILEA-South) were under way in Costa Rica as of early 2004. INL argues that the ILEAs encourage strong partnerships among regional countries to address common problems associated with criminal activity and that they also develop an extensive network of alumni who will exchange information with their U.S. counterparts and assist in transnational investigations.[77]

The descriptions of ILEA-South's training make clear that drug control training will be a major focus of the academy, although other training will also cover "attacking international terrorism," as well as "alien smuggling, financial crimes, and accountability in government." DEA instructors would likely teach a large percentage of the counterdrug classes. According to an October 2002 job posting, instructors are expected to have "practical DEA experience and academic expertise."[78] The training programs include drug identification, worldwide trafficking trends, case initiation, informant handling, intelligence operations, undercover operations, firearms, toll analysis and link charting, clandestine laboratory operations, raid planning and execution, interviewing and interrogation, surveillance, evidence collection and handling, precursor chemical control, international controlled deliveries, and officer safety and survival.

ILEA-South's establishment is controversial. Members of the Costa Rican Congress approved a proposal to increase national and civil society input into the governance of the academy and to make explicit the nonmilitary nature and goals of training conducted there. The original version of the treaty establishing the academy specified that it was for training of law enforcement officials, but there was no explicit ban on military trainees or military-style training. This is an issue of great sensitivity in Costa Rica, a country that abolished its military and maintains a constitutionally mandated neutrality. Human rights organizations have also argued that all training at the academy should be characterized by adherence to the principles of democratic policing, including transparency.[79] In March 2004, the U.S. embassy informed the Costa Rican government that proposed changes to the agreement were unacceptable, particularly the ban on military training.[80]

• U.S. Assistance for Institutional Development

In contrast to the programs described so far, which are directed at operational capability, institutional development aid has focused on building democratic policing practices such as police accountability, as well as improving investigative skills in order to prevent the use of torture to extract confessions from detainees. The main U.S. provider of such assistance has been the International Criminal Investigative Training Assistance Program, primarily funded with foreign aid monies for specific country programs and with some INC funds. USAID's rule of law program is another major actor, and has provided extensive support for legal reforms in Latin America since the 1980s. Although there are valid criticisms of all of these programs, the approach and principles underlying U.S. support for institutional reforms and professionalization offer a striking contrast to most of the training described in this chapter. They provide a model on which to build and improve if U.S. policy is to make a serious effort to develop professional, accountable, and effective law enforcement partners in the region.

ICITAP and OPDAT

In 1986, under an exemption to Section 660, USAID transferred funds to the Department of Justice to design, develop, and implement projects to improve and enhance the investigative capabilities of law enforcement agencies in Latin America and the Caribbean. The Department of Justice created the International Criminal Investigative Training Assistance

Program to carry out this mission. ICITAP's initial training focused on building specialized investigative skills of foreign police. In 1999, ICITAP trained 8,000 foreign law enforcement officials with a budget of U.S.$35 million. ICITAP is now a joint program with the Justice Department's Office of Professional Development and Training (OPDAT), which trains and assists foreign prosecutors' offices.

ICITAP's past programs in Bolivia and Honduras, and ongoing work in Colombia, provide technical assistance and training in such areas as enhancement of forensic capabilities, expansion of criminal investigation skills and techniques, and development of internal discipline.[81] However, starting with the effort to reform Panamanian security forces following the 1989 U.S. intervention, ICITAP became a key player in postconflict efforts to rebuild—or build from the ground up—new police forces and practices. This has included the establishment of new academies and training curricula, as well as the creation of accountability mechanisms such as offices of professional responsibility and internal affairs.

In postconflict settings, police reform is often central to the broader effort to establish democracy; internal security needs to be demilitarized, and political guarantees must be provided to all parties. The emphasis on institutional reform tends to override other U.S. policy objectives, at least in the immediate postconflict period, and despite the challenges of these difficult environments there have been important advances. The reformed police force in El Salvador, though far from perfect, is a vast improvement on the old Salvadoran National Police and is often cited as an important success story.[82]

Unlike counterdrug police assistance, ICITAP's mission explicitly includes a human rights focus. It aims "to support U.S. policy by providing law enforcement development assistance, based on internationally recognized principles of human rights and the rule of law, to foreign criminal justice systems."[83] ICITAP and OPDAT's rule of law assistance projects are funded from various parts of the annual foreign aid budget appropriation, and Leahy Amendment background vetting requirements apply (see Appendix 1). In addition, a "human dignity" course, developed jointly with the John Jay College of Criminal Justice in New York, was made an integral part of ICITAP programs in the early 1990s. The human dignity course has been given in most Latin American countries.[84]

Nevertheless, there have been criticisms—including in a Justice Department inspector general's inquiry—of ICITAP's training, of the quality of some employees and contractors, and of departmental management. Indeed, as a result of such flaws and interagency competition for police assistance programs and funds, police aid programs in Bolivia and Honduras were recently removed from ICITAP and are now being run by the INL.

USAID's Rule of Law Program

In the mid-1980s, the United States launched an ambitious initiative—first called the Administration of Justice program (AOJ) and now the Rule of Law (ROL) program—to support judicial reforms in Latin America. Initially, ROL projects often tried to work directly with the actors and institutions that were standing in the way of change. As a result, they were criticized for failing to address structural issues and for being overly technical.[85] The programs evolved and improved significantly, however, as USAID began to recognize the need for political will in recipient countries as essential to success. ROL assistance is today an important component of a broader U.S. democracy promotion program.[86] Greater attention is now given to the role of civil society and citizen participation in ensuring successful and sustained reforms, and more focus is put on related human rights and democratization efforts.

Common components of ROL projects include support for the design and implementation of new criminal procedure codes; improved efficiency and management of the justice sector; the provision of training and technical assistance to judges, prosecutors, and public defenders; increased access to justice through mediation, alternative dispute resolution, and other mechanisms; and reform of law school curricula.[87]

Various analyses agree that USAID has supported reform efforts that have brought about important changes in the justice systems of the region.[88] However, the goal of fair, equitable, and effective justice remains elusive. Reform efforts still often falter due to lack of sustained support from host country governments, the difficulty of reforming and reeducating entrenched bureaucracies, and the low levels of domestic, U.S., and other international funding. According to one USAID official, "By the end of 1999, USAID, and allied programs in the Departments of State and Justice, had provided about $300 million in grants to Latin America for work in justice and police reform, through regional and bilateral assistance programs in 19 countries."[89] The relatively small amounts of funding provided to each country for judicial reform stand in stark contrast to the more substantial sums for direct drug control and other assistance.

As in its 1992 report on police assistance, GAO reported in 2003 that democracy programs also suffer from lack of coordination and collaboration between the various U.S. agencies involved, leading to "fragmented programs that are not always mutually supportive in achieving common goals."[90] This is particularly acute in Latin America, where the operational imperative of fighting drugs has repeatedly outweighed the broader democratization mandates of USAID and U.S. foreign policy. In a number of cases, drug control strategies pursued by other U.S. agencies such as the INL or DEA have further discredited or weakened already dysfunctional and mistrusted judicial systems, even as the AOJ and ROL programs run by

USAID sought to address the structural problems underlying judicial weakness in Latin America.

When rule of law programs are developed and carried out in conjunction with U.S.-backed drug control efforts, moreover, the results are often deeply problematic, undermining the very human rights and due process guarantees that the ROL program is designed to protect. U.S. embassy personnel and antidrug officials have pressed for legal reforms and initiatives, including harsh drug control legislation and special antidrug courts, that have violated basic due process rights and national constitutional standards. USAID assistance is sometimes provided to ensure efficient enforcement of antidrug laws that lack due process guarantees. Judges, prosecutors, and other judicial personnel in antidrug courts have often received their salaries and monthly bonuses from USAID.

Bolivia provides a case in point. In 1988, under intense U.S. pressure, the Bolivian congress passed Law 1008. The legislation violated basic standards of due process in a variety of ways, among them by reducing the amount of evidence needed for a conviction to the point where a defendant essentially had to prove innocence. As bail was banned for drug offenses, even if a defendant was acquitted in the first court, the defendant remained in jail while the case was appealed through two higher courts. In practice, this meant that all arrests resulted in jail time of two to five years spent in appalling prison conditions, even if the defendant was innocent.[91] Some of the worst pieces of Law 1008 were finally corrected by the 2001 reform of the Bolivian criminal procedure code—a process supported by USAID.

ROL officials were clear about how the short-term and heavy-handed tactics used in counterdrug programs competed with the objectives of ROL programs, which were ostensibly aimed at creating fair and effective judiciaries that would improve respect for human rights. A USAID Bolivia project paper noted that: "Failure to differentiate between [the AOJ program and drug control efforts] places the program at risk of being perceived by the Bolivian public opinion as subordinate to narcotics control programs and possibly raising serious political complications for it."[92]

Colombia presents another example. USAID funds were directly used to support the creation of Colombia's regional courts—initially called Public Order Courts—which operated for a decade beginning in 1987 to prosecute crimes of drug trafficking and terrorism. The regional courts were a response to murders and threats against judges and court officers, and they provided protection and anonymity to judicial officials and witnesses. They also permitted the military to conduct investigations and make arrests and allowed convictions based on the testimony of a single, secret witness. Interestingly, the 1993 law that permitted the use of secret witnesses also allowed for cross-examination by defense lawyers. These processes revealed that the same witnesses appeared in repeated trials around the country, apparently on the military payroll.[93] Human rights groups reported that these mechanisms were used primarily to criminalize social protest under an excessively broad definition of "terrorism" and that many of the defendants before the regional courts were peasant leaders, human rights activists, and labor leaders.[94]

While less egregious in other cases, harsh antidrug legislation advocated by the United States continues to have negative impacts in other Latin American countries where "both law enforcement and judicial institutions are extremely weak and permeated by corruption, [and] major traffickers are rarely sanctioned while poor, low-level offenders fill the jails."[95] Latin American governments and the U.S. government routinely use arrest statistics as indicators of success. So while these arrests have very little impact on the flow of drugs to the United States, they continue to fill local jails with nonviolent, small-time drug offenders as countries strive to cooperate with U.S. policies and to avoid the threat of U.S. retaliation via cuts in trade benefits or aid.

• Tactical Success, Strategic Failure

Short-term tactical successes have yet to translate into long-term gains in thwarting the efforts of international drug-trafficking organizations and networks. Three fundamental steps could be taken to develop more effective policing in drug source countries. First, more emphasis should be placed on institutional development, with a focus on accountability and transparency mechanisms to root out corruption and abuse. Second, democracy-building measures, particularly related to the justice sector, need far more resources. And third, the development of clear mechanisms for ensuring effective oversight of U.S. police assistance and its impact is crucial to long-term success.

Limits of Drug Control

U.S. drug control policies in drug source countries have two key components that involve local counterparts. The first is law enforcement, particularly bilateral investigations into major traffickers, trafficking routes, and networks. Here one of the major obstacles is corruption. The second is coca eradication. The role of the police in eradication varies by country, but such campaigns are typically associated with human rights abuses, violence, and social or even political upheaval. Eradication policies overcriminalize activities viewed locally as legal or inoffensive and lead to resistance because they threaten local livelihoods.

Corruption is a particularly acute problem in police operations against drug traffickers. Sometimes police strike deals with one group of traffickers to go after a rival group. One of the most notorious cases is that of the U.S.-backed operation set up to track down Medellín cartel leader Pablo

Escobar. In the process, the U.S.-funded unit carrying out the search struck an informal alliance with Los Pepes, a notorious death squad linked to the competing Cali cartel. Escobar was eventually killed, and the Cali cartel quickly moved in to take the place of the Medellín cartel.[96] In March 2004, the Colombian press reported that the U.S.-backed unit is to be reestablished, almost a decade later, this time targeting the Cali drug traffickers.[97]

The U.S. response to problematic antidrug units has not been to address the institutional and structural issues of weak accountability, transparency, and oversight that bedevil the police across Latin America but to create SIUs. The goal of such units is to create a skilled cadre of police officers that can be insulated from the vices of the larger police force. These programs create U.S. proxy units, which have not generally made any contribution to national police reform—though the recent adoption by the Mexican attorney general's office of integrity testing based on SIU practices suggests one of the ways in which such programs can support increased local accountability.

Experiences in other regions also suggest that the question is not whether to use special units or not but rather how to create accountable and effective units. It also shows the importance of creating structural mechanisms of transparency and accountability. In Europe, questions about the legality of many practices, including buy-and-bust tactics, plea bargaining, and the use of undercover agents, were gradually overcome as police sought to respond to the internationalization of crime dynamics and, in some measure, to U.S. pressures.[98] These investigative practices are now used across the European continent with little controversy. The crucial difference between late-twentieth-century Europe and Latin America, of course, is that in Europe democratic practices and accountability mechanisms are already consolidated. The excesses of state regimes based on powerful police intelligence apparatuses and disruption of opposition through agents provocateurs were a thing of the past.

In Latin America as elsewhere, special antidrug units are necessary to gather intelligence and to conduct counterdrug investigations. Police need special skills and capabilities in order to overcome the financial clout and coercive power wielded by traffickers, in particular when it comes to combating money laundering and the provision of precursor chemicals. It is extremely difficult to go after the big fish—the major traffickers and cartel leaders—without cultivating good intelligence. This is generally achieved through the development of paid informers and the use of undercover techniques such as wiretaps and controlled deliveries. Without these approaches, police actions will continue to focus on small producers, consumers, and mules. However, Latin America must first improve law enforcement accountability if it is to use these strategies successfully and avoid further abuses. U.S. policymakers should be giving far more consideration to strategies that can address these structural issues in a systematic fashion rather than as a belated second thought.

Even police reform and professionalization, however, cannot change the fundamentally counterproductive dynamics of eradication, the other aspect of drug control. Coca and poppy eradication will continue to generate social upheaval as long as large numbers of people are economically dependent on their cultivation. As noted above, when poor farmers view their activities as legitimate and have no viable alternative livelihood, they will oppose eradication campaigns and any force that conducts them, whether the police, military, or another agency. In such cases, simply carrying out eradication more professionally is most unlikely to change the fundamental dynamic, although it could reduce the number of abuses associated with these efforts—an achievement worth striving for.

Potential for Institutional Reform

The United States has a growing box of tools to use in improving the human rights record and accountability of personnel taking part in U.S.-supported antidrug programs. The institution-building programs discussed here—ROL, ICITAP/OPDAT, and democracy assistance more broadly—have important contributions to make. More could easily be done through vigorous application of the Leahy Amendment, which requires human rights screening of all members of units receiving U.S. military and police assistance. With greater attention and resources, as well as political backing, all of these U.S. policy tools could be applied to beneficial effect in Latin America.

More effective policing tactics in the drug control effort require institutional reforms that start to tackle the deep malaise that characterizes most Latin American police forces. The track record of the SIUs suggests that greater success is certainly possible when corruption is controlled. However, in the absence of structural reforms to enhance accountability, SIU successes cannot produce more than short-term tactical gains. The arrests of cartel leaders and other important traffickers and the seizures of drugs represent significant achievements, but as repeated experience has demonstrated, there are always new entrepreneurs happy to fill deposed traffickers' shoes. In both Colombia and Mexico, the capture of major cartel leaders led to the proliferation of smaller, and sometimes more violent, trafficking organizations.

The potential for reform, even within the context of U.S. counterdrug policy, is illustrated by one positive experience in Colombia. In the mid-1990s, the Colombian National Police undertook a major reform process. While direct U.S. assistance for the reform was limited, enthusiastic U.S. support for police chief and reform leader General José Rosso Serrano gave him important political backing to attack corruption in the police. The result was an important short-term reduction in police corruption and abuse. The Colombian police continue to be implicated in human rights abuses and providing support to paramilitaries, and recently the police were again implicated in major corruption scandals. Nonetheless, the fact that a reform effort could achieve results—albeit with problems in consolidating and sustaining those results—implies that far more could be done in less adverse circumstances, a category that would include almost every other country in Latin America.

It is possible that reformed police will still fail to make a serious dent in the flow of drugs, but it is unlikely that they would do a worse job than the region's current police forces. The collateral benefits of police reform—enhancing the rule of law and democracy, strengthening safety and public order, and thus contributing to other U.S. foreign policy objectives such as improved conditions for trade and foreign investment—make reform worthwhile independent of its potential counterdrug impacts.

A Critical Imbalance

The fact is, however, that there is a critical imbalance in resources going into the two separate tracks of democratization and counterdrug law enforcement. This is combined with failures of coordination because of inadequate accountability and oversight. The funding imbalance is shown clearly in Table 3.2, based on the INL budget presentation for FY2003. Bolivia was slated to receive U.S.$33.2 million for narcotics law enforcement (NLE) programs and U.S.$4 million for ROL and ICITAP. Peru was to receive U.S.$42.2 million for NLE and just U.S.$600,000 for ROL (Peru has no ICITAP program or police reform support). Colombia was to receive U.S.$120.5 million for the Colombian police and a further U.S.$47.25 million for drug interdiction (whether for police or military programs or both is not specified). Colombia also receives massive military assistance under Plan Colombia. It does receive nearly U.S.$46 million for Rule of Law and ICITAP, but in this case both the ICITAP and ROL programs are largely counterdrug-oriented.[99]

Table 3.2 FY2003 Funding for Narcotics Law Enforcement, Rule of Law, and ICITAP Programs (millions of U.S. dollars)

	Narcotics Law Enforcement (NLE)	Rule of Law and ICITAP	Rule of Law/ICITAP as % of NLE
Bolivia	33.20	4.0	12.00%
Peru	42.20	0.6	0.01%
Colombia	167.25	46.0	27.50%

Source: FY2003 INL budget presentation.

The implications of this pattern of funding are apparent in Table 3.3, which outlines the typical impacts of the two kinds of programs.

Accountability and Oversight
Building more effective public security policies in countries increasingly beset by crime and social violence requires greater transparency and accountability at all levels. To varying degrees, these issues are addressed by U.S. and other donor assistance for institutional reform. However, they tend to be given little or no attention in U.S. counterdrug policy. The remedy must begin at the top, with congressional responsibility for oversight.

Budgets for both institutional reform and drug control are reviewed and voted on every year by the U.S. Congress. Congressional drug warriors continue to demand short-term results according to a timetable set by the annual congressional budget appropriations process and a political debate driven by a bipartisan fear of looking soft on drugs. In private, many agency officials blame Congress for setting impossible goals and for failing

Table 3.3   Impacts of Reform Strategies Versus Counterdrug Strategies on Policing

Area of Impact	Police Reform	U.S. Counterdrug Policy
National Government	Civilian oversight and accountability of police to parliaments, local elected officials, courts, and prosecutors is strengthened.	Erosion of national civilian authority and accountability through support for military role in internal counterdrug activities; creation of proxy units under direct U.S. control; imposition of counterdrug legislation.
Police Force	Institutional reforms orient police away from regime protection toward public service. Programs include new training and skills building, creation of internal accountability mechanisms, improved management and supervision, and improved police-community relations through greater attention to policing local communities and crime prevention.	Police are trained in military-type counterdrug skills and thus less apt to carry out policing duties correctly. Overall strengthening of police force neglected in favor of the formation of special units. Accountability and oversight of these units are negligible, often undermining civilian governmental authority. Short-term efforts to improve operational performance crowd out long-term institutional strengthening.
Civil Society / Local Communities	Relations improved through increased contact, dialogue and transparency; greater police responsiveness to community concerns.	Community relations profoundly damaged by overcriminalization, eradication policies, and harsh antidrug laws.

to provide a better framework in which the many competing U.S. policy priorities in the region can be coordinated and assessed. In public, in congressional hearings, and in other official reckonings, these officials are eager to point to successes in order to maintain agency mandates and budgets.

It is still true that there is little congressional scrutiny and oversight of the varied programs that make up U.S. police assistance. The complexity of these programs, with their different and sometimes competing goals, hinders transparency and accountability. So does the multiplicity of both funding routes and agencies implementing programs (reportedly more than fifty)[100] combined with weak reporting mechanisms. It is extremely difficult to uncover all the U.S. government programs that are involved in providing police assistance and even more difficult to obtain figures for how much each agency spends on those programs. In 1992 the GAO found that even it "could not determine the total extent or cost of U.S. assistance to foreign police because some agencies do not maintain such data."[101] Seven years later, the GAO reported that "data on rule of law funding was not readily available, and some entities could not provide funding data" and noted that the different agencies do not even have an agreed-upon definition of what constitutes rule of law activities.[102]

Basic principles of good program management, transparency, and accountability should require a comprehensive mechanism for reporting to Congress on U.S. police assistance programs. Such reporting would facilitate congressional oversight and could support efforts to develop a more coherent, coordinated, and cost-effective strategy for police assistance, with improved outcomes in promoting police development and improved law enforcement cooperation.

• The Bottom Line

In some countries, U.S. drug control policies have directly contributed to human rights violations and undermined democracy. In Bolivia, for example, a poor and aid-dependent nation, the political class has almost no capacity to reject U.S. demands, and as coca production is the single predominant issue in bilateral relations, U.S. drug warriors have had close to a completely free hand. The strategies and programs they have chosen to pursue have had serious negative effects on human rights, on the livelihoods of the rural poor, and on the political stability of the country.

In other countries with larger economies, strategic or regional importance, or other factors that create greater capacity to resist U.S. pressures, direct impacts of U.S. policies are far harder to identify, particularly given the history of corrupt, inefficient, and abusive policing across the region. This is certainly the case with Colombia and Mexico. Despite the challenges of drawing clear causal connections, there is little doubt that U.S.

drug warriors have pursued their goals with little concern for human rights and democratization processes. While the promotion of democracy and human rights are also long-standing U.S. policy objectives, democratization programs run on a separate track in Washington. When the two sets of programs clash on the ground, the operational imperatives of and massive funding for counterdrug programs override long-term, low-resource democratization programs.

Given the amply documented failure of U.S. drug control policy in Latin America to reduce the availability or purity of drugs on U.S. streets, U.S. policymakers must face up to the problems with the current approach to counterdrug police assistance. Its alleged benefits are too elusive to justify the political, financial, and ethical costs. It is time to invest in the development of a new policy framework, one rooted in partnership and international cooperation rather than imposition. U.S. policy should be guided by an understanding of drug production, trafficking, and consumption as shared problems. Most important, it should focus on strengthening democratic institutions, the rule of law, and police accountability and should foster investment in development policies that can offer viable alternatives to impoverished rural farmers and to marginalized and alienated urban youths.

• Notes

Research for this chapter was carried out by Lora Lumpe, independent consultant and author of "Unmatched Power, Unmet Principles: The Human Rights Dimensions of U.S. Training of Foreign Military and Police Forces," Amnesty International USA, 2002; and by Rachel Farley at the Washington Office on Latin America. Thanks to Charles Call, Laurie Freeman, Adam Isacson, Joy Olson, Robert Perito, Eileen Rosin, and Coletta Youngers for their comments and insights.

1. See, for example, Paul Chevigny, *Edge of the Knife: Police Violence in the Americas* (New York: The New Press, 1995); and Paulo Sergio Pinheiro, "Democracies Without Citizenship," *Report on the Americas* (New York: NACLA, September/October 1996).

2. David H. Bayley, "What's in a Uniform? A Comparative View of Police-Military Relations in Latin America," paper prepared for the Conference on Police and Civil-Military Relations in Latin America, Washington D.C., October 1993, sponsored by the Latin America and Caribbean Center, Florida International University.

3. Gustavo Palmieri, "Themes and Debates in Public Security; Criminal Investigations," Washington Office on Latin America, July 2000; Rachel Neild, "From National Security to Citizen Security; Civil Society and the Evolution of Public Security Debates," an occasional paper commissioned by the International Centre for Human Rights and Democratic Development, Montreal, Canada, December 1999.

4. Charles T. Call, "War Transitions and the New Civilian Security in Latin America," *Comparative Politics* 35, no. 1 (October 2002): 20.

5. Mayra Buvinic and Andrew Morrison, "Living in a More Violent World," *Foreign Policy* (Spring 2000); The World Bank, *Crime and Violence as Development Issues in Latin America and the Caribbean* (seminar on The

Challenge of Urban Criminal Violence, Rio de Janeiro, March 1997); World Health Organization, *World Report on Violence and Health* (Geneva, 2002).

6. Gustavo Capdevila, "Drugs: Fight Against Narco-Trafficking Goes Local," *Inter Press News Service*, 3 March 2004.

7. Bratton is the former police commissioner of New York City, now chief of the Los Angeles Police Department; Giuliani Associates is the consulting firm of former New York City mayor Rudolph Giuliani.

8. WOLA, *Demilitarizing Public Order: The International Community, Police Reform and Human Rights in Central America and Haiti*, November 1995, p. 5.

9. Martha K. Huggins, *Political Policing: The United States and Latin America* (Durham, N.C., and London: Duke University Press, 1998).

10. All information in this paragraph from Thomas Lobe, "The Rise and Demise of the Office of Public Safety," *Armed Forces and Society* 9, no. 2 (Winter 1983): 187.

11. Huggins, *Political Policing*, p. 192.

12. WOLA, *Demilitarizing Public Order*, p. 5.

13. Lobe, "The Rise and Demise."

14. It is worth noting that a number of OPS agents subsequently transferred into the DEA. Ethan A. Nadelman, *Cops Across Borders; The Internationalization of U.S. Criminal Law Enforcement* (University Park: Pennsylvania State University Press, 1993), p. 119.

15. Charles T. Call, "Institutional Learning Within ICITAP," in Robert B. Oakley et al., eds., *Policing the New World Disorder: Peace Operations and Public Security* (Washington, D.C.: National Defense University, 1999), p. 318.

16. WOLA, *Demilitarizing Public Order*.

17. U.S. General Accounting Office (GAO), *Foreign Aid: Police Training and Assistance*, GAO/NSIAD-92-118, 5 March 1992.

18. Charles C. Call, "Pinball and Punctuated Equilibrium: The Birth of a 'Democratic Policing' Norm?" paper prepared for annual conference of the International Studies Association, Los Angeles, 16 March 2000.

19. David Bayley, *Democratizing the Police Abroad: What to Do and How to Do It* (Washington, D.C.: U.S. Justice Department, Office of Justice Programs, National Institute of Justice, 2001).

20. See, for example, Christopher Stone and Heather Ward, "Democratic Policing: A Framework for Action," *Policing and Society* 10, no. 1 (2000): 11–47.

21. The author was a participant at a meeting to discuss a draft policy paper prepared by USAID's Program and Policy Coordination Office.

22. Roger F. Noriega, Assistant Secretary of State, Bureau of Western Hemisphere Affairs, "Foreign Assistance Priorities for the Western Hemisphere," remarks to U.S. Senate Committee on Foreign Relations, Washington, D.C., 2 March 2004.

23. Cynthia Gorney, "U.S. Proposes Ambitious Plan to Limit Coca Production in Peru," *Washington Post*, 19 June 1981. Cited in JoAnn Kawell, "Going to the Source: A History of the U.S. War on Cocaine," unpublished draft manuscript.

24. Peter Zirnite, "Under Fire: The Drug Enforcement Administration in Latin America," unpublished monograph, Washington Office on Latin America, 1998.

25. Description of training given by Southcom to Adam Isacson and Joy Olson, June 2002.

26. Letter from Otto J. Reich, U.S. State Department, to Lisa Haugaard, director of the Latin America Working Group, 13 August 2002.

27. U.S. State Department, Bureau for International Narcotics and Law Enforcement Affairs (INL), *International Narcotics Control Strategy Report (INCSR) 2001*, "USG Assistance."

28. INL, *Congressional Budget Justification (CBJ), FY2004*.

29. INL, *CBJ FY2003*. See Table 2.2 in this volume.

30. Author interview with Steve Peterson and James Pulio, INL, U.S. State Department, 15 September 2001.

31. GAO, *Foreign Aid*, 5 March 1992.

32. Author interview with Elizabeth Carroll and Edmund Sutow, U.S. State Department, 12 December 2003.

33. Faye Armstrong, U.S. State Department, Office of Policy Planning, interviewed by Rachel Farley and Rachel Neild, Washington, D.C., 22 May 2001.

34. U.S. Justice Department, Drug Enforcement Administration (DEA), "Domestic and Foreign Offices," on the DEA website, www.dea.gov/agency/domestic.htm#foreign.

35. Statement of Asa Hutchinson before the Senate Judiciary Committee, Subcommittee on Technology, Terrorism, and Government Information, 13 March 2002. Hutchinson said DEA was requesting U.S.$7 million for antiterrorism upgrades at foreign facilities, "such as in Cartagena, Colombia."

36. DEA, "Aviation," www.usdoj.gov/dea/programs/aviation.htm.

37. DEA, "Intelligence," www.usdoj.gov/dea/programs/intelligence.htm. See also Nadelman, *Cops Across Borders*, pp. 207–208.

38. See *INCSR 2001*, "USG Assistance," pp. 9–10, for examples of overseas intelligence-gathering operations in 2001.

39. GAO, *Drug Control: DEA's Strategies and Operations in the 1990s*, July 1999, GAO/GGD-99-108, p. 37. See *INCSR 2001*, "USG Assistance," pp. 7–9, for some examples of recent investigations in Latin America.

40. Named after its sponsor, Senator Mike Mansfield. First passed as an amendment to the International Security Assistance and Arms Export Control Act, it was codified in 1978 as Section 481c of the Foreign Assistance Act.

41. Adam Isacson, interview with House Armed Services Committee staff, June 1998.

42. *INCSR 2001*, "USG Assistance," p. 6.

43. DEA, "Training," www.usdoj.gov/dea/programs/training.htm.

44. INL, *CBJ FY2002*, "Other Latin America."

45. *INCSR 2002*, "Canada, Mexico and Central America."

46. GAO, *Drug Control*, July 1999, p. 56.

47. "Drug Enforcement Administration," hearing of the Subcommittee on Crime of the House Committee on the Judiciary, 29 July 1999, published as serial no. 65 (Washington, D.C.: U.S. Government Printing Office, 2000), p. 9.

48. Statement of Asa Hutchinson, 13 March 2002.

49. Statement of Asa Hutchinson, 17 September 2002; and statement of Rogelio Guevara, DEA Chief of Operations, before the House Judiciary Committee, Subcommittee on Crime, Terrorism, and Homeland Security, 9 July 2003.

50. Author interview with former Andean country senior official, on background, 22 January 2004.

51. Statement of Rogelio Guevara, DEA, to the House Judiciary Committee, 9 July 2003.

52. Author interview with Interior Ministry senior official, 22 January 2004.

53. DEA Mission Statement, www.usdoj.gov/dea/agency/mission.htm.

54. Nadelman, citing police scholar Antony Simpson.

55. Zirnite, "Under Fire."

56. "Drug Enforcement Administration," hearing, 29 July 1999. Several congressional committee staff have been on delegations to visit DEA missions, in particular, Colombia and Mexico.

57. In 1999, the GAO report reviewed the DEA's performance through the 1990s. GAO, *Drug Control*.

58. Interview with GAO evaluator Allen Fleener in 1997, cited in Zirnite, *Under Fire*.

59. OMB Performance and Management Assessments, FY2004, on OMB website.

60. For the FY2005 budget, the OMB said this: "A follow-up review found that DEA has made significant progress in addressing these performance measurement shortcomings," and OMB upgraded its assessment of DEA from results not demonstrated to adequate. They also increased the budget by U.S.$49 million.

61. Statement of DEA Administrator Asa Hutchinson before the House Committee on International Relations, April 24, 2002. Please see Appendix 1 for full quote.

62. *Financial Times*, "Colombian Rebels Indicted," 19 March 2002.

63. The FBI's mandate, which is the broadest of all federal investigative agencies, authorizes it to investigate all federal criminal violations that have not been specifically assigned by Congress to another federal agency. The FBI's investigative functions fall into the categories of civil rights; counterterrorism; foreign counterintelligence; organized crime/drugs; violent crimes and major offenders; and financial crime.

64. Statement of William Sessions, in "FBI Oversight and Authorization Request for FY1992," hearings before the Subcommittee on Civil and Constitutional Rights of the House Judiciary Committee, 13 and 21 March 1991, published as serial no. 24 (U.S. Government Printing Office, 1992), p. 91.

65. Submission to Laurie Freeman, Washington Office on Latin America, 18 February 2004, by David M. Hardy, Section Chief, Records Management Division, FBI's International Operations in Latin America, FOIAPA no. 0982064-000.

66. Statement of Robert S. Mueller III, Director, Federal Bureau of Investigation, before the Subcommittee for the Departments of Commerce, Justice, and State, the Judiciary, and Related Agencies of the House Appropriations Committee, 21 June 2002.

67. Statement by U.S. Customs Commissioner Robert C. Bonner, hearing on U.S. Customs FY2003 Budget Request, House Appropriations Committee, Subcommittee on Treasury, Postal Services and General Government, 27 February 2002.

68. *INCSR 2001*, "USG Assistance."

69. Comments of U.S. Customs Commissioner Raymond Kelly, 1999 National HIDTA Conference, Capital Hilton Hotel, Washington, D.C., 14 December 1999, www.customs.ustreas.gov/xp/cgov/newsroom/commissioner/speeches_statements/archives/dec141999.xml.

70. Statement by Robert C. Bonner, hearing on U.S. Customs FY2003 Budget Request, 27 February 2002.

71. According to a 1994 State Department bulletin, governments in Latin America requested that the United States be more careful in licensing small arms and ammunition for export. Concerned about the quantity of firearms entering their countries, and the possibility for diversion to terrorists, drug traffickers, and criminals, they requested that the U.S. government demand more extensive documenta-

tion for firearms export license applications to protect against fraud and diversion. U.S. State Department, *Defense Trade News* 5, no. 3 (July and October 1994): 6.

72. U.S. Treasury Department, Bureau of Alcohol, Tobacco, and Firearms, *ITAR: International Traffic in Arms, Annual Report FY1993* (Washington, D.C.: 1994).

73. U.S. Transportation Department, U.S. Coast Guard (USCG), "Drug Interdiction," www.uscg.mil/hq/g-o/g-opl/mle/drugs.htm.

74. USCG, *Coast Guard Publication 1: U.S. Coast Guard—America's Maritime Guardian*, 1 January 2002, p. 6.

75. USCG, Testimony of Rear Admiral Ernest R. Riutta, before the House International Relations Committee, on Anti-Narcotics Efforts in the Western Hemisphere, 3 March 1999.

76. *INCSR 2001*, "USG Assistance."

77. INL, *CBJ FY2004*.

78. DEA, Office of Acquisition Management, job posting for "International Law Enforcement Academy Instructors," 16 October 2002.

79. See WOLA letter and background memorandum on ILEA-South, www.wola.org/security/public_security.htm.

80. Specifically, training with the U.S. Coast Guard was mentioned as a potential problem because of the dual military/law enforcement nature of that body. Conversations on background with U.S. officials in the State Department, Washington D.C., and U.S. Embassy, Costa Rica. In addition, several Latin American police forces, including the Colombian, remain under ministries of defense. However, as it stands, the clause proposed by Costa Rica is written in broad terms—"The Academy will not conduct any type of training, instruction or activity that is military or has military ends"—and would not appear to preclude training with the Coast Guard, as it is military content and goals that are prohibited, not quasi-military trainees.

81. *Interagency Working Group on U.S. Government Sponsored International Exchanges and Training*, FY1999 Annual Report, inventory of Department of Justice programs, www.iawg.gov/info/reports/reports/fy99inventory/doj.html.

82. See WOLA, *Sustaining Police Reform in Central America*, Washington, D.C., October 2002.

83. www.usdoj.gov/criminal/icitap/.

84. Call, "Institutional Learning," p. 352.

85. Coletta Youngers, "Administration of Justice Programs in Andean Countries: Do They Make Any Difference?" paper prepared for delivery at the 1995 meeting of the Latin America Studies Association, Washington, D.C., 28–30 September 1995, p. 1. On file in WOLA offices.

86. For an analysis of U.S. democracy promotion, see Thomas Carothers, *Aiding Democracy Abroad: The Learning Curve* (Washington, D.C.: Carnegie Endowment for International Peace, 1999).

87. GAO, *U.S. Democracy Programs in Six Latin American Countries Have Yielded Modest Results*, GAO-03-358, March 2003, p. 22.

88. Ibid.

89. Margaret J. Sarles, "USAID's Support of Justice Reform in Latin America," in Pilar Domingo and Rachel Sieder, eds., *Rule of Law in Latin America: The International Promotion of Judicial Reform* (London: Institute of Latin American Studies, University of London, 2001), p. 47.

90. Ibid., p. 13.

91. Human Rights Watch, *Human Rights Violations and the War on Drugs* 7, no. 8 (New York: July 1995), pp. 2 and 19–20.

92. U.S. Agency for International Development, *1999 Annual Report*, 1 January–31 December 1999: Bolivia Administration of Justice Project, project no. 511-0626, supplement, p. 87.

93. See Youngers, "Administration of Justice Programs," p. 23.

94. Ibid, p. 22; Human Rights Watch, *State of War: Political Violence and Counterinsurgency in Colombia* (New York: Human Rights Watch, December 1993); Robert Wiener, "Colombia's Faceless Courts," *NACLA Report on the Americas* 30, no. 2 (September/October 1996).

95. Sandra G. Edwards, *Illicit Drug Control Policies and Prisons; The Human Cost*, special update, Washington Office on Latin America, November 2003, p. 2.

96. See Mark Bowden, *Killing Pablo* (London: Atlantic Books, 2001).

97. *El Colombiano*, "Renació el Bloque de Búsqueda," 8 March 2004.

98. See M. G. W. den Boer, "Internationalization: A Challenge to Police Organization in Europe," in R. I. Mawby, ed., *Policing Across the World* (London: UCL Press, 1999), pp. 59–75. Also Nadelman, "The DEA in Europe," chapter 4 in *Cops Across Borders*.

99. INL, *Congressional Budget Justification, FY2003*.

100. GAO, *Foreign Aid*, 5 March 1992.

101. Ibid., p. 2.

102. GAO, *Foreign Assistance: Rule of Law Funding Worldwide for Fiscal Years 1993–98*, GAO/NSIAD-99-158, p. 2.

4

Colombia:
A Vicious Circle of Drugs and War

María Clemencia Ramírez Lemus, Kimberly Stanton & John Walsh

D rug control issues have long been central to the agenda of U.S.-
Colombian relations. Indeed, the U.S. public identifies Colombia,
more than any other country, with the "war on drugs." In the Andean
region, Colombia is now the focus of U.S. international drug control policy.
When Colombians were consolidating their preeminent role in cocaine trafficking during the 1980s, Bolivia and Peru served as the major sources of
coca, the plant from whose leaves cocaine is produced. In the mid-1990s,
though, Colombia also emerged as the world's leading coca producer and a
major producer of opium poppy, the raw material for heroin. By 2003,
Colombia supplied an estimated 90 percent of the cocaine and a significant
proportion of the heroin consumed in the United States.

Colombia is often described as one of the oldest democracies in Latin
America, yet it is also a country racked by more than forty years of internal
armed conflict. The cost of political exclusion for the majority of the population was the growth and consolidation of insurgent guerrilla movements,
two of which are still engaged in armed insurrection against the Colombian
state: the Revolutionary Armed Forces of Colombia (FARC), and the
National Liberation Army (Ejército de Liberación Nacional, or ELN). In
addition, right-wing paramilitaries, illegal armed groups with origins in
Colombia's U.S.-aided counterinsurgency strategy, compete with the guerrillas for control of territory, resources, and support. Since the mid-1990s,
the paramilitaries have been loosely organized under the umbrella of the
United Self-Defense Forces of Colombia (Autodefensas Unidas de
Colombia, or AUC). Evidence indicates that they continue to receive training, intelligence, and logistical support from members of the Colombian
security forces. The FARC, the ELN, and the AUC are currently on the U.S.
State Department's list of foreign terrorist organizations due to their systematic use of tactics that target noncombatants.[1] And they benefit, in different ways, from the resources provided by the illicit drug trade.

Colombia's history since the 1970s is marked by repeated attempts to

Colombia

Population	42,800,000
GDP	U.S.$82.4 billion
GDP per capita	U.S.$1,915
Share of Income	
• Poorest 10 percent of population	0.8%
• Richest 10 percent of population	46.5%
• Ratio of income of richest 10% to poorest 10%	57.8 times
Percentage living in poverty (<$2/day)	26.5%
Percentage living in extreme poverty (<$1/day)	14.4%
Public perception of corruption among public officials and politicians (0=more, 10=less)	3.7

Sources: UNDP, *Human Development Report 2004;* World Bank, *Inequality in Latin America: Breaking with History?;* Transparency International, *Corruption Perceptions Index 2003.*

Notes: Population and GDP data from 2001; share of income data 2000; poverty data 1990–2001.

come to terms with the scourge of drug trafficking and the threat of insurgency but without addressing effectively the underlying structural problems that feed both phenomena. These include the absence of land reform or a strategy for rural development that would ensure sustainable livelihoods for Colombia's small farmers and limit the attraction of growing coca. Although political participation is more open, only recently have new political movements begun to weaken the hegemony of the Liberals and Conservatives, after years in which serious opposition candidates were simply assassinated. And justice remains elusive. Impunity is nearly absolute, both for common crimes and for violations of human rights and international humanitarian law committed in the context of the armed conflict. The Colombian military has committed direct violations of human rights, including massacres, extrajudicial executions, and forced disappearances, and it has been complicit in or has tolerated these same abuses when committed by the notorious paramilitary forces.

U.S. foreign policy has played a key role in shaping Colombia's internal responses to its problems. Colombian leaders have sought U.S. engagement as well as economic and military assistance. However, the nature of

U.S. engagement and the composition of aid packages have been shaped far more by the political agenda in Washington than by Colombian interests and preferences. In spite of the fundamentally political nature of the problems Colombia confronts, the United States has viewed the country primarily through a security lens, privileging engagement with the armed forces and the police—a trend that has accelerated in the post–September 11 environment.

The U.S. government provided increasing levels of counterdrug assistance to Colombia beginning in the late 1980s and into the 1990s, initially to combat the Medellín, Cali, and other drug cartels. In the mid-1990s, as coca production began to soar, the United States increased funding for aerial eradication, where coca crops are sprayed with a potent herbicide intended to kill the crops. Highly controversial in Colombia, aerial eradication has led thousands of poor farmers to flee the areas being sprayed, often leading to coca production in new areas. Though a thorough and objective evaluation of the program's impact has yet to be carried out, numerous reports point to the negative consequences for people's health, food crops and cattle, and the environment. Nonetheless, aerial eradication remains the centerpiece of U.S. counterdrug efforts in Colombia.

Although for years the primary U.S. ally was the Colombian police, the bulk of U.S. assistance began flowing to the Colombian military after July 2000. The U.S. Congress approved a massive U.S.$1.3 billion aid initiative termed Plan Colombia after an earlier initiative with the same name by the president of Colombia at the time, Andrés Pastrana. The U.S. package included U.S.$860 million for Colombia, with the rest going to neighboring countries potentially threatened by Colombia's internal conflict and its booming illicit drug trade. Of the aid destined for Colombia, the vast majority was—and continues to be—provided to the security forces. Human rights conditions placed on U.S. assistance have largely failed to end recipient forces' complicity in human rights violations.

The rationale put forward by U.S. policymakers for the growing role of the Colombian military in what was, at the time, still considered a counterdrug mission, was guerrilla involvement in the drug trade. The "narcoguerrilla" terminology—though in use for many years previously—became the dominant discourse. After the September 11 terrorist attacks, U.S. policymakers shifted their language again. Colombia's guerrillas became "narcoterrorists," and the U.S. Congress authorized the use of counterdrug assets for counterterrorist purposes. Through a variety of programs and forms of assistance, the U.S. government now provides direct support to the Colombian counterinsurgency effort. Yet four years after the approval of Plan Colombia, the country is no closer to overcoming its structural problems, drug trafficking continues unabated, and peace remains a distant dream.

• Prelude to Plan Colombia

Colombia is a country racked by more than forty years of internal armed conflict, rooted in a period of intense nationwide strife known as La Violencia. Between 1947 and 1953, some 300,000 Colombians died during struggles over land rights and in armed clashes between the two main political parties, the Liberals and the Conservatives. The violence receded following a 1953 military coup. Six years later the civilian elite regained formal control under a power-sharing agreement in which elections continued to be held, but the two parties alternated the presidency between themselves. The agreement expired in 1974; in the meantime, however, the exclusion of other groups from the political process had contributed to the development of a number of insurgent guerrilla movements. Several of the groups, including the once-predominant M-19, disarmed and joined the electoral process in 1990. Two groups are still engaged in armed insurrection against the Colombian state: the 17,000-strong FARC, and the ELN, with perhaps 3,000 members.

Cold War and Counterinsurgency

During the Cold War, the United States fostered a close relationship with the Colombian military that it has maintained to the present. At the height of the East-West conflict during the 1960s, the administrations of John F. Kennedy and Lyndon Johnson considered Colombia a key front in the effort to stop the Cuban revolution from spreading throughout the Western Hemisphere. They lavished counterinsurgency assistance on the Colombian armed forces—including aid that supported the 1964 attack on Marquetalia, an armed peasant commune. That attack led to the formation of the FARC. U.S. assistance for Colombia's military continued at moderate levels throughout the Cold War, complemented by training programs.

The Colombian paramilitary groups of today also have their origins in the 1960s, when U.S. military advisers first recommended the organization of "indigenous irregulars" as a fundamental component of Colombian counterinsurgency strategy.[2] The legal basis for state sponsorship of paramilitary organizations, officially called "self-defense forces," was a 1965 decree law that had enshrined the U.S. Doctrine of National Security in Colombian law and allowed the government to "mobilize the population in activities and tasks" to restore public order. (The doctrine, described more fully in endnote 1 in Chapter 2, defined threats to national stability and development very broadly, and implicitly legitimized the use of any measures deemed effective against such threats.) Self-defense groups became part of military doctrine: the army was "to organize in military form the civilian population, to protect itself against the action of guerrillas and support the execution of combat operations."[3] From the mid-1960s on, the armed forces actively sought the involvement of businessmen, landowners, and political leaders in the creation and financing of such groups.[4] Today the loosely organized paramilitary network, the AUC, is said to number about 13,000.

Over time, both the guerrilla and the paramilitary forces became major players in the drug trade. As described in more detail below, key paramilitary groups have been, from the outset, closely linked to drug traffickers. In the 1980s, the FARC began taxing coca production by small farmers in territories under its control. Over time, the drug trade became a major source of financing for the FARC, as its role expanded to include control of laboratories, marketing, and trafficking, at least in some regions.[5] In the mid-1990s, the paramilitaries decided to challenge FARC control of coca territory and markets, and they gained increasing resources from the illicit drug trade as well. Statements by paramilitary leaders suggest that they currently earn 40–70 percent of their income from the drug trade.

Beginnings of Colombia's Drug War

Colombia's war against drugs had its origins in the late 1970s, when eradication programs in Mexico pushed the cultivation of marijuana to Colombia's Atlantic coast. Beginning with the administration of Jimmy Carter (1977–1981), the United States pressed Colombian authorities to eliminate illegal drug crops and to pursue drug traffickers within a law enforcement framework that included the possibility of extraditing Colombian traffickers to the United States. Colombia's first aerial eradication campaign took place during the government of Julio Cesar Turbay (1978–1982), when thousands of acres of marijuana were sprayed with the chemical herbicide paraquat. Turbay also signed a 1979 extradition treaty that was quickly ratified by the U.S. Senate and went into effect in 1982.

During the 1980s, the Medellín and Cali cartels, which managed the marijuana trade, expanded their business into processing Peruvian and Bolivian coca and then trafficking the cocaine they produced. The power of these family-based criminal networks grew quickly and dramatically. As the cartels consolidated control over a billion-dollar drug industry, their leaders sought political power through legal and illegal means—all backed by the threat of violence. Colombian authorities pursued the cartels because of their drug trafficking, and the authorities strongly resisted cartel efforts to penetrate the state. In August 1983, President Belisario Betancur (1982–1986) appointed Rodrigo Lara Bonilla as minister of justice. Lara Bonilla launched an intense campaign against the cartels. On March 10, 1984, in a major joint operation with the U.S. Drug Enforcement Administration (DEA), the Colombian government captured ten metric tons of cocaine and destroyed 101 coca-processing laboratories.[6] Six weeks later, Lara Bonilla was assassinated on the orders of the Medellín traffickers.

In response, Betancur declared "total war" against the cartel. He gave up his principled opposition to extradition and refused offers from cartel leaders to give up their drug businesses in exchange for, among other things, a promise that they would not be extradited to the United States. The traffickers, who came to be known as the "extraditables," then unleashed a series of brutal attacks that left hundreds of judges, police investigators, journalists, and other public figures dead. The victims included presidential candidate Luis Carlos Galán, assassinated in August 1989.[7]

The killings did not prevent Betancur or his successor, Virgilio Barco (1986–1990), from proceeding with extradition. When Colombia captured Medellín cartel leader Carlos Lehder in February 1987, he was immediately extradited. But extradition went forward by means of "a complex and judicially dubious process,"[8] as the executive branch sought ways around court decisions—some made as a result of threats and intimidation by the traffickers—that voided the extradition treaty.

With extradition at risk, the United States asserted that Colombia was not doing enough against the illicit drug trade. On the day that Galán was murdered, however, Colombia's Council of Ministers restored extradition by administrative decree, and the action was subsequently upheld by the Colombian Supreme Court.[9] Shortly thereafter, the United States sent an additional U.S.$65 million in counterdrug aid.[10] By February 1990, fourteen extraditions had taken place, although a subsequent evaluation of these found that they had no effect in reducing drug trafficking.[11] When Colombia adopted a new constitution in 1991, extradition was prohibited.

The bruising experience with extradition shaped a proposal by the government of César Gaviria (1990–1994) in which drug traffickers who turned themselves in, and confessed to a crime that allowed a judge to open a case against them, would be spared extradition and benefit from a reduced sentence. Backed by increased resources provided through President George H. W. Bush's Andean Initiative, the strategy produced the surrender in January 1991 of three Ochoa brothers, leaders of the Medellín cartel. Pablo Escobar, the notorious head of the Medellín cartel, turned himself over in June 1991.[12] (He escaped from jail in July 1992 and was later killed in U.S.-assisted operations in December 1993.) By the end of Gaviria's presidency, the Medellín cartel had been virtually dismantled.

The government of Gaviria's successor, Ernesto Samper (1994–1998), was marked by a crisis in U.S.-Colombian relations due to allegations that the Cali cartel, which benefited from the dismantling of the Medellín organization, had financed his presidential campaign. Samper was eventually cleared in a formal investigation by the Chamber of Representatives that began in June 1994, but the investigation provoked a severe crisis within the government. The United States canceled Samper's U.S. visa and decertified Colombia for lack of cooperation in drug control, although it continued to provide counterdrug aid. Ironically, in part because of the scandal, Samper pursued a highly aggressive and punitive counterdrug policy. Investigations by the police and the attorney general's office led to the arrests of five leaders of the Cali cartel in the summer of 1995. By September 1996 all the Cali leaders were imprisoned.[13] A year later, seeking to improve the relationship with the United States, the Colombian Congress amended the constitution to restore extradition.

However, the breakup of the two largest cartels by the mid-1990s did not lead to a long-term decline in Colombian drug trafficking. Rather, it presaged a new phase in the drug war; the cartels were quickly replaced by smaller organizations that lacked the capacity to operate transnationally, and coca production in Colombia increased dramatically. In December 1994, Colonel Leonardo Gallego, head of the counternarcotics police, described the south-central province of Guaviare as "a sea of coca."[14] Colombia's National Narcotics Directorate (Dirección Nacional de Estupefacientes, or DNE) reported a total of 43,000 hectares of coca in 1994, 67,200 in 1996, and 79,500 in 1997, at which point Colombia became the largest producer of coca in the Andean region.[15]

Samper responded to the expansion of coca production by increasing aerial eradication, or fumigation, as it has come to be known. Large-scale fumigation of coca began in the province of Guaviare, at that time the zone of greatest coca cultivation. From 1995 through 1997, pilots sprayed more than 38,000 hectares. The total area sprayed increased to more than 65,000 hectares in 1998, when operations were extended to the neighboring province of Caquetá.[16] By the end of Samper's presidency, as drug trafficking continued apace, the counterdrug strategy had shifted decisively toward attacking the cultivation of coca, which in practice meant targeting peasant producers. Fumigation became the centerpiece of the U.S. aid package negotiated by President Andrés Pastrana (1998–2002), known as Plan Colombia; it remains at the heart of U.S. and Colombian counterdrug efforts.

• Plan Colombia

In the late 1980s and early 1990s, during the heyday of Colombia's infamous drug cartels, U.S. military assistance to Colombia increased significantly over Cold War levels. By 1991, Colombia had surpassed El Salvador as the region's largest recipient of military and police aid. In this period the primary beneficiary of counterdrug aid was the Colombian police. As late as 1997, as much as 90 percent of the aid went to the police for interdiction efforts and for fumigation of illegal crops. With the initiation of Plan Colombia, however, the Colombian military surpassed the police as the primary beneficiary of U.S. assistance.

After the FARC handed the Colombian armed forces important defeats in the mid-1990s, some U.S. policymakers sought consideration of counterinsurgency aid. Winning support for this proved politically difficult given the controversial U.S. involvements in Vietnam and Central America. However, by reframing Colombia's internal armed conflict as being integrally connected to the issue of drug control, U.S. policymakers were able to garner support for Plan Colombia.

Designing Plan Colombia

Andrés Pastrana was elected president in 1998 on a platform that pledged control of the drug trade as well as a negotiated end to Colombia's forty years of conflict. A series of meetings with FARC leaders led to formal peace negotiations and to the government's withdrawal from five municipalities in the provinces of Meta and Caquetá, creating a "cleared zone" (*zona de despeje*) completely under FARC control. Though it had inspired great hope, the peace process collapsed in February 2002.

Late in 1998, however, as he prepared for negotiations with the FARC, Pastrana unveiled his Plan Colombia, described "as a policy of investment for social development, reduction of violence and the construction of peace."[17] The proposal recognized the need for social investment directed toward small cultivators engaged in producing coca to offset their lack of economic alternatives. Pastrana hoped that the international community, including the United States, would make major financial contributions to the plan. However, over the course of the next year, Plan Colombia would be fundamentally altered to reflect U.S. analysis and priorities, and the new, U.S.-influenced version would downplay development in favor of military aid. Other countries were to show themselves unwilling to support the U.S.-dominated plan.

At the time Pastrana was elected, the FARC controlled or operated freely in 40–60 percent of Colombian territory and had de facto control over much of the southwestern part of the country. Much of Colombia's coca was being produced in FARC-controlled areas, and half of the FARC's income, some U.S.$200–400 million, was believed to come from its involvement in drug trafficking.[18] Drug income helped finance the FARC's improved military capacity.

Some officials in the administration of President Bill Clinton (1992–2000), particularly Clinton's drug czar, General Barry McCaffrey, and leaders of U.S. Southern Command (Southcom), viewed the FARC and its role in the drug trade with growing concern and sounded alarms within the executive branch. "We have an emergency situation in Colombia and it requires a broad-gauge response which may require additional resources," McCaffrey warned in mid-1999.[19] As the administration debated what to do about Colombia, these officials strongly urged a revival of assistance to Colombia's armed forces. At the same time, the administration remained cautious about diving into an outright counterinsurgency mission in Latin America: "The issue raises too many human rights concerns and has been a searing experience for us in Central America," wrote Ambassador Myles Frechette in a January 1997 cable in apparent reference to the hundreds of thousands of people who were tortured, killed, dispossessed, or disappeared during U.S.-backed counterinsurgency efforts in El Salvador, Guatemala, and Nicaragua during the 1980s.[20]

Meanwhile, the Colombian armed forces had avoided any significant role in drug control efforts—a mission for which the Clinton administration had much more enthusiasm. The armed forces viewed illegal drugs as a law enforcement issue, to be dealt with by the police, while their primary adversaries were the guerrillas.

U.S. defense officials sought a way to help Colombia's armed forces stave off the guerrillas within the confines of the drug war. The answer lay in using the promise of aid to encourage Colombia's military to help fight drugs in Putumayo, a center of coca cultivation and guerrilla activity. In December 1998, Colombian defense minister Rodrigo Lloreda and U.S. Defense Secretary William Cohen agreed to form an elite, highly mobile counternarcotics battalion within the Colombian army.[21] Endowed with thirty-three Huey helicopters, the 950-man battalion was to guarantee security conditions for aerial eradication in the provinces of Putumayo and Caquetá, which in 1999 accounted for the greatest part of the coca cultivated in Colombia. "Guaranteeing security conditions" was clearly understood to mean confronting armed groups directly on the ground—something not contemplated in the previous police-aid model.

The brigade completed training at the end of 1999, without the U.S. Congress ever specifically appropriating money for it. The new military aid strategy was already well under way by the time the Clinton administration asked Congress for a large appropriation to continue and expand it.

The basis for the administration's request was the revised version of Plan Colombia. The Colombian government had produced the new plan—in English—in September 1999, after U.S. diplomats promised President Pastrana that the United States would "sharply increase aid if he develop[ed] a comprehensive plan to strengthen the military, halt the nation's economic free fall and fight drug trafficking."[22] In the revised version, investment in social capital, infrastructure, and productive projects gave way to a new mission: "to assure order, stability and compliance with the law; guarantee national sovereignty over territory; protect the State and the civilian population from threats by groups in arms and criminal organizations; [and] break the links existing between these groups and the drug industry that supports them."[23] The new Plan Colombia, with its explicit counterdrug and implicit counterinsurgency focus, was only minimally circulated in Colombia, received spotty media coverage, and was never discussed in the Colombian Congress. Nevertheless, in July 2000, the U.S. Congress approved a special supplemental appropriation of U.S.$1.3 billion for the initiative, of which U.S.$860 million was designated for Colombia.

Pastrana's original Plan Colombia had included no mention of military aid. But in the version funded by the U.S. Congress, 75 percent of Colombia's share—$642.3 million—went to the armed forces and the police, and most of that to the military (Figure 4.1).[24] The centerpiece, which administration documents called the "push into southern Colombia," involved the addition of two more counterdrug battalions to form the Counternarcotics Brigade within the Colombian army. Equipped with forty-five helicopters, communications and intelligence gathering equipment, arms, and ammunition, and provided with light infantry training, the 2,300-man brigade would ease the way for massive fumigation in Putumayo. Additional assistance went to Colombia's navy to expand the riverine program, while the air force and the police were given more aircraft and equipment.

The initial U.S. aid package did provide U.S.$218 million for alternative development, aid to the internally displaced, human rights, judicial reform, and rule of law programs. While the amounts marked a significant increase over prior levels of U.S. social and economic aid, they fell far

Figure 4.1   U.S. Aid to Colombia, 1997–2005

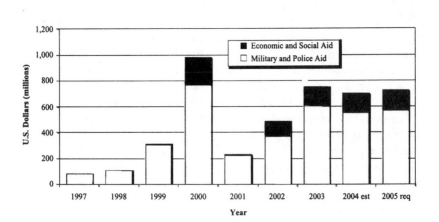

Source: Data from the U.S. State Department, Bureau for International Narcotics and Law Enforcement Affairs, *International Narcotics Control Strategy Report*, various years. Please see WOLA website, www.wola.org, for full listing.

short of the levels of social investment that President Pastrana had originally called for.

Those critical of the U.S.-backed Plan Colombia also pointed out that
it underplayed paramilitary involvement in the drug trade, despite the fact
that the U.S. government has requested the extradition of numerous paramilitary leaders on drug-trafficking charges. The AUC is also, as pointed
out previously, on the U.S. State Department's list of terrorist organizations. Nonetheless, to date U.S. military aid under Plan Colombia has not
been directed at combating paramilitary forces. Instead, these illegal groups
have expanded their presence and consolidated their control of territory
throughout the country.

The Pastrana government had estimated the full cost of its Plan
Colombia at U.S.$7.5 billion, of which U.S.$3.5 billion in contributions
was to come from the international community. But as of June 30, 2002,
Colombia's comptroller general reported that non-U.S. grant contributions
to Plan Colombia had totaled only U.S.$106.32 million.[25] European disap-
pointment at being excluded from discussions of the plan, fundamental dis-
agreements with the United States over drug control strategy, and lack of
interest in a country outside Europe's sphere of influence were the reported
reasons for the scanty contributions.[26]

The name Plan Colombia continues to be widely used to refer to the
U.S. aid package to Colombia, even though since FY2002 the funds have
actually been provided under the rubric of the Andean Counterdrug
Initiative (ACI), which also includes counterdrug assistance for neighboring countries. Although Plan Colombia was presented as a five-year program, its funds must be approved annually through the foreign operations
appropriations process and related supplemental appropriations legislation.
Since 2000, Colombia has received U.S.$3.15 billion; U.S.$2.52 billion has
gone to Colombia's military and police.[27] The George W. Bush administration requested an additional U.S.$724 million for FY2005, in principle the
final year of the program. The security focus of the aid package has been
maintained; in any given year, between 68 percent and 75 percent of
Colombia's ACI aid has gone to the military and police. Additional aid provided through U.S. Defense Department accounts has increased the security
forces' share to 75–80 percent annually. Economic and social aid peaked at
U.S.$218 million in the first appropriation in 2000 and has remained level
at U.S.$150 million since 2003, despite the efforts of some in the U.S.
Congress to increase the amount.

The Counterinsurgency Mission

While the composition of the U.S. aid has not changed, the counterinsurgency objectives have become more and more explicit. To enforce the distinction between counterdrugs and counterinsurgency, the Clinton adminis-

tration issued an executive order banning the U.S. military from sharing nondrug intelligence with its Colombian counterparts. Before the September 11 attacks, the Bush administration was also somewhat reluctant to officially endorse involvement in counterinsurgency, and the U.S. Congress was still on record that fighting drugs should remain the U.S. priority.[28]

September 11 substantially undercut opposition to an explicit counterinsurgency mission. In August 2002, Congress granted the Bush administration's request for "expanded authority" for a "unified campaign" in Colombia against drug trafficking and activities by organizations designated as foreign terrorist groups, that is, the FARC, the ELN, and the AUC. The following November, Bush reversed Clinton's executive order banning the sharing of nondrug intelligence. Expanded authority has since been renewed twice, in the FY2003 and FY2004 foreign operations appropriations legislation. The broadened authority has allowed U.S. aid to pay for a host of new nondrug military and police aid initiatives in Colombia, including a new army commando unit to pursue the leaders of guerrilla and paramilitary groups. New police units are being deployed, with U.S. support, in many conflict areas. U.S. funds are supporting antikidnapping units, presidential security, and an expanded signals intelligence gathering effort. The aerial interdiction program was revived for Colombia in August 2003 (it had been placed on hold after a 2001 incident in Peru in which a U.S. missionary and her child were killed). The Colombia program's scope has broadened to include interdiction of aircraft suspected of trafficking arms.

In a second step toward an explicit counterinsurgency role, at the end of 2002 the U.S. Congress approved a U.S.$99 million program to help the Colombian army protect an oil pipeline in the conflict-ridden province of Arauca, located along the Venezuelan border in the northeastern part of the country. The Caño Limón–Coveñas pipeline, of which the U.S. firm Occidental Petroleum owns a major share, was bombed 170 times by guerrillas in 2001 and about forty times in 2002.[29] By mid-2003, dozens of U.S. Special Forces were in Arauca, training members of the Colombian army's 18th Brigade and the new 5th Mobile Brigade. According to Southcom operations chief General Galen Jackman, "I think that these brigades that we're talking about will be very offensively oriented. That is, focused on the enemy, as opposed to a static defense around the pipeline."[30]

The pipeline protection program is funded through Foreign Military Financing (FMF), the main nondrug military aid program under the Foreign Assistance Act. In April 2003, only a couple of months after the U.S.$99 million was approved and despite strong opposition in the House of Representatives,[31] Congress approved an additional U.S.$37 million in FMF for Colombia (and U.S.$68 million in International Narcotics Control and Section 1004 funds) as part of a bill to fund the Iraq War. During

FY2004, the Bush administration planned to spend U.S.$110 million more in FMF for Colombia, only a portion of which is for the pipeline protection effort. Most is not earmarked for specific projects—it can be spent to meet contingencies as they arise, as was the case for most U.S. aid to Cold War allies like El Salvador years ago. The Bush administration requested an additional U.S.$108 million in FMF for FY2005.

The third indicator of the growing counterinsurgency emphasis in U.S. policy is the recent effort to increase the "troop cap," the limit on the number of U.S. military personnel and contractors who can be deployed in Colombia at any one point in time. When the U.S. Congress approved Plan Colombia in 2000, some members were concerned that the United States could be drawn into a growing military commitment in Colombia. As a result, deployment was limited to 800, including a maximum of 500 troops and 300 private contractors. In the FY2002 appropriation, the overall limit of 800 was retained, but the composition was changed to a maximum of 400 troops and 400 private U.S. citizen contractors. The same cap was retained for FY2003 and FY2004.

Since late 2003, Southcom has been developing a proposal to nearly double the cap, to 800 U.S. troops and 600 military contractors. The rationale is support for the Colombian government's Patriot Plan, designed to expand military presence in parts of southwestern Colombia—territory that remains under FARC control two years after the collapse of peace talks. The U.S. Defense Department proposes to provide direct support to the Colombian military in the form of communications, intelligence, and logistical support at the brigade level, at an initial estimated cost of U.S.$320 million over three years. There is no pretense of a counterdrug objective.

The Uribe Government

Even as the post–September 11 global war against terrorism has facilitated the U.S. shift toward a counterinsurgency emphasis in Colombia, the Colombian president, Alvaro Uribe, who took office in 2002, has wholeheartedly embraced the language of counterterrorism, and he has implemented the U.S. aid package he inherited under the logic of counterinsurgency.

Uribe was elected in May 2002 in reaction to the deep popular disillusionment that followed the collapse of Pastrana's negotiations with the FARC. Colombians who had voted for peace in 1998 opted in 2002 for a hard-line approach to dealing with guerrillas. The FARC reacted to Uribe's inauguration on August 7, 2002, by launching gas cylinder bombs that missed the new president but killed several people in nearby neighborhoods. Within days, Uribe declared a "state of internal unrest" and placed large regions of the country under military control. During 2002 and 2003, he increased the number of combat troops, established programs to draw the civilian population into collaborating with the military, and pursued legal and constitutional reforms that expand the military's powers or weaken civilian and judicial oversight of the security forces. At the same time, Uribe pursued fumigation with a vengeance. In 2003, 127,000 hectares of coca were fumigated, the highest number in the history of Colombia's fumigation program.

Uribe's actions, which have enjoyed the full and unconditional support of the Bush administration, distanced Plan Colombia even more from Pastrana's original vision. While counterterrorism has become another objective of U.S. policy in Colombia, the impact of Plan Colombia should be evaluated according to the original U.S. goals. Foreign policy discourse has changed, but at the end of 2003 Colombia was still the leading producer of cocaine in the Western Hemisphere, and the internal armed conflict was still raging.

• The Fumigation Strategy

Aerial eradication has been conducted in Colombia with U.S. support since the 1980s, when the primary target was marijuana. In the mid-1990s, as coca and opium poppy cultivation surged in Colombia, U.S.-backed fumigation efforts intensified. But cultivation continued to expand, alarming U.S. policymakers and setting the stage for a far more significant escalation of fumigation as the central strategy of Plan Colombia.

U.S. support for the fumigation campaign is delivered through the State Department's Bureau of International Narcotics and Law Enforcement Affairs (INL) and the U.S. embassy's Narcotics Affairs Section (NAS) in Bogotá. The spraying operations are conducted by a police unit, the Colombian Antinarcotics Directorate (known as DIRAN), with NAS funding technical support, herbicide, fuel, and spray aircraft. By the end of 2003, twenty-four fixed-wing aircraft were flying spray missions. The planes are piloted by U.S. citizens, Colombians, and third-country nationals contracted by the INL through Virginia-based DynCorp Aerospace Technologies. DynCorp contractors also provide maintenance, training, and logistical support.[32]

The spray flights are accompanied by armed, NAS-provided helicopters to protect them from potential attack by the FARC or other armed groups active in the drug production zones. Despite these armed escorts, spray planes have frequently been targets of ground fire; 194 were hit by hostile fire in 2002, and 380 were hit in 2003, resulting in the loss of four INL planes.[33] Five U.S. civilian contractors died in Colombia in three separate incidents related to the fumigation campaign in 2003, a year in which one helicopter and four spray planes either crashed or were severely damaged because of ground fire. In February 2003, a plane carrying U.S. and Colombian personnel crashed in FARC-controlled territory. One

Colombian and one U.S. citizen were murdered, and as of mid-2004, three other U.S. citizens were still being held by the FARC.[34] In September 2003, one pilot was killed when his spray plane crashed due to ground fire.[35]

The pilots spray a chemical mixture whose active ingredient is glyphosate, a nonselective systemic herbicide that kills most plants and trees if a sufficient dose is applied. The glyphosate used for coca fumigation is manufactured by the St. Louis–based Monsanto Corporation and sold under variations of the trade name Roundup.[36] The mixture applied in Colombia consists of a glyphosate formulation, water, and a surfactant, Cosmo-Flux 411F, which increases the effectiveness of the herbicide.

Rapid Expansion

Under Plan Colombia, fumigation has been conducted on an unprecedented scale: from 2000 through 2003, the U.S.-backed fumigation program sprayed herbicide on more than 380,000 hectares of coca, equivalent to more than 8 percent of Colombia's arable land.

Although the spraying began in December 2000, its full impact was not felt until 2002. In 2001, 94,127 hectares were fumigated, but new plantings brought total coca production to 169,800 hectares that year. In 2002, a record 122,695 hectares of coca were sprayed, and though new planting continued, total coca cultivation reportedly dropped 15 percent to 144,450 hectares. According to the State Department, the spraying of 127,000 hectares in 2003 led to a further 21 percent decline, to 113,850 hectares (Figure 4.2).

Dubious Claims of Success

The U.S. and Colombian governments trumpeted these reductions as evidence of the success of Plan Colombia. In March 2004 testimony to Congress, Robert Charles, assistant secretary of state for the INL, maintained that U.S.-Colombian fumigation efforts "brought us close to the tipping point where sustained suppression of illegal crops and alternative employment incentives together will convince growers that further cultivation is a futile proposition."[37] Time will tell whether even the steep declines in 2002 and 2003 will translate into strategic success, namely, deep and sustainable reductions in the production of coca leaf in Colombia and in the availability of cocaine in the United States. But there are several reasons for skepticism. First, even the sharp reductions in 2002–2003 did not bring cultivation back down to the 1998 level: 101,800 hectares, according to State Department estimates. Colombia remains the largest coca-growing country in the world.[38]

Second, in the past, when coca cultivation has declined in one geographic area, it has increased in another, in what is known as the "balloon effect" (see Chapter 1). Past experience suggests that eradication success in

Figure 4.2   Colombian Coca Cultivation, 1995–2003

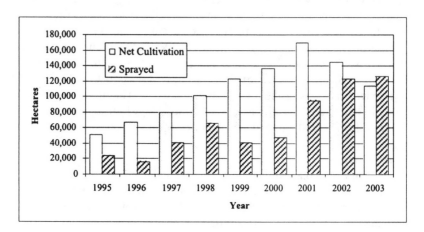

Source: U.S. Department of State, *International Narcotics Control Strategy Report* (INCSR), years 1995–2003.

Note: One hectare is equivalent to 2.47 acres.

Colombia will likely be frustrated in the future by stepped-up coca production in other countries. In the wake of eradication, coca cultivation has spread within Colombia as well: the Colombian government reported that the number of provinces in which coca was known to be cultivated rose from twelve to twenty-two between 1999 and 2002.[39] According to the State Department, the emphasis placed on Putumayo under Plan Colombia resulted in a marked decline in cultivation in that province, from a peak of 47,400 hectares in 2000 to 8,200 hectares in 2002. As Figure 4.3 shows, however, the reductions in other regions have been not been nearly as impressive, and the State Department reported that in the Guaviare region the land under coca cultivation actually rose from 38,200 hectares in 2000 to 78,500 hectares in 2002.[40]

Coca survey data for 2000–2002 compiled by the United Nations Office on Drugs and Crime (UNODC) also reveal "the high degree of mobility of coca cultivation, both within and across department boundaries."[41] Significant declines in overall cultivation were led by sharp drops in Putumayo and Caquetá. But the UNODC also found increases in coca cultivation in ten provinces. While most of the increases were fairly small in absolute terms, in Nariño, the province on Putumayo's western border, coca cultivation was nearly two-thirds higher in 2002 than in 2000.[42] And in Guaviare—the province from which coca cultivation migrated south toward Caquetá and Putumayo under the pressure of aerial eradication in

Figure 4.3   Colombian Coca Cultivation by Region, 1998–2002

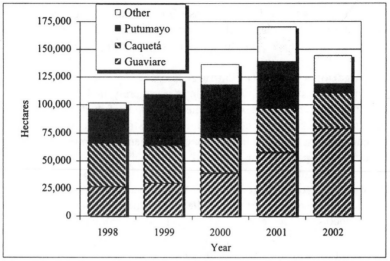

Source: U.S. State Department, Bureau for International Narcotics and Law Enforcement Affairs, "Colombian Coca Cultivation," INL, 14 March 2003. www.state.gov/g/inl/rls/other/18650.htm.

the mid- to late 1990s—cultivation rose 55 percent. It is worth noting that neither U.S. nor UN surveillance methods are considered accurate in detecting newly planted fields or in measuring the extent of coca fields outside the major established coca-growing zones.[43]

Another reason for skepticism about the effectiveness of the fumigation strategy is its high cost. According to the INL's Robert Charles, after 2004 the United States "expects to enter a maintenance phase of spraying smaller, more isolated coca fields, instead of the larger fields we have sprayed since our program began. The endgame will then involve a ramp down to maintenance levels."[44] But the State Department has yet to define the level of cultivation it believes will be manageable for the Colombian government to handle without significant infusions of U.S. aid. In June 2003, the U.S. General Accounting Office (GAO) observed that:

> Neither the Colombian Army nor the Colombian National Police can sustain ongoing counternarcotics programs without continued U.S. funding and contractor support for the foreseeable future.... As GAO noted in 2000, the total costs of the counternarcotics program in Colombia were unknown. Nearly three years later, the Departments of State and Defense have still not developed estimates of future program costs, defined their

future roles in Colombia, identified a proposed end state, or determined how they plan to achieve it.[45]

As the costs to the United States of the global war against terrorism mount, and as U.S. budget deficits grow, the financial feasibility of maintaining a large-scale, ongoing fumigation program is highly questionable.

• Fumigation's Collateral Damage

The fumigation strategy in Colombia is not merely ineffective; it is also counterproductive. It has destroyed the livelihoods of thousands of peasant farmers who lack viable economic alternatives to producing illicit crops, also endangering their health and the environment. The implementation of the fumigation program in disregard of Colombian legal principles, and against the will of local and regional elected officials, has undermined the rule of law and government authority. And as coca cultivation has dispersed in response to the fumigation, the illegal armed actors have followed the new production, further extending the reach of the internal armed conflict.

Alternative Development: Too Little, Too Late

The spray program targets coca fields of all sizes, from industrial-size plantations to plots of less than two hectares grown by peasant farmers and indigenous people.[46] The Colombian government's attitude toward such small cultivators has been ambiguous. On the one hand, Law 30 of 1986 specified that the cultivation of marijuana, coca, and opium poppy in excess of twenty plants was a crime. Law 599 of 2000, which revised Colombia's penal code, reaffirmed that growing these crops is illegal and increased the penalties for violations. On the other hand, policy initiatives throughout the 1990s differentiated between "industrial" or "commercial" production (extensions of land as large as 300 hectares or more, directly controlled by drug traffickers) and "small cultivators" (peasant and indigenous farmers cultivating coca on parcels of land between two and five hectares).[47] The latter were to be assisted with programs for crop substitution and alternative development, in recognition of the economic, social, and political conditions that foster reliance on illicit crops.

When fumigation intensified in the mid-1990s, the expectation of differential treatment led to protests that culminated in a march of 200,000 coca farmers in July 1996. The participants called for voluntary eradication accompanied by long-term development projects. They also demanded that the government fulfill agreements promising social investment and development infrastructure that it had signed in 1994 and 1995 with peasant organizations in the Guaviare and Putumayo regions.

Plan Colombia was also shaped by the distinction between small-scale and large-scale cultivators. As the U.S. Congress was debating whether to support the aid package in 2000, Clinton administration officials asserted that most of Colombia's coca was produced on industrial plantations. The claim helped persuade many members of Congress to accept the heavy reliance on fumigation. At the same time, the first appropriation for Plan Colombia included U.S.$68.5 million to support alternative development projects, with an additional U.S.$15 million to provide emergency assistance to small producers likely to be displaced by the spraying.

UNODC estimated that in 2002 and 2003 more than 60 percent of Colombia's coca crop was grown on plots less than three hectares in size.[48] Though large-scale producers are known to fragment their coca fields in order to avoid detection, most small coca plots are cultivated by individual farmers for their own subsistence. Moreover, the highest concentrations of coca are in provinces with especially high indicators of poverty. Even so, the amount of development aid provided under Plan Colombia was inadequate from the beginning. Between 2001 and 2003, nearly 340,000 hectares of coca were sprayed, but the U.S. Agency for International Development (USAID) supported the cultivation of fewer than 39,000 hectares of legal crops.[49]

In addition, the disbursement of aid under Plan Colombia has been marked by significant delays, and the models for aid delivery have changed frequently. Between December 2000, when fumigation began, and July 2001, the Colombian government signed thirty-three "social pacts for voluntary eradication and alternative development" with 37,775 families in nine municipalities in Putumayo. The agreements imposed a one-year deadline for families to eradicate their coca in exchange for aid. According to the Latin America Working Group, "More than two years later, only 21 percent of the aid for food security projects had been delivered, and only 24 percent of those participating in social pacts had received all or a portion of the promised aid."[50]

Over the years, the lack of follow-through on development aid has left many farmers skeptical that the Colombian government will actually provide aid once their coca is eradicated and doubtful that aid programs that do commence will be sustained long enough to make a difference. They are therefore reluctant to voluntarily eradicate their coca.

In Putumayo in 2001 and 2002, because so much of the aid was not delivered, many families did not eradicate their coca, leading the Pastrana government and USAID to declare the social pacts a failure.[51] In July 2002, the Colombian government began a major punitive fumigation campaign in which areas covered by the pacts were sprayed. Meanwhile, USAID was already implementing a different model, known as "early eradication," in which communities had to commit to eradicating 100 percent of their coca, subject to verification, before receiving assistance. From 2000 to 2003 there were also numerous reports, official and unofficial, that fumigation had caused significant damage to legal food crops, pasture, fish, livestock, and agricultural development projects. This damage exacerbated the problems related to aid delivery.

According to the State Department, the fumigation program is designed to avoid harm to humans and other crops, and officials say herbicide spraying is carefully targeted and done only under conditions that minimize spray drift. They cast aspersions on the motives of those who report such damage and accuse farmers of having intermingled coca with other crops.[52] However, the sheer number and consistency of the reports of damage lend them credibility, and many complaints have been verified by Colombian state agencies, intergovernmental commissions, or independent parties. Herbicide spray drift is a probably a major cause of the damage; models created by the U.S. Environmental Protection Agency (EPA) show that herbicides can drift up to 600 feet downwind from their targets. Although, on paper, a procedure exists to compensate small farmers whose legal crops are destroyed by spraying, in practice it has not functioned. Anecdotal reports suggest that some farmers left destitute by fumigation are joining the guerrillas or the paramilitaries out of economic necessity.[53]

Fueling Displacement

The clearest indication that the fumigation strategy is having a devastating effect on the livelihood of small farmers is found in statistics on the movement of people out of fumigated regions. UNODC reports that, with the exception of Nariño, all the coca-growing areas "show very high levels of forced displacement of population."[54] Much of this displacement is evidently due to the armed conflict. However, according to the Colombian government's ombudsman, fumigation was one of the causes of the displacement of more than 17,000 people from Putumayo in 2001; the spraying deprived them of their subsistence income from coca and threatened their food supply.[55] According to the Social Solidarity Network, in 1999 415 people were displaced from Putumayo by political violence.[56] By August 2003, after the fumigation operations had been launched, the population displaced from the province had risen to nearly 56,000.[57]

Colombia's nongovernmental Council for Human Rights and Displacement estimates that in 2001 and 2002 alone fumigation led to the displacement of more than 75,000 people nationwide.[58] This process has deepened the crisis affecting small farmers and indigenous groups in Colombia and along the border with Ecuador. Displaced families typically live in poverty and profound insecurity. Those displaced by fumigation are not eligible for emergency food aid and other services provided by the Social Solidarity Network to those displaced by political violence. Since many small farmers do not hold title to their land, they often forfeit their right to return when forced to abandon their homes.[59] While most of the displaced remain in Colombia, some have fled to neighboring Ecuador (see Chapter 7). Of those who remain in the country, some had settled recently in the coca-producing zones and have now returned to their regions of origin.[60] Others have moved more deeply into tropical forests, including indigenous reserves. Dispossessed and without other options for survival in their new locales, many displaced people become engaged in coca cultivation and harvesting, as well as the processing and transporting of coca paste and cocaine.[61]

Health and Environmental Risks

Beyond fumigation's direct impact on farmers' livelihoods, there are numerous reports of adverse health and environmental effects. Spray zone residents say frequent exposure to the spray mixture has caused a variety of skin, respiratory, and other ailments. Concerns have also been raised about the impact that widespread spraying may have on Colombia's diverse and fragile tropical ecosystems, which are home to one in every ten known species on earth. About one-third of Colombia's approximately 50,000 known plant species are found nowhere else, and about one-third of all known vertebrate species live in Colombia.

The U.S. State Department has consistently downplayed health and environmental concerns, however. Officials argue that the ill health suffered by many people in the spray zones is the result of generally poor conditions or exposure to agricultural and drug-processing chemicals. They say glyphosate, the herbicide used, has been shown to be fairly benign in its environmental effects. They are silent on the effects of the surfactant.

However, concern about the health effects and environmental impact of fumigation led the U.S. Congress to set conditions on the disbursement of aid for the aerial eradication program. Passed as part of the annual foreign aid appropriations bills for FY2002, FY2003, and FY2004, the conditions have varied somewhat each year, but all made the disbursement of U.S. aid contingent on reports by the secretary of state, in consultation with the EPA, on the effects of fumigation.

As a result, the EPA has provided the State Department with assessments of the health and environmental impacts of the fumigation campaign, and the State Department has interpreted the EPA's findings in a favorable light. However, there are major gaps in the information available to the EPA. Most important, the EPA analysis is based strictly on information about the spray program provided by the State Department. EPA cannot collect its own primary data or contact other organizations with relevant expertise. What's more, the EPA assessments were conducted without the benefit of any information specific to the local environment in Colombia. Meanwhile, the State Department submits little specific information to the EPA on how spraying operations are actually implemented. As a result, fundamental questions about the effects of the spray program remain unanswered.

The State Department cites the environmental destruction wrought by drug crop cultivation as justification for the aerial eradication program, maintaining that spraying "discourages the cultivation of illicit crops and thereby slows the rate of deforestation."[62] The evidence to date, however, suggests that spraying has actually encouraged the spread of coca farming to new areas, including relatively pristine forests and national parks. These have in turn been subjected to deforestation and pollution as farmers clear additional forest areas to replace eradicated croplands, and those processing the coca pollute new soil and waterways with processing chemicals. Although not quantified precisely, deforestation due to illicit crop cultivation has greatly increased the risk of extinction for many Colombian bird and plant species.[63]

In short, assertions that the spray program is essentially harmless to human health and the environment are questionable at best. Health and environmental monitoring, and studies specific and rigorous enough to measure the impact of the spraying as it is being implemented in Colombia, have not yet been conducted.

Disregarding Colombian Laws

From the moment fumigation began, it also provoked controversy and dissension within the Colombian government. Although the police and the president's office have supported the spraying, agencies charged with protecting the environment and public health have consistently voiced concern about or opposition to it.

Colombia's key antidrug statute, Law 30 of 1986, required the prior approval of health and environmental agencies for aerial eradication. National Narcotics Council Resolution 0001 of February 1994 laid out procedures to be followed for that approval process to take place. On the environmental front, the National Narcotics Directorate (DNE) was to contract an environmental auditor to control and supervise the implementation of the fumigation. In August 1996, the Ministry of Environment ordered DNE to produce an environmental management plan for carrying out fumigation with glyphosate. Not until January 2002, however, after six years of back-and-forth among the relevant agencies, including litigation, was the Environmental Management Plan (EMP) finally put in place. The plan has not been strictly enforced, and under the Uribe administration its original provisions have been weakened.

The fumigation policy has also been seriously questioned on other legal and constitutional grounds. The comptroller general and the public ombudsman have repeatedly urged that aerial eradication be suspended for contravening various Colombian legal and constitutional guarantees pertaining to public health, environmental protection, and prior consultation with affected communities.[64] The grounds for the challenges include government failures to implement an epidemiological monitoring plan, to develop contingency and mitigation plans, to comply with spray buffer zones, and to refrain from spraying sensitive environments such as water bodies and protected areas. The recommendations to suspend spraying have not been followed by the National Police.

In June 2003, the Administrative Court of Cundinamarca ruled that the fumigation program violates citizens' constitutionally guaranteed rights to public health, security, and a healthy environment. It found the government to be in violation of numerous laws, including compliance with the EMP. The court ordered DNE to suspend the aerial eradication program completely until it has achieved full compliance with the EMP and conducted rigorous studies to measure the impact of fumigation on human health and the environment. President Uribe promptly denounced the ruling, declaring, "While I am president, fumigation will not be suspended."[65] The government appealed the ruling and refused to comply with the court order to suspend spraying.

Nor have the objections of local and provincial elected leaders succeeded in slowing or significantly modifying implementation of the spraying program. In 2001, the governors of the departments of Putumayo, Nariño, Cauca, and Tolima met with members of the U.S. Congress and Bush administration officials in Washington, requesting that fumigation be suspended in favor of manual eradication and increased development assistance. Charging ahead with fumigation, the governors predicted, would simply promote the migration of illegal crops and the spread of armed conflict. But as of early 2004, even the minimal funds for community-based development projects were coming to an end, and the Uribe government communicated to USAID its interest in focusing on large-scale industrial projects, which are of doubtful feasibility or benefit to the peasants most affected by fumigation. In 2003 Colombia's inspector general opened disciplinary investigations against several of the governors for their opposition to the national policy of fumigation.

Notwithstanding the concerns of regional governments, the affected communities, government agencies, or the courts, President Uribe has considered implementation of the fumigation program to be nonnegotiable. The minimal safeguards that had been put in place are either being dismantled or disregarded in practice. In particular, in close cooperation with the U.S. State Department, the Uribe government has rolled back many of the environmental protection measures included in the 2001 Environmental Monitoring Plan. The modified EMP reduces the buffer zones required to avoid spraying environmentally sensitive areas and settlements and allows for aerial spraying in Colombia's national parks. The newest version of the

U.S. fumigation conditions also accepts spraying in national parks, although the issue provoked such a public outcry that the Colombian government was forced to backtrack. In March 2004, the Colombian environment minister said that the government will resort to fumigation in national parks only if manual eradication fails.

The significant reductions in coca cultivation recorded since 2002 are attributed by the State Department almost exclusively to the record-setting pace of the fumigation program. By contrast, UNODC agrees that fumigation has been central to the overall decline, but it takes pains to put events into a broader context and to recognize that other factors come into play, including voluntary eradication, the dynamic of the armed conflict, and the prices for legal agricultural products. According to UNODC,

> The armed conflict, which was fueled by narcotics production, deteriorated the security situation ... to a point that in some parts of the country it prevented farmers from even planting coca. Moreover, a recovery of the prices of some key farm products, such as cocoa and sugar cane in 2002, seemed to have reduced the incentives for farmers to switch to coca cultivation.[66]

The high-profile political commitment to fumigation on the part of both the U.S. and Colombian governments precluded serious consideration of very different but more promising options, such as a concerted effort at integral rural development. While fumigation has alienated potential allies, a genuine and ambitious effort to promote rural development would likely attract more support in the region and from potential donor governments in Europe.

• Plan Colombia and Human Rights

In 1999, as President Pastrana was in conversations with the Clinton administration about U.S. support for Plan Colombia, the Inter-American Commission on Human Rights (IACHR) reported that "the situation of human rights in Colombia—which involves massive and continuous violations of the most fundamental human rights—is currently one of the most difficult and serious in the Americas."[67]

Despite the fact that Colombia is a formal democracy and its 1991 constitution contains strong human rights protections, the nation's continuing insurgency and counterinsurgency efforts provided a context in which serious abuses have occurred. Government security forces have been regularly accused of massacres, extrajudicial executions, forced disappearances, and violations of due process and civil liberties. Guerrillas as well as paramilitary members have been charged with other massacres and executions and with indiscriminate attacks that affected civilian noncombatants—all violations of international humanitarian law. Impunity for those responsible for the abuses, especially members and officers of the armed forces, has been nearly absolute.

The 1991 constitution was a by-product of negotiations between 1988 and 1990 that had led some guerrilla movements, including the M-19 and several smaller groups, to give up armed struggle and to take part in electoral politics.[68] The constitution recognized and guaranteed the full range of human rights. It also established new institutional spaces to ensure protection of those rights, including a strong constitutional court and a public ombudsman. It gave international human rights treaties ratified by Colombia precedence over domestic law, and it created *la tutela*, the right to request the immediate intervention of the courts if an individual believed his or her rights were being violated. This institutional framework was shaped by the deep involvement of the human rights movement in the writing of the constitution, but the dramatic human rights crisis Colombia faced at the end of the decade reflected the deeply rooted nature of the obstacles to progress in this area.

Military Autonomy

These obstacles included a military accustomed to significant autonomy and empowered to play an essentially unconstrained role in maintaining public order. The origins of the military's autonomy lie in the perception of its neutrality during La Violencia, when the army initially declined to be pulled into partisan conflict. In exchange for maintaining nominal civilian control of the government, the military was granted authority to design and implement national security policy largely independent of any civilian oversight.

The military's power grew as a result of the executive branch's almost permanent invocation of state of siege powers during the counterinsurgency campaigns of the 1960s through the 1980s. Under state of siege decrees, legal rights were suspended even though constitutional guarantees were not formally modified. The military was given power to investigate and judge civilians for many crimes, including rebellion and carrying arms. The Security Statute of 1978, informed by the U.S. National Security Doctrine, created the crime of "attacking the public order" and made the military's jurisdiction over civilians permanent.[69] The use of state of siege became a defining characteristic of Colombian political culture and "the means through which the Armed Forces ... significantly increased their presence in the political process and their power within the regime."[70]

Between 1984 and 1989, in the context of the war against the drug cartels, a state of siege was invoked 139 times. In 1986 President Barco decreed laws extending the military's extraordinary powers to include trials of those accused of drug trafficking.[71] The 1988 Defense of Democracy Statute sought to repress both the guerrilla movements and narcoterrorism and ratified the extension of national security concerns to include drug trafficking.[72] The statute led to the creation of special judicial procedures for trying drug traffickers and guerrillas, in what came to be known as "justice without a face." These remained in place until the mid-1990s.

Civilian control over the military had been further eroded by the military's penal code, under which the members of the armed forces charged with crimes were investigated and judged by the military itself; thus, members of the armed forces were protected from civilian courts regardless of the nature of their crimes. At the same time, the military justice system lacked any pretense of impartiality. Commanding officers served as military judges in cases involving soldiers in their units. Accusations of misconduct were likely to be dismissed, particularly if soldiers alleged that their commanding officers acted improperly. In practice, the military's jurisdiction over its own members guaranteed impunity, even as denunciations of human rights violations increased.

The military used its extraordinary powers to carry out widespread detentions throughout Colombia in the 1970s and 1980s and tried civilians in secret hearings without due process protections. The first Colombian human rights organizations were founded to investigate and report on military abuses and to defend those detained. The groups documented hundreds of cases of torture in military detention centers and brought legal cases challenging the military's practices. In 1987 the Colombian Supreme Court ruled that military jurisdiction over civilians and the secret hearings were unconstitutional.[73] The rejection of the military's practices as abusive and ineffective by large sectors of the Colombian public was reflected in the decisions of a 1991 constitutional assembly, when strict limits were placed on the use of states of exception such as state of siege or any other legally declared suspension of constitutional guarantees. But the military retained its autonomy and involvement in maintaining public order, and impunity was deeply entrenched.

The Paramilitary Phenomenon

A second key human rights issue as Plan Colombia was under consideration was the structural relationship between the armed forces and paramilitary organizations. The paramilitary organizations—first established at U.S. urging in the 1960s to complement military counterinsurgency efforts—expanded dramatically in the 1980s. As guerrilla pressure forced large landowners in the rich central regions of the country to abandon their estates, these were acquired by drug traffickers who sought to launder their profits and buy social standing. The drug traffickers joined with the military and local elites to form private armies. The expansion of the paramilitaries took place as the Betancur government was opening the door to peace negotiations with the FARC and other guerrilla groups. The paramilitary growth reflected local elites' fear that an agreement with the insurgents would leave them unprotected, as well as the military's sense that it was being marginalized by the peace process.[74]

The result was that the military's relationship with paramilitaries deepened even as the cartels unleashed their war against the Colombian state. As the paramilitaries grew, so did human rights violations involving the armed forces. Military doctrine referred to the "internal enemy" and characterized civil society actors as potentially subversive.[75] By the late 1980s, high-ranking military officials and military spokesmen were publicly linking unions, universities, judicial authorities, human rights defenders, and even the church to the guerrillas.

Small leftist parties—including the Patriotic Union (Unión Patriótica, or UP)—founded by the FARC in 1985 after the inconclusive end of that group's dialogue with the Betancur government—had enjoyed significant success in Colombia's first popular elections of mayors and other local officials in 1987. But paramilitary groups, with the support of drug traffickers, worked closely with local military commanders to eliminate "guerrilla sympathizers," thus decimating leftist political organizations. UP was a particular target; some 3,000 UP members have been assassinated since its founding.

In the La Rochela massacre of January 1989, paramilitary gunmen with military support massacred eleven members of a judicial team investigating paramilitary operations linked to local military commanders. As a result of this case, President Barco issued a series of decrees declaring the self-defense groups illegal.[76] Shortly thereafter the Colombian Supreme Court declared unconstitutional the provision of the decree that had authorized self-defense forces.[77] But five years after La Rochela, a new decree law revived the self-defense forces under the name Convivir.[78] By the time the right of these new groups to carry military arms was struck down in November 1997, the paramilitary phenomenon in Colombia had expanded qualitatively and had become well entrenched.[79]

In the mid-1990s, paramilitary activity in Colombia had changed in several ways. First, and coinciding with the dismantling of the cartels, the paramilitaries had begun to challenge the FARC for direct control over coca-producing territories. Second, a national coordinating body, the United Self-Defense Forces of Colombia, was created. Following a July 1997 summit, the groups adopted an offensive strategy that entailed expanding operations into new regions of the country. Finally, the share of human rights abuses committed directly by the paramilitaries increased sharply, as the number of violations directly attributable to the armed forces declined (Figure 4.4).

These changes were interrelated. The newly targeted regions were traditional guerrilla strongholds. Increasing their control of the drug trade

Figure 4.4   Share of Responsibility for Noncombatant Deaths and Forced Disappearances

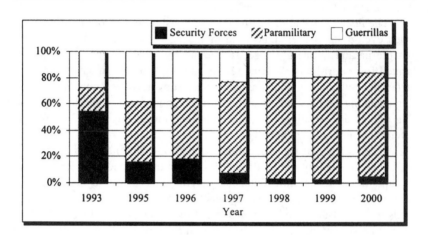

Source: Reports of the Colombian Commission of Jurists, available on the Center for International Policy website, www.ciponline.org/colombia/infocombat.htm.

allowed the paramilitaries greater autonomy and fed further expansion of their operations. The offensive campaign, announced in public documents and press statements, was carried out through massacres that also caused other residents to flee, thus clearing territory. Although members of the armed forces continued to be involved directly in killings, the military's role moved more toward that of intelligence and logistical support to the paramilitaries. The military was also increasingly involved in acts of omission—failing to act to prevent atrocities carried out against noncombatants, even when forewarned. Thus, even as the numbers of dead and displaced went steadily up, the military's human rights record appeared to improve.[80]

The new operational relationship was visible in the first massacre that took place after the paramilitaries announced their new military strategy. During the period of July 15–20, 1997, AUC gunmen held control of the town of Mapiripán in the province of Meta and executed several dozen people. (The exact death toll was never established, as many of the bodies were dismembered and thrown into a nearby river.) Subsequent investigations showed that the military escorted the paramilitary killers to private planes, allowed the paramilitaries to pass through three highly militarized zones en route to Mapiripán, and failed to respond to reports of the massacre once it began. Hundreds of similar massacres followed, carried out throughout the country and affecting thousands of people.

The Mapiripán case was investigated by the military and the civilian justice systems. Military courts sentenced Brigadier General Jaime Humberto Uscátegui to forty months in jail for dereliction of duty. Lieutenant Colonel Hernán Orozco, who testified against him, was also sentenced to thirty-eight months in prison. However, both sentences were subsequently annulled. The response of the civilian justice system has been more appropriate. A civilian court sentenced the local commander, Lieutenant Colonel Lino Sánchez, to forty years in prison for his role.As of mid-2004, both Uscátegui and Orozco were being tried in civilian courts for aggravated homicide and kidnapping, and the case is pending before the Inter-American Court of Human Rights.

A Changing Landscape for Human Rights

The consolidation of the paramilitaries, and the changing division of labor between them and the military, took place against the background of the crisis in U.S.-Colombian relations that followed accusations linking President Samper to the drug trade. Some U.S. officials recognized that isolating Samper had only served to weaken the Colombian state, although the object of their concern was the growing strength of the guerrillas, rather than the paramilitaries.[81] As some U.S. officials began to discuss the possibility of increased funding for the Colombian military, the military's human rights record was a clear liability. At the same time, challenges to the armed forces from the Colombian courts and the human rights movement were gaining traction.

In 1993, the new Constitutional Court had confirmed the Supreme Court's 1987 decision striking down military jurisdiction over civilians.[82] In 1997, the court issued a landmark ruling that violations of human rights and crimes against humanity could in no case be considered acts of service and therefore fell outside the jurisdiction of the military justice system.[83] The decision went to the heart of military impunity for human rights abuses and opened the door to public debate over reform of the military penal code. A bill revising the code was introduced during the Samper government and became law a few days after President Pastrana took office.[84] The revisions were imperfect in that the new code specified only torture, genocide, and forced disappearance as human rights crimes falling outside military jurisdiction. But the military understood that the new code represented a setback to its autonomy. General Manuel Bonnet, commander of the armed forces at the time, characterized the new penal code as seeking to "criminalize" the army and complained that "society should not send [troops] to combat unarmed, because the *fuero* is our shield."[85]

These advances were due in no small part to the work of the Colombian human rights movement.[86] Two strategies were key: litigation and international advocacy. Seeking to make full use of the new protections for human rights in the 1991 constitution, Colombian groups pressed spe-

cific cases of human rights violations in the civilian, military, and administrative justice systems, sought reports and resolutions from the public
ombudsman, and brought constitutional challenges to elaborate rights or to
enforce limitations on the security forces.

At the same time, the groups put Colombia's human rights record on
the international agenda. They participated regularly in the IACHR, bringing key cases that had stagnated in the Colombian courts and providing
semiannual updates on the overall human rights situation. In 1996 the sig-
nificance of this strategy was reinforced by approval of Law 288, which
recognized the obligatory character of recommendations handed down by
the IACHR and the UN Committee on Human Rights.[87] The human rights
groups also engaged the UN human rights system. Among their most significant achievements was the 1996 opening of the Office of the UN High
Commissioner for Human Rights (OHCHR) in Colombia.

In spite of the advances made by the human rights community during
the 1990s, the human rights situation remained critical as the U.S. policy
debate on Plan Colombia got under way. The OHCHR reported 402 massacres in 1999, a 50 percent increase over the previous year.[88] Many of the
"collective executions" had been announced in advance by paramilitary
forces who were advertising the creation of "new war fronts." Testimonies
pointed to the involvement of members of the armed forces in the organization of new paramilitary blocs.

At the same time, rates of impunity for all crimes in Colombia exceeded 90 percent. For human rights crimes, the figure was nearly 100 percent.
Therefore, two key actions were required prior to the provision of U.S.
security assistance: the structural relationship between the paramilitaries
and the armed forces had to be severed, and impunity had to be ended.

However, only a few provisions in the version of Plan Colombia
approved by the U.S. Congress were directly relevant to these two points.
Of particular importance were human rights conditions added to the legislation by Congress, along with funding provided explicitly for programs to
strengthen human rights and rule of law. Senators Patrick Leahy (D-
Vermont), Ted Kennedy (D-Massachusetts), and Paul Wellstone (D-
Minnesota) and Representative Jim McGovern (D-Massachusetts) were
among the leaders on these issues.

U.S. Human Rights Conditionality

Human rights conditions focused on the military-paramilitary relationship
have been included in the Plan Colombia appropriation every year. The
conditions provide that a stated percentage of military assistance may not
be disbursed until the U.S. secretary of state certifies to Congress that
Colombia's military is suspending officers credibly alleged to have committed human rights violations or to have aided and abetted paramilitary

forces, that Colombia's government is cooperating with civilian human rights investigations, and that steps are being taken to sever links between the military and the paramilitaries.

Prior to making the certification, the State Department is required to meet with internationally recognized human rights organizations. In every such consultation, the groups have presented detailed information and benchmark cases relevant to evaluating Colombia's compliance.[89] With the exception of the first certification, however, when Secretary of State Madeleine Albright chose to waive most of the conditions, the State Department has consistently certified compliance. The State Department has relied on a narrow, legalistic interpretation of the conditions in which any cases or actions consistent with the conditions, no matter how minimal, constitute compliance.[90] As a result, the State Department is able to argue that Colombia is complying with the letter of the law, even though its own annual human rights report documents continuing collaboration between the Colombian armed forces and the paramilitaries, and even though impunity for human rights crimes remains nearly absolute.[91]

The human rights conditions are complemented by another legal provision inserted annually into U.S. foreign operations appropriations bills, known as the Leahy Amendment (see Appendix 1). The provision prohibits military assistance to foreign military units implicated in human rights violations, although aid may be resumed if the foreign government takes steps to bring the responsible members of the unit to justice. U.S. embassies are charged with implementing the Leahy Amendment by vetting potential beneficiaries of military assistance. Though interpretation of the provision has been subject to debate, particularly over the definition of a unit and what constitutes appropriate corrective measures, in practice the provision is probably an incentive to establish new, clean military units. In Colombia, the soldiers and officers recruited to staff the three new counterdrug battalions were vetted as individuals prior to assignment.

The case of the Santo Domingo massacre demonstrates the promise of the Leahy Amendment. In December 2002, the United States suspended aid to the 1st Air Combat Command of the Colombian air force, the unit involved in launching a rocket attack on the village of Santo Domingo, Arauca, during a December 1998 clash with the FARC. Seventeen civilians, including children, were killed when the unit dropped cluster bombs on the village and shot already-wounded passengers being transported in a truck. Pressure from the U.S. government concerning the case also led to the forced retirement of General Héctor Fabio Velasco, the commander of the air force. General Velasco had delayed investigation of the case to the point of obstructing justice. Velasco did not succeed completely, however. In the fall of 2002, Colombia's inspector general suspended from duty for three months a captain and a lieutenant in the case. In December 2003 the attorney general charged the helicopter crew with involuntary manslaughter; as of May 2004 the case was also pending before the IACHR.

The strong pro–human rights message that should have been sent by General Velasco's retirement was undermined by President Uribe when the new commander of the air force was installed on September 8, 2003. Uribe, speaking before a military audience with high-ranking U.S. officials present, used the occasion to attack human rights defenders as "politickers at the service of terrorism."[92] His targets included "collectives and lawyers," a reference to the Lawyers' Collective, the nongovernmental organization that brought the Santo Domingo case to the IACHR. Uribe concluded his remarks by urging that the incoming air force commander not allow the "traffickers in human rights" to deter him. Neither the State Department nor the U.S. embassy in Colombia publicly condemned or clearly distanced the U.S. government from Uribe's statements. Paramilitaries publicly embraced the president's position and in a communiqué issued on September 17 congratulated the president on his statements and identified several human rights groups as façades for the FARC and involved in "guerrilla diplomacy."

More generally, U.S. human rights policy under Plan Colombia has sent a mixed message. Even though imperfectly implemented, the human rights conditions have established a frame of reference for analyzing the military's human rights behavior. Some members of the Colombian armed forces—probably a growing number—have a clear interest in a clean and professional institution. According to a leading Colombian political analyst, the worst thing that can happen to a rising military commander is to be confronted with credible allegations of human rights violations.[93] U.S. behind-the-scenes pressure has likely been instrumental in ending the careers of some other high-ranking military leaders with highly problematic human rights records, including Generals Rito Alejo del Río, Fernando Millán, and Rodrigo Quiñones.[94] U.S. officials insist that they regularly discuss human rights concerns with Colombian officials. U.S. embassy officials have been responsive and genuinely helpful to threatened human rights defenders.

The links between the paramilitaries and sectors of the armed forces, however, have not been severed. The State Department and the OHCHR, among others, continue to document new cases of military-paramilitary collusion.[95] One egregious example is the killing of more than sixty members of the Kankuamo indigenous community, in the Sierra Nevada de Santa Marta region, since President Uribe assumed office in August 2002. Major military operations have coincided with paramilitary expansion in the same zones.[96] Paramilitaries currently have political control of several provinces and are visibly present in urban areas, including municipalities such as Barrancabermeja, where security forces also have a strong presence. The basic goal of the human rights conditions has simply not been achieved.

U.S. Support for Human Rights and Rule of Law Programs

From the outset, Plan Colombia included funding for programs to strengthen key human rights institutions, both governmental and nongovernmental. Examples include support provided to the human rights units of the attorney general's office, the inspector general, and the public ombudsman; the Early Warning System (EWS), an interagency program coordinated by the Office of the Public Ombudsman and created to protect the civilian population from massacres, forced displacement, and other massive human rights violations; other protection programs for human rights defenders, trade unionists, and journalists; and the office of the OHCHR. The funding for these programs is provided by State Department counterdrug accounts, although the implementation of the programs is through USAID (and in some cases through the Justice Department). While it is beyond the scope of this chapter to provide a comprehensive analysis of the impact of human rights and rule of law programs, a few observations are in order.[97]

By the time Plan Colombia was approved, the United States had provided more than a decade of support for judicial reform.[98] U.S.-backed reforms focused on increasing the efficiency of judicial processes, sometimes at the expense of due process protections. A key example was the highly controversial "faceless justice" system implemented in the early 1990s. Designed to protect threatened judges and lawyers, the system allowed for anonymous witnesses and secret trials. The human rights community documented cases in which individuals were prosecuted without legal recourse.[99] The U.S. government also supported the establishment of an accusatorial, jury-based system, which was approved by the Colombian Congress in December 2002 and is scheduled to be fully operational as of 2005.

Past experience with these reform efforts, however, underscore the importance of the Colombian government's political will in implementing the reforms effectively as well as the importance of its commitment to human rights and due process guarantees. When these are lacking, even well-planned efforts can fail to achieve their intended aim.

A case in point is the effort to provide protection for civil society leaders at risk because of their work on behalf of democracy and human rights. The protection program works with the Ministry of Interior to evaluate the risk faced by threatened human rights workers, union leaders, and local government officials and makes and implements recommendations for protection measures. The program was initially controversial because potential beneficiaries were suspicious of funding provided through Plan Colombia. Over time, acceptance has grown; as of February 13, 2004, 3,364 individuals had benefited.[100]

But while the program has increased security for individuals, it has been criticized for failing to address the broader issue of accountability for attacks and for significant operational problems.[101] In some cases, these difficulties have contributed to the program's inability to protect threatened activists. To cite just one example, on January 12, 2003, presumed paramilitaries killed Enoc Samboni, a community leader from Cauca who was participating in the protection program. According to a coalition of human rights NGOs, the protection program has "played an important role in specific cases to safeguard the life and integrity of some people ... but has not developed a strategy for the program or policies that address the causes of risks."[102] President Uribe's recent attacks on human rights defenders clearly reinforced skepticism about the government's political will to stop attacks on civil society leaders.[103]

The EWS raises a different issue. From June 2001 through August 2002, according to official reports, 150 alerts were emitted, and the security forces responded to 107.[104] As of early 2004, the cumulative figures were 220 alerts and 170 responses.[105] The number of responses, however, fails to indicate the lag time between alert and response. Early in the implementation of the program, USAID circulated charts that showed a minimum two- to three-month lag time before any action was taken, and central government authorities and the security forces had a long history of ignoring warnings about pending atrocities.

Recommendations by human rights activists to sanction military authorities if they failed to respond to an alert were not accepted. Although the director of the EWS asserted that the system had saved 90,000 people from being victimized, it was impossible to evaluate the claim because no actual results indicators had been developed.[106] Still, the program benefited from the personal credibility of Public Ombudsman Eduardo Cifuentes. It did provide a mechanism for alerting authorities about potential atrocities, and it came to be seen as a positive step by international agencies.

Under President Uribe, however, the clearly preventive nature of the program is perceived to have been lost. Now, EWS issues "risk assessments" instead of alerts, and they are reviewed by a committee that includes the Ministry of Defense. U.S. and Colombian authorities assert that the committee is a mechanism to ensure a more effective response.[107] But some staff at the Office of the Public Ombudsman, and many in the human rights community, believe that the presence of the Ministry of Defense in the process has fundamentally altered the nature of the EWS. Instead of the EWS serving as a mechanism to ensure that the security forces act, the power of decision is again in the hands of security forces.

Some believe that the EWS has become an intelligence gathering tool for the military.[108] As of February 13, 2004, the EWS had issued a total of 104 risk assessments to the review committee, and it had in turn issued only thirty-seven alerts to local authorities to take preventive action.[109]

A third example of the vulnerability of human rights initiatives in Colombia is the deteriorating ability of the Office of the Attorney General to investigate and prosecute human rights cases since coming under the leadership of Luis Camilo Osorio in July 2001.[110] Since 2000, the U.S. Department of Justice has invested more than U.S.$25 million in training, equipment, and the creation of satellite human rights units designed to facilitate the investigation of cases. However, many key justice officials who worked on sensitive human rights cases, including many who were trained with U.S. funds, were forced out of their jobs in the first year after Osorio assumed his position. Human rights cases that had gathered momentum under his predecessor, and are critical to the goal of severing the military-paramilitary relationship, have been severely undermined. News articles in 2004 have documented charges that the attorney general's office is infiltrated by paramilitaries.[111]

While U.S. efforts to support human rights and rule of law initiatives in Colombia are clearly important, these examples suggest the limitations of efforts to create "a culture of respect for human rights" when a country's highest-ranking political leaders send equivocal messages.[112] Moreover, U.S. funding for these programs is extremely modest compared to the much larger security assistance program. In fact, some view U.S. assistance for human rights initiatives as a way of gaining congressional and public support for security assistance. These perceptions continue to undermine U.S. programs to promote human rights and the rule of law in Colombia.

The Government-Paramilitary Dialogue

Another issue that has raised questions about the Uribe government's commitment to human rights is the dialogue it has initiated with the AUC leadership concerning paramilitary demobilization. The Santa Fe de Ralito Agreement, signed in July 2003, is described as a peace process by Colombian and U.S. officials, who argue that removing a key actor from the conflict will save the lives of hundreds of innocent civilians. Sectors of the paramilitary movement that refuse to enter the dialogue will be targets of military action, according to the government. U.S. officials have indicated a willingness to provide resources in support of the demobilization.

If the dialogue with AUC held real promise for dismantling the paramilitary groups, it could be a significant contribution toward eliminating a major structural cause of the violation of human rights in Colombia. However, as of mid-2004 the focus was on the demobilization and social reintegration of a specific set of paramilitary fighters without affecting their underlying structures of support, in particular their relationship with the armed forces and thus the Colombian state.[113]

To date, the dialogue process has not ended paramilitary violence. On the contrary, more than 600 killings have been attributed to the paramilitaries since the AUC declared a ceasefire in December 2002.

Nor is there a framework in place to ensure the return of assets illegally acquired by paramilitaries, including lands stolen from displaced populations. Instead, apparently anticipating that they will be allowed to retain their territorial gains through the demobilization process, paramilitaries have continued to forcibly displace the rural population.[114] Colombian observers argue that the dialogue will facilitate the consolidation of paramilitary economic and political gains made over the last twenty years, including control over land in resource-rich regions of the country.

Of particular concern is the Uribe government's apparent willingness to forgo investigating the past or ensuring justice for victims of paramilitary crimes. In August 2003, the Uribe government proposed legislation to the Colombian Congress that, at the discretion of the president, would have allowed grave human rights crimes to be punished not with prison sentences but with a series of milder sanctions: preventing the violators from serving in public office or carrying arms for some period of time, limiting their freedom of movement, and requiring that they contribute to reparations for the victims. The legislation would not have ensured serious, impartial investigations or prosecutions and would not have required or compelled a truthful accounting of past actions. The bill provoked so much opposition within and outside of Colombia that the government was forced to modify it; however, a new version introduced in March 2004 also failed to meet the government's obligation under international law to respect the rights of victims to truth, justice, and reparations.

Those who would benefit from such measures include figures such as Carlos Castaño, the primary spokesman and self-styled political theorist of the AUC. Castaño is the subject of dozens of criminal cases and has more than two dozen formal arrest warrants issued against him. He is wanted in connection with the assassination of two presidential candidates and one senator, as well as multiple massacres involving the torture and death of hundreds of people. In some cases, like the Mapiripán massacre, he has already been convicted in absentia. Castaño himself admitted to many of these crimes in his best-selling autobiography. In April 2004, Castaño was the target of an assassination attempt, allegedly by rival paramilitaries, that killed six of his bodyguards. At this writing, his whereabouts are unknown.

If the legislation proposed by the Uribe government is passed, all those who participated in, collaborated with, facilitated, or failed to prevent the actions of the paramilitaries would also be spared by a less-than-thorough examination of Colombia's brutal history. As previously described, the paramilitaries have their origin in state policy, and in spite of occasional efforts from the mid-1980s forward, the Colombian government has failed to stop the growth of paramilitary presence and power.[115] Cases already before the courts have begun to provide details of the intimate relationship between the state and paramilitary violence. One general summoned in the Mapiripán case has threatened to reveal all he knows about the links between other military officials and paramilitarism if his trial goes forward.[116] Ultimately, a full accounting will be the most effective, and perhaps the only, means for dismantling the paramilitary networks and finally severing the military-paramilitary link.

Other Security Measures

Since taking office, President Uribe has implemented a series of controversial security initiatives, including antiterrorist legislation that has been repeatedly declared unconstitutional by the Constitutional Court and criticized by the United Nations.[117] He has sought to return judicial police powers to the military and to restrict Constitutional Court oversight of states of emergency. These measures would undo the advances of the 1990s in curtailing the military's autonomy and in limiting practices that contribute to impunity. At the same time, his administration is undercutting the ability of civilian oversight agencies to ensure that human rights are respected by slashing their budgets and publicly questioning their role. Public confidence in the judicial system, a fundamental component in strengthening the rule of law, has been eroded by the lack of independence demonstrated by the attorney general.[118]

At the end of 2003, the Colombian government reported significant reductions in some categories of violence—including murders, kidnappings, and forced displacement—and concluded that the overall human rights situation in the country had improved. These reported advances were attributed to the government's policies. However, it is far from clear what the long-term impact will be. Already, the policies' impact on the institutions and actors that promote and defend human rights is deeply disturbing.

Of particular concern is the practice of *señalamiento*, publicly seeking to discredit the work of human rights groups by linking them to the guerrillas. This is not new in Colombia: in 1988, the commander of the armed forces argued that human rights lent itself to political action by subversion.[119] But whereas President Pastrana took action to penalize such statements by public officials, Uribe has embraced the tactic and combined it with judicial harassment. Detentions of human rights and civil society leaders and the judicial investigations against them have been based on unverified intelligence provided by paid informants. Organizations targeted include those that provide legal defense to individuals accused of political crimes.

The U.S. government's public silence in the face of these measures strengthens the hand of antidemocratic actors in Colombia and weakens many of the same institutions that it seeks to strengthen through its foreign aid programs.

• Conclusion: Plan Colombia and Democracy

A Colombian human rights organization recently observed that:

> Currently it is the Congress of the United States that determines how much money goes for the war in Colombia and what the conditions are for war "assistance," it is the Environmental Protection Agency that determines the benefits of glyphosate, it is the Department of State that says whether human rights are being complied with or not, it is the Bureau of Political Affairs that says whether Colombia is or is not a regional or global threat. In this cycle of determinants, the only one who doesn't express an opinion is the Colombian Congress and it abstains voluntarily from doing so ... the blow to Colombian democracy is obvious.[120]

As harsh as this statement is, however, the problem is not merely that key decisions lie in the hands of U.S. policymakers, most of whom know little of Colombia or its history. There are myriad other ways in which the implementation of Plan Colombia risks undermining democratic actors and institutions in Colombia.

For example, a continued focus on the importance of fumigation has undermined existing legal and constitutional limitations on the aerial spraying program, as well as the authority of the public ombudsman, the inspector general, the Ministry of Environment, and the courts. It also contradicts broader national development objectives. The failure to take into account the comprehensive regional development proposals of the elected governors of the southern provinces, which rely on manual eradication, weakens local government. Meanwhile, because citizen participation and transparency are lacking in the control and oversight of Plan Colombia development resources, much of the development aid does not even directly reach the affected communities.[121]

The cumulative effect of giving greater weight to outcome than to process is especially worrisome as counterinsurgency becomes an explicit goal of the U.S. aid package. From one perspective, real democracy in Colombia dates from the 1991 constitution. But the institutional and judicial advances of the 1990s have not fully overcome the legacy of military autonomy, much less put an end to impunity. Yet President Uribe is attempting to roll back those advances, while the U.S. government fails to use fully its leverage to defend either the achievements or those who made them possible.

Plan Colombia in its existing form will not achieve its drug control objectives. Most likely, either coca production will increase in new areas, or sustaining the reductions of 2002 and 2003 will require a permanent fumigation campaign. Yet the collateral damage from the fumigation strategy, and from privileging engagement with the military, is undermining the consolidation of democracy and rule of law.

The moment for debate on the next phase of Plan Colombia is rapidly approaching as its initial five-year mandate comes to an end. U.S. policymakers have an opportunity to engage Colombia on restructuring the aid package for FY2006 and beyond in order to achieve lasting, sustainable solutions to the country's structural problems. That could provide an opportunity to return to the original vision of Plan Colombia, with its emphasis on rural development, social investment, and strengthening of democratic institutions and practices.

• Notes

1. The FARC and the ELN were placed on the list on 9 October 1997 and the AUC on 10 September 2001.

2. For detailed analyses of the armed forces-paramilitary relationship, see Ediciones NCOS, *Tras los Pasos Perdidos de la Guerra Sucia, Paramilitarismo, y Operaciones Encubiertas en Colombia* (Brussels: Ediciones NCOS, 1995), and the following Human Rights Watch reports: *Colombia's Killer Networks: The Military-Paramilitary Relationship* (1995); *The Ties that Bind: Colombia and Military-Paramilitary Links* (February 2000); and *The "Sixth Division"—Military-Paramilitary Ties and U.S. Policy in Colombia* (September 2001).

3. "Reglamento JC 3-10, Reservado, de 1969," army regulations cited in *Tras Los Pasos*, p. 21.

4. Ediciones NCOS, *Tras los Pasos.*

5. Drug Enforcement Administration Director Donnie Marshall, testimony before the Subcommittee on Criminal Justice, Drug Policy, and Human Resources, House Committee on Government Reform, 2 March 2001.

6. Juan G. Tokatlian, Eduardo Sarmiento, Luis Orjuela, and Carlos Arrieta, *Narcotráfico en Colombia* (Bogotá: Tercer Mundo Editores, Ediciones Uniandes, 1995).

7. See Jonathan Hartlyn, "Drug Trafficking and Democracy in Colombia in the 1980s," Working Paper no. 70, Barcelona, 1993.

8. Ibid.

9. Decree no. 1860 went into effect on 18 August 1989 and was declared valid by the Supreme Court on 3 October 1989.

10. Russell Crandall, *Driven by Drugs: U.S. Policy Toward Colombia* (London: Lynne Rienner Publishers, 2002), p. 34.

11. Tokatlian et al., *Narcotráfico en Colombia*, pp. 346–352.

12. Frontline, "Drug Wars: Thirty Years of America's Drug War, a Chronology," PBS Online and WGBH/Frontline, 2000, www.pbs.org/wgbh/pages/frontline/shows/drugs/cron/.

13. Ibid.

14. *Revista Semana*, "La Batalla del Glifosato," no. 659 (Bogotá: 20 December 1994), p. 23.

15. Dirección Nacional de Estupefacientes, *La Lucha de Colombia Contra las*

Drogas Ilícitas, Acciones, y Resultados 2001 (Bogotá: DNE, March 2002), p. 16.

16. U.S. State Department, Bureau for International Narcotics and Law Enforcement Affairs (INL), *International Narcotics Control Strategy Report (INCSR) 1999* (Washington, D.C.: 1 March 2000); *INCSR 1998* (Washington, D.C.: 1 March 1999).

17. Observatorio para la Paz, "Plan Colombia: Juego de Máscaras," in *Cultivos Ilícitos, Narcotráfico, y Agenda de Paz*, Darío Posso, ed. (Bogotá: Mandato Ciudadano por la Paz, la Vida y la Libertad, 2000), p. 167.

18. www.ciponline.org/colombia/infocombat.htm.

19. Transcript of hearing before the House of Representatives Government Reform Subcommittee on Criminal Justice, Drug Policy and Human Resources (Washington, D.C.: U.S. House of Representatives, 6 August 1999).

20. U.S. Embassy, Bogotá, to Secretary of State, "Ambassador's January 12 Meeting with New MOD Designate," cable, 13 January 1997. Available on website of National Security Archives, electronic briefing book no. 69, "War in Colombia: Guerrillas, Drugs and Human Rights in U.S.-Colombia Policy, 1988–2002," www.gwu.edu/~nsarchiv/NSAEBB/NSAEBB69/col51.pdf.

21. William S. Cohen, U.S. Secretary of Defense, and Rodrigo Lloreda, Minister of Defense of Colombia, briefing, (Washington, D.C.: Defense Department, 1 December 1998). Available at Defenselink.mil under News Archives.

22. Douglas Farah, "U.S. Ready to Boost Aid to Troubled Colombia," *Washington Post*, 23 August 1999.

23. Government of Colombia, Contraloría General de la República (CGR), *Plan Colombia: Primer Informe de Evaluación* (Bogotá, Contraloría General de la República, August 2001), p. 13.

24. See Center for International Policy (CIP), "The Colombia Aid Package By the Numbers," 5 July 2002, www.ciponline.org/colombia/aid0001.htm.

25. Government of Colombia, Contraloría General de la República, *Plan Colombia: Tercer Informe de Evaluación* (Bogotá: CGR, August 2002), p. 14.

26. See Transnational Institute, *Europe and Plan Colombia,* Drugs and Conflict Debate Paper no. 1 (Amsterdam: TNI, April 2001), www.tni.org/drugs/index.htm.

27. CIP, "U.S. Aid to Colombia Since 1997: Summary Tables," www.ciponline.org/colombia/aidtable.htm.

28. "The managers strongly express reservations and objections to any mission creep in Colombia beyond ongoing counterdrug efforts," Conference Report on H.R. 4506, Foreign Operations, Export Financing, and Related Programs Appropriations Act, 2002, Section on Andean Counterdrug Initiative.

29. U.S. State Department, "Report to Congress: Caño Limón Pipeline," December 2002, www.ciponline.org/colombia/02120001.htm.

30. Brigadier General Galen Jackman, U.S. Southern Command J-3 (Operations), media roundtable, 4 October 2002, www.ciponline.org/colombia/02100401.htm.

31. An amendment cosponsored by Reps. James McGovern (D-Mass.) and Ike Skelton (D-Mo.) to cut the FMF aid lost narrowly.

32. Connie Veillette and Jose E. Arvelo-Velez (Congressional Research Service [CRS]), *Colombia and Aerial Eradication of Drug Crops: U.S. Policy and Issues*, updated 28 August 2003.

33. Testimony by Robert Charles, Assistant Secretary of State for International Narcotics and Law Enforcement Affairs before the House Government Reform

Committee, "U.S. Policy and the Andean Counterdrug Initiative (ACI)," 2 March 2004.

34. Connie Veillette (CRS), *Colombia: Issues for Congress*, 1 March 2004.

35. Government Accountability Office (GAO), *Drug Control: Aviation Program Safety Concerns in Colombia Are Being Addressed, but State's Planning and Budgeting Process Can Be Improved*, report to the Honorable Charles E. Grassley, Chairman, Caucus on International Narcotics Control, U.S. Senate (Washington, D.C.: GAO-04-918, July 2004).

36. U.S. State Department, "Aerial Eradication of Illicit Crops: Frequently Asked Questions," 24 March 2003.

37. Testimony by Robert Charles, 2 March 2004.

38. U.S. State Department, *INCSR 2003*, "South America."

39. Dirección Nacional de Estupefacientes, based on the Integrated System for Monitoring Illicit Cultivation (SIMCI).

40. U.S. State Department, "Colombia: Net Coca Cultivation by Region, 1998–2002," 14 March 2003, www.state.gov/g/inl/rls/other/18650.htm.

41. United Nations Office on Drug Control (UNODC), "Colombia Coca Survey for December 2002 and Semi-Annual Estimate for July 2003," p. 17.

42. Parmenio Cuellar, governor of Nariño from January 2000 until December 2003, asserts that during his period in office coca cultivation increased threefold, from approximately 10,000 hectares to more than 43,000. Interview with Kimberly Stanton, February 2004.

43. Latin America Working Group (LAWG), "Going to Extremes: The U.S.-Funded Aerial Eradication Program in Colombia," March 2003, p. 6 and n. 37.

44. Testimony by Robert Charles, 2 March 2004.

45. U.S. General Accounting Office, *Drug Control: Specific Performance Measures and Long-Term Costs for U.S. Programs in Colombia Have Not Been Developed* (GAO-03-783), June 2003.

46. Colombian National Narcotics Office (DNE), Resolution 005, 2000, cited in LAWG, "Going to Extremes," 2003, p. 3 and n. 13.

47. Defensoría del Pueblo, "La Ejecucion de la Estrategia de Erradicacion," p. 47.

48. Information in this paragraph, unless otherwise noted, is from UNODC and Government of Colombia, *Colombia: Coca Survey for December 2002 and Semi-Annual Estimate for July 2003*, September 2003, pp. 27 and 46.

49. U.S. State Department, *INCSR 2003*.

50. LAWG, "Going to Extremes," p. 22.

51. Defensoría del Pueblo, "Derechos Humanos y Derecho Internacional Humanitario en el Marco del Conflicto Armado y de las Fumigaciones de los Cultivos de Coca en el Departamento del Putumayo," resolution no. 026, 9 October 2002.

52. U.S. State Department, "Aerial Eradication of Illicit Crops: Frequently Asked Questions," 24 March 2003, www.ciponline.org/colombia/03032401.htm.

53. This paragraph and next in LAWG, "Going to Extremes," 2003, p. 25 and n. 177 and 178.

54. UNODC and Government of Colombia, *Coca Survey*, p. 29.

55. Defensoría del Pueblo, "Derechos Humanos," p. 11.

56. The Red de Solidaridad Social is the Colombian government agency responsible for providing aid to displaced people.

57. LAWG, "Going to Extremes," p. 26 and n. 190.

58. Government of Colombia, Ombudsman's Office, Resolution 028, 21 May 2003, cited in LAWG, "Going to Extremes," p. 26 and n. 182.

59. Ibid., p. 26 and n. 192 and 198.

60. Note that many of those living in Putumayo at the beginning of Plan Colombia were colonists or day laborers who had come from Nariño and Cauca; they returned to those provinces, bringing drug cultivation and violence with them.

61. UNODC and Government of Colombia, *Colombia: Coca Survey*, p. 29.

62. U.S. State Department, "Aerial Eradication," 24 March 2003.

63. LAWG, "Going to Extremes," pp. 28–29.

64. Anna Cederstav, Earthjustice and AIDA, "Memorandum to Honorable Members of Congress on the Department of State report to Congress regarding aerial eradication in Colombia," 23 September 2002, cited in LAWG, "Going to Extremes," 2003, p. 38 and n. 285.

65. *El Tiempo*, "'Mientras Yo Sea Presidente No Serán Suspendidas las Fumigaciones,' advierte Alvaro Uribe," 29 June 2003.

66. UNODC and Government of Colombia, *Colombia: Coca Survey*, p. 17.

67. Inter-American Human Rights Commission, "Tercer Informe Sobre la Situación de Derechos Humanos en Colombia", OEA/Ser.L/V/II.102 Doc. 9 rev. 1, 26 February 1999, reprinted by the Comisión Colombiana de Juristas, 15 April 1999, p. xix.

68. See Mauricio García-Durán, ed., *Accord Issue 1—Alternatives to War, Colombia's Peace Processes* (London: Conciliation Resources and CINEP, 2004).

69. Francisco Leal, *El Oficio de la Guerra: La Seguridad Nacional en Colombia* (Bogotá: Tercer Mundo Editores and IEPRI, 1994), p. 104.

70. Andrés Dávila Ladrón de Guevara, *El Juego del Poder: Historia, Armas, y Voto* (Bogotá: Editorial Cerec and Unidades, 1998), p. 86.

71. Decree 3655 of 17 December 1986 increased the role of the military and the police in the fight against drugs. Decree 3671 of 19 December 1986 granted the military jurisdiction over civilians accused of drug offenses.

72. Dávila, *El juego del poder*, p. 112.

73. The relevant rulings were issued on 5 March 1987, decree no. 3671 of 1986, and on 23 April 1987, decree no. 340 of 1987.

74. Ibid.

75. Ediciones NCOS, *Tras Los Pasos*, p. 15ff.

76. Daniel García-Peña Jaramillo, "La Relación del Estado Colombiano con el Fenómeno Paramilitar: Por el Esclarecimiento Histórico," manuscript, April 2004, p. 3.

77. The Supreme Court ruling was issued on 25 May 1989.

78. Decree 356 of 11 February 1994.

79. Consitutional Court ruling no. C-572/97, 7 November 1997.

80. For detailed analysis of how the military/paramilitary relationship functioned, see the HRW reports, the IACHR reports, and UNHCHR reports for 1998 forward.

81. Crandall, *Driven by Drugs*, p. 131.

82. Constitutional Court ruling no. C-034/93, 8 February 1993.

83. Constitutional Court ruling no. C-357/98, 5 August 1997.

84. Law 533 of 12 August 1999.

85. *Revista Cambio*, "Conejo a la ONU y Micos," *Cambio*, no. 255 (Bogotá: 4 May 1998), p. 36.

86. The Colombian human rights groups that led the way in these efforts include: the Colombian Commission of Jurists, founded to bring international

human rights law to bear in Colombia; the Colectivo de Abogados José Alvear Restrepo, the leading NGO in national and international litigation; the Committee in Solidarity with Political Prisoners, Colombia's first human rights group; Minga, known for its work in conflict zones and with the displaced; and the Association of Family Members of Disappeared Prisoners of Colombia (ASFADDES), the only nationwide victims' organization in the country.

87. The committee is the enforcement mechanism for the International Covenant on Civil and Political Rights and is empowered to hear individual cases.

88. UN report E/CN.4/2000/11, 9 March 2000, paragraphs 28ff., citing statistics from the Office of the Public Ombudsman.

89. See in particular Human Rights Watch, Amnesty International, and WOLA, "Colombia Human Rights Certification Briefing Paper," August 2000; "Colombia Human Rights Certification II Briefing Paper," January 2001; "Colombia Human Rights Certification III Briefing Paper," February 2002; and "Colombia Human Rights Certification IV Briefing Paper," September 2002.

90. For example, see "State Department Memorandum of Justification on 2002 Human Rights Conditions, May 1, 2002"; and Robin Kirk, "Rebuttal of Colombia Human Rights Certification," memorandum to interested aides and Colombia specialists, 16 May 2002.

91. See the U.S. State Department's annual *Country Reports on Human Rights Practices,* released each February by the State Department's Bureau of Democracy, Human Rights, and Labor.

92. Álvaro Uribe, speech delivered at the installation of General Édgar Alfonso Lesmez Abad as commander of the Colombian Air Force, Bogotá, Colombia, 8 September 2003, www.presidencia.gov.co/discursos/framdis.htm.

93. Conversation with Daniel García Peña, 18 February 2004.

94. See HRW/Amnesty International/WOLA reports cited above. Cf. García Peña, "La Relación del Estado Colombiano," April 2004, pp. 8–9.

95. Compare the U.S. State Department human rights report, March 2004, and the UNHCHR report of March 2004.

96. *Revista Semana,* "Meras Coincidencias?" no. 106 (Bogotá: 14 July 2003).

97. For a comparative review of U.S. democracy, human rights, and rule of law programs, see U.S. General Accounting Office (GAO), *Foreign Assistance: U.S. Democracy Programs in Six Latin American Countries Have Yielded Modest Results,* GAO-03-358, March 2003.

98. For a review of judicial reform efforts, see Luz Estella Nagle, "The Search for Accountability and Transparency in Plan Colombia: Reforming Judicial Institutions—Again," Implementing Plan Colombia Special Series, Strategic Studies Institute, U.S. Army War College, May 2001.

99. For a systematic analysis of the faceless justice program, see UNIJUS-Unidad de Investigaciones Jurídico-Sociales "Gerardo Molina," *Justicia sin Rostro: Estudio Sobre la Justicia Regional,* Gabriel Ricardo Nemogá, ed. (Bogotá: Universidad Nacional de Colombia, Facultad de Derecho, Ciencias Políticas y Sociales, 1996).

100. Management Sciences for Development, Inc., "USAID/MSD Human Rights Program," summary sheet, 19 February 2004.

101. UNHCHR, "Report on the Human Rights Situation in Colombia," UN Doc. E/CN.4/2003/13, p. 29, 24 February 2003, www.hchr.org.co/documentosein-formes/informes/altocomisionado/informe2002_eng.pdf.

102. "Seguimiento a las Recomendaciones del Alto Comisionado de Naciones Unidas para los Derechos Humanos Correspondiente al Informe Presentado en

Marzo de 2003 (E/CN.4/2003/13), en el Marco de los Compromises Adquiridos por el Gobierno Colombiano en la Pre-Mesa de Donantes en Londres, Julio de 2003," July 2003, p. 2. Signed by the Alianza, 114 Colombian human rights groups, with the Colombian Commission of Jurists as primary author.

103. This is the case even though the government's statistics show, for example, a decline in killings of union leaders during 2003. Union leaders attribute this to a change in paramilitary tactics in the context of the dialogue, not to the government's policies.

104. GAO, *Foreign Assistance*, March 2003, p. 66.

105. USAID, "Strategy in Colombia, 2003–2004."

106. Ibid.

107. MSD summary sheet, 19 February 2004.

108. Remarks of a former counsel for defense and national security in the forum Violence Prevention Measures in Colombia held at the University of the Andes, 7 February 2003.

109. MSD summary sheet, 19 February 2004.

110. See Human Rights Watch, "A Wrong Turn," November 2002.

111. *El Tiempo*, "El Diario 'The Miami Herald' Pide la Renuncia del Fiscal General Luis Camilo Osorio," 23 April 2004.

112. USAID, "Strategy in Colombia, 2003–2004."

113. García Peña, "La Relación del Estado Colombiano."

114. Scott Wilson, "Cease-Fire Becomes Land Grab," *Washington Post*, 20 September 2003, p. A25.

115. García Peña, "La Relación del Estado Colombiano," April 2004.

116. *Cambio,* "Uscátegui Acusa," no. 561, 29 March–5 April 2004.

117. For more details, see Latin America Working Group, *The Wrong Road: Colombia's National Security Policy*, July 2003. Also, Amnesty International, *Colombia: Security at What Cost? The Government's Failure to Confront the Human Rights Crisis*, 9 December 2002. UNHCHR, Colombia office, "Observaciones Sobre los Cambios Constitucionales 'Para Combatir el Terrorismo,'" press release, 12 December 2003, available on UNHCHR/Colombia website, www.hchr.org.co/publico/comunicados/2003/comunicados2003.php3?cod=45&cat=16. Also, Amnesty International, "Constitutional Reform Undermines Human Rights," press release, 11 December 2003, web.amnesty.org/library/Index/ENGAMR230772003.

118. Human Rights Watch, *A Wrong Turn: The Record of the Colombian Attorney General's Office*, report, November 2002.

119. Ediciones NCOS, *Tras Los Pasos,* p. 16.

120. Colectivo de Abogados "Jose Alvear Restrepo," *Plan Colombia No* (Bogotá: Colectivo de Abogados, 2003), p. 150.

121. Government of Colombia, Contraloría General de la República, *Tercer Informe*, July 2002, pp. 47, 57.

5

Bolivia:
Clear Consequences

Kathryn Ledebur

Although the scale of social conflict and human rights violations in Bolivia does not approach that of neighboring Andean nations, an examination of the impact of U.S.-funded drug control programs in Bolivia provides an important case study. In Colombia, and to a certain extent Peru, it can be difficult to attribute phenomena directly to official drug control forces because of the complexities created by guerrilla and paramilitary actions. In Bolivia, by contrast, there are no guerrilla movements or paramilitary groups. Thus the ineffectiveness of antidrug programs and the outright harm they generate are clearly evident. This direct causality provides a unique opportunity to explicitly assess the effects of policy, without the confounding influence of other factors.

Since the 1970s, drug control policy has been the main focal point of U.S.-Bolivian relations—and the main point of contention. Bolivia's most important role in the international drug trade has always been, and continues to be, that of coca leaf producer. By the 1980s, in addition, Bolivia had become an important producer of refined cocaine, and some Bolivians played leading roles in the international cocaine distribution network. Bolivia then became a key target of U.S international drug control operations, at that time still almost entirely the province of the Drug Enforcement Administration (DEA) and other law enforcement agencies. The "cocaine coup" of 1980 brought to power a short-lived military government that had strong links to cocaine producers.[1] U.S. diplomatic ties and aid were briefly severed as a result.

Since the early 1980s, the continued viability of Bolivia's desperately poor national economy has depended at least in part on illicit returns from international cocaine sales. Tens of thousands of small farmers in Bolivia have relied on coca cultivation for economic survival. Nevertheless, the United States has continued to insist on drug control measures, in particular coca eradication, that most affect the poorest Bolivians. The United States has promoted forced eradication, accompanied by the involvement of the

Bolivia

Population	8,500,000
GDP	U.S.$8.0 billion
GDP per capita	U.S.$936
Share of Income	
• Poorest 10 percent of population	0.3%
• Richest 10 percent of population	42.3%
• Ratio of income of richest 10% to poorest 10%	143.5 times
Percentage living in poverty (<$2/day)	34.3%
Percentage living in extreme poverty (<$1/day)	14.4%
Public perception of corruption among public officials and politicians (0=more, 10=less)	2.3

Sources: UNDP, *Human Development Report 2004;* World Bank, *Inequality in Latin America: Breaking with History?;* Transparency International, *Corruption Perceptions Index 2003.*
Notes: Population and GDP data from 2001; share of income data 2000; poverty data 1990–2001.

military in drug control operations. In the coca-growing regions and elsewhere, social conflict has escalated in tandem with this process.

The Chapare region, where much of Bolivia's unauthorized coca is grown, has been convulsed by recurring cycles of protest and repression, interrupted by temporary periods of conciliation. Periods of negotiations between growers and government on a range of issues have alternated with eradication operations marked by increasingly violent confrontations between coca growers and security forces. Since 1987, Bolivia's Permanent Human Rights Assembly has documented dozens of grower deaths at the hands of the security forces.[2] Human rights groups have also reported numerous indiscriminate arrests and unlawful detentions, arbitrary searches and theft of property, abuse of local residents, and the suppression of peaceful demonstrations.[3]

The problems came to a head with Plan Dignidad, a forced-eradication operation that began in 1998 with the goal of eliminating all "illicit" coca within five years. This was carried out by combined military and police forces. The United States hailed the plan as a success when it resulted in the destruction of about half of the reported coca crop. However, thirty-three coca growers and twenty-seven members of the security forces were killed in the escalating series of confrontations provoked by Plan Dignidad operations between 1998 and late 2003. The human rights violations committed by the military and militarized police forces have never been thoroughly investigated, nor has any member of these forces faced serious legal consequences. Cases of human rights violations are routinely transferred to Bolivian military courts, in violation of both Bolivian and international laws.

The foundation for Bolivia's increasingly forceful eradication operations was laid by the 1988 passage of Law 1008, a sweeping revision of Bolivian drug control legislation undertaken at U.S. behest.[4] This law criminalized new coca production in most of the country. Previously, growing coca had been legal throughout Bolivia, though sales were regulated. Harsh provisions in the law led to the establishment of antidrug courts and violated fundamental due process and constitutional guarantees.

The presence of U.S. military forces and the expanding role of the Bolivian military in drug control have also been sources of contention. This is particularly sensitive because Bolivia's history has been marked by long periods of military rule. The most recent return to civilian government came only in 1982, and democratic civilian control of the military is still not regarded as fully consolidated. The high-profile participation of U.S. troops in Operation Blast Furnace, a 1986 drug control operation, was seen by most Bolivian analysts as a violation of the Bolivian constitution and national sovereignty. Although less visible subsequently, U.S. military personnel participation in drug control activities since then continues to provoke similar concerns.

The United States has done little to address the issue of impunity for the forces it backs in Bolivia. The State Department has yet to implement in Bolivia the Leahy Amendment, which prohibits funding for security forces whose members have been credibly implicated in human rights violations. U.S. supervision of and control over police and military forces used in drug control operations often circumvent supervision and control by civilian Bolivian government officials. Furthermore, the U.S.-promoted militarization of the antidrug police has confused the roles of the Bolivian police and military and intensified competition between the institutions.

In recent years, both the U.S. and Bolivian governments have pointed to a potential terrorist threat and have attempted to link the coca grower movement and its leaders to terrorist activity. So far, however, there is no evidence of insurgent activity in Bolivia. This stands in contrast to neighboring Peru, where Shining Path guerrillas found a ready base in areas that had been subject to forced eradication. The Bolivian coca growers continue to be organized in legally recognized unions, and their leaders increasingly stress participation in electoral politics. The growers have become a powerful national political force; indeed, coca grower leader Evo Morales ran a close second in the 2002 presidential race. Concerns about the economic and social effects of eradication were among the issues that in 2003 fed mass protests across Bolivia that forced the resignation of President Gonzalo Sánchez de Lozada. Continued militarization and continued U.S. insistence that Bolivia meet strict drug war goals could further destabilize Bolivia's still fragile democracy.

• Poverty and Coca Production

Bolivia is the third-poorest nation in the Western Hemisphere, ranking ahead of only Haiti and Nicaragua. Income inequality is extreme; the richest 10 percent of the population receives income more than ninety times greater than that of the poorest 10 percent.[5] The estimated 56–70 percent of Bolivians who are indigenous largely overlap with the two-thirds who live in poverty; many of these are subsistence farmers.[6] Nearly 30 percent of the population subsists on less than a dollar a day, and 23 percent are considered by the United Nations Development Program to be undernourished (the average for all Latin America is 12 percent).[7] Bolivia also has the second-highest infant mortality rate in Latin America.[8]

This precarious economic situation has made the country extremely dependent on foreign aid, especially that from the United States, which totaled almost U.S.$171 million in 2003 (Figure 5.1).[9] Bolivia also relies on funds from international lenders like the Inter-American Development Bank and the World Bank, institutions in which the United States wields great influence.

Access to loans and grants previously depended on the results of the yearly certification process in which the U.S. executive branch would determine whether or not a country has complied with U.S. counterdrug objectives. As a result of recent reforms to the law, the U.S. administration no longer issues a certification for each country but can decertify any country deemed to have failed to make substantial efforts to meet its international counterdrug obligations. President Sánchez de Lozada complained during his first administration in 1993, "The dependency is terrible; the International Monetary Fund comes, the United States Embassy comes, the World Bank comes, and they all tell us what to do."[10] Because of this dependency, Bolivian governments view compliance with U.S. antidrug goals as indispensable.

Income from coca has provided a safety net for Bolivia's poor. In addition, cocaine dollars circulating in the Bolivian economy helped replace export earnings lost after the 1985 tin market crash and continued to supply foreign exchange that helped the government cope with heavy international debt.[11] At its peak, the cocaine industry in Bolivia contributed more to national income and employed more people than that in any other country.[12] Until the late 1990s, when intensive eradication programs began,

Figure 5.1   U.S. Aid to Bolivia, 1997–2005

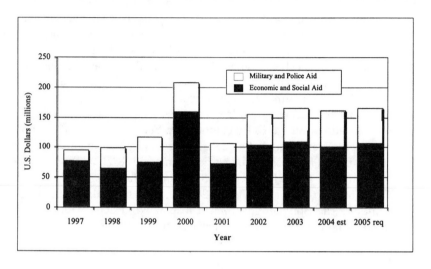

Source: Data from the U.S. State Department, Bureau for International Narcotics and Law Enforcement Affairs, *International Narcotics Control Strategy Report*, various years. Please see WOLA website, www.wola.org, for full listing.

growing coca provided subsistence for approximately 45,000 Chapare families, while profits from cocaine production helped stabilize the country's currency and greatly stimulated the national economy.

Since coca leaf accounts for only about 2 percent of cocaine's value, coca growers have hardly been the greatest beneficiaries of the trade.[13] But in the face of Bolivia's widespread poverty, many families turned to growing coca to generate enough income to guarantee their survival.[14] The coca leaf has many uses other than as an ingredient of cocaine. It is chewed as a mild stimulant and appetite suppressant, and it plays an important role in Andean social and religious life. Its production has, for centuries, been an economic mainstay of Bolivia's two main coca-growing areas, the Yungas region near the capital of La Paz, and the Yungas Vandiola, a small area partly within the Chapare region.

Throughout much of the twentieth century, successive Bolivian governments regarded the Chapare as a frontier area that needed settling and encouraged migration there, but they neglected to establish a state presence or provide basic services. Instead, migrants created agrarian unions (*sindicatos*) that made up the basic societal organization in the Chapare. The *sindicatos* distributed land, imposed community sanctions, and facilitated planning and supplies for the public works most needed by the population. They also organized the local coca trade. This system continues to function.

Each *sindicato* belongs to one of six Chapare federations, all of which then come together in the body known as the Six Coca Growers' Federations.

In the 1970s, while the Yungas continued to mainly supply nearby markets patronized by traditional coca users, the Chapare became the main source of coca for the cocaine industry that was developing in the neighboring Santa Cruz and Beni regions. Migration to the Chapare accelerated in the mid-1980s in response to massive layoffs of tin miners and government austerity measures mandated by international financial agencies.

The Chapare became an epicenter of conflict in the wake of later forced eradication operations. By contrast, the Yungas and a small portion of the Chapare were regarded as zones of traditional production. Under Law 1008, 12,000 hectares of Yungas coca remained legal, and social conflict was minimal there. However, U.S. officials claim that Yungas coca cultivation has expanded rapidly since 2000 and that the additional production is illicit. The Bolivian government responded in 2001 with a failed forced eradication attempt that threatened to turn the Yungas into another conflict zone.

• Drug Control Before 1997:
History and Organizational Structures

Bolivia has had more military coups than any other nation in the world. These have generated political instability and weakened the country's civilian institutions. Throughout most of the twentieth century, the nation experienced alternating periods of civilian and military rule. The populist 1952 revolution initiated a period of civilian rule marked by significant, though incomplete, land and labor reforms.[15] The civilian revolutionary government briefly disbanded the armed forces and replaced them with citizen militias but reestablished the military at U.S. urging. Another period of successive military dictatorships, with a range of political orientations, began in 1964 and continued until 1979.

The reformist leanings and anti-U.S. rhetoric of some Bolivian military leaders of this era periodically cooled U.S.-Bolivian relations, but these were revived during more conservative regimes. As it did elsewhere in the region, the United States continued to encourage, and provide aid for, the Bolivian military's involvement in internal security and counterinsurgency. In 1967, the Central Intelligence Agency (CIA) and U.S. military trainers helped a Bolivian military unit put an end to a brief insurgency headed by Ernesto "Che" Guevara, famous for his role in the Cuban Revolution.[16] U.S.-Bolivian relations were especially good during the seven-year military regime led by Hugo Banzer (1971–1978), despite the fact that the coup that brought Banzer to power was relatively bloody, and U.S. aid, including military aid, increased significantly.[17] A number of close Banzer associates were later linked to the then-developing cocaine industry.[18]

In July 1980, an even more brutal coup ended another fleeting period of civilian rule. The notorious dictatorship of Luis García Meza participated directly in drug trafficking and committed widespread human rights violations.[19] The United States cut virtually all economic, military, and even drug control aid to Bolivia shortly after the coup. García Meza relinquished control to other military officials in May 1981. During their brief regimes, his two successors tried to improve relations with the United States by conducting high-profile drug control operations, including a series of combined police-military raids on cocaine factories and coca fields.[20]

The 1982 election of President Hernan Siles Suazo restored civilian rule and allowed the United States to fully reopen the flow of aid to Bolivia, including drug control aid. In 1983, the United States provided U.S.\$4 million to create, train, and outfit a rural drug police unit, UMOPAR, modeled on a unit of the same name created in Peru several years earlier.[21]

The U.S. and Bolivian Militaries in Drug Control

In 1986, Bolivia became the scene of the first major antidrug operation on foreign soil to publicly involve U.S. military forces. One hundred sixty U.S. troops took part in Operation Blast Furnace, carried out primarily in the departments of Beni, Pando, and Santa Cruz in July through November 1986. U.S. planners said the well-publicized operation had been designed to shut down cocaine laboratories, seal off river routes used to transport coca and other raw materials used to make cocaine, and intercept drug-carrying planes. Though Blast Furnace did little to stanch the flow of cocaine from Bolivia, the presence of U.S troops on Bolivian territory without the required approval by the Bolivian National Congress touched off widespread public outcry against the violation of national sovereignty.

One incident that occurred during Blast Furnace particularly raised Bolivian concerns about the objectives of the operation. Well-known botanist Noel Kempff and two other men were murdered when they mistakenly landed their small plane near a huge drug-processing facility in Huanchaca, in the Beni region. U.S. forces reportedly knew about the factory and had targeted it for destruction but had not yet done so. There were accusations that Bolivian officials had been corrupted by the traffickers and were protecting it. In the years following the Huanchaca incident, critics pressed the Bolivian and U.S. governments to investigate the matter. A member of the Bolivian Congress who was heading up an investigation was murdered. To date the case has never been clarified.

The U.S. military continued to play a growing role in drug control in Bolivia. In the wake of the protests over Blast Furnace, however, it took on a lower profile. U.S. Special Forces trained the UMOPAR police force, and the Pentagon lent helicopters and other equipment during ongoing drug

control activities conducted under Operation Snowcap.[22] At U.S. instiga-
tion, the Bolivian military was also given a larger part in drug control. In
1988, the U.S. government funded the creation of a Bolivian air force unit
called the Red Devils, and a naval group called the Blue Devils, to carry
out drug interdiction operations.[23] The trend continued with the launching
of the Andean Initiative, under which the U.S. government began "a deliberate incorporation of host country military forces into the counternarcotics
effort and an expanded role for the U.S. military throughout the region."[24]

In May 1990, Bolivian president Jaime Paz Zamora (1989–1993)
signed a secret agreement with the United States that formalized the
Bolivian military's counterdrug role. The Bolivian Congress was completely left out of the approval process. The agreement, known as Annex III,
stipulated a direct U.S.-funded role for the armed forces, in particular the
army, which the Bolivian government had previously kept out of drug control.

Fears that increased military participation would weaken the nation's
democracy were paired with well-founded concerns that greater participation of the institution in drug control efforts would further augment opportunities for widespread corruption. Corruption was known to be prevalent
within both military and police antidrug units; the United States often kept
these forces out of the planning process for U.S.-backed operations for just
this reason.[25]

U.S. Influence and Law 1008

Throughout this period, the United States continued to use its political and
economic leverage to shape Bolivian drug policy. U.S. officials used the
certification process, which required Bolivia to meet set eradication and
other targets or risk the loss of economic support, to pressure Bolivian officials into backing U.S. strategies. Although Bolivia has never been decertified, in 1994 and 1995 the United States invoked a national interest waiver
that allowed for certification even though Bolivia had not met U.S. antidrug
goals.[26] The lack of effective oversight mechanisms in the Bolivian political system aggravated the problem, allowing the United States to negotiate
with a handful of high-level officials and minimizing both public debate
and independent legislative action on drug control policies.

The United States justified circumventing Bolivian authorities as necessary to avoid corruption. However, the practice gave U.S. policymakers
disproportionate influence over both the development and implementation
of policy. The lack of effective oversight mechanisms made the problem
worse, allowing the executive branch, under pressure from Washington, to
dictate policy with little public scrutiny or input into the policymaking
process. The weakness of Bolivia's Congress and political parties exacerbated the problem. The Bolivian government failed to consult congress on a

number of occasions even when such was constitutionally mandated, as was the case with Operations Blast Furnace and Snowcap and the signing of Annex III.

In some cases, the Bolivian government acted primarily because of pressure from the United States. The passage of the Law to Regulate Coca and Controlled Substances (Law 1008) is a prime example. U.S. officials in La Paz pushed especially hard for its passage. U.S. legal experts reportedly helped draft the law, which was approved by the Bolivian Congress in July 1988.[27] Bolivia's vice president admitted that he had promised U.S. Attorney General Ed Meese that the law would be approved.[28] In 1986 U.S. embassy spokespersons affirmed that the adoption of the antidrug law was essential to win the release of economic assistance that had been temporarily withheld.[29]

This harsh counterdrug legislation provided a legal foundation for U.S.-funded interdiction and eradication programs.[30] Law 1008 delineated the zones within which coca production was legal and made it illegal to initiate coca cultivation in new areas. Transitional zones were slated for eradication within ten years. Coca's designation as a controlled substance turned "peasant coca leaf producers into societal delinquents,"[31] and the law's approval in the Bolivian Congress set off intense protests by coca growers. Coca growers, legal experts, and human rights monitors also criticized certain provisions of Law 1008 as violating protections and procedures contained in the Bolivian constitution and legal code. The law was eventually revised in 2001 in response to some of these criticisms. But, as noted below, the changes have not altered the basic thrust of the law, which is to criminalize peasant coca production.

Building Up the Drug Police

After Law 1008 was passed, the United States provided funding to beef up existing drug police forces. In 1987 President Victor Paz Estenssoro (1985–1989) issued a supreme decree—a presidential act bypassing the legislative process—that created the Special Drug Police Force (known by its Spanish acronym FELCN).[32] This new force was given the mission of interdicting cocaine and precursor chemicals. The FELCN continues to receive funding, including salary bonuses, weapons, and training, directly from the United States.[33] In 2001 the U.S. government began a two-year program to expand the size of the FELCN and its specialized operational units. This expansion included an increase in personnel of more than 15 percent, upgrading the FELCN's existing physical infrastructure and building at least fourteen new bases throughout the country.[34]

The Rural Mobile Patrol Unit (UMOPAR), the police unit charged with interdiction in rural areas, became a FELCN division. UMOPAR specializes in jungle patrol, reconnaissance, air insertions, mobile roadblocks, and river operations. UMOPAR units are now stationed throughout Bolivia but based primarily in Chapare, Yungas, and another department, Trinidad.[35] They also have posts at key border areas that have been identified as drug transit zones.

UMOPAR's budget is largely managed by the Narcotics Affairs Section (NAS) of the U.S. embassy, and the DEA plans and supervises interdiction activities.[36] Close consultation and collaboration between UMOPAR and the DEA has existed since the former's inception, and the groups share a base in the Chapare region. Until 1997, DEA officers were frequently observed supervising interdiction missions and even participating in interrogations of detainees.[37] Since that time, the DEA has refrained from direct participation in missions and operations that would bring its personnel into contact with suspects and detainees.

In the Chapare, UMOPAR makes use of more than fifty undercover informants who provide information on drug production sites and shipments.[38] Human rights monitors have expressed concerns that some of these informants may themselves be involved in drug trafficking and may engage in entrapment of individuals who would not otherwise have participated in the drug trade.[39]

From UMOPAR's creation in 1983 until the formation of the Joint Task Force in 1997, the great majority of human rights violations and arbitrary detentions were attributed to this special police unit. The FELCN's Office of Professional Responsibility investigates corruption and human rights violations committed by UMOPAR and other FELCN agents. It is funded and directly supervised by the DEA.[40] Human rights monitors have objected that the DEA, a law enforcement agency, cannot effectively supervise human rights investigations; according to the constitution, such investigations should be carried out within the civilian legal system. Officers implicated in five cases ranging from physical abuse to the death of a detainee received internal disciplinary sanctions instead of referral to the civilian justice system. Investigations tend to be superficial and rarely result even in internal sanctions for accused officers.[41]

Originally some UMOPAR officers received training at the School of the Americas in Panama. In-country training began with the 1987 opening of the Talons of Valor school in the Chapare. Initially designed as a jungle operations training center exclusively for UMOPAR agents, the school, which is funded by NAS, now also trains police and military officers from other nations, including Panama, Colombia, Peru, and Ecuador. The training includes a brief human rights module, and there is an instructor for human rights, but the great bulk of the training time is spent on military tactics and strenuous exercise. Although the objective is to teach how to perform in dangerous situations, human rights monitors fear that training exercises may provoke insensitivity to detainees. They also charge that training exercises violate the basic human rights of students. Course participants routinely work from 5 A.M. until 10 P.M. They are assigned numbers and referred to as "elements."[42]

The FELCN, and especially UMOPAR, have been directly and indirectly linked with corruption. The first known cases of FELCN corruption were publicized in the media in the late 1980s, as kilograms of drugs meant for incineration inexplicably disappeared from the care of FELCN officials. Another case that cast a particularly dark shadow over the legitimacy of the agency was the 1995 seizure in Peru of a plane loaded with thousands of kilos of drugs. The plane had originated in Bolivia, allegedly taking off with FELCN knowledge.[43] Although fewer high-profile cases have received media attention recently, accusations made in December 2003 indicate that the problem continues: the special presidential representative to fight corruption announced that for a period of fifteen years there had been "absolute corruption" in the FELCN office in charge of properties and goods confiscated during drug interdiction. Authorities were unable to provide conclusive accounting of confiscated items, including real estate, vehicles, cash, and jewelry; nor were they able to explain what had happened to these items.[44]

Although drug interdiction had been the centerpiece of early U.S.-funded counternarcotics programs, by the mid-1990s the United States was placing increased emphasis on the eradication of coca crops. Bolivian government officials generally complied with minimum eradication goals to earn U.S. certification in order to maintain funding and access to international aid, but the eradicated coca was quickly replaced. The Bolivian government would often step up eradication efforts just prior to the certification deadline. The administrations of Paz Estenssoro and Paz Zamora and the first Sánchez de Lozada administration (1993–1997) were reluctant to push too hard for fear of triggering widespread clashes with coca growers, who maintained some degree of popular support. Instead, successive governments negotiated a series of agreements with the coca growers that called for alternative development funding (discussed below) in conjunction with voluntary eradication. The government's failure to comply with these agreements caused resentment and mistrust among growers.

Conflict periodically erupted between security forces and coca growers. In 1995, the United States threatened to cut aid if the Bolivian government did not meet coca eradication targets. The government's intensified eradication efforts met with resistance from coca growers. In the resulting confrontations, Human Rights Watch reported, four civilians were killed and at least twelve civilians and two police were injured. The group also documented "excessive use of force, arbitrary detention and the suppression of peaceful demonstrations."[45] It charged that UMOPAR members were the primary agents of the abuses.

• Plan Dignidad and Drug Control, 1997–2003

When former military dictator Hugo Banzer was elected to the presidency in 1997, he abandoned the balancing act of trying to meet U.S. requirements without causing conflict. Instead, his administration proposed an all-out, no-holds-barred approach to eradication through the five-year Plan Dignidad. The prime goal was to reduce illegal coca production to zero. The Defense Policy Analysis Unit (UDAPDE), a think tank within the Ministry of Defense, warned in 1999 that the plan had been written and implemented without consolidating the long-term support of nongovernmental actors or taking into account the social and political effects of its implementation. UDAPDE criticized the government for "underestimating the costs implied ... [by the] context of instability and recurring conflict in coca-growing regions."[46] This criticism proved correct, as the plan was implemented in the absence of productive dialogue and resulted in the use of heavy repression.

Plan Dignidad proposed four pillars of action based on "shared responsibility" with the international community: *alternative development* (programs intended to provide new sources of income that would allow farmers to stop growing coca); *prevention and rehabilitation*; *eradication* of illegal excess coca; and *interdiction*. In practice, the Bolivian government focused primarily on the forced eradication of 38,000 hectares of coca. To the surprise of critics and supporters, the plan almost reached its goal of total eradication—zero coca—in the Chapare in 2000. The United States lauded this success, but the trend was quickly reversed. U.S. figures showed that Bolivian coca production increased 23 percent over the course of 2002, even after 12,000 hectares had been eradicated.[47] In November 2003, the State Department reported that coca production in Bolivia had increased about 17 percent over 2002 estimates.[48] Meanwhile, the government's inability to provide subsistence for "eradicated families" through viable alternative development provoked intense protest and confrontation that threatened the stability of Banzer's administration as well as those of his successors—Jorge Quiroga, who took office in 2001 after Banzer resigned for health reasons, and Gonzalo Sánchez de Lozada.

The cornerstone of the widespread eradication strategy was a direct role for the Bolivian military in forced eradication. The 1998 creation of the Joint Task Force (JTF), a combined military and police eradication unit, gave the Chapare region the highest ratio of security forces to population in the country and aggravated conflict there. By the end of 2001, approximately 4,500 members of the security forces were stationed in the

Chapare.[49] As of late 2003, even during periods of relative tranquillity there were approximately 2,500 members from various forces stationed in the region.[50] This combination of different forces presents a confusing chain of command and complicates the identification of units and individuals for investigations and prosecutions.

An October 2000 agreement between leaders of the Six Coca Growers' Federations and government officials stated that no new bases would be installed in the Chapare.[51] In November 2001, nonetheless, the Bolivian government confirmed a total of eighteen combined forces camps in the region. Construction of new installations continued. Coca growers interpret ongoing large-scale construction and remodeling at existing military bases, as well as the construction of new antidrug posts, as a violation of this agreement. Both the U.S. and Bolivian governments officially state that a long-term, sustained military presence in the region is indispensable to maintaining eradication goals and preventing a resurgence of the coca crop.[52]

The Expeditionary Task Force

The U.S. embassy's Narcotics Affairs Section began funding a paramilitary counterdrug force, the Expeditionary Task Force (ETF), in January 2001. Although its commanders were Bolivian military officers, its troops were neither police officers nor soldiers. The State Department claimed that the force members were part of a military reserve that had completed mandatory service, but no such reserve actually exists. The force received funding for transportation, food, uniforms, a monthly salary bonus of approximately U.S.$100 from NAS, and training from the U.S. military.[53] The human rights ombudswoman at the time, Ana María Romero de Campero, characterized the ETF's troops as mercenaries and stated that the Bolivian military was not authorized to increase its ranks without approval from Congress.[54] Unit commanders and troops admitted that the rank and file of the unit were "hired hands."[55]

During its eighteen months of operation, the ETF was implicated in a significant percentage of human rights violations in the Chapare region, including the deaths of five coca growers. Human rights monitors, and even military officers, expressed concern about the irregular status of this group. In March 2002, five members of the U.S. Congress requested that funding for the ETF be suspended due to credible allegations of gross human rights violations.

Despite this criticism from U.S. congressional representatives and both national and international human rights organizations, the United States increased funding to expand the ETF to 1,500 members in January 2002. However, as a result of continuing negative publicity and inquiries by members of the U.S. Congress, U.S. funding for the force was ended in mid-2002 and the ETF was disbanded. Some military personnel viewed the dissolution of the unit as a positive step, privately stating that the ETF had let things "get out of hand."[56] Nevertheless, this episode heightened concern about civilian control over military units involved in drug control efforts.

Conflict Within the Military

Bolivia's weak civilian authorities still have tenuous control over the military, which has a long history of intervention in politics. Within such a context, the enhanced power of the military under Plan Dignidad—and in ongoing drug control efforts, which continue along the lines laid out in that five-year plan—is problematic. Questions about the military's new role have been raised even within the institution itself. With the return to democracy in 1982, the armed forces were eager to escape the stigma of having participated in dictatorships and to clean up an institutional reputation sullied by accusations of involvement in drug trafficking during the García Meza dictatorship. At the same time, elected leaders had cut the budget for the armed forces. Within the military, participation in drug control efforts was widely viewed as an opportunity to regain legitimacy and to restore lost funding by making use of U.S. antidrug aid.

The direct participation of the armed forces in Plan Dignidad's accelerated forced eradication program, however, brought problems as well as advantages. Although the Joint Task Force gained public acclaim for successful eradication, it was also harshly criticized for human rights abuses. The direct influence and control of U.S. military and drug control authorities over the Bolivian participants became abundantly clear, and this was difficult for the Bolivian military to swallow. The military's increasing role in internal law enforcement functions, along with the militarization of the antidrug police, provoked conflict and heightened traditional rivalries between the two institutions; competition for U.S. drug control funds exacerbated this situation.

Bolivian military personnel involved in the counterdrug mission, as well as retired officers, expressed growing disenchantment with the institution's role. There was increasing realization in military circles that participation in drug control programs had a high price in terms of national sovereignty. Officers became increasingly uncomfortable with direct U.S. dictates to drug control officials, which often circumvented civilian authorities and the military's national command structure. One retired military officer noted, "They [the armed forces] are irritated with the Americans, because they are militarizing the police. They send police officers to Fort Benning and other places, and military officers are adopting police techniques for anti-drug efforts."[57]

The strict control of funding by NAS and the military's economic dependence on the U.S. embassy also became increasingly evident. For example, JTF commanders had to obtain permission from NAS for each helicopter flight, for visits to installations, and before meeting with the press or human rights monitors.[58] One retired officer said in an interview that the embassy's role in decisionmaking had "reached a grotesque level, because lieutenant colonels and majors from Milgroup today make more decisions than Bolivian generals." He added, "Many [Bolivian] officials are beginning to question the U.S. occupation of the Bolivian armed forces."[59]

A 1998 survey of the Bolivian military, carried out by the country's defense ministry, found that 73 percent of those surveyed felt that the armed forces participated in antidrug efforts as a result of U.S. pressure. More than one-third believed that participation in drug control efforts forced the military to neglect its traditional duties. Fewer than 8 percent felt that internal security and drug control should be the most important roles for the military, with 66 percent stating that the most important mission is the external defense mission stipulated by the Bolivian constitution, which does not authorize internal law and drug enforcement.[60] In a later interview, one JTF official stated bluntly, "We are perfectly aware that what we are doing here is not constitutional."[61]

Some officers criticized dependence on U.S. dictates and the inefficacy of Plan Dignidad. One eradication official stated, "We are completely conscious that if we eradicate everything we are out of a job." He jokingly added, "At this rate we may have to begin planting coca ourselves."[62] Another former officer explained, "The reality is that the military feels in part guilty for being so efficient, so disciplined in eradication. They are conscious that eradication and the speed with which they acted have created economic and social conflict in the country."[63] A member of the JTF noted, "We know that what we are doing here causes these people to go hungry. Alternative development projects don't provide income. This makes us the bad guys."[64] Some members of the armed forces observed that they lacked options: "Where else are we going to get training and equipment? We'll never get out from under the gringos; we might as well take advantage of it."[65]

Resentment within both the military and police about overlapping roles, mixed mandates, and shared resources sowed the seeds for further conflict at the national level. This was to have a dramatic impact on future administrations. The authority and legitimacy of the national government itself was greatly weakened as institutional conflict came to a head with street clashes between the military and police in early 2003.

Cyclical Patterns of Violence and Conflict
The use of military conscripts to manually eradicate coca plants did lead to dramatic advances in coca eradication, which destroyed more than 70,000

acres between 1998 and 2001. But this came at a high social cost. With the exception of 1999, violent conflicts of increasing intensity have occurred every year since the implementation of Plan Dignidad in 1998. The initiation of forced eradication operations by the Joint Task Force that year sparked three months of violence in the region, leaving thirteen coca growers and three members of the security forces dead. Violence recurred in September 2000, when coca growers blocked the main highway between Santa Cruz and Cochabamba for one month. Clashes between security forces and coca growers left one of the growers dead and many others seriously injured, and five members of the security forces and one of their wives were killed. The blockades were suspended after the Bolivian government agreed to scrap plans to build three military bases with U.S. funding.

By 2001, as a result of intense eradication in the Chapare, production in the Yungas was increasing. The United States was pressing for extending eradication to that region, which had been designated under Law 1008 as a traditional zone where coca cultivation was legal. In June, Yungas coca growers violently resisted the incursion of the JTF into the region. In response, the Bolivian government agreed to suspend forced eradication and remove eradication forces from the area. Nevertheless, the Yungas operation diminished public support for Plan Dignidad, and critics expressed concern about the shifting parameters for compliance with antidrug goals.

In September 2001 Chapare coca growers, frustrated by the government's lack of compliance with the agreement signed the previous year, blocked troops' access to replanted coca fields. Tensions grew, and two months later members of the Expeditionary Task Force killed three of the protesters who were attempting to block the Santa Cruz–Cochabamba highway. In the weeks that followed, dozens of coca growers were beaten by security forces.

By the end of October, the escalating confrontations led both parties to accept dialogue, and eradication efforts were suspended for four days. Throughout the course of the negotiations, both security forces and coca growers appeared willing to make concessions. However, the U.S. government opposed any break in eradication or retreat of the security forces. An embassy cable stated, "We were quite concerned by the agreement in November to halt eradication and withdraw troops from the front lines in the Chapare where they had been so effective."[66] Both sides, as well as members of groups trying to mediate, cited strong U.S. pressure to resume eradication as the cause of the breakdown in dialogue.[67]

The Chapare coca growers attempted to block the highway again, and violence resumed. On November 15, the ETF fired into a crowd of protesters near the town of Ivirgarzama, killing three and wounding five. On December 6, the same day that President Jorge Quiroga met with President George W. Bush, the ETF teargassed a peaceful roadside protest in the town of Chimoré. Following the teargassing, witnesses said, an ETF member shot and killed union leader Casimiro Huanca after Huanca entered a nearby union office. Another man, Fructuoso Herbas, was shot at close range in his leg, which later had to be amputated.

In January 2002, two months before the announcement of U.S. antidrug certification decisions, the Bolivian government made aggressive moves to clamp down on coca growers. The no-holds-barred approach marked a dramatic change in the cyclical give-and-take between the two sides. In response to U.S. pressure, the government began to enforce Supreme Decree 26415, which prohibited the drying, transport, and sale of coca leaf grown in the Chapare region in previously legal markets.[68] The move to control coca sales provoked an overwhelmingly violent response from growers and merchants. In January, several thousand coca growers entered and sacked the governmental General Coca Directorate offices and the central coca market in Sacaba, which had both been closed by the government. Clashes between protesters and security forces continued, and the next day four security officers were found dead, their bodies showing evidence of torture. These brutal murders turned Bolivian public opinion against coca growers and caused the Bolivian government to clamp down further, creating an environment in which negotiations and any resolution appeared impossible.

Government forces detained more than eighty union leaders. A majority of the lower house of the Bolivian Congress voted to remove coca grower leader Evo Morales, a presidential candidate, from his congressional seat. The move backfired, however, and heightened public support for Morales and the growers' demands. Tensions in the Chapare seemed to be reaching a climax in late January after an ETF commander allegedly shot and killed a coca grower as the ETF was dispersing a highway roadblock in the town of Shinahota.

In February 2002, however, coca grower leaders and the government arrived at a new agreement. The pact stipulated that the congress would reevaluate Morales's removal from his seat in that body, suspend the supreme decree prohibiting the drying, transport, and sale of Chapare coca, release jailed union leaders, reopen the local radio station that had been closed during the conflict, investigate human rights violations, and pay compensation to victims. This surprising shift in the Bolivian government's approach was an attempt to avoid further substantial economic and human losses. Government representatives also apparently feared that sustained violence would further erode the ruling coalition's already substantially deteriorated credibility in upcoming elections. U.S. policymakers, however, criticized the Quiroga administration for backing down from full compliance with U.S. drug control objectives in the region.

Due to the sustained political unrest and the worsening economic crisis, which many Bolivians attributed to forced eradication, the June 2002 presidential election produced unexpected results. Former president Gonzalo Sánchez de Lozada won by a narrow margin. Outgoing President Quiroga's party fared particularly poorly. Coca grower leader Evo Morales finished in second place, only 1.5 percent behind Sánchez de Lozada. This dramatically restructured the political landscape and sent a clear message to traditional parties that the nation's voters were anxious for change. Representatives from Morales's party, Movement Toward Socialism (Movimiento al Socialismo, or MAS), became the second-largest bloc in congress and a formidable opposition force.

A statement by U.S. Ambassador Manuel Rocha just four days before the election apparently provoked voter outrage and increased support for Morales. Rocha had warned that U.S. aid would be cut off if Morales were elected.[69] After the election, the director of the State Department's Office for Andean Affairs echoed Rocha's sentiments, stating that the U.S. government wanted Bolivians to understand precisely what was at risk—the cutoff of U.S. aid and the branding of Bolivia as a pariah state—if the Bolivian electorate decided to "play footsie with coca growers."[70]

The Fall of Sánchez de Lozada

Given the popular protest that had erupted around Plan Dignidad and the strong electoral showing for MAS, Sánchez de Lozada initially sought to modify existing drug control policy. During his campaign, he said that he opposed forced eradication and would demilitarize antidrug efforts. He had previously expressed his distrust and disdain for the military, and during his first term as president he worked to limit military power.[71] For example, in June 2000 he stated that in government "you don't change the military; the military changes you!"[72] After the first year of his second administration, however, he was forced to make substantial concessions to the armed forces.

Soon after taking office in September 2002, Sánchez de Lozada initiated a 100-day dialogue with coca growers that reached consensus on some key issues. During the talks, coca growers called for a sustained pause in forced eradication efforts in order to study legal markets. They also demanded a reevaluation of alternative development efforts and the right to legally grow a small amount of coca per family. Of particular importance was the prospect of agreement to have an independent institution carry out an in-depth study of legal coca consumption markets in Bolivia in order to determine how much coca was actually necessary to meet traditional needs. Law 1008 stipulates that 12,000 hectares of coca may be grown for legal, traditional uses, but growers maintain that internal consumption and export of legal coca to Argentina has increased well beyond those limits. In exchange, coca growers were ready to agree to abide by eradication targets for coca crops surpassing the new legal consumption limit.

Such an agreement would have given the Bolivian and U.S. governments significantly more legitimacy in future eradication efforts. If concluded, the agreement would have represented a significant step forward in meeting coca grower demands while allowing the government to eradicate coca production not destined for the legal market. But after U.S. officials expressed opposition to a temporary suspension in coca reduction efforts, the talks stalled and eventually broke off altogether.

In January 2003, coca growers and other groups began new protests and blockaded roads across the country. In the ensuing conflict, eleven people were killed, including two members of the security forces, and many were injured. Dialogue began again, but violence continued.

Dramatic events that exploded in the country's capital soon thereafter marked the beginning of the end for Sánchez de Lozada. On February 12, the La Paz police force mutinied, echoing other groups' protests against a new income tax and negligible pay raises. This police force had been a traditional ally of the governing party, but such ties had been weakened by the economic crisis and by resentment over increased military participation in counterdrug efforts and domestic law enforcement. Police protesting in front of the capitol building clashed with the military, which had been deployed by the president. Thirty-two people died, including police and military troops, and almost 200 were wounded.

Sánchez de Lozada's failure to respond effectively to the violent events of "Black February" fueled public doubts about his capacity to govern. After the crisis, it appeared that he felt forced to grant considerable concessions to the armed forces and to adopt a promilitary public discourse to maintain the institution's support.

In September, political turmoil was sparked once again by the government's proposal to export Bolivian natural gas to the United States through a Chilean port. The widespread protests that ensued ultimately encompassed a range of concerns. These included demands for better wages, reform of antidrug legislation, rejection of a law imposing prison terms for people participating in road blockades, and repudiation of the proposed Free Trade Area of the Americas.

As the protests gained momentum from mid-September to mid-October 2003, the paralyzed government coalition refused to engage in dialogue with most of the protesters or otherwise to address their concerns. As social unrest increased, legislators continued to bicker over party control of appointments. In response to government inaction, more and more Bolivians took to the streets.

Finally, the administration resorted to heavy repression in lieu of dialogue. During the month after the new round of protests began, security forces killed at least sixty people and injured several hundred, the great majority of whom were shot. The armed forces and police killed almost as many people during the fourteen-month Sánchez de Lozada presidency as during the seven years of General Banzer's dictatorship, considered one of the bloodiest of Bolivia's military governments since the 1952 revolution. Popular outcry against the government's violent response to largely peaceful protests ultimately provoked widespread calls for the president's resignation, even from some high-ranking government officials. Carlos Mesa, Sánchez de Lozada's vice president, withdrew his support for the president on October 13, explaining: "If the government does not have the capacity to understand [the concept of] unconditioned dialogue, it will not be able to be a valid participant in the process to address popular demands."[73]

At first Sánchez de Lozada refused to resign, saying that he was going to preserve democracy and not succumb to "a huge subversive project from outside the country which is attempting to destroy Bolivian democracy." The president alleged that Peruvian Shining Path guerrillas, Colombian insurgent groups, and nongovernmental organizations were organizing among the coca growers and financing the protests.[74] These statements provoked even more popular anger. After more than a month of growing demonstrations, violent conflict, and a near breakdown in public order, the president resigned on October 17. Vice President Mesa assumed the presidency in accordance with the country's constitution.

Like his predecessors, Mesa was caught between two opposing forces. Immediately after he assumed office, U.S. officials began pressuring him to maintain the very counterdrug policies that had helped bring down the previous government. At the same time, Mesa faced domestic social pressure to confront the legacies of the past cycles of conflict and violence, including human rights violations, unpopular antidrug laws, and ongoing impunity.

• Human Rights and Justice

Pressure to meet U.S. antidrug objectives has led to a continuing series of human rights violations, the majority of these committed by Bolivian security forces stationed in the Chapare. A 1995 Human Rights Watch investigation found that arbitrary detentions, beatings of Chapare residents, and the use of excessive physical violence by antidrug police were common.[75] With the implementation of Plan Dignidad in 1998, levels of violence and unrest increased. Pressure to meet eradication goals continued to take precedence over human rights, resulting in a growing number of deaths. The justice and human rights minister bluntly stated the government's priority at the height of the 2001 conflict: "Human rights are not the key issue. The main issue is coca eradication in the Chapare."[76] Reports of excessive use of force, and the killings and shootings of unarmed civilians during confrontations, have not been fully investigated by representatives of the district attorney's offices in the Chapare.

The contradiction between U.S. pressure to meet antidrug goals and the embassy's formal discourse of respect for human rights provoked outrage in the Bolivian human rights community. In March 2001 Waldo Albarracín, then-president of the Permanent Human Rights Assembly, a national NGO that documents human rights violations, told the press that the United States "talks about human rights and pressures the Bolivian state to carry out forced eradication, which is a synonym for violence, death, murdered campesinos, and tortured soldiers and police officers. They put up the funds and we offer up the dead."[77]

Two principal human rights institutions maintain a permanent presence in the Chapare: the Human Rights Ombudsman's Office, and the Justice and Human Rights Center, which is part of the Vice Ministry of Justice and Human Rights.

The Human Rights Ombudsman's Chapare office opened in November 1998. The office is independent of government control but receives funding from the Bolivian treasury as well as a number of European governments. The institution works as an advocate for the public in its efforts to prevent human rights and other abuses by government officials. Its officials have the right to enter any government installation at any time and to have access to documentation and information from any state employee.[78] The ombudsman directly participates in mediation, conflict resolution, and documentation and investigation of human rights violations.

The justice ministry opened its first Chapare human rights office in December 1995. The center's most important contribution at this writing is the provision of medical certificates and autopsy reports prepared by its forensic doctor. These official documents confirm cause of death and could be extremely useful in prosecuting human rights violators, except that the vice ministry in La Paz restricts access to them. This, along with U.S. financial support for the office and the limited follow-up on cases, has created mistrust on the part of the Chapare population, reducing the office's potential impact.

An active Bolivian human rights community has identified abuses and succeeded in gaining some commitment to reforms. However, the effectiveness of these reforms is still limited in practice, as the imperative of drug eradication has continued to take priority over human rights and conflict resolution.

Collateral Damage

The cumulative evidence of damage resulting from drug eradication efforts is substantial. Table 5.1 summarizes the quantitative data from the Human Rights Ombudsman's Office in Chapare.

Other accounts document incidents of excessive use of force by the police, the military, the combined Joint Task Force, and the Expeditionary Task Force. As the death toll mounted, scores of people were wounded or suffered respiratory damage from tear gas inhalation. In a number of cases, eyewitnesses, video recordings, or forensic evidence showed that unarmed victims had been shot from behind or at very close range.

One of the most notorious incidents occurred on December 6, 2001, after a small group of coca producers in Chimoré stacked fruit on the side of the highway to protest the lack of markets. Video records show the ETF used tear gas to disperse the peaceful protesters. Soldiers followed the growers into nearby coca grower union offices where, according to eyewitness testimony, ETF member Juan Eladio Bora shot union leader Casimiro Huanca twice. Huanca later died. Another grower was shot at close range and wounded just outside the office. Another well-known case is the January 29, 2002, shooting death of Marcos Ortiz Llanos during a highway blockade in Shinahota. Eyewitnesses said ETF commander Colonel Aurelio Burgos, easily identifiable because of his missing right forearm, fired directly at Ortiz.

Other incidents showing the character of the violence include the following:

November 15, 2001: Members of the ETF fired into a crowd of coca

Table 5.1 Deaths and Injuries Incurred During Drug Control Efforts in the Chapare

Year	Coca grower fatalities	Coca growers injured	Coca growers detained[a]	Police and military fatalities	Police and military injured
1997	5	65	135	2	6
1998	9	62	171	4	19
1999	0	0	82	0	0
2000	2	72	47	10	10
2001	7	193	88	0	5
2002	5	145	66	5	69
Jan.–Aug. 2003	5	30	104	6	26
Total	33	567	693	27	135

Source: Chapare Human Rights Ombudsman's Office, January 2004.
Note: a. Security forces often carry out mass detentions and liberate detainees within twenty-four hours.

growers attempting to block a Chapare highway near Ivirgarzama; three people died from shots from behind.

October 6, 2002: Coca grower union leader Sabino Toledo was fatally shot when the JTF broke up a small gathering near Entre Ríos. According to eyewitness reports, the coca growers were unarmed and there was no confrontation.

January 26, 2003: Coca grower Roberto León was shot four times and died during a JTF eradication operation in the community of Litoral. Burn marks around his wounds suggest that he was shot at extremely close range.

May 8, 2003: Coca grower Hilaria Pérez was shot in the back as she was entering her field to collect coca before it was eradicated by the JTF. She suffered serious lung damage.

Attacks Against Security Forces

In retaliation for the eradication campaign, there have also been attacks against members of the security forces in the Chapare. By far the most coca grower resistance to the implementation of drug control policy has consisted of roadblocks, marches, and other forms of protest. In the early 1990s, though, coca grower unions began to form self-defense committees to block forced eradication in their communities. These small groups, generally armed with sticks and machetes, primarily function as a deterrent to eradication efforts.

In 1998, some of the growers began to retaliate against members of the security forces. As shown in Table 5.1, the total number of police and military killed has almost equaled the number of growers killed. During confrontations in 1998, three members of the security forces were killed. In October 2000, during the monthlong Chapare roadblocks, five security officers and one of their wives disappeared. Two coca growers confessed to the killing of one of these officers and his wife in July 2003. Intense press coverage of the incidents generated public indignation against the coca growers.[79]

In 1998, JTF commanders and other government officials began to report the discovery of booby traps placed in areas slated for eradication. In a series of incidents, security forces and civilians sustained injuries as a result of explosions. For example, in October 2001, a nine-year-old girl triggered the tripwire of a booby trap as she crossed the main road. Officials have also reported an increase in random gunfire aimed at the eradication forces' camps. During the last few months of 2001, five soldiers sustained gunshot wounds from snipers. During this time, government officials claimed that coca growers had fired rifles and set off dynamite around three eradication camps; coca growers also shot at a pickup truck belonging to the government's eradication control agency, DIRECO. During the coca market conflict in Sacaba, four members of the security forces were brutally beaten and killed. During 2002 and 2003, fire from unidentified snipers and the use of booby traps in and around coca fields continued. In early 2003 three military conscripts were shot and killed by snipers and at least thirteen others suffered bullet wounds. During the first months of the Mesa administration in late 2003, two members of the security forces were killed by booby-trap bombs and another died from a bullet wound. At least eight others were injured in these incidents.

Security forces and the Bolivian and U.S. governments complain that these violent responses place antidrug security officers in frequent danger. The death and serious injury of officers has provoked a greater militarization of the region and has been used as a justification for a permanent military presence. Tension and fear provoked by these attacks have also caused members of these forces to react with increased use of excessive force, aggravating the conflict. With the exception of the cases in 2000, district attorneys in the Chapare have failed to seriously investigate deaths and injuries of either security officers or coca growers. The sense of impunity and insecurity this creates has led to higher tensions on both sides.

• Reforms Fall Short

Recent legal reforms have sought to provide greater protection against abuses than initially offered by Law 1008; however, the failure to prosecute offenses still promotes impunity. Military trials are used to evade civilian judicial proceedings, and the United States has failed to use the Leahy Amendment to deter human rights abuses by security personnel.

Revisions in Law 1008

Bolivian and international human rights organizations criticized many provisions of Law 1008. From 1998 until 2001, the law violated the presumption of innocence mandated by the nation's constitution by effectively placing the burden of proof on the accused.[80] A police report, often poorly prepared and containing scant evidence, was considered sufficient evidence for conviction.[81] Law 1008 also violated existing Bolivian law stipulating that an investigative judge supervise all investigations. Under Law 1008, antidrug prosecutors determined whether or not to press charges, and judges were forced to try the accused on the basis of this determination.[82] As a former interior minister stated, "We put human rights on a scale to see if drug trafficking caused more harm to the country than adhering to an orthodox [legal] procedure. We broke the rules and tried to find an efficient mechanism that would really battle drug trafficking."[83]

Bolivia's notoriously weak, corrupt, and slow judiciary also contributed to abuses under the law.[84] Trials often lasted five years or more before a sentence was declared. Those accused under Law 1008 were not eligible for bail, and even if acquitted by a district court, they had also to be acquitted in two higher courts in order to obtain their release. Human Rights Watch wrote in 1995: "Innocent or guilty, a person charged with drug trafficking offenses faces years of imprisonment."[85] The law also set harsher sentences for drug-related crimes than for other offenses and did not permit parole. Sentences for drug production ranged from five to fifteen years, and those convicted of trafficking received ten to twenty-five years.[86] These numbers still apply today. The maximum legal sentence in Bolivia—for premeditated murder—is thirty years. There is no death penalty or life sentence.

A new criminal procedures code, fully enacted in June 2001, eliminated some of Law 1008's most egregious problems while providing key due process guarantees for Bolivian citizens. Enactment of the new code was part of a regional effort to modernize Latin American justice systems and involved the participation of Bolivian legal experts, the U.S. Agency for International Development (USAID), and GTZ, the German government's development agency. USAID played a key role in the formulation and implementation of the code. The USAID consultant in charge of the project "was actively engaged in the revision process, assembling a team of lawyers and legal experts to review and revise the [criminal procedures] Code, training justice sector officials to interpret the new Code, training police and prosecutors to enforce the new Code."[87] Among other things, the new code sets specific deadlines for trials and investigations and requires police and district attorneys to carry out expeditious investigations under the supervision of an investigative judge. The code establishes pretrial release for certain charges if the accused can present guarantees. It also establishes the presumption of innocence and guarantees humane treatment for detainees. Deadlines imposed by the code benefited prisoners who were awaiting sentencing and led to the release of many inmates.

The new code, however, does not eliminate all the problems with the antidrug law. Judicial authorities trying drug-trafficking cases continue to protest the pressure they receive to convict the accused.[88] Disproportionately long sentences under Law 1008 still limit the new code's benefits. Convicts receiving sentences of fifteen years or more under the law are ineligible for certain considerations. Most of those arrested on narcotics charges are extremely poor and are generally unable to present guarantees, such as a house or work contract in their name or high cash sums, to make bail. The right to defense is also restricted because of extreme budget and personnel constraints in the public defender's office. In the Chapare, the lack of access to a public defender has led many detainees to hire unscrupulous private lawyers who often charge high fees without providing adequate representation.

Law 1008's implementation dramatically increased the number of men, women, and children in Bolivia's already overcrowded prisons. In one Cochabamba prison that receives prisoners from the Chapare, twenty times more prisoners entered the prison in 1994 than in 1987, the year before Law 1008 was passed.[89] Since the reforms took effect, the overall prison population has diminished substantially. For example, in June 2001 there were 2,439 inmates in the Cochabamba prison; in April 2003 there were only 1,262, almost a 50 percent reduction.[90]

Even after the judicial reforms, however, in mid-2003 approximately 78 percent of the Cochabamba prison population was serving time under Law 1008 charges.[91] Poor Bolivians accused of minor trafficking offenses and without the means to hire capable legal counsel still represent the great majority of Law 1008 detainees and convicts.[92] Large-scale traffickers with the means to buy their way out of jail and hire expensive private lawyers are rarely detained or convicted.

Impunity Prevails

Despite the reforms contained in the new code, the Bolivian justice system remains notoriously weak. The United Nations Development Programme noted in 2002 that "in practice the new judicial institutions are completely subordinated to political powers, immersed in a world of corruption, inefficiency and professional mediocrity."[93] Few security force members have yet been tried or found responsible for human rights violations committed while engaged in drug control activities.

The UN Committee Against Torture, Amnesty International, and the UN Human Rights Committee have all highlighted the failure to investigate human rights violations and the systematic impunity in Bolivia. The UN Human Rights Committee wrote in 1997 that "the current legislation for combating impunity has proven to be ineffective in the identification, trial and punishment of those responsible for human rights violations." The committee also expressed concern about the delays and failures of the process of law and about noncompliance by the police with minimum UN standards.[94]

Although fifty-seven coca growers died at the hands of the security forces between 1987 and 2002, only four of these cases have made it into court.[95] Of these, only one was ever concluded. Macario Beltran Condori, a member of the Ecological Police, was accused of the 2002 shooting death of Ramón Pérez, who had been leading a group of journalists toward a military camp in the Chapare. A civilian judge sentenced Beltran to two years' probation and forbade him to drink alcohol. He will serve no jail time. One U.S. embassy official called the abbreviated trial process, with its multiple irregularities, a "kind of a slap on the wrist."[96]

In spite of the availability of eyewitness testimony and documentation, the Chapare district attorneys' offices have not completed a single serious investigation of human rights violations committed during the roadblocks from 2000 to 2003. These offices remain a weak link in the judicial chain, as investigative judges cannot open cases without a completed report. Although they are technically autonomous, the district attorneys' offices are subject to constant political pressure and are under the control of the powerful government ministry. Bolivian government officials have reacted strongly to efforts to investigate human rights cases. Those few district attorneys who attempt to prosecute human rights offenders have been pressured not to do so by their superiors and other high-ranking Bolivian government officials. One prosecutor received intense criticism from government ministers and military commanders when he moved to have ballistics tests performed to determine who shot two coca growers in October 2001.[97] Another received pressure from superiors to retract a request for the detention of Colonel Aurelio Burgos in the 2002 killing of coca grower Marcos Ortiz.[98]

Initially there was only one district attorney in the region. However, the opening of two other regional offices and the hiring of new staff have not led to an improved completion rate for investigations. Even military personnel complain that the prosecutors do not investigate crimes. One officer lamented, "The head district attorney hasn't made any effort to investigate the death of the soldiers [in July 2003]. He didn't even go to the crime scene. All he cares about is getting his contract renewed!"[99]

The Use of Military Trials

The lack of investigations and follow-through in the civilian court system is not the only source of impunity. In addition, civilian inefficiency and inefficacy have been used to justify holding human rights trials in military courts. Since 2001, the Bolivian government has begun to refer high-profile human rights cases to its military court, despite stipulations in the Bolivian constitution and in international law requiring such cases to be tried in civilian courts.[100]

Article 12 of the constitution states, "All types of torture, duress or coercion, or any form of physical or psychological violence are prohibited under penalty of immediate dismissal." Article 34 establishes that "those who violate constitutional rights and guarantees are subject to prosecution by the civilian court system." Furthermore, article 48 of the new criminal procedures code provides that when there is doubt about which jurisdiction is appropriate, the case must be handled within the civilian system; in addition, civilians can never be submitted to military jurisdiction.

Military personnel have refused to cooperate in investigations carried out by the attorney general's representatives, asserting that they are answerable only to internal military investigations. Moreover, there are no laws that provide for transparency in military court proceedings. None of the human rights cases that have gone to the military court has resulted in a conviction.

Although some military commanders state that military jurisdiction in human rights cases is essential to protect the institution, a 1998 study revealed that the great majority of members of the armed forces lack faith in the military courts' decisions and operations. For example, 88 percent of members surveyed felt that the military court was not at all or not very impartial. Ninety-five percent stated that the court was not at all modern or not sufficiently modern, and 86 percent believed that the military justice authorities were not sufficiently competent or were completely incompetent.[101] This vote of no confidence from members of the armed forces themselves further calls into question the legitimacy of the system. According to a defense expert and retired military officer:

> The military court is basically a tool to cover up and drag out legal processes against officers that have committed human rights violations. Many trials have absolved those who were primarily responsible. ... Almost none of them received any punishment; when they did, it consisted of internal disciplinary measures.... As a result, the trials are just a simulation to give the appearance that justice is being administered within the armed forces.[102]

Cases in which military commanders face criminal prosecution are now routinely passed to the military courts. In 2000, the judge in Villa Tunari, a town in the Chapare, initiated legal proceedings against two JTF commanders for negligent homicide in the deaths of three coca growers.[103] The judge was pressured by high-ranking government officials and UMOPAR officers to drop the cases.[104] In 2001, a Cochabamba district court transferred the first two cases to the military tribunal, while the third case continued to languish in the civilian courts. The cases in the military court were later dropped for lack of evidence—the court's investigator had neither interviewed witnesses nor conducted an investigation.[105]

In yet another case, a military tribunal acquitted ETF member Juan Eladio Bora in the 2001 killing of coca grower leader Casimiro Huanca and the wounding of another person. In a textbook example of impunity, the Bolivian military tribunal took only two weeks to conclude that Bora shot Huanca in self-defense, even though video footage of the incident clearly demonstrated the peaceful nature of the protest.[106] Military judicial investigators questioned only military personnel involved in the incident and did not obtain statements from coca growers and eyewitnesses.[107]

Although an arrest warrant was issued in June 2002 for ETF commander Burgos for the killing of coca grower Marcos Ortiz in January of that year, Burgos's lawyers argued that he had already been tried in a military court and that continued prosecution in civilian courts would constitute double jeopardy. The district attorney in charge of the investigation at first recommended that the judge issue the order. Later, however, he requested that it be withdrawn, citing pressure from the attorney general's office.[108]

Members of the armed forces have categorically refused to give testimony in civilian investigations of the February 2003 confrontations. A lawyer for the armed forces prematurely concluded, "No military [personnel] committed criminal acts" and stated that members of these forces would be judged by the military, not the civilian justice system.[109] In February 2004, the public was outraged when the military tribunal acquitted four members of the armed forces accused of shooting and killing a nurse assisting a wounded person on February 13, 2003.[110]

The State Department recognized problems with military courts in the 2001 and 2002 *Human Rights Practices Country Report* on Bolivia. The 2001 report concluded that "the military justice system generally is susceptible to senior-level influence and corruption and avoids making rulings that would cause embarrassment to the military."[111] In spite of this observation, embassy officials continue to assert that the decision to move cases to the military court is in accordance with Bolivian law.[112]

The United States and the Leahy Amendment

Since 1997, the Leahy Amendment has provided the U.S. government with a means to ensure that U.S. funds do not go to security forces that commit gross human rights violations. Application of the amendment would greatly facilitate the fight against endemic impunity for violations committed by Bolivian security forces. However, U.S. officials have yet to withhold funds as stipulated by the amendment; nor have they pressured for the removal of accused personnel from U.S.-funded units. Embassy and State Department officials maintain that they vet units as well as they can with their limited resources. Embassy officials state that they lack the staff and budget necessary to determine whether gross human rights violations have been committed, in spite of the extensive documentation provided to them by human rights monitors.[113]

U.S. embassy officials commonly adopt the Bolivian authorities' version of events, routinely citing the Bolivian government and security forces as their principal sources. For example, in late 2002, the U.S. embassy official in charge of narcotics affairs stated in a BBC interview that abuses will occur and that he was unsure whether the recent ones constituted "gross" human rights violations.[114] When a high-ranking State Department official told NGO representatives in 2002 that extensively documented killings by the Expeditionary Task Force were not "gross" human rights violations, one human rights monitor angrily responded, "What could be grosser than dead!"[115]

The killing of Casimiro Huanca, mentioned above, provides a clear example. The State Department provided the military version of the events to members of the U.S. Congress as an explanation for the incident, stating that coca growers had blocked the road and that the ETF had acted in self-defense. The U.S. Defense Intelligence Agency contradicted this assessment:

> The video tape is clear enough to show that the military's version of the events of 2001-12-06 is inaccurate at best and a complete fabrication at worst. This video tape could be used by military and medical personnel as an excellent example of "what not to do" in terms of crowd control, military discipline and medical care.[116]

In early 2002, a State Department official told an interviewer from the Washington Office on Latin America that the shooting of Huanca did not constitute a gross human rights violation because he did not die from being shot but had bled to death. If Huanca had received adequate medical attention he might have survived, the official said. The official failed to note the lack of adequate medical facilities in the region. Embassy officials also claimed that Fructuoso Herbas, shot in the same incident, had only been "wounded slightly above the right ankle," although his leg had to be amputated above the knee. An embassy official blamed the need for amputation on the failure of human rights monitors and the NGO community to provide assistance.[117]

The explanation presented by the State Department for the death of Marcos Ortiz in early 2002 repeated almost verbatim the version provided by Colonel Burgos, who was accused of the killing.[118] The State Department wrote:

> According to the Bolivian military, Colonel Burgos saw Ortiz lying on the road wounded and Burgos pointed while at the same time holding a pistol. Because [Burgos] has only one hand ... he apparently was using this hand both to hold his pistol and to point/gesture/give orders. The Bolivian military reports that military authorities examined Burgos and his pistol after the incident and determined that it had not been fired recently and that Burgos had not recently fired any weapon.[119]

The Human Rights Ombudsman's Office collected eyewitness testimony from numerous individuals. For example, two witnesses gave testimony identifying Burgos as the shooter and describing how he beat and kicked them when they tried to approach the body of Ortiz to offer assistance. The existence of any documentation of the tests done to determine whether Burgos fired his weapon could not be ascertained. Although a civilian judge issued an arrest warrant in June 2002 for Burgos, the State Department asserted: "The Attorney General's office opened a parallel investigation into the case but concluded that there was insufficient evidence to bring charges against Colonel Burgos."[120]

Embassy officials claim that they cannot gain access to the medical certificates and autopsy reports that would allow them to evaluate whether or not credible evidence of violations exists, but this seems implausible, considering the level of influence the United States enjoys. The United States provides funding and administrative support to the Ministry of Justice's Human Rights Office, which issues the certificates.

Neither the Leahy Amendment nor international law permits the substitution of military tribunals and internal disciplinary measures for the civilian legal system's jurisdiction over human rights violations. Seven members of the U.S. House of Representatives made the same point to the U.S. ambassador to Bolivia, Manuel Rocha, on November 15, 2001: "As you are aware, neither internal disciplinary measures by the security forces, nor economic compensation for the victims' families, will satisfy U.S. law. It is also our assessment that military jurisdiction in such cases is not satisfactory."[121] In addition, the U.S. Congress approved report language in its 2004 foreign operations bill requiring that

> funds appropriated under this heading that are available for the Bolivian military and police may be made available if the Secretary of State determines and reports to the Committees on Appropriations that (1) the Bolivian Government is vigorously investigating and prosecuting members of the Bolivian military and police who have been credibly alleged to have committed gross violations of human rights and is promptly punishing those found to have committed such violations; and (2) the Bolivian military and police are cooperating with such investigations and prosecution.[122]

Another government agency also highlighted problems with the military tribunal. In the Huanca case, the U.S. Defense Intelligence Agency observed that

> the [military] tribunal's findings appear to simply rubberstamp and thereby vindicate the military's own version of what occurred. The Bolivian military's refusal to take action against the soldier whose weapon discharged and simply restrict the officer in charge to his quarters is likely to generate a further outcry against the Bolivian government's policies in the Chapare.[123]

Despite more than ten U.S. congressional letters of inquiry pressing for the application of the Leahy Amendment, the State Department continues to circumvent the spirit of the law, permitting impunity for the security forces it funds. The U.S. embassy in La Paz downplays even the most serious abuses, despite the probability that a few successful prosecutions of well-documented cases would increase the legitimacy of both the U.S. and Bolivian governments and thus serve to further U.S. counternarcotics goals.

• Coca Growers, Politics, and U.S. Policy

As a result of recent events and their own organizing efforts, Bolivian coca growers have become a formidable force in national politics. Chapare growers' unions now represent approximately 45,000 families in the region, organized within the Six Coca Growers' Federations. Faced with the threat presented by drug control efforts in the region, the unions have become a skillful advocacy group for their rights, interests, and livelihoods.

The growers' organizations have filled the void left by the decline of Bolivia's traditional labor unions and have gained influence and key positions in the umbrella groups organized by peasant farmers and others.[124] However, support from other sectors for the coca growers sometimes wavers when the government negotiates separately with those sectors and offers them concessions it cannot make to coca growers because of U.S. opposition to doing so.

The conflict generated by the implementation of drug policy has raised the national profile of the coca growers' movement and is changing the political landscape in Bolivia. But it remains doubtful that alternative development programs will generate sufficient income for Chapare families' subsistence. Strong U.S. pressure continues to maintain forced eradication, while the United States is also seeking to link coca growers with terrorism.

With traditional coca use and national sovereignty as their banners, coca growers use direct mass action to pressure the Bolivian government.[125] However, in the Chapare, coca growers have also turned to participating directly in Bolivian politics, generally following existing laws and ground rules, to further their goals. The party that would later become the MAS was formed in 1995. It made use of the high level of social organization within the existing union structure to overwhelmingly sweep the 1995 municipal elections in the Chapare and to gain control of the five municipal governments there. During two consecutive terms, coca grower mayors skillfully used the new Popular Participation Law, which mandated decentralization and the disbursement of funds to municipalities, to carry out public works projects for their communities. Directly answerable to the unions that placed them there, these local governments were viewed as much more cost-efficient and less corrupt than municipalities run by traditional parties. As a result, MAS has maintained control of Chapare local governments, and MAS candidates have been elected in other rural areas, especially in the department of Cochabamba.

Successes at the local level inspired MAS to campaign actively during the 2002 presidential and congressional elections. Funding its operation with government funds given to each established political party, as well as a contribution of ten pounds of coca from each union family, MAS ran a low-budget and highly successful campaign.[126] After the elections, the party returned unused government campaign funds to the treasury, a practice unheard of in Bolivia, which further increased support for the party. MAS candidates included coca grower leaders from the Chapare and the Yungas, other farmer leaders, and progressive intellectuals.

Widespread frustration with traditional political parties' lack of responsiveness to the needs of the population as well as opposition to current neoliberal economic policies have also contributed to MAS's popularity. The party's electoral gains also signal a rejection of U.S.-backed coca eradication policies while providing Morales with the opportunity to widen his base of support.[127] During 2002 and 2003, the party broadened the scope of its activities to include other issues, such as opposition to the Free Trade Area of the Americas. The MAS strategy is now to combine legislative work with direct mobilization and protest. As Morales told the press in August 2003, "We've learned that proposals without protest just don't work."[128] The litmus test for the political movement, however, will be its ability to obtain concessions and concrete benefits for its Chapare constituents, given the government's failure to comply with past agreements.

Alternative Development

When Law 1008 laid the foundation for forced eradication, it also required that alternative development programs be implemented simultaneously. Article 27 specified that eligibility for receiving international alternative development aid could not be conditioned on the beneficiaries' previous eradication of their coca crops. Ten years later, Plan Dignidad stipulated as one of its key pillars that forced eradication should be accompanied by alternative development.

USAID has provided substantial and sustained funding for alternative development programs. Unfortunately, aggressive eradication efforts have consistently outpaced the income-generating capacity of alternative development schemes. Despite the contrary provision of Law 1008, U.S.-funded programs have required that a farmer completely eradicate all coca before being eligible for this assistance. Poor soils and inappropriate conditions for other crops, combined with a lack of transportation and markets, have meant that most of the projects carried out with U.S. funding since the mid-1980s have failed to generate sufficient income to ensure subsistence for families growing coca. Moreover, until 2004, the United States refused to work directly with coca producers' unions, in spite of their high level of organization. This, too, has hampered the success of the programs. This failure in turn has led coca producers to replant coca on a large scale. In any case, coca producers and development workers agree that no other crop can compete with coca in terms of the income it generates.

Chapare residents also complain that a disproportionate amount of U.S. funds go to sustaining a military presence instead of providing development and much-needed social services.[129] The United States pays approximately U.S.$2.80 per soldier per day to feed the security forces in the region. On average, 3,000–3,500 people a day are fed through this program, many more during times of conflict. "The amount spent daily on food for security forces is enough to build three classrooms, a health center or to pay the salary for a government-employed anesthesiologist for a year and a half."[130]

Coca growers remain skeptical about the Bolivian government's ability to implement current proposals.[131] This skepticism is well founded in light of past experience. The Bolivian government has repeatedly signed accords with the coca growers in an effort to stem conflict and then failed to comply with their terms. In 1998, the vice minister for alternative development stated that eradication authorities had not complied with more than 1,000 agreements made with coca growers during past administrations.[132] This constant violation of agreements has created mistrust and reluctance on the part of growers to participate in alternative development projects.

However, the potential for improvement does exist. In 2003, USAID devoted greater funding to the improvement of health care in the region. More significant, the organization began to reevaluate its stance against collaboration with coca growers' associations. It has made initial efforts to begin work with coca grower–controlled municipal governments in the Chapare on limited projects. Bolivian decentralization laws cede responsibility for local development efforts to these local governments, which have the support of the growers' unions, are responsive to the needs of their constituents, and have generally used available funds efficiently to provide public works in their communities. Cooperative efforts through the local governments provide a key opportunity to refocus and improve U.S.-funded development efforts in the region.

A Terrorist Threat in Bolivia?

Working against this potential is the fact that both the U.S. and Bolivian governments have stepped up their rhetoric about a potential terrorist threat. In particular, they have attempted to link Morales and the coca growers' movement to terrorist activity. In April 2003 police detained a Colombian, Francisco Cortés, along with two coca grower leaders, stating that they had "found evidence linking the detainees to subversive activities and drug-trafficking, constituting a narco-guerrilla organization."[133] Although the Colombian embassy confirmed that Cortés was a human rights worker participating in its witness protection program, prosecutors did not drop the charges of espionage, terrorism, and armed uprising.

Contradicting government spokesmen, the commander of the armed forces affirmed that there were no guerrilla groups operating in the Chapare at that time and that attacks on eradication forces were isolated incidents.[134] In response, a high-ranking U.S. embassy official quickly asserted that members of Colombia's insurgent groups had been in the country during 2002. "We know that last year the Colombian FARC and ELN were present [in Bolivia], and they weren't tourists.... Terrorism is a risk in the future, but the United States will work closely with the government to avoid this evil." Fighting this "terrorist" presence in Bolivia became an increasing priority for the U.S. government. For FY2004, the George W. Bush administration requested that Congress double the foreign military funding account, citing two new areas: "security for drug eradication and interdiction operations," and "equipment and training for the Bolivian army's new counterterrorism unit."[135]

• Conclusion

U.S. counterdrug policy in Bolivia is destabilizing the country's fragile democracy and empowering the very forces that Washington is seeking to combat. Threats by U.S. State Department officials that aid would be cut if Evo Morales became president caused his popularity to soar and substantially strengthened the coca grower movement. Continued U.S. pressure on President Sánchez de Lozada, in spite of widespread social upheaval, impeded his efforts to reach negotiated solutions with the coca growers. As a result, coca producers and other groups, increasingly frustrated with attempts to change policy through the existing party system, relied on direct protests as a way of articulating their interests.

In the end, Sánchez de Lozada proved to be "out of touch with a poor and angry country."[136] The U.S. government suffers from the same shortsightedness: it has yet to learn from the mistakes that have characterized its antidrug policy, culminating in the crisis during Sánchez de Lozada's most recent term. The drug war's collateral damage is evident in the increasing power of military forces, frequent human rights abuses, continued impunity for those responsible, and economic hardship both for those directly affected and for the population as a whole. The failure of alternative development, in the context of extreme poverty and inequality, has ensured that eradicated coca is quickly replanted. The lack of viable alternatives combined with the short-term eradication targets dictated by Washington make new cycles of conflict and violence predictable.

Moreover, despite the high political, social, and economic costs of eradication, there is no evidence that sustained reductions in coca crop cultivation have been achieved. According to the U.S. State Department, Bolivian coca production reached its high point of 52,900 hectares in 1989. In December 2000, the Bolivian government announced that it had met its zero coca goal in the Chapare region, claiming that all coca destined for the illicit drug trade had been wiped out.[137] Since then, widespread replanting of coca and active grower resistance have reversed this trend. In 2003, the State Department reported that forced eradication led to a 15 percent reduction in Chapare coca production. But Yungas production went up by 26 percent, for an overall increase of 17 percent over 2002 estimates, bringing total Bolivian coca production to 28,450 hectares.[138]

Sustainable economic development that generates adequate income for coca grower families is an essential element of any lasting solution to the recurring cycles of conflict. Funding priorities should shift to benefit poor farmers and to promote economic development more broadly. Development programs must work directly with the local population and their existing organizational structures. They must directly engage coca growers in planning and implementing the projects to improve the chances that these will be relevant and sustainable. Prioritizing the building and supplying of schools and health clinics over the expansion of military and police facilities will also contribute to providing new opportunities for the next generation.

The Bolivian government should take effective steps to investigate, sanction, and prevent abuses committed by U.S.-funded security forces in Bolivia. Moreover, the U.S. government, in accordance with U.S. law, should suspend funding to those units that commit abuses when the members responsible are not sanctioned. Rather than the current short-term focus on meeting coca eradication goals, U.S. international drug control policy would be better served in the long run by ensuring a stable civilian government in Bolivia. Toward that end, the U.S. government should allow the Bolivian government greater political flexibility, publicly supporting dialogue between the Bolivian government and coca growers as a way to avert further violence and to address social concerns. It should also support a greater role for civil society and Bolivian public opinion in determining the government's antidrug policies, including public debate and legislative revision of unpopular antidrug legislation.

These are necessary steps toward a lasting, concrete, and peaceful solution to Bolivia's long-standing coca conflict. Any government will face the dilemma of pressure to continue eradication and the need to avoid prolonged social upheaval. However, as long as success is measured in terms of coca eradicated and not by the well-being of the Bolivian people, repeated cycles of protest, repression, and temporary conciliation will continue indefinitely.

• Notes

1. Franciso Thoumi, *Illegal Drugs, Economy, and Society in the Andes* (Washington, D.C.: Woodrow Wilson Center Press, 2003), pp. 253–254.

2. *La Razón*, "El Gobierno es Acusado de Violar los DD.HH.," 14 February 2002.

3. Human Rights Watch (HRW), "Human Rights Violations and the War on Drugs," *Human Rights Watch* 7, no. 8 (July 1995); and "Bolivia Under Pressure: Human Rights Violations and Coca Eradication," *Human Rights Watch* 8, no. 4 (B) (May 1996).

4. Eduardo A. Gamarra, "U.S.-Bolivian Counternarcotics Efforts During the Paz Zamora Administration: 1989–1992," in Bruce M. Bagley and William O. Walker III, eds., *Drug Trafficking in the Americas* (Coral Gables, Fla.: University of Miami, North-South Center; New Brunswick, N.J.: distributed by Lynne Rienner Publishers, 1994), p. 220.

5. UN Development Programme (UNDP), *Human Development Report 2001 (HDR2001)*, pp. 182–185.

6. U.S. State Department, Bureau of Western Hemisphere Affairs (WHA), *Country Information*, Bolivia, "Background Notes," November 2003.

7. UNDP, *HDR2001*, pp. 150 and 164–165.

8. *El Deber*, "Bolivia Ocupa el Segundo Lugar en Mortalidad Infantil," Santa Cruz, 12 December 2002.

9. U.S. State Department, *FY2005 Congressional Budget Justification for Foreign Operations*, "Western Hemisphere," released 10 February 2004, p. 470.

10. *Presencia*, 9 April 1994, cited in "El Enigma Boliviana: Bilateralizar la Agenda Bilateral," in *Democracias Bajo Fuego*, Martin Jelsma and Theo Roncken, eds. (Uruguay: Impresora Editorial, 1998), p. 291.

11. Roberto Laserna, *Las Drogas y el Ajuste en Bolivia: Economía Clandestina y Políticas Públicas* (La Paz: CEDLA, 1993), pp. 89–90.

12. Barbara Leóns and Harry Sanabria, *Coca, Cocaine, and the Bolivian Reality* (Albany: State University of New York Press, 1997), p. 3.

13. James Painter, *Bolivia and Coca: A Study in Dependency* (Boulder: Lynne Rienner Publishers, 1994), p. 139.

14. U.S. State Department, "2003 Coca Cultivation Estimates for Bolivia and Peru," press statement, Richard Boucher, Washington, D.C., 17 November 2003.

15. Cornelius H. Zondag, *The Bolivian Economy, 1952–1965: The Revolution and Its Aftermath* (New York: Praeger, 1966).

16. Peter Kornbluh, *The Death of Che Guevara*, National Security Archive, electronic briefing book no. 5.

17. James Dunkerley, *Rebellion in the Veins* (London: Verso, 1984), p. 205.

18. Thoumi, *Illegal Drugs*, pp. 251–253.

19. Clare Hargreaves, *Snowfields: The War on Cocaine in the Andes* (New York: Holmes and Meier, 1992), pp. 104–107.

20. Dunkerley, *Rebellion*, pp. 323–325.

21. Sewall Menzel, *Fire in the Andes: U.S. Foreign Policy and Cocaine Politics in Peru and Bolivia* (New York: University Press of America, 1996), p. 8. On Peruvian unit, see Chapter 6 in this volume.

22. Operation Snowcap was the umbrella name applied to U.S. drug control activities in twelve Latin American countries after 1987.

23. Sewall Menzel, "Southcom in the Andes," *Hemisphere* 6, no. 3, Latin American and Caribbean Center, Florida International University; Jacqueline

Williams, *Waging the War on Drugs in Bolivia* (Washington, D.C.: Washington Office on Latin America, April 1997), p. 6.

24. Menzel, *Fire*, p. 47.

25. Ibid., p. 14.

26. Human Rights Watch, "Human Rights Violations and the War on Drugs," *Human Rights Watch* 7, no. 8 (July 1995): 14–15.

27. Ibid., p. 23.

28. Eduardo Gamarra, *Entre la Droga y la Democracia* (La Paz: Ildis, 1994), p. 62.

29. *Presencia*, 10 February 1986, quoted in Jelsma and Roncken, 1998.

30. Gloria Rose Marie de Achá, "Violaciones a los Derechos Humanos Civiles bajo la Ley 1008," Andean Information Network, Centro de Documentación e Información Bolivia (CEDIB), 1 December 1996, p. 1.

31. Kevin Healy, "Coca, the State, and the Peasantry in Bolivia, 1982–1988," *Journal of Interamerican Studies and World Affairs* 30 (Summer–Fall 1988).

32. CEDIB, *Information Dossier: The FELCN*, Cochabamba, June 1996.

33. Author interview with UMOPAR officers, September 2002; and Painter, *Bolivia and Coca*, p. 81. Note: numerous informants requested anonymity for fear of reprisals against their person or their livelihood.

34. Lora Lumpe, Bolivia, WOLA research 2002, www.wola.org/ddhr_documents.htm, p. 1.

35. Ibid.

36. Painter, *Bolivia and Coca*, p. 81.

37. See Andean Information Network (AIN), "The Weight of Law 1008," 1997; and Painter, *Bolivia and Coca*, p. 81.

38. Author interview with Chapare human rights ombudsman, Dr. Godofredo Reinicke, 2 June 2003.

39. Author interviews with human rights monitors, 17 April 2002 and 29 January 2003.

40. Author interview with U.S. Embassy officials, 23 March 2000.

41. FELCN, "Memoria Anual de la Gestión 1999," La Paz, 2000.

42. Author interview with guest instructor in "Talons of Valor" (Garras) Human Rights Module, 15 October 2002.

43. All preceding information in this paragraph is from CEDIB, *Dossier*, June 1996.

44. *La Prensa*, "No Se Conoce en Manos de Quiénes Terminaron Fortunas de Narcotraficantes," 4 December 2003.

45. Human Rights Watch, 1996, p. 1.

46. UDAPDE, "Programa de Prevención, Gestión, y Resolución de Conflictos en el Marco de la Lucha Contra las Drogas en Bolivia" (La Paz: Ministerio de Defensa Nacional, June 1999), p. 2.

47. *INCSR 2002*, "Bolivia."

48. *INCSR 2003*, "Bolivia." While production in the Chapare had decreased by 15 percent, the yield from the Yungas region had increased by 26 percent, leading to an overall increase in Bolivia of 17 percent.

49. AIN interview with Bolivian army officer, 16 January 2001 and 15 August 2001.

50. Author interviews with military personnel and Chapare human rights ombudsman, 12 August 2002 and 23 January 2003.

51. "Acuerdo Entre el Gobierno y la Coordinadora de las Federaciones del Trópico de Cochabamba," photocopy of agreement in possession of author, Chimoré, 15 October 2001.

52. AIN interview with U.S. government official, 15 August 2001, and Bolivian government official, 16 January 2001.

53. Letter from Paul V. Kelly, Assistant Secretary of Legislative Affairs, to Representative Maurice Hinchey (D-New York), 28 March 2002.

54. *Los Tiempos*, "La Nueva Fuerza Hace el Trabajo Sucio en Chapare," 22 November 2001.

55. Author interview with members of the Expeditionary Task Force, 15 June 2002.

56. Author interview with member of the eradication forces, 15 January 2002.

57. AIN/WOLA interview with Juan Ramón Quintana, 18 November 2002.

58. Author interview with eradication official, 13 March 2003, and with a Chapare human rights monitor, 13 October 2002.

59. AIN/WOLA interview with retired Bolivian military officer Juan Ramón Quintana, La Paz, 18 November 2002.

60. Defense Ministry, Defense Policy Analysis Unit (UDAPDE), "Encuesta de Opinión. Fuerzas armadas: 'Realidad y Perspectiva Institucional,'" 1998, p. 2. This study is based on the survey of a representative sample of approximately 10 percent of the members of the armed forces, with even distribution in terms of force membership, rank, age, and posting.

61. Author interview with member of the Joint Task Force, 14 April 2000.

62. Author interview with eradication official, 12 May 2000.

63. AIN/WOLA interview with Juan Ramón Quintana, 18 November 2002.

64. Author interview with eradication official, 29 September 2002.

65. Author interview with retired military officer, 15 August 2003.

66. U.S embassy in La Paz, cable, "Talking Points for Quiroga Visit," 6 December 2001.

67. Author interviews with participants in mediation process, 30 November 2002; *Opinión,* "Diálogo de la Coca Queda Roto por Falta de Voluntad Política," 28 November 2001.

68. U.S embassy cable, "Talking Points for Quiroga Visit," 6 December 2001.

69. Public speech given by U.S. Ambassador Rocha, 26 June 2002.

70. AIN/WOLA interview with Phil Chicola, U.S. State Department, 15 July 2002.

71. *Pulso,* "Goni y las FF.AA.: Del Desprecio al Amor," 22 August 2003.

72. Gonzalo Sánchez de Lozada, speech at the Interamerican Dialogue, Washington, D.C., May 2000.

73. *El Diario*, "Carlos Mesa Gisbert: No Tolero que Muerte Sea Respuesta a las Protestas Populares," La Paz, 14 October 2003.

74. *CNN Español,* "Presidente de Bolivia Anuncia Intento Golpista," 13 October 2003.

75. See Human Rights Watch, "Human Rights Violations," July 1995; and AIN, "The Weight of Law 1008," 1997.

76. *Los Tiempos,* "Derechos Humanos en Chapare a Segundo Plano," 31 October 2001.

77. *Los Tiempos,* "EE.UU. Ahora Deplora a las Violaciones de DD.HH," 5 March 2002.

78. See Law 1818, "La Ley del Defensor del Pueblo."

79. Author interviews with Cochabamba residents, 22 July 2003 and 15 August 2003.

80. Constitución Política del Estado, Ley 1615, Artículo 16, 2002.

81. Human Rights Watch, "Human Rights Violations," July 1995.

82. Ibid., p. 20.

83. SEAMOS, "Problemas Jurídicos-Legales Asociados a la Aplicación de la Ley 1008: Procesos, Encausamiento, y Penalidades al Narcotráfico," in SEAMOS, ed., *Drogas: El debate Boliviano* (La Paz: SEAMOS, 1991), pp. 60–61.

84. Linda Farthing, "Social Impacts Associated with Antidrug Law 1008," in *Coca, Cocaine, and the Bolivian Reality*, Madeline Barbara Léons and Harry Sanabria, eds. (New York: SUNY Press, 1997), p. 256.

85. HRW, July 1995, p. 19.

86. República de Bolivia, "La Ley del Régimen de la Coca y Sustancias Controladas: Ley 1008," Title III, articles 47, 48, 19 July 1988.

87. From the website of Management Sciences for Development, Inc., www.msdglobal.com/law_bol.html.

88. Author interview with judicial employees, 23 August 2002.

89. Juzgado de Vigilancia, *Informe Anual 1995*, Cochabamba, Bolivia. In 1987, eight men were imprisoned; in 1994, 175 began serving time. This is one of four prisons in Cochabamba housing inmates on drug charges.

90. Statistics courtesy of Régimen Penitenciaria de Cochabamba, 29 May 2003.

91. Author interview with Dr. Charles Becerra, director of the Cochabamba prison system, 29 May 2003.

92. Roberto Laserna, Gonzalo Vargas, and Juan Torrico, "La Estructura Industrial del Narcotráfico en Cochabamba" (Cochabamba: UNDCP/PNUD, unpublished manuscript, 1995).

93. PNUD, *Informe de Desarrollo Humano en Bolivia, 2002*, p. 122.

94. Amnesty International (AI), "Concluding Observations of the Human Rights Committee: Bolivia," CCPR/C/79/Add.74, 1 April 1997, par. 24, cited in AI, "Bolivia, Torture, and Ill-Treatment: Amnesty International's Concerns," AI index: AMR 18/008/2001, June 2002, p. 15.

95. *La Razón*, "El Gobierno es Acusado de Violar los DD.HH.," 14 February 2002.

96. Telephone conversation with U.S. embassy official, 20 October 2002.

97. Author interview with Chapare District Attorney's Office staff, 6–7 October 2001; *La Prensa*, "El Gobierno y el MNR Respaldan la Decisión de las Fuerzas Armadas: Militares no Entregarán Sus Armas al Ministerio Público," 6 October 2001.

98. Author interview with judicial employees, 17 March 2003.

99. Author interview with military officer, 20 July 2003.

100. Bolivia has been a state party to the American Convention on Human Rights since 19 July 1979 and has recognized the obligatory jurisdiction of the Court since 27 July 1993. See also Susan Lee, Amnesty International Regional Director, letter to Leopoldo Fernández, minister of government, 22 October 2001.

101. UDAPDE, "Encuesta," p. 15.

102. AIN/WOLA interview with Juan Ramón Quintana, 18 November 2002.

103. Case file and court documentation, Alberto Coca Coyo murder case, May 2000.

104. Author interview with judge, Villa Tunari courthouse, December 2000.

105. AIN, *Análisis Jurídico*, 3 December 2001.

106. *Pulso*, "En Proceso de Paramilitarización Las Fuerzas Armadas Han Perdido el Control," 17 December 2001.

107. AIN interview with witnesses in the Casimiro Huanca case, 16 January 2002.

108. AIN interview with Chapare court officials, 6 February 2003.

109. *Los Tiempos*, "Febrero: Los Militares No Cometieron Delitos," 2 May 2003.

110. *El Diario*, "Febrero Negro: Justicia Militar Declara Inocentes a 4 Militares," La Paz, 17 February 2004.

111. U.S. State Department, *Country Reports on Human Rights Practices, 2001*, "Bolivia," p. 8.

112. AIN/WOLA meeting at the U.S. Embassy in La Paz, 19 November 2002. Present were the chargé d'affaires, a political officer, and representatives of Milgroup, USAID, three WOLA staff members, and the author.

113. Ibid.

114. Interview with Stanley Shraeger on "Newsnight," *BBC Television*, 21 October 2002.

115. AIN/WOLA interview at the State Department, 15 July 2002.

116. U.S. Defense Intelligence Agency memo, Document I.D. number 189636551, 20 December 2001.

117. AIN/WOLA meeting at the U.S. Embassy, November 2002.

118. Author interview with an eradication official, June 2002.

119. State Department response to congressional inquiry, signed by Paul V. Kelly, Assistant Secretary, Legislative Affairs, 28 March 2002.

120. U.S. State Department, *Country Reports on Human Rights Practices 2002*, "Bolivia."

121. Letter to U.S. Ambassador to Bolivia, Manuel Rocha, 15 November 2001.

122. U.S. Senate, 2004 Foreign Operations Appropriations bill, report no. 108-106, 17 July 2003.

123. U.S. Defense Intelligence Agency Memo, Document I.D. number 189695174, 28 December 2001.

124. Kevin Healy, "Ascent of Bolivia's Peasant Coca Leaf Producers," *Journal of Interamerican Studies and World Affairs* (Spring 2001): 112–113.

125. Kevin Healy, "The Coca-Cocaine Issue in Bolivia: A Political Resource for All Seasons," in *Coca, Cocaine, and the Bolivian Reality,* Madeline Barbara Léons and Harry Sanabria, eds. (New York: State University of New York Press, 1997), p. 233.

126. Interview with MAS and coca grower leaders Leonida Zurita and Feliciano Mamani, 22 March 2003.

127. Robert Albro, "A New Evo-lution? Prospects for Bolivia's Popular Movement," draft submitted to *Hemisphere: A Magazine of the Americas,* July 2003.

128. Interview on *Periodistas Asociados de Television* newscast, 2nd edition, 29 August 2003.

129. Author interviews with Chapare residents, 20 May and 17 July 2003.

130. Author interview with Chapare's human rights ombudsman, Godofredo Reinicke, 23 March 2003.

131. Author interviews with coca growers, 17–20 November 2001.

132. Oscar Coca et al., *Cifras y Datos del Desarrollo Alternativo en Bolivia* (Cochabamba: CEDIB, 1999).

133. *Los Tiempos*, "Cae un Supuesto Guerrillero Junto a Dos Cocaleros," 11 April 2003.

134. *El Diario*, "FFAA Descarta Presencia de Grupos Irregulares en el Chapare," 6 May 2003.

135. U.S. State Department, *Congressional Budget Justification for Foreign Operations, FY2004*, pp. 450–451.

136. *The Economist*, "Bolivia: After the Uprising," 25 October 2003.

137. *INCSR 2000*, "Bolivia," 1 March 2001. Also, this claim was premature, since satellite photos showed a remaining 600 hectares of coca.

138. *INCSR 2003*, "Bolivia," 1 March 2004.

6

Peru:
Drug Control Policy, Human Rights,
and Democracy

Isaías Rojas

During his annual message to congress at the start of his third year in office in July 2003, Peru's president, Alejandro Toledo, announced that his administration would initiate a "new strategy against terrorism" and stressed that the new strategy would target areas where terrorism and drug trafficking were closely linked. His announcement was intended to calm fears among the Peruvian population about a reported resurgence of the Shining Path insurgency, a tiny splinter of which had recently attacked some workers on an oil pipeline in a remote zone of the Apurímac and Ene River Valley (VRAE), currently the highest producer of coca leaf in Peru. But the message was also directed at Washington. U.S. officials, placing regional policy in the context of September 11, had voiced concerns about the supposed reappearance of the Shining Path, saying it was a "serious threat" that represented an "immediate danger" to Peru, and urged the Peruvian government to "increase its efforts to bring the narcoterrorists under control."[1]

The debate about the alleged resurgence of Shining Path, however, masked from public sight a set of more complex questions related to U.S.-Peruvian drug control policy in the aftermath of the downfall of President Alberto Fujimori. In September 2002, the Peruvian and U.S. governments had signed a new drug control agreement that had as its principal goal the total eradication of illegal coca crops in Peru over the next five years, continuing what they had viewed as a successful policy since the Fujimori era.[2] The United States offered U.S.$300 million in alternative development aid that was strictly conditioned on meeting coca eradication targets and on a state security presence being restored to the coca-growing areas.[3] The new agreement set higher goals in coca leaf eradication than those demanded by Washington during the Fujimori regime.

Moreover, the agreement was signed in the midst of widespread protests against eradication in the coca-growing areas. First initiated during the final phase of the Fujimori regime in late 2000, these protests continued

185

Peru	
Population	26,400,000
GDP	U.S.$54.0 billion
GDP per capita	U.S.$2,051
Share of Income	
• Poorest 10 percent of population	0.8%
• Richest 10 percent of population	36.9%
• Ratio of income of richest 10% to poorest 10%	46.2 times
Percentage living in poverty (<$2/day)	41.4%
Percentage living in extreme poverty (<$1/day)	15.5%
Public perception of corruption among public officials and politicians (0=more, 10=less)	3.7

Sources: UNDP, *Human Development Report 2004;* World Bank, *Inequality in Latin America: Breaking with History?;* Transparency International, *Corruption Perceptions Index 2003.*

Notes: Population and GDP data from 2001; share of income data 2000; poverty data 1990–2001.

into the Toledo administration, resulting in a tense dynamic of negotiation and confrontation between the government and the coca growers' organizations.

The Toledo government's ability to deal effectively with the protests was undermined by two major problems. First, it was unable to meet the pent-up social demands that had accumulated during Fujimori's authoritarian rule. Second, the political fragility of the Toledo regimen limited its options—President Toledo's approval ratings had declined rapidly, primarily as a result of his own political mistakes and the population's growing perception of the government's inability to solve the crucial problems of the country. Also significant, a diminishing level of action against corruption allowed for the reconstitution of the political forces that had supported the regime of Alberto Fujimori.

The frightening possibility of a Shining Path revival provided Toledo's socially and politically besieged regime with the necessary rationale for allowing the new drug control agreement to be implemented. In reality, the Shining Path had almost completely disappeared many years earlier and posed no current threat to Peru, but the renewed menace of "narcoterrorism" served to justify the reinforcement of the military presence in the coca-growing areas. In fact, at the time of the president's speech, the VRAE was one of the coca-growing areas where the protests were strongest; an increased military presence would also serve to quell the protests.

Faced with the complexity of the coca issue, the weak Toledo government seemed to be walking a thin line, where social protest might be conflated with terrorism, and the demand to "restore security" transformed into "militarization." Indeed, the recent history of Peruvian drug control suggests that Peruvian governments have believed that militarization and authoritarianism are necessary elements of law enforcement.

In order to determine the prospects for such developments under the Toledo government, it is useful to examine the evolution of U.S.-inspired drug control policies in Peru during the authoritarian rule of President Alberto Fujimori (1990–2000). The details of this history have only recently begun to come to light with the declassification of documents by the U.S. State Department. This chapter focuses on U.S. policies and their relationship to the evolution of Peruvian drug control, democracy, and human rights policies during the Fujimori era and its immediate aftermath.

What this history shows is that to date, unfortunately, democratic governance and respect for human rights have clashed with the implementation of Peruvian drug control policy. First under Bill Clinton and then George W. Bush, U.S. administrations have prioritized drug policy over strengthening democracy or ensuring compliance with the principles of human rights. This is most clearly illustrated by the role Vladimiro Montesinos played during the Fujimori years. As the de facto head of Peru's intelligence services, he acquired broad powers and became a key broker between Peru and the United States. He used this position to enrich himself while setting up a broad network of corruption, many members of which held important positions within the Peruvian government for more than a decade while U.S. officials largely turned a blind eye.

Stipulations on human rights, included in U.S.-Peruvian drug control agreements in the early 1990s, disappeared in later agreements signed after the unexpectedly impressive achievements of the mid-1990s in decreasing the area under coca cultivation. However, among the many paradoxes found in Peru's history of drug control efforts, these achievements were less the result of policy implementation than of external factors such as fluctuations in the international drug trade and market. The successes, moreover, were greatly outweighed by the massive collateral damage that the implementation of drug control policy caused to Peru's democratic process, its respect for human rights, and the nature and quality of its governance.

While the U.S. government has provided both diplomatic and econom-

ic support to the democratic transition now under way in Peru, paradoxical-
ly its drug control efforts are an additional source of political instability in
the Andean country. U.S. pressure to achieve drug policy goals is fostering
a volatile social climate in Peru's coca-growing regions, where vigorous
protests by coca growers are challenging the old eradication-based drug
control schemes. The complex and delicate social and political situation in
Peru requires that a balance be struck between a resolute struggle against
the criminal activity of drug trafficking on the one hand, and close attention
to the social and economic problems that shape the life of impoverished
farmers in the Andean Amazonian areas in Peru on the other.

• Antidrug Policies, Militarization, and Authoritarianism
At the end of the 1980s, just before President Fujimori came to power,
Peru's problems of drug trafficking, political violence, weak democracy,
and human rights violations were reaching a crisis point. In response to
Shining Path's armed insurgency, two successive Peruvian governments
ceded control of counterinsurgency strategy to the military. By the end of
the 1980s, about half of the country's territory and more than half the population had been placed under a state of emergency that suspended basic
civil liberties and subordinated civilian officials to the military. In these
parts of the country, massacres, disappearances, and extrajudicial executions carried out by the armed forces were commonplace; the insurgents
also committed horrendous atrocities. Although poor peasants were the primary victims of attack by both sides, the violence was increasingly felt in
more affluent urban areas as well.

    At the time, Peru was the world leader in coca leaf production and was
believed to supply 60 percent of the raw material worldwide used to make
cocaine. The estimated 18,000 hectares of coca that existed in the mid-
1970s increased in a decade to more than 200,000 hectares, mainly in the
Upper Huallaga Valley in the highland jungle of the departments of
Huánuco and San Martín.[4] Landless Andean peasants migrated to these
areas during the 1960s and 1970s when settlement programs were carried
out by reformist governments. The subsequent abandonment of the jungle
regions by later governments, the lack of markets for traditional crops, and
above all the increasing international demand for cocaine made coca cultivation a way for Peruvian farmers to meet their subsistence needs.

    The U.S.-inspired drug control policies of the 1980s, consisting mainly
of police interdiction and the forced eradication of coca crops, were not
only incapable of putting the brakes on increased coca farming; they actually seemed to contribute to it. In response to government pressure, farmers
began moving deeper into the jungle, planting coca in the Middle and
Lower Huallaga Valleys and Aguaytía. In addition, the valleys around the

Ene and Apurímac Rivers, where coca had been grown for traditional use, entered the cocaine production cycle in the 1990s when the prices for other products collapsed.[5]

Even more serious than the expansion of coca crops was the fact that police interdiction and forced eradication helped create favorable conditions for Shining Path to gain a foothold in the Upper Huallaga Valley. Police actions were generally accompanied by extortion and abuses committed against farmers, and the farmers saw forced eradication as a direct attack on their livelihood. The drug traffickers, meanwhile, instilled a climate of fear through the violence their hired guns perpetrated against the population. Shining Path members took advantage of the situation to present themselves as protectors of the coca farmers. Ultimately they were able to build a political and military force in the valley larger than those in any other parts of the country.[6]

Shining Path systematically attacked the police and unleashed a campaign against forced eradication that included killing members of eradication brigades. To prevent traffickers from abusing or cheating coca growers, the insurgents became middlemen in transactions between the two.[7] The United States labeled Shining Path members "narcoguerrillas." However, the insurgents were not just after the fast money to be made within the drug business. Their "uneasy working relationship" with the drug trade was part of their long-range goal of taking over the Peruvian state.[8]

By the late 1980s, the growth of Shining Path in the Upper Huallaga Valley, as well as nationally, had become a major problem for Peru. The military was generally opposed to the drug control operations that the police were carrying out in the Huallaga, arguing that these operations contributed to conflicts with the population. Much of the Peruvian military (and many others in government) distinguished clearly between coca farmers, drug traffickers, and Shining Path cadres. Most military officials maintained that the principal enemy was Shining Path and that defeating the insurgents meant depriving the insurgents of the population's support, even if this meant the temporary suspension of antidrug actions. Meanwhile, U.S. concern over Shining Path's advance was growing, but the United States refused to accept that drug control policies were somehow feeding the growth of the insurgent movement.

A Former Lawyer for Drug Traffickers
Takes on the Role of De Facto Drug Czar

At the end of President Alan García's term (1985–1990), the general perception both inside Peru and abroad was that the country was becoming ungovernable. This served to create fertile ground for the hard-line policies of President Alberto Fujimori. His election as a political independent represented a rejection of the traditional politicians and parties who had been incapable of resolving the country's problems, especially the spread of Shining Path and hyperinflation.

Fujimori dealt with the crisis he inherited from García in July 1990 by turning to the armed forces. The military had been extremely skeptical as to whether Fujimori, an inexperienced politician with no platform or party, could manage a country in the midst of crisis. Since the final days of García's term, military sectors had been plotting a coup to put themselves in power. The election of Fujimori, however, afforded them an opportunity to see their vision realized without resorting to a coup; together they negotiated a new path for the government. In return, Fujimori received from the military the political support that he otherwise lacked. Thus, from the time Fujimori took office, military officers enjoyed even more power than they had had during the two previous administrations. They soon became the principal political operators in the new regime.[9]

Former army captain Vladimiro Montesinos had a central role within this new regime. He had been expelled from the army in the 1970s for disobedience and falsification of documents, although his real crime had been to pass information on Peruvian military armaments to the U.S. Central Intelligence Agency (CIA). The original charge of treason was reduced in order to avoid creating problems for the high-ranking officers under whom Montesinos had served. The treason charges were reopened in the 1980s, however, and Montesinos fled the country.

He made his reappearance as a defense attorney for big-time drug traffickers. He also defended high-ranking police officials implicated in the Villa Coca case, one of Peru's biggest drug-trafficking and police corruption cases of the 1980s. Montesinos was also the principal legal strategist for army generals who ultimately escaped serious scrutiny or punishment for human rights violations committed during the counterinsurgency campaign.[10] He became Fujimori's top adviser after resolving some serious legal problems that had arisen for Fujimori during his presidential campaign.[11]

From his position as the new government's chief adviser on security and drug trafficking, Montesinos began his manipulation of the military and intelligence services. By the end of 1998, this process gave him complete control over the armed forces. Montesinos revamped the National Intelligence Service (SIN) and had an army general named as interior minister. He brought all the files and information on drug trafficking and subversion that had been collected by the Ministry of Interior's Intelligence Bureau (Digimin) to the SIN offices for his own use.

These events did not go unnoticed in Washington. One cable sent by the U.S. embassy in Lima stated, "There is substantial circumstantial evidence linking Montesinos to past narcotics activity." The cable added,

"Among the police and military figures recommended to the president by Montesinos are men with possible ties to drug-trafficking."[12] U.S. Ambassador Anthony Quainton reported that Montesinos was the "man behind the Fujimori throne" and noted that this former lawyer for drug traffickers had placed himself in charge of making policy on subversion, drug trafficking, human rights, and the military despite holding no official appointment.[13]

According to the respected Peruvian investigative journalist Gustavo Gorriti, the U.S. Drug Enforcement Administration (DEA) was extremely concerned about Montesinos's growing power. The CIA, however, had maintained a close relationship with Montesinos since 1990. It was happy to see one of its old collaborators attain such a high position, thus providing an opportunity to reestablish close contact with the Peruvian intelligence services. The CIA won the battle over the DEA. Increasing U.S. concern about the growth of Shining Path, and the perception that the Peruvian state in general and the military in particular were incapable of containing the threat, worked in Montesinos's favor.[14]

Montesinos took advantage of this scenario and of his links to the CIA to become a key interlocutor on security issues. There were people in Washington who were not at all uncomfortable with the idea of Montesinos taking "direct or indirect control of the principal nodes of Peruvian intelligence and the security forces." When others expressed concern, the response was: "As a former army officer, Montesinos is well equipped to advise President Fujimori on just how far he can deviate from the traditional promotion hierarchy in order to secure his hold over the country's military and police components."[15] Nevertheless, the relationship between Montesinos and Washington was full of tension and ambiguity because of issues related to democracy, human rights, and corruption.

From the Fujimori Doctrine to the Montesinos Doctrine

Despite his support from the CIA, Montesinos was not the head of Peruvian drug control policy at the beginning of Fujimori's regime. That position was first held by Hernando de Soto, a renowned economist who was chosen by Fujimori not only for his abilities but also for his top-level contacts in Washington.

Fujimori's original stance on U.S. drug control policy echoed that of the Peruvian military. He feared that strongly repressive measures against coca cultivation, especially forced eradication, would alienate the coca farmers and drive them into the arms of Shining Path. In September 1990, Fujimori refused to sign an antidrug agreement with Washington because it required measures he considered too harsh, even though it meant sacrificing U.S.$36 million in military aid.

De Soto drafted what became known as the Fujimori doctrine, which advocated the incorporation of coca farmers into the formal economy by granting them titles to their lands, which would then allow them to obtain credit for planting substitute crops. The coca growers and their organizations were also recognized as "valid interlocutors" for participation in drug control policy discussions. De Soto managed to keep Peru from being decertified during that year's annual U.S. evaluation of countries' antidrug efforts and represented Peru in negotiating a new drug control agreement signed in May 1991.

This agreement was a curious mix of U.S. demands and the Peruvian view: It recognized the need to provide the farmers with alternatives for income generation, but it also inserted the Peruvian military into antidrug operations to provide security.[16] Significantly, the United States was willing to see eradication suspended even while it continued to be the central principle of U.S. policy. The trade-off was that Peru would militarize its drug control activities. The militarized U.S. drug control strategy as embodied in the Andean Initiative found a perfect match in the militarization of the Peruvian state by Fujimori as part of his civil-military project.

The administration of George H. W. Bush also downplayed issues of corruption and human rights in order to be able to justify the continuation of drug control and economic aid to Peru. Immediately after signing the agreement, Washington affirmed that the Peruvian government showed no "systematic pattern of violations of human rights." However, the human rights situation continued to be dire under the Fujimori government. The U.S. Congress had begun to closely monitor the Peruvian situation and objected to releasing the counterdrug funding. The dispute between Congress and the administration resulted in the withholding of U.S.$10 million for counterinsurgency training, arms, and military equipment. The rest, nearly U.S.$25 million, was conditioned on specific improvements in human rights.[17]

Meanwhile, Montesinos had begun to manage the Peruvian side of the drug war from the shadows. Secure in his CIA connections—he regularly met with the CIA station chief in Lima at the time—he used his power in April 1991 to displace the DEA from its leadership position in the drug war in Peru, replacing it with the CIA.[18] In September of that same year, Montesinos called the heads of the National Police and Ministry of Interior to a meeting at the SIN offices to inform them that President Fujimori considered drug trafficking to be an issue of national security. He announced that the army would have primary responsibility for fighting it, that the two existing antidrug police units (the Antidrug Police and the Bureau of Illegal Drug Trafficking Investigations) would be combined into a single organization known as Dinandro, and that an antidrug section, known as Dinin, would be created within the SIN.[19] It appears that the decision to create the SIN antidrug unit was discussed not with the U.S. embassy in Lima but in

Washington.[20] The merger of the two police antidrug units to form Dinandro was also done on the recommendation of the United States.[21]

The SIN's Antinarcotics Intelligence Bureau, Dinin, began operations in September 1991 with CIA support. Montesinos later told Peruvian judicial authorities that the CIA supplied money and espionage equipment to three SIN departments, including the Dinin, each of which had special agents working under CIA supervision.[22] The U.S. embassy never confirmed nor denied the CIA support, but it did eventually reveal that the State Department had channeled small amounts of funding to SIN for its antidrug work.[23] Retired National Police general Dennis del Castillo, who headed the Dinin in 2000, testified that his office received training support and intelligence-gathering equipment from the United States.[24]

Montesinos also created a parallel intelligence network in the Upper Huallaga Valley. General Jaime Ríos Araico, head of the Peruvian army's Huallaga Front at the time, has stated that an intelligence unit from Lima operated in his area from early 1991, but he was never informed what their mission or their functions were. According to Ríos Araico, SIN established direct contacts with the regional military intelligence officers. Other intelligence services over which Montesinos was gaining influence and control also stepped up operations in the Huallaga. In 1993, the Army Intelligence Service (SIE) set up eight intelligence units used exclusively for gathering information on drug trafficking in the Upper Huallaga.[25]

In September 1991, the police in the Upper Huallaga were placed under the command of the Upper Huallaga Political-Military Command for antidrug and antiterrorism operations.[26] Two months later, President Fujimori issued a decree formally incorporating the military into the drug war.[27] A military presence had existed in the Upper Huallaga since the end of the 1980s, but it was restricted to fighting Shining Path. The new decree not only broadened the military's mandate and powers but also confused the role of the police with that of the armed forces. Counterinsurgency was officially combined with drug control activities.

De Soto resigned his post in January 1992, claiming that the Fujimori doctrine was being corrupted and sabotaged from within the government. He said that state agents were responsible for the widely publicized murder of Walter Tocas, a coca grower leader who had supported the government's original, less aggressive approach. De Soto also reproached Fujimori for repeatedly rebuffing his requests for a meeting to coordinate counterdrug policy.[28] It appears that Fujimori's priorities changed in response to a convergence of interests. The militarization of the state and of drug control, with Montesinos as the principal operator, together with the Peruvian government's need for U.S. political support, led to the abandonment of the initial priority given to alternative development for coca farmers.

Nevertheless, Washington continued to be suspicious of Montesinos and of corruption within the armed forces. The military's participation in drug control activities allowed its members to move at will throughout the coca-growing zones. As they did so, they formed alliances with drug traffickers and the coca-growing population in order to isolate Shining Path. The Fujimori regime in turn blackmailed high-ranking military officers involved in drug trafficking and other criminal activities in order to obtain political control over them.[29]

The first Bush administration was aware of the extent of military corruption in the Upper Huallaga. A May 1991 report noted that while corruption was endemic to Peru, corruption linked to drug trafficking was rampant in the coca-producing areas. Police and judicial authorities were implicated as well as the army, according to the report, but army corruption was "more organized." "Unit commanders offer protection to airports and safe passage for traffickers. In some cases, the profits from narcotics skimming are used to feed the troops.... The skim may be in the form of contributions from local merchants with narcotics interests or direct payment from traffickers."[30] Washington policymakers considered, correctly, that corruption weakened drug control efforts, but they did not appear to accept that this was the result of misguided policies. They continued to claim that corruption existed only at the individual level, not as an institutional problem.

Tensions between Peru and the United States increased during the final year of the Bush administration. Before the January 1992 presidential summit in San Antonio, Texas, Washington again raised questions about Montesinos's background. The U.S. embassy in Lima reported that there were recurring allegations against Montesinos but that the evidence was inconclusive.[31] In San Antonio, Fujimori reacted strongly against Bush's proposal to create a multinational counterdrug force and criticized U.S. funding for alternative development as insufficient.[32] When asked about corruption in the Peruvian military, he responded by accusing the DEA of being corrupt.

The Autogolpe: Antidrug Policy as Escape Valve

The civil-military regime headed by Fujimori assumed its true shape on April 5, 1992. In what came to be known as the *autogolpe* (a coup against oneself), he shuttered congress and the judiciary, suspended the constitution, and installed a "government of national reconstruction." The sense conveyed by the term *autogolpe* is that Fujimori in effect staged a coup d'état against his own government. It became clear that the military officers were not only Fujimori's most important source of political support but also had an active role in governing the country. Fujimori implemented the military's long-standing demands for dealing with Shining Path. He reorganized the state to create mechanisms that would guarantee impunity for officials involved in the counterinsurgency campaign. He also enacted antiterrorism legislation providing for severe punishment of anyone even remotely suspected of terrorism, clearly violating fundamental human rights norms.

The authors of the autogolpe miscalculated the reactions of the international community. Assistant Secretary of State for Inter-American Affairs Bernard Aronson arrived in Lima the very day of the autogolpe. He immediately distanced himself from Fujimori and declared the Bush administration's strong opposition to the Peruvian president's action. This ultimately led to the suspension of all aid to Peru with the exception of humanitarian and antidrug disbursements.[33]

The Fujimori government's reaction was to give the Peruvian air force control of all the airstrips in the coca-growing regions and the authority to intercept any and all national or foreign aircraft in those areas.[34] He also ordered the army to double the number of battalions assigned to the Upper Huallaga Valley. This reinforcement of military control in the coca-growing regions was meant to neutralize U.S. resistance to the "coup" through the show of increased drug control efforts.

A few days after the April 5 autogolpe, the Peruvian air force opened fire on a U.S. C-130H plane engaged in photographing clandestine airstrips and cocaine laboratories in the Upper Huallaga. The plane was forced to land, and one crew member was killed. According to a cable from the U.S. embassy in Lima cited in *Newsweek*, there was no doubt that the Peruvian pilots knew they were firing on a U.S. military plane. According to *Newsweek*, "Some Pentagon officials speculated that the Peruvians fired because they suspected the Americans of spying on secret dealings between corrupt Peruvian military officers and traffickers."[35]

However, as *Newsweek* pointed out, neither the Peruvian nor the U.S. government wanted to dwell on the incident and risk further compromising their relationship. There was too much at stake: the United States wanted to maintain its drug control program, and the Peruvians desperately needed U.S. support to avoid international isolation in the wake of the autogolpe. Nevertheless, the incident weakened the Fujimori government's standing in the U.S. Congress. A rare consensus between Republicans and Democrats emerged. Republicans were not only upset by the plane incident but also skeptical of Peru's commitment to the drug war, and Democrats were critical of Fujimori's human rights record.

The result was the suspension for several years of the bulk of military aid to Peru. Only drug control aid continued, managed by the State Department's Bureau for International Narcotics and Law Enforcement Affairs (INL). This financed the Peruvian air force's airport control program through an agreement signed in July 1992.[36]

U.S. pressure on Peru to return to the democratic fold was reduced after the annual meeting of the Organization of American States (OAS) in the Bahamas in June 1992. Fujimori unexpectedly attended the meeting and committed himself to a timeline for "democratic reinstitutionalization," including seating a constituent assembly to draft a new constitution. For many of Fujimori's opponents, however, the only true show of "democratization" would have been the removal of Montesinos from government. In fact, Montesinos retained his power and used the autogolpe to consolidate military (and his own) control over Peru's drug control policy. On July 21, he ordered that from that date forward, all agencies involved in drug control would have to follow orders from the Armed Forces Operational Command. A second decree published that same day consolidated Montesinos's absolute control over the armed forces and police intelligence services.[37]

The arrest in early September 1992 of Shining Path founder and leader Abimael Guzmán provided the Fujimori administration with some crucial breathing room. While the autogolpe itself did not appear to have helped contain the insurgents, after Guzmán's arrest Shining Path was no longer perceived as a threat to the Peruvian state. Soon after the arrest, on November 13, the government easily quashed an alleged attempted coup led by the retired general Jaime Salinas. With Salinas and his allies behind bars, Montesinos had eliminated the last significant group within the armed forces opposed to his growing influence and power.[38] Meanwhile, General Nicolás Hermoza Ríos, army commander and head of the joint chiefs of staff, joined Fujimori and Montesinos as the third member of a governing triumvirate. Recognizing that he controlled the nation's firepower, the general quickly began to carve out his own power niche and "his own brand of corruption."[39] With all obstacles out of the way, the triumvirate consolidated itself: Fujimori as political boss, Hermoza Ríos as military commander, and Montesinos as intelligence chief.

In late 1992, the administration held elections for the eighty-member Constituent Assembly. The arrests of Shining Path's Guzmán and of the founder of a smaller rebel group, the Tupac Amaru Revolutionary Movement, several months earlier helped Fujimori and his allies win a majority of contested seats. The new constitution written by the Constituent Assembly was approved in a 1993 referendum. For Fujimori and Montesinos, its most significant new provision was one that allowed the president to run for immediate reelection. This opened the door for Fujimori to seek the presidency again in 1995.

The Rise of Peru's Drug Czar

In 1993, the new Clinton administration in Washington began to make strategic changes in drug control policy toward Peru. It suspended funding for the principal antidrug base in the Upper Huallaga.[40] This was replaced by the concept of mobile bases for interdiction operations, which consisted mainly of bombing clandestine airstrips in the Upper Huallaga Valley and controlling river and air traffic. At the same time, the Justice Department began its Support Justice IV program, which consisted of a ground radar system in Yurimaguas and air radar installed at several Peruvian military bases in the jungle. Operated by U.S. military personnel, the radars were intended to monitor drug trafficking activity and to aid in planning and carrying out air interdiction operations.[41]

An air interdiction program had existed in Peru since the early 1990s, but operations were temporarily suspended several times for different reasons. It was suspended after the C-130H aircraft incident in 1992 and again in 1994 on the recommendation of the Justice Department because of possible legal problems with the programs. The border war between Ecuador and Peru that began in early 1995 forced yet another suspension. The program resumed in October 1995. With assistance from the CIA and the Pentagon, Peruvian air force fighter planes began intercepting aircraft suspected of transporting drugs or money for drug traffickers.

Montesinos actively collaborated with the revised U.S. antidrug policy, apparently attempting to neutralize doubts about himself as well as questions about Peruvian government policies deemed undemocratic or inimical to human rights. A new crisis had surfaced in 1993, when General Rodolfo Robles, number three in the army hierarchy, publicly denounced the existence of a death squad, the Colina Group, which he claimed was directly linked to Montesinos and General Hermoza Ríos. He accused the death squad of the 1992 kidnapping and killing of nine students and a professor from La Cantuta University and of the Barrios Altos massacre the year before, where fifteen people were murdered at a party in downtown Lima only a few blocks from the presidential palace. Robles was forced to flee the country. General Hermoza Ríos brought tanks into the streets of Lima to intimidate the Peruvian Congress, which was investigating the accusation by Robles.

The Clinton administration took a critical view of these events. Clinton had named people sensitive to human rights issues to key high-level posts, including on the National Security Council. Nevertheless, the concern over human rights abuses was never sufficient to outweigh the commitment to drug control policy in U.S. government discussions on Peru.

Internal debate within the Clinton administration continued, however. At the request of Representative Dan Glickman, then head of the Permanent Select Committee on Intelligence in the U.S. House of Representatives, an interagency working group was created in late 1994 to examine the U.S. relationship with Vladimiro Montesinos and SIN. The administration officials participating in the group weighed the benefits of ongoing collaboration—continued access to the most powerful elements in the Fujimori administration as well as intelligence information—against the possible risks of U.S. association with individuals and agencies implicated in human rights abuses, drug trafficking, and other forms of corruption. According to one former official, when the CIA was questioned about links between Montesinos and drug trafficking, it maintained that it had "no credible information" to substantiate such claims.[42]

The CIA, which defended the working relationship with Montesinos, won the internal debate within the administration. Guidance was issued to "downgrade slightly" the relationship and to exert greater control over U.S. officials' contact with Montesinos via the ambassador. However, for all practical purposes the relationship was maintained and continued to flourish over the next five years. The internal debate over Montesinos within the administration largely subsided. During this same time, however, the Peruvian army intelligence service, SIE, came under scrutiny because of its suspected ties to the Colina death squad, and a decision was made to suspend all U.S. support for the unit.

Despite lingering doubts, Fujimori's 1995 reelection helped assuage concerns in Washington that the country was moving out of the democratic orbit. Fujimori handily won the election, which was certified as free and fair by OAS observers, receiving more than double the votes of his closest competitor, former UN Secretary-General Javier Pérez de Cuéllar. In addition, his political coalition won nearly two-thirds of the 120 seats in the country's unicameral legislature.

Over the course of President Fujimori's second five-year term, U.S. counterdrug assistance to Peru steadily increased (see Figure 6.1). A plethora of U.S. agencies were then operating in the country, including the DEA, the CIA, the U.S. Customs Service, and the National Security Agency. The Pentagon supported the operation of counterdrug bases and riverine interdiction programs, trained local forces, and maintained equipment, working primarily with the Peruvian air force and navy. More than 100 U.S. personnel were assigned to the air interdiction program and "as many as 175 U.S. military and intelligence personnel were deployed for short intervals in order to train Peruvians for anti-drug missions."[43]

The Clinton White House began placing increased priority on drug control, taking advantage of the political will of the Peruvian government to cooperate with such programs. A steep and continued drop in coca prices in the Upper Huallaga Valley began in mid-1995, attributed by the drug control bureaucracy to the air bridge denial program. The State Department reported that drug flights had been reduced by 47 percent compared to 1994 and that total land used for coca cultivation had also dropped.[44] This supposed success added to the regime's political capital.

That same year Fujimori accepted a number of U.S. demands in a new drug control agreement. The most significant demand was to restart the

Figure 6.1   U.S. Aid to Peru, 1997–2005

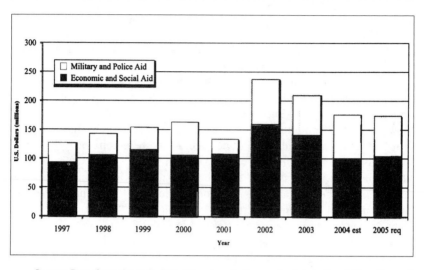

Source: Data from the U.S. State Department, Bureau for International Narcotics and Law Enforcement Affairs, *International Narcotics Control Strategy Report*, various years. Please see WOLA website, www.wola.org, for full listing.

eradication campaigns, and these indeed began again in August 1996.[45] The new agreement, unlike those signed in the early 1990s, contained no references to human rights. In another change specified in the new agreement, the Peruvian army was pulled out of drug control activities in April 1996, while the air force and navy continued to play a role.

Montesinos's role as a broker for Peruvian antidrug policies gained greater acceptance as the U.S. government began to see results. Although he never held an official title within the Fujimori administration, by the mid-1990s Montesinos was commonly referred to as the Peruvian "drug czar." He took full advantage of this reputation to consolidate his role as the primary interlocutor with U.S. officials on drug policy issues.

Montesinos made his first public appearance as a representative of the Fujimori government in October 1996 during a visit to Peru by the U.S. drug czar, the retired general Barry McCaffrey, director of the White House's Office of National Drug Control Policy. Illustrative of Montesinos's power is the fact that he had selected the Peruvian authorities who were to meet with McCaffrey.[46] During his stint as head of the U.S. Southern Command, McCaffrey had met with Fujimori several times and often praised the Peruvian president. "I have tremendous admiration for Alberto Fujimori," he once said. He had dubbed what was happening in

Peru "revolutionary," "without historical precedent," and "impressive."[47] At the October 22 meeting, he went even farther when, in halting Spanish, he congratulated Montesinos for his role in the drug war.[48]

McCaffrey's visit came in the midst of a string of scandals affecting the Peruvian administration. On May 10, a shipment of 170 kilograms of cocaine was discovered on the air force plane that Fujimori normally had used as his presidential aircraft and whose pilot was close to the president. Shortly thereafter, on July 3, 45 kilograms of cocaine were seized from a Peruvian navy ship in Vancouver, Canada, and another 92 kilograms were found when the ship returned to Peru.[49] Accusations linking Montesinos to drug trafficking surfaced at the same time. At the beginning of August, the Mexican daily *La Reforma*, citing U.S. antidrug sources, wrote that Montesinos had protected a Peruvian drug-trafficking clan, the López Paredes, until their organization was dismantled in 1995. Finally, in mid-August, accused kingpin Demetrio Chávez, known as "El Vaticano," told a court that he had been paying Montesinos U.S.$50,000 a month for protection of his drug-trafficking operations.

In response to the allegations published in *La Reforma*, the U.S. embassy in Lima sent a letter to the Peruvian government denying that a U.S. drug control source had information linking any "high-ranking Peruvian authorities" to drug trafficking. The U.S. ambassador also sent a cable to Washington stating that after a careful investigation the diplomatic mission had reached the conclusion that Chávez's accusations against Montesinos were spurious. The cable speculated that behind the accusations there might be large drug-trafficking interests seeking to destroy a powerful enemy and tarnish the intelligence service, perhaps even "rogue military or police officials jealous of Montesinos' power or who, like the traffickers, hoped to remove a check on their corrupt practices."[50] When asked about the issue, McCaffrey said that Peru had the sovereign right to chose its own authorities and that the United States had no reason to intervene.[51] Given the circumstances, McCaffrey's visit was seen as public support for Montesinos, a "gringo blessing," according to the weekly magazine *Caretas*.[52]

The dust from McCaffrey's visit had not yet settled when rival drug control forces clashed in an event similar to the force-down of the C-130H by the Peruvian air force in 1992. On October 26, 1996, a SIN counterintelligence team raided a radio listening post operated by the Dinandro drug police that was part of Operation Pajarito. This operation, run by the DEA, tracked drug traffickers' radio communications to and from their bases in the coca-growing areas. SIN claimed to believe that the post was being run by drug traffickers or terrorists. The head of Dinandro and his police commander in charge of the operation, however, later testified that SIN was perfectly aware that it was raiding a DEA center.[53]

The motivation behind the raid remains unclear. A number of theories were tendered. Some said that the SIN suspected that its telephone communications were being monitored by the listening post. Others speculated that it was a ruse of Montesinos to deflect attention from investigations into his doings, or revenge for the DEA raids on the presidential plane and the cocaine-laden boat earlier in the year. Yet others hypothesized that its objective was to paralyze aerial interception and give the trafficking groups time to regroup, or that it stemmed from competition between the CIA and the DEA.

Whatever the explanation for the raid, it is clear that the listening post was absolutely crucial to air interdiction operations. It transmitted information to the military radar bases in the jungle that then tracked suspect aircraft. The police commander stated that after the SIN raid, during the few months that Operation Pajarito was out of commission, the operational capacity of the air interdiction program was severely curtailed in its ability to intercept suspicious aircraft. The two officials mentioned above stated that Montesinos feared the DEA;[54] the U.S. agency had reopened its investigation of him in the wake of Vaticano's accusations.[55] The DEA complained bitterly about the raid.[56] As with the earlier C-130H incident, however, there were few repercussions. In fact, the raid only became public several years later.

The high point of Montesinos's visible power came in March 1997 when he called a meeting of Peru's top authorities to discuss drug control, inviting the new U.S. ambassador, Denis Jett, to participate. Attending the meeting were the presidents of congress and the supreme court, the attorney general, the interior and defense ministers, the commanders of the three military branches, and other high-level authorities. Jett commented in a report to Washington, "SIN sponsorship and organization of this extraordinarily high-level meeting suggests counterdrug coordination is increasingly and more effectively being handled by the intelligence agency, headed in practice by powerful SIN principal adviser Dr. Vladimiro Montesinos."[57]

Montesinos was perfectly aware of how much power he was accumulating through the drug issue and how he could use it for not only personal but also political gain. In a meeting with the commanders of the three military branches at SIN offices, Montesinos said, "We have shown that when we get tough on the drug trafficking issue, they [the United States] lower their guard."[58] In other words, Montesinos realized that the implementation of drug control policies gave him leverage with the United States—whenever he threatened to suspend some forms of collaboration, the United States would quickly reach an accommodation on the matter at hand.

Decline, Authoritarianism, and Fraud

The Fujimori government used its control over the legislative and judicial branches to pave the way for yet a third electoral bid. In 1996 the congress passed an "authentic interpretation law" providing a reinterpretation of the Peruvian Constitution, despite its lack of any formal authority to enact such a measure. This law asserted that Fujimori had been elected in 1990 under one constitution but that since his 1995 election was under another constitution he could still run for reelection one more time. Congress thwarted a petition drive to allow a referendum on this issue. In 1997, lawmakers also impeached three members of the Constitutional Court who voted to declare the authentic interpretation law unconstitutional. The court, for all practical purposes, was rendered inoperative.

That same year, a Peruvian TV station reported that an officer with SIE had been murdered and one of her colleagues brutally tortured by fellow SIE agents after the victims had been accused of leaking sensitive information to the media. The station also reported that Montesinos, who claimed to receive no salary from the Peruvian government, had millions of dollars in undisclosed bank accounts. Not only did these revelations go uninvestigated by the justice system and congress; the TV station that had aired the story was illegally confiscated from its owner.

Although Washington strongly criticized the Fujimori government in internal communications, it maintained public silence. A State Department cable sent to embassies in Latin America noted: "These latest incidents conform to a pattern of arrogant, authoritarian behavior evident in Montesinos' large and unexplained income, continuous harassment of opposition figures and journalists, and the grisly murder of an army intelligence agent and the torture of another by their own organization."[59] Ambassador Jett sent a cable from Lima to Washington describing the situation in Peru as "a slow-motion coup d'état" aimed at eliminating all individual and institutional opposition to Fujimori's reelection.[60] After Jett's arrival in Lima, the embassy began making strong general statements on democracy and human rights. Jett's position on these issues, however, was counterbalanced by Washington's praise of the positive results in drug control and public silence concerning Montesinos. Several years later, Ambassador Jett admitted that he had no alternative but to negotiate with Montesinos, as he was designated by the Peruvian government as the principal interlocutor on drug policy.[61]

In April 1998, U.S. drug czar McCaffrey made a return visit to Peru. This time, Montesinos leaked a video to the media that showed him allegedly briefing McCaffrey on the drug situation. In response, McCaffrey publicly criticized Montesinos—who was then coordinating Fujimori's second reelection bid—for using the visit for political purposes and to strengthen his own image, and he distanced himself from his Peruvian counterpart.

Montesinos reacted to what he called "severe and unjust" criticism from McCaffrey by temporarily suspending the exchange of intelligence with the United States. He informed the embassy that no information would change hands until the United States officially recognized the contribution he had made to the war on drugs.[62] This was one of the lowest moments in diplomatic relations between the two nations since 1992, and relations remained frosty until Ambassador Jett left in mid-1999.

However, criticism of human rights policies and antidemocratic measures under Fujimori began to grow toward the end of the 1990s as the Peruvian president's reelection effort intensified. In mid-1999, the U.S. Congress harshly criticized the SIN for carrying out actions incompatible with human rights, the rule of law, and democracy, and expressed concern about U.S. aid going to SIN.[63] For the first time, the U.S. Senate asked to be informed before any funds were sent to the Peruvian intelligence agency.[64] At the same time, Peru's image as successfully prosecuting the drug war began to tarnish. In August 1999, in testimony to the U.S. Congress, McCaffrey admitted that there had been "a deterioration in the fight against drugs and in alternative development in Peru." He attributed the setbacks to an increase in coca prices, meaning more farmers would return to coca cultivation, and changes in drug-trafficking routes, as traffickers adapted their methods to evade the interdiction apparatus currently in place.[65]

A few days after his testimony to Congress, McCaffrey paid another visit to Peru. The U.S. embassy in Lima insisted that, in spite of events during the previous visit, it was crucial to U.S. interests that McCaffrey meet with Montesinos. The statement argued that "there is no one who stands toe-to-toe with Montesinos in the Peruvian government and nothing that the government does on intelligence, enforcement, and security issues occurs without his blessing." It also noted that Montesinos had made overtures toward a new meeting with McCaffrey, "presumably to clear the air."[66] McCaffrey agreed to meet with Montesinos in private, after which he again expressed his "admiration" for the Peruvian government's drug control efforts and his "recognition" of the contribution by the country's intelligence services. He did also refer to human rights concerns, saying: "I have met with Mr. Montesinos to hear his opinions and ideas, to praise the achievements of the Peruvian government, and to categorically and publicly express my close relationship with the human rights community."[67]

The effects of McCaffrey's visit were felt a few weeks later. SIN took charge of the Commission to Fight Drug Consumption (Contradrogas), the Peruvian agency in charge of combating drug use and promoting alternative development. Named as its new executive director was General Ibsen del Castillo of the National Police, who had worked in SIN's antidrug section between 1992 and 1997. One of the new tasks of Contradrogas under del Castillo was to support the coca eradication efforts carried out by the Ministry of Interior, although this did not fall within its area of responsibility. That year, Peru eradicated more coca than ever before (13,800 hectares compared to 7,825 in 1998).[68]

The new U.S. ambassador, John Hamilton, took a much more conciliatory approach to the Peruvian government than had Ambassador Jett, and the embassy's public criticism of Peruvian antidemocratic actions ceased. Montesinos had asked McCaffrey if the United States could intercede on his behalf to facilitate a meeting with human rights activists. In response, Hamilton attempted to bring Montesinos together with the Human Rights Ombudsman's Office and human rights groups. While the ombudsman's office accepted the offer, the National Human Rights Coordinating Committee rejected the idea of negotiating in private with the man they believed to be the principal source of corruption and human rights violations in Peru.[69]

The Fall of Peru's Drug Czar

In June 2000, Fujimori won a third presidential term in elections held in spite of allegations of electoral fraud and enormous popular protest. He had the open support of the country's armed forces. OAS election observers at first refused to validate the elections, and the international community did not recognize the legitimacy of his mandate. After intense negotiations, however, the OAS agreed not to question the elections if Fujimori promised to negotiate with opposition groups to draw up a timetable for the "democratization" of Peru. The United States, which had declared its neutrality during the controversial electoral cycle, supported this solution.

Protests continued at home, however, led by Alejandro Toledo, who had been Fujimori's principal opponent in the 2000 elections and who would become president himself in 2001. Fujimori's third inauguration was one of the most violent in the country's history, with six people killed and scores injured. Still on shaky ground because of the questionable election and violent inauguration, Fujimori and Montesinos held a press conference in the Presidential Palace on August 21, 2000. They announced that Peru had dismantled a criminal gang that had, since 1999, funneled 10,000 AK-47 assault rifles to the Revolutionary Armed Forces of Colombia (FARC) guerrillas. They claimed that the operation had involved corrupt members of the Peruvian military, international arms brokers, and operatives in Jordan, where the weapons had originally been purchased.

Fujimori attributed the success in discovering and dismantling the smuggling ring to Montesinos and SIN. He also praised them for contributing to a significant reduction in drug trafficking, as recognized even by the U.S. government. Fujimori also criticized U.S. Secretary of State Madeleine Albright for not stopping in Peru during her Latin American tour in spite of the contribution Peru had made to regional security by capturing the arms.

The Jordanians immediately rejected Fujimori's version of events. The Colombian government discounted the story as fantasy, and soon it appeared that Montesinos himself was linked to the alleged smuggling operation.[70] Montesinos's star was on the decline. The final blow came in mid-September 2000, only six weeks after the inauguration, when a small opposition party made public a videotape that showed Montesinos paying an opposition lawmaker U.S.$14,000 to switch political sides in congress and thereby swell the ranks of Fujimori's majority. Fujimori accepted defeat. On September 16, 2000, he announced that he would call new elections, deactivate the SIN, and fire Montesinos.

A week later, Montesinos fled to Panama, where the Organization of American States, the U.S. government, and several South American heads of state were working hard to convince the Panamanians to grant Montesinos political asylum. Only then did the U.S. government break off its ties with him. The secretary of state issued a directive to U.S. embassies, saying, "We no longer view Montesinos as having any role in the Peruvian government. Furthermore, there should be no [U.S. government] contact with Montesinos."[71] Despite the continuing efforts of Ambassador Hamilton to help Montesinos find political asylum, the latter returned to Peru in October 2000 after spending only a month in Panama. He was not seen during his brief stay in Lima, fleeing again aboard a yacht and eventually making his way to Venezuela. In June 2001 he was arrested in Caracas, the Venezuelan capital, with the help of the FBI and was quickly extradited to Peru. He has been in prison since, facing more than sixty separate court cases. Despite Montesinos's removal from the government, antidrug cooperation between the United States and Peru remained unchanged.

• Paradoxes in Peru's Drug Control Policy

After the fall of Fujimori, the extent of the web of corruption spun by his regime became increasingly clear. Of particular importance for U.S. policy were the level of corruption within the armed forces and the charges of drug trafficking, arms smuggling, and human rights abuses against Montesinos. But other paradoxes also emerged. The reduction in coca production that was put forward by both the U.S. and Peruvian governments to show the "success" of counterdrug efforts was a result of outside market forces—not eradication efforts. Eradication campaigns, moreover, also produced reactions from growers that ultimately made them unsustainable.

From Campanilla to Tijuana

Under Montesinos's management of Peruvian drug control policy, the armed forces were officially responsible for pursuing not only Shining Path insurgents but also drug traffickers. Though there had been many earlier accusations of involvement by members of the Peruvian military in drug

The CIA and Drug Traffickers

The case of Peru's Vladimiro Montesinos was not the only time in Latin America that an individual or organization involved in criminal activity, including drug trafficking, maintained a working relationship with the CIA. During the Cold War, the CIA partnered with individuals involved in drug trafficking throughout the region—generally high-level military and police officials—often rewarding their service as intelligence assets directly and by turning a blind eye to their criminal activities. Following are some of the most notorious examples of CIA connections in Central America:

Nicaragua

After the leftist Sandinistas overthrew Nicaragua's Somoza dictatorship in 1979, the CIA hatched a plan to form, finance, and train a counterrevolutionary force, known as the Contras, to dislodge them. A Senate investigation found that the CIA was fully aware of drug smuggling carried out by the Contras and their suppliers:

> Individuals who provided support for the Contras were involved in drug trafficking, the supply network of the Contras was used by drug trafficking organizations, and elements of the Contras themselves knowingly received financial and material assistance from drug traffickers. In each case, one or another agency of the U.S. government had information regarding the involvement.[72]

Panama

The dictator Manuel Noriega, a paid CIA informant since 1968, was a staunch anticommunist ally in the region. He was particularly helpful in the early to mid-1980s against the Sandinistas, smuggling guns to the Contras and allowing the CIA to establish a Contra training camp in Panama.[73]

In 1986 reporter Seymour Hersh wrote in the *New York Times* that Noriega "is extensively involved in illicit money laundering and drug activities" and that an unnamed White House official "said that the most significant drug running in Panama was being directed by General Noriega." He was implicated in arms-for-cocaine deals with Colombian cartels, whom he allowed to operate cocaine processing labs in the Panamanian jungle bordering Colombia. The CIA knew of his involvement in drug trafficking as early as 1972.[74]

Even so, it was not until the U.S. intelligence community discovered that Noriega was sharing intelligence with Fidel Castro that the ties were finally broken; in December 1989, U.S. armed forces invaded Panama and brought Noriega to Miami to stand trial for drug crimes. He was convicted on eight counts of racketeering, drug trafficking, and money laundering.

Guatemala

The CIA has a long and sordid history in Guatemala, where it supported a military coup against democratically elected president Jacobo Arbenz in 1954 and later financed a 1982 coup led by General Efraín Ríos Montt.[75] Throughout the forty-year civil war and in the decade since it ended, members of the Guatemalan military have enjoyed absolute impunity for human rights violations and criminal dealings, including drug trafficking.

An extensive network of military officers waging the counterinsurgency war took advantage of their positions to engage in trafficking along air, land, and sea routes. Two top drug traffickers were Generals Manuel Callejas y Callejas and Luis Francisco Ortega Menaldo, both of whom worked in Guatemalan intelligence and covert operations against guerrillas. Guatemalan military intelligence received surveillance equipment from the CIA and DEA, allegedly using it to further their own smuggling activities and to spy on their opponents. Many of the same military personnel involved in drug trafficking were the perpetrators of serious human rights crimes; some of them were on the CIA payroll.

—Laurie Freeman and Eileen Rosin

trafficking, military corruption linked to drug trafficking in Peru probably reached its highest level ever during this time. At least two factors contributed to this phenomenon. First, under Fujimori, corruption was used as a tool for gaining political control over the armed forces. Second, the militarization of the war on drugs brought the armed forces into closer contact with the drug traffickers with whom they collaborated against their common enemy, Shining Path.[76]

As detailed above, Washington was kept informed about such practices of corruption and presumably pushed the Peruvian government to investigate those allegations. However, the Fujimori administration never undertook a vigorous investigation. One of the major objectives of Fujimori's autogolpe in April 1992 was to gain absolute political control over the judiciary and the congress; this control allowed Montesinos to manipulate the law and the institutions charged with upholding it to block investigations of his actions and secure impunity for them. He averted any official independent investigation into his bank accounts and into other accusations such as human rights violations.

Montesinos also controlled the sectors within the judiciary and attorney general's office in charge of hearing drug trafficking cases. In September 1996, a system of special courts for drug trafficking cases was established. When its judges demonstrated a surprising amount of independence, the special courts were quickly replaced by a new criminal court division in the supreme court, visibly under his control. Using his control over the justice sector, Montesinos created an extortion network that sold judicial rulings.[77] He was also able to control high-profile cases, such as the ones involving drugs found on the presidential plane and a navy ship mentioned above. Only low-level military personnel were prosecuted for these cases.[78]

Only with the advent of the democratic transition were official investigations initiated into the activities of the former adviser and others in the Fujimori government. At least three congressional commissions appointed by the Peruvian Congress after Fujimori's fall to investigate corruption in the previous government unveiled the extent to which drug-related corruption proliferated during the Fujimori era and Montesinos's role in it.[79]

As documented by these commissions, the case of Demetrio Limoniel Chávez Peñaherrera, the drug trafficker known as El Vaticano, amply illustrates the depth of involvement by Montesinos and the military in corruption linked to the drug trade. Vaticano testified before the Peruvian Congress that between 1990 and 1992 he operated the Campanilla airstrip, one of the most important drug trafficking routes in the Upper Huallaga for supplying raw material to Colombia. According to his account, he did so with the protection of Montesinos and Hermoza Ríos and with the complicity of lower-ranking officers stationed at the Punta Arenas military base.[80]

Vaticano testified that he paid Montesinos U.S.$3,000–5,000 per flight for a total of 280 flights over that period, plus U.S.$50,000 per month from July 1991 through May 1992. He said that the deal also included lending his help against Shining Path, and his men worked with the military to keep the insurgents from entering the zone. Finally, Vaticano claimed that his money bought him information that allowed him to evade DEA raids.[81]

The Herrera Commission, following earlier findings of the Waisman and Townsend Commissions, concluded that cases such as Vaticano's show how Montesinos used his position of power within the government to form "a network to engage in illicit drug trafficking and money laundering."[82] The commission also sustained that "the management of information was Vladimiro Montesinos' principal instrument of participation in the illicit drug trade."[83] Accusations were made not only against Montesinos, however. According to the commission, the SIN also played a role in the drug-trafficking network, as did former president Fujimori, who "permitted . . .

the development of this network which connected the state with illicit drug trafficking."[84]

Several of the more than sixty legal proceedings against Montesinos involve direct and indirect links to drug trafficking.[85] The most serious accusation is that Montesinos himself was a major drug trafficker in Peru between 1994 and 2000. Although most of the cases are only now coming to trial, these charges are gradually being verified. Some court cases came to trial in early 2004, and others were continuing to make their way through the courts.

Earlier, in May 2003, a judge in the anticorruption court began legal proceedings in which Montesinos was accused of being the Peruvian connection to Mexico's Tijuana cartel, allegedly heading up the cartel's operations in Peru. According to the initial proceedings, Montesinos trafficked cocaine under cartel auspices to Europe disguised as exports made by phantom companies. Court documents claim that Montesinos used army helicopters to ferry supplies for producing cocaine and the finished product between the coast and the coca-growing valleys. He also allegedly used army installations and the SIN offices to meet with the heads of Peruvian and international drug cartels, including Tijuana.[86]

Another serious accusation against Montesinos is the case of dealing arms to the Colombia guerrillas. Among the many testimonies directly linking him to the FARC deal mentioned earlier is that of Sarkis Soghanalian, the Lebanese-born arms dealer who brokered the agreement with Jordan. He claimed to have negotiated directly with Montesinos in the belief that it was the Peruvian government that was buying the AK-47s.[87] According to statements from a former FARC guerrilla, the Colombian rebels directly paid Montesinos U.S.$8 million for the weapons.[88] Many in Peru question what the CIA in particular knew about the illicit arms sale and when they knew it.

The Herrera Commission's report states that there is sufficient evidence to determine that the trafficking of arms to the FARC was an operation "designed, planned and executed within the National Intelligence Service with the direct participation of Vladimiro Montesinos." Moreover, government funds were illegally diverted from the armed forces to SIN to facilitate the operation. Finally, the commission concluded that individuals and networks involved in illegal activity connected to Montesinos and the armed forces were brought in to help carry out the arms trafficking deal. They were, according to the commission, "involved in suspicious activity related to drug trafficking and money laundering, for which they were under the surveillance of the DEA ... and the SIN."[89]

Market Adjustments and Coca Reduction

The U.S. government repeatedly used Peru as a drug control "success" story, pointing to the reduction in the amount of coca under cultivation. Yet much of this reduction in fact seems to have come from other causes. At the beginning of the 1990s, a strain of the soil fungus known as *Fusarium oxysporum* affected at least 12,000 acres of coca in the Huallaga.[90] Then a steep drop in price in the Upper Huallaga Valley that began in the mid-1990s led many farmers to voluntarily abandon their coca fields (Figure 6.2).

The decisive factor contributing to the drop in prices was the decline of Colombia's dependence on Bolivian and Peruvian coca. At the start of the 1990s, Colombians began planting their own coca crops, and by mid-decade Colombian coca production had skyrocketed. Being able to obtain coca leaf at home reduced the cartels' risks and their costs for importing coca or semiprocessed cocaine paste from Bolivia and Peru.[91] The immediate impact was felt in the Upper Huallaga Valley, which had been a chief supplier of raw material for the Colombian cartels (Figure 6.3).

The dismantling of the largest Colombian cartels in the 1990s also affected Peru's illicit drug trade. The Medellín cartel collapsed with the death of Pablo Escobar, and the leaders of the Cali cartel, which had become the principal buyer of Peruvian coca paste, were later imprisoned. This vacuum led to Mexican cartels entering the South American markets, while small Peruvian drug-trafficking outfits ratcheted up their operations from supplying coca leaf and coca paste to producing refined cocaine. In 1995, the State Department reported evidence of cocaine being produced in Peru that bypassed the Colombian connection, especially for Mexico and European destinations. The following year it noted that traffickers had

Figure 6.2   Average Price of Coca Leaf Paid to Peruvian Farmers, 1995–2002

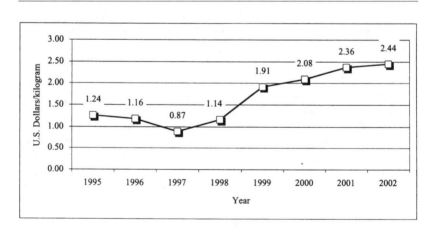

Source: Government of Peru, from the Devida website, Alternative Development Section, www.devida.gob.pe/programa2.asp#.

Figure 6.3   Net Coca Cultivation and Eradication in Peru, 1990–2002

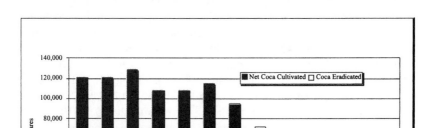

Source: U.S. State Department, Bureau for International Narcotics Law Enforcement Affairs, *International Narcotics Control Strategy Report 2002.*

begun using new routes for moving cocaine.[92] While some analysts pointed to the air bridge denial program as having achieved the disruption of Peruvian trafficking routes, in reality the traffickers continued to move their product, shifting to alternate routes by land, river, and sea instead of by air.

In sum, many factors contributed to the reduction in Peru's role as a major supplier of coca leaf to the cocaine industry, most of which were more closely related to market forces and agricultural shifts than to eradication programs.[93] What the United States and Peru touted as achievements of their drug control programs was not necessarily the result of that policy's impact on the cocaine trade. Instead, the trade was simply reconfigured, as assorted national and transnational groups and cartels took on new roles or reshuffled old ones in the production and distribution of their illicit and extremely profitable product. In the end, the successes attributed to Fujimori and Montesinos were illusory.

The Return of Forced Eradication and Social Protest

The Peruvian government's approach to drug control policies also resulted in the failure of alternative development programs in the 1990s. The collapse of coca prices provided a golden opportunity to initiate programs for providing viable income-generating alternatives for coca growers. These might well have discouraged them from returning to coca cultivation once prices recovered. This was particularly so in the Upper Huallaga Valley, where the coca growers themselves requested help from the United States in the identification of such alternatives. Embassy officials visiting the area reported that "coca growers repeatedly reiterated a strong desire to switch to other crops." These same officials were also aware of the difficulties faced by the farmers: "Without credit, title to lands, seeds and technical assistance, many farmers simply cannot make the transition."[94]

U.S. alternative development funding for Peru totaled U.S.$10 million between 1991 and 1994. With the new 1995 drug control agreement, this reached U.S.$60.8 million for the period 1995–1999. The Fujimori regime had committed itself to provide counterpart funding, but despite the priority given to alternative development in Peru's 1994 national drug control strategy, this never occurred. Contradrogas was not an important player within the government's drug control structure and never received enough funding to carry out significant alternative development programs. Efforts to establish an international donors' group to finance alternative development produced little response.[95]

Most of the assistance available, therefore, came from the U.S. Agency for International Development (USAID). This focused mainly on infrastructure projects and technical assistance rather than on directly aiding the farmers in production or in identifying potential markets. As a result, farmers did not perceive enough direct benefits to persuade them to give up their reliance on the coca economy. Furthermore, the perception among coca growers was that the nongovernmental organizations implementing the alternative development programs were using up most of the funds in administrative costs. This fueled growing resentment.

Despite these limitations, USAID focused its attention on development while other U.S. agencies were emphasizing eradication. General Ibsen del Castillo, head of Contradrogas under Fujimori, said there were tensions between the proponents of development and the eradicators. Development workers said forced eradication hindered their work, whereas the eradicators countered that alternative development strategies had not achieved the elimination of a single hectare of coca.[96] In effect, eradication policies had initiated a conflict in coca-producing regions that culminated in confrontations between farmers and eradication brigades.

Toward the end of the 1990s, eradication won out over development. The order was given to intensify forced eradication in order to help Peru retain its image as a successful partner in drug control. As mentioned earlier, General Ibsen del Castillo, formerly of SIN's narcotics intelligence unit, took the helm of Contradrogas, and the commission began to participate more actively in eradication. In 1999, 13,800 hectares of coca were eradicated, the largest amount over the course of the decade. Eradication efforts were concentrated in the Upper Huallaga Valley and Padre Abad regions in the departments of Huánuco, San Martín, and Ucayali.

This new push was devastating to the local population. Nancy Obregón, leader of one of the coca growers' federations in the area, recounted that "the eradication was brutal ... several people were injured. ... Seven people committed suicide after the eradication campaign. The people lost everything."[97] Around this time there were renewed accusations that fumigation had been used, particularly in Huánuco's Monzón Valley. No serious investigation was ever carried out to either prove or disprove these allegations.[98] Nevertheless, pressured by mobilization of coca growers in the Monzón Valley in January and February 2000, Fujimori signed a decree prohibiting the use of chemical or biological defoliants for eradication.[99]

The coca growers continued the protests, which reached their height in late 2000. On October 30, only three weeks before Fujimori would abandon his presidency and flee Peru, farmers in the Monzón, Upper Huallaga, and Padre Abad Valleys called for massive protests. The mobilization of coca growers was the largest in two decades. Gaining support from nearby urban areas as well, they paralyzed all movement in the regions of Lencio Prado, Padre Abad, and Monzón. The administration negotiated an agreement to initiate new talks with the coca growers, which began on November 9, 2000, in the city of Tingo María. The central issues on the twenty-point agenda included the immediate suspension of forced eradication during the dialogue process, an investigation into the damages caused by forced eradication from 1996 to 2000, and, most important, replacement of the forced eradication program with a plan, approved by the farmers, for gradually reducing coca production.

The coca growers thus again raised the prominence of demands that had been pushed to the backburner by the government. Coca cultivation could not be eliminated through law enforcement or military approaches when the reasons for its existence were so much more complex. As the farmers saw it, widespread poverty pushed them into growing coca, and international demand pulled them. Coca was a relatively profitable crop, especially during times of agricultural downturns. The income it produced went to satisfy basic family needs, provided seed money for other crops, and, in short, was the foundation of the economic and social structure for more than 200,000 families. The protests also restored the coca farmers to roles as "valid interlocutors." The farmers sought participation in policy decisions that directly affected them. They forced the Fujimori regime to sit down at the negotiating table to discuss coordinated solutions to the coca problem other than forced eradication. They had brought the issue out of SIN's shadow and into the light of public oversight and debate, ensuring that they would have to be taken into account by future governments.

• **Antidrug Policies in the Post-Montesinos Era**

The civilian government that followed Fujimori's downfall and embarked upon the "democratic transition" inherited a complicated situation. On the one hand, it had to deal with the coca farmers and their demands. On the other hand, the United States insisted on continuing eradication policies viewed by Washington as successful. This required keeping forced eradication as the centerpiece of the country's drug policy and complying with the targets previously agreed to by the Fujimori administration. On these issues, the new administration of George W. Bush was adamant from the start. The shifts in U.S. policy after the September 11 terrorist attacks, with reintroduction of the "narcoterrorism" discourse, only reinforced the hardline approach.

After Fujimori fled the country in November 2000, the head of the Peruvian Congress, Valentin Paniagua, was named interim president. He held office until Alejandro Toledo was inaugurated in July 2001. During his eight months in office, Paniagua continued to negotiate with the coca growers, but he was trapped by the need to comply with the 2000 eradication targets. Thus, the negotiations were only able to quiet the protests temporarily. Moreover, the government, which was short-lived by nature, was largely based on easily shattered political coalitions, yet it faced the enormous tasks of dismantling the authoritarian and corrupt machine left behind by Fujimori and rebuilding democratic institutions. Moreover, few financial resources were available to meet the social demands that had accumulated over a decade, including those of the coca farmers. As a result, from the start of the democratic transition the coca issue was locked into a cycle of negotiations and conflict.

Dialogue and Conflict: The New Government's Inheritance[100]

While negotiations continued under the new administration on the coca farmers' twenty-point agenda, the failure to reach concrete agreements left open the door for tensions. Lack of funds made it impossible to reach agreement on specific social and economic measures for the neediest sectors of the population. In fact, the only real progress was to formalize the negotiating process itself as a space for bringing the state together with civil society organizations in the coca-growing valleys. The government recognized "farmers in general and the coca producers [in particular] as valid interlocutors," but there was no mechanism established for farmers to actively participate in alternative development planning.[101]

Meanwhile, forced eradication continued in several areas, and in May 2001 new protests exploded in Aguaytía. A high-level government delegation traveled to the zone to negotiate with the farmers, and an agreement was reached to limit eradication to protected areas such as national forests.[102]

The accidental downing of a small plane in April 2001, in which a U.S. missionary and her infant daughter were killed, complicated the picture. The plane, mistaken for a drug transport flight, was shot down by the Peruvian air force. The CIA was implicated in the incident, as it supervised some of the mission's personnel and had monitored the events from a nearby aircraft. The air interdiction program was suspended pending an investigation of the case and a redesign of the policy. Despite repeated requests by Peruvian authorities for the program to resume, as of March 2004 it was still suspended.

The war on drugs was not a high priority for the Paniagua government. It was consumed by other serious tasks, including investigating the rampant corruption left behind by the Fujimori administration, organizing free and fair elections, and reconstructing Peruvian state institutions. But it also needed international assistance to manage the transition and for that reason chose to avoid conflict with the U.S. government over drug control policy.

The Toledo Doctrine

After winning the presidential election, Alejandro Toledo took office in July 2001. He demonstrated the political will to confront drug trafficking by strengthening the relevant agencies. He formally created the position of drug czar and named a businessman rather than a military or police official to the post. The czar was to be the executive director of Contradrogas, which was transformed into a high-profile, decentralized public agency answering to the cabinet chief. In addition, congress created a commission responsible for alternative development and for control of drug trafficking and money laundering.

The administration declared alternative development a top priority but did not appear to have a clear plan to implement it. The new drug czar, Ricardo Vega Llona, said that previous alternative development programs had failed because they had not succeeded in reducing poverty in the coca-growing valleys. The new programs' effectiveness, he said, would depend on the existence of a broad network of roads and highways that would allow access to national and international markets for what the farmers produced.[103]

Vega Llona lasted on the job only a few months before being replaced by Nils Ericsson Correa. Contradrogas was renamed the National Commission to Develop Life Without Drugs (Devida), and its executive directorship was elevated to a cabinet-level post. Ericsson proposed programs to provide jobs to growers who agreed to eradicate their coca, including large-scale agricultural production. However, even as the government discussed its alternative development plans, forced eradication was restarted in order to meet the targets for 2001. The Toledo administration maintained the decision to eradicate coca located in national parks only but added exceptions: new plantings and crops located near maceration pits and cocaine laboratories would also be eradicated. A total of 3,900 hectares of coca were eradicated in 2001.[104]

In practice, negotiations with the coca farmers languished despite the government's promise to continue them. The October 2001 round of discussions produced no concrete results, and a timid attempt to restart the talks in March 2002 also failed. The result was an explosion of conflict in the coca-growing valleys. In second week of June 2002, coca farmers in the Monzón Valley began a march to Lima. The next week, coca farmers in the Upper Huallaga once again called for mass protest. Even though no eradication was taking place in their area at the time, coca farmers in VRAE joined in on June 26 in solidarity with the demand for an immediate halt to all eradication throughout the country. Surpassed in size only by the mobilization of November 2000, the demonstrations in June were an impressive demonstration of the coca growers' capacity for organization at the national level.

Toledo's government acceded to the farmers' basic demands. These were: a temporary end to forced eradication while a new policy was being developed; the formation of a commission to investigate the rumors of fumigation; an examination of the alternative development programs, with at least a temporary halt to project implementation; and lastly, changes in the government's policies for legal coca sales and purchases.[105]

The Toledo administration came up with a plan that theoretically incorporated the coca growers' demands. The plan mandated gradual eradication, to be agreed on and carried out by the coca farmers themselves. However, the proposal was still subject to the 1978 law (Decree 22095) mandating the complete eradication of all coca except for 12,000 hectares for traditional consumption. It was also understood in different ways by the government and the farmers. For the government, "participatory gradual eradication" meant reaching agreements with the coca farmers on how they would meet the eradication targets, then determining what an appropriate set of incentives would be.[106] For the coca growers, it was understood as moving forward on alternative development first, with eradication to begin only after that was well established. USAID, for its part, maintained that eradication had to occur before the disbursement of any such incentives.

Renewed failures by Devida to comply with commitments on alternative development provoked a new round of protests by coca farmers in August 2002. This time, growers in the Apurímac Valley took the lead, calling for mass mobilization while beginning their march to Lima. The country was shaken by the coca growers' protest. Many sectors of the population felt cheated by the lack of adequate governmental response to their needs and demands since the democratic transition began. Caught between the demands of the coca growers and the eradication targets agreed upon with Washington, Toledo's government returned to negotiations with the farmers, hoping at least to quell the unrest. But the government's support was rapidly eroding because of its inability to follow through on its commitments.

U.S. Drug Control Policy: The Time for Zero Coca

The Toledo government's proposal for negotiated gradual eradication was opposed by the U.S. ambassador, John Hamilton, who insisted that forced eradication was needed in order to "defeat drug trafficking." He did not accept the arguments that farmers could not live without growing the "illicit crop," or that poverty and unemployment justified this "illegal activity," or that eradication needed to be gradual, negotiated with the farmers, and linked to the introduction of other crops and income-producing activities. "This focus," Hamilton said, "does not take into account a fundamental element: that illegal crops are the principal ingredient drug traffickers use to make coca paste and cocaine. Coca growers, as such, become the suppliers of drug trafficking."[107]

Hamilton's forcefulness reflected Washington's new hard-line foreign policy after September 11 and a conviction that terrorism was partly funded by drug trafficking. Hamilton reminded the Toledo government that, from the U.S. government's point of view, the problem of coca is principally a police and law enforcement issue, and interdiction and eradication are the principal tools for dealing with it. Eradication, he insisted, is the more important of the two, since it "allows for the elimination of drug trafficking at its source before the product moves as coca paste or cocaine toward the country's vast borders." He added that eradication was more cost-efficient than interdiction.[108]

The ambassador began to use much harsher language when referring to coca growers. Unlike the Peruvians, who differentiated between coca growers, drug traffickers, and terrorists, Hamilton blurred the lines, using terms like "coca-growing narcofarmers."[109] In so doing, coca growers were categorized as criminals instead of valid interlocutors, thereby dooming to failure any efforts toward finding negotiated solutions. Moreover, this discourse marginalized the coca growers, equating them with drug traffickers and with the terrorists of Shining Path.

Prices that farmers received for coca reached an all-time high at the beginning of 2002, averaging nearly U.S.$5 per kilogram.[110] Washington turned up the pressure again, saying that the rising prices were caused by slowed eradication. The hardening of U.S. rhetoric and the new demands played on the weakness of the Toledo government, which needed U.S. support to survive the intense political and social pressures threatening to bring it down. U.S. officials did recognize that for the continuity of the democratic transition it was vital that Toledo remain in office and that chaos could ensue if he were forced out. Every time new calls were made for Toledo to step down, the U.S. embassy publicly declared its support for him and the completion of his full five-year term.[111] But it also made full use of U.S. leverage to insist he comply with U.S. drug policy demands.

That leverage relied on Peru's dependence on the United States for economic assistance and the development of its foreign trade. The Andean Trade Preference and Drug Eradication Act (ATPDEA), signed into law by George W. Bush in August 2002, provided yet another tool to be used. ATPDEA updated the earlier Andean Trade Preference Act, which had expired in December 2001 after ten years, allowing thousands of products from the Andean nations of Bolivia, Ecuador, Colombia, and Peru to be exported tariff-free to the United States as a way of developing legal activities for coca farmers. Richard Brown, who ran the U.S. embassy for a short time after Hamilton departed, explained that the difference between the two acts was that APTDEA placed much more emphasis on a country's meeting its drug targets before it could benefit from trade preferences.[112]

Washington's commitment to apply the zero coca strategy in Peru was specified in the new drug control agreement signed by the two countries in September 2002, which aimed for the complete eradication of illegal coca crops within five years. The agreement stated, "Although the rate of reduction has slowed in the last two years, Peru—with the support of the United States government—can move toward the elimination of illicit coca production within the next five years."

To help meet this goal, the United States increased its aid to U.S.$300 million over the five-year period to "improve the quality of life for people living in coca-growing zones."[113] Disbursement of this aid, however, was specifically conditioned on meeting eradication targets, with progress to be evaluated annually. Richard Brown was explicit that in order for Peru to participate in ATPDEA it would have to speed up its eradication program, as well as to resolve several outstanding commercial disputes it had with U.S. companies operating in the country.[114] Thus, in the midst of its tenuous and complex transition to democracy, Peru signed, for the first time, a "Bolivian-style" drug control agreement conditioning all of its aid on coca eradication.[115]

A Collision Course and the Path to Negotiation

The new agreement with the United States had direct implications for the government's relations with coca growers. The most attractive components of the participatory coca eradication program (such as emergency loans and incentives for reforestation), previously agreed to by the government and coca growers in negotiations in Lima, were eliminated. The program, now referred to as the "participatory eradication of illegal coca crops,"[116] included wages of about U.S.$16 per day, up to a total of U.S.$500, for coca farmers who eradicated all of their coca. It also provided food packages and the possibility of construction jobs in community infrastructure projects. The program was strictly tied to eradication. In order to receive benefits, farmers had to sign agreements to fully eradicate their coca crops. If a farmer did not sign, eradication would be carried out by government agents, with no benefits forthcoming for the farmer. In other words, with or without the cooperation of the farmers, eradication was going to happen.

The program did not recognize the coca growers' associations as legitimate participants in negotiations. Instead it substituted other actors such as local mayors and non–coca farmers, all grouped together in the vague category of the "community." The development projects were largely oriented toward constructing infrastructure such as health clinics, schools, and roads rather than developing agricultural or other income-generating productive projects that farmers could use to replace coca cultivation. The infrastructure projects were, however, attractive to the mayors. The idea was that in return for these projects the mayors would try to convince their communities to eradicate their coca.

While some communities in Aguaytía accepted the program, the majority of coca growers rejected it as not conforming to previously negotiated commitments. They saw it as yet more government deception.[117] New protests broke out in February 2003 when the government proceeded with forced eradication in those communities that had not signed the new eradication agreements. Then farmers in Aguaytía also joined the mobilization. More than fifty people were injured in confrontations with security forces, and the protests quickly spread to other coca-growing valleys. A month earlier, in January 2003, coca growers had held their first national meeting where they formed the National Confederation of Farmers in the Coca-Growing Valleys of Peru (CONPACCP).

Toledo's administration hardened its position against the coca farmers. Nelson Palomino, CONPACCP's secretary general and the head of the Federation of Farmers in the Apurímac and Ene River Valley, was arrested in February 2004 and sentenced to ten years' jail time, accused of abetting terrorism. The government also launched a campaign to try to link the coca growers' protests with drug trafficking and terrorism.[118] Palomino's arrest radicalized the coca growers' protests, and farmers from all of the coca-growing valleys began a nationwide march on Lima. Finally, almost two months after the protests began, negotiations were reopened. The president met with CONPACCP's leaders, resulting in new agreements. By this time, the short-lived unity within the coca growers' movement began to crumble, with some supporting the new agreements while others opposed them. While the movement is far more cohesive than it was some years ago, internal divisions continue to hamper its effectiveness.

USAID and Devida began looking more actively for allies for their program. Offering investment for "integrated development" in exchange for coca eradication, they approached regional and local governments in coca-growing areas to try to persuade them to sign a "common agenda" and to participate in eradication plans. Several regional governments, won over by the hope of obtaining resources for their own projects, signed on to the agenda. However, some local coca farmers complained that they were neither consulted nor were their criticisms of the plan taken into account. The local governments in the VRAE, however, refused to participate, saying the decision whether or not to eradicate belonged to coca farmers and their respective organizations.[119]

Violence: Waiting for the Crash

The situation was tense at the end of 2003, with analysts publicly discussing the possibility of a new outbreak of violence in coca-growing regions. The economic situation in these areas remained desperate for many families, and the possibilities for negotiated accords with the government seemed increasingly unlikely. At least one group sought to use the situation to its advantage: the faction of Shining Path known as Proseguir, whose thinned ranks had survived mainly in the VRAE, began to proselytize among coca growers under the banner of defending coca, even advocating the use of arms to repel threats to the crops.

Proseguir had changed its approach to peasant farmers years earlier after becoming very small and weak. It no longer committed the indiscriminate massacres and political assassinations that had characterized the insurgents in the past. Instead, it tried to cultivate a respectful relationship with peasant communities. Proseguir members now paid for what they consumed in a community, using resources obtained by extorting illicit loggers and drug traffickers. Their rhetoric also changed, and they claimed to recognize that they had been wrong to use violence to impose their control in the past. Now they offered themselves as the farmers' protectors during the inevitable eradication campaigns.

The coca growers in the VRAE, however, did not trust this new incarnation of Shining Path. Despite some common ideas regarding the defense of coca, the growers were clear that they did not want to return to the violence and death unleashed by Shining Path in the 1980s and early 1990s. It was one thing to continue growing coca as long as there were no viable alternatives, but it would be something else altogether to join an armed struggle to overthrow the state.

However, anxiety was growing in the VRAE that eradication, whether participatory or forced, would begin as soon as conditions permitted. Residents did not want Shining Path to return, but it was not impossible that they would allow the insurgents to operate in the zone and attack the eradicators as they had during the 1980s in the Upper Huallaga Valley. It was also possible that some farmers would take up arms to defend their crops. One leader of the local peasant civil defense patrols said that if eradication brigades entered the area without the farmers' prior consent, "they would be met with a Mauser [hunting rifle]."[120] At the height of Peru's fight against Shining Path, the civil defense patrols had been the communities' first line of defense and were often used to back up the military. Hence, such declarations could not be taken lightly.

In 2003, Proseguir insurgents carried out a few spectacular actions, including the mass kidnapping of workers laying the Camisea gas pipeline. The group also carried out a number of incursions into local communities and ambushed a military patrol, killing five army and navy officers and two civilians. As a result, the government extended a month-long state of emergency—declared in May to stem a nationwide wave of protest that threatened to spill over into violence—in nine highland and jungle provinces, including the VRAE. The state of emergency was still in force in August 2004.

In July 2003, Toledo announced that his administration would launch "a model of peace and development" in which the civil defense patrols would be reactivated and the operational capacities of the armed forces and police would be strengthened. To achieve the latter, the budget would be increased to reinforce the twelve existing counterterrorism bases and create four more, plus two new navy posts,[121] in areas where, according to Peruvian officials, terrorism and drug trafficking went hand-in-glove.[122] In March 2004, Peru's National Defense Council announced a proposal to reactivate, over the medium term, forty-two counterinsurgency bases, both military and police, in coca-growing regions. According to one journalist, the plans under way "unite antiterrorist and antidrug objectives."[123]

Washington also expressed its concern about the "resurgence of narcoterrorism," calling on Peru to combat it energetically. After the kidnapping of the pipeline workers, Asa Hutchinson, assistant secretary of the U.S. Department of Homeland Security, said the reappearance of Shining Path was a "serious threat" representing an "immediate danger" for Peru. He added that the government needed to "increase efforts to control narcoterrorists."[124] The U.S. drug czar, John Walters, followed up by saying that coca cultivation had increased in Peru and that the government needed to be more aggressive to prevent actions by "organizations [that] look for alternative means to produce drugs and carry out terrorism."[125]

Proseguir's actions led to a definition of "narcoterrorism" in Peru that dangerously blurred the lines between social protest, drug trafficking, and the political activities of terrorist groups. Such characterizations placed the VRAE coca growers in a perilously ambiguous zone where human rights abuses could be rationalized in the name of reestablishing the law.

The hardened rhetoric, the stigmatization and criminalization of coca growers by labeling them "narcofarmers," and the elimination of the distinctions between farmers, drug traffickers, and terrorists all set the stage for the potential return to political violence. Pushing a large number of people into legal, social, economic, and political marginality could lead to a repeat of the 1980s, when drug control policies helped ignite a social conflagration in Peru.

• Conclusion

As this chapter demonstrates, the history of Peruvian drug control is full of paradoxes and contradictions. At times, the unanticipated results of drug control efforts were the opposite of those intended, producing new sets of problems. Moreover, the alleged success of U.S. and Peruvian drug control efforts—as measured in terms of reduced coca production—did not necessarily stem from counterdrug policies per se but rather from a variety of factors largely having to do with changes in the illicit drug trade. Perhaps most disturbingly, the protector of the henhouse turned out to be a fox.

The United States has often had a positive impact on human rights in Peru. In fact, Peruvian human rights groups were often heard in Washington at critical times for the country's democracy and the defense of human rights.[126] Nevertheless, the impact of U.S. support for human rights and democracy in Peru was limited by a pragmatism that avoided conflict with the Fujimori administration in order to ensure the continuity of what Washington considered to be a successful antidrug program.[127]

This pragmatism also led Washington to tolerate or support Vladimiro Montesinos, who was seen by U.S. drug control authorities as key to the successful pursuit of antidrug policies in Peru. Montesinos used this recognition as one more tool for consolidating his power. This in turn allowed him to set up, with President Alberto Fujimori, one of the most corrupt and authoritarian regimes in Peruvian history. Even at the moments when Montesinos's seeming invulnerability was shaken by plausible accusations of corruption, he continued to receive crucial U.S. support from some U.S. officials who wanted to avoid conflict with the man who pulled the strings of Peruvian drug control policy.

Peruvian drug control policy has aimed not only to reduce coca crops but also, as described in this chapter, to strengthen the state's authority. Yet Montesinos, who ordered the eradication of coca fields and the interdiction of drug trafficking flights in order to please the U.S. government and keep the funds flowing, also manipulated Peru's military, police, and intelligence apparatuses to set up and run a parallel criminal network that allowed him to engage in and benefit from the very crimes he was supposed to be preventing. As this volume went to press in mid-2004, the Peruvian justice system continued to build its case on Montesinos's alleged ties to drug trafficking, and Peruvian congressional investigating commissions have documented serious accusations that he used the state apparatus and his access to information to run the illicit drug business in Peru.

As mentioned earlier, the large drop in Peruvian coca leaf production in the mid-1990s was not so much a result of eradication and interdiction as of adaptations in the international drug market and a new division of labor in the production and trafficking of illicit drugs. Ironically, though, just as coca cultivation decreased, Peru's involvement in the production of refined cocaine increased. These realignments were at least partly brought on by the seeming successes of U.S. drug policy elsewhere, such as when the dismantling of Colombian cartels made room for new Peruvian and Mexican groups. Meanwhile, effective forced eradication programs may have pleased the United States, but they also engendered an extensive organized protest movement of coca growers throughout the country's coca-growing regions that further complicated the already difficult and delicate situation faced by the post-Fujimori governments. In the end, the "successes" attributed to Fujimori and Montesinos were nothing more than illusions—smoke and mirrors that diverted attention from the true nature of the regime.

Despite U.S. recognition of the fragility of Peru's return to democracy and the nation's limited ability to withstand new pressure or conflict, Washington's current drug control goals for Peru are set even higher than they were under Fujimori. The United States has clearly expressed its support for the Toledo administration and the ongoing democratic transition, but its insistence on achieving zero coca within five years could touch off a new wave of militarization and violence in the coca-growing valleys. As of early 2004, no significant violence has yet occurred during the coca growers' mass mobilizations, meaning that it is not yet too late for negotiated solutions and the peaceful resolution of conflict.

But if violence is to be avoided, imaginative and audacious new approaches and new conceptualizations of the problems of coca and drug trafficking are required. Clear distinctions must be made between coca farmers, drug traffickers, and terrorists. Coca cultivation should be viewed primarily as a product of social exclusion and poverty and as a matter of basic subsistence.

Peru's drug control policy must begin to incorporate the lessons of both its failures and its successes. A change in focus could lead to new definitions of successful drug control, moving away from the sole measure of eradication. This should include the design of integrated development strategies in which coca growers participate in planning, implementation, and evaluation. Drug control policy should become an issue for public debate and incorporate input from civil society organizations and other sectors of the population. Efforts should be reoriented toward the capture of drug traffickers, as opposed to small farmers, as well as toward disruption of money-laundering networks and the illegal trade in precursor chemicals.

The benefits and incentives of programs such as ATPDEA should be extended to coca-growing areas, and local and regional governments, as well as the population, should have a central role in planning local development efforts. Finally, the current bilateral U.S. approach to drug policy throughout the region should be replaced by the development and use of multilateral mechanisms for dealing with what is a transnational phenomenon. With these fundamental shifts, drug control policies could become not only more effective in the long run but also more humane and just.

• Notes

1. *La República*, "Toledo Hace Autocrítica y Lanza Ambicioso Paquete de Medidas," 29 July 2003; *La República, Domingo*, "Hay Alianza Entre Sendero y Los Narcotraficantes. Ministro de Defensa Loret de Mola: La Postura Oficial Sobre el Terrorismo," 6 July 2003, supplement; *La República*, "Narcoterrorismo Está en Fase Inicial en Perú," 30 June 2003; comments from Asa Hutchinson, Undersecretary of Homeland Security, in *La República*, "Sendero es un Peligro Inmediato," 23 June 2003.

2. Government of Peru, Presidency of the Council of Ministers, "Gobiernos del Perú y Estados Unidos Firman Convenio de Donación Especial," press release no. 120, 12 September 2002. Also, U.S. embassy, Lima, "Nuevo Convenio para el Financiamiento del Objetivo Estratégico para el Desarrollo Alternativo por 300 millones de dólares," available on the embassy website in Spanish only, peru.usembassy.gov/wwwsdesaltconv.shtml.

3. U.S. White House, Office of National Drug Control Policy (ONDCP), *National Drug Control Strategy 2003*, February 2003, p. 35.

4. Juan Zárate Gambini, "Políticas Gubernamentales: Perú," in *Narcotráfico: Realidades y Alternativas* (Lima: Comisión Andina de Juristas, 1990), p. 49. One hectare equals nearly 2.5 acres. Please note that beginning in the 1980s, official Peruvian and U.S. statistics for coca production often differed by as much as 100 percent: JoAnn Kawell, unpublished manuscript, "Going to the Source: A History of the U.S. War on Cocaine," chapter 1.

5. Ponciano Del Pino, "Tiempos de Guerra y Dioses: Ronderos, Evangélicos y Senderistas en el Valle del Río Apurímac," in *Las Rondas Campesinas y la Derrota de Sendero Luminoso*, Carlos I. Degregori et al., eds. (Lima: Instituto de Estudios Peruanos, 1996), p. 174.

6. José E. Gonzáles Manrique, "Perú: Sendero Luminoso en el Valle de la Coca," in *Coca, Cocaína, y Narcotráfico: Laberinto en los Andes* (Lima: Comisión Andina de Juristas, 1989), pp. 210–217.

7. Truth and Reconciliation Commission (TRC), *Report of the Truth and Reconciliation Commission,* Lima, 28 August 2003, pp. 740–744.

8. Human Rights Watch, *World Report 1989*, Peru.

9. Fernando Rospigliosi, *Montesinos y las Fuerzas Armadas: Cómo Controló Durante una Década las Instituciones Militares* (Lima: IEP, 2000).

10. For more background on Montesinos, see Rospigliosi, *Montesinos*; Gustavo Gorriti, "The Betrayal of Peru's Democracy: Montesinos as Fujimori's Svengali," *Covert Action*, no. 49 (Summer 1994); Luis Jochamowitz, *El Comercio*, "Vladimiro: Vida y Tiempo de un Corruptor, Expediente I," Lima, 2002. For a good summary, see Coletta Youngers, *Deconstructing Democracy: Peru Under Alberto Fujimori* (Washington, D.C.: WOLA, 2000), p. 24.

11. Joint Staff, Washington D.C., to Army Intelligence and Threat Analysis Center, Counterintelligence Periodic Summary [Extract], *Who Is Controlling Whom?* 23 October 1990. Many declassified documents referred to in this chapter can be found in "electronic briefing books" on the website of the National Security Archive (NSA), www.gwu.edu/~nsarchiv/NSAEBB/NSAEBB37/. Please look for the specified report, in this case, "Fujimori's Rasputin."

12. U.S. embassy, Lima, to the State Department, "Narcotics Corruption in Peru: Several Shades of Black," 22 May 1991, pp. 16–17. Some of the declassified documents referenced in this chapter are available on the website of the U.S. embassy, Lima, Peru, hereafter referred to as "Lima embassy website," peru. usembassy.gov/wwwsclasse.shtml.

13. Quainton also said, "We will report separately how Montesinos has used the new president's trust to shape the [Government of Peru]'s budding anti-subversive/narcotics and military policy." U.S. embassy, Lima, to the State Department, "The Man Behind Fujimori's Throne: A Bio Report on Vladimiro Montesinos," 16 August 1990, p. 1. Lima embassy website.

14. Gorriti, "Fujimori's Svengali," 1994. For information on Washington's view of the Peruvian political situation at the end of the 1980s, see Coletta Youngers, *Violencia Política y Sociedad Civil en el Perú: Historia de la Coordinadora Nacional de Derechos Humanos* (Lima: IEP, 2003), p. 192.

15. Quotes in this paragraph are from the Army Intelligence and Threat Analysis Center, Counterintelligence Periodic Summary [Extract], *Peru: Does Fujimori's Unofficial Adviser Control the Peruvian National Intelligence Community?*, 27 July 1991. NSA collection, "Fujimori's Rasputin."

16. U.S. embassy, Lima, "Nuevo Convenio."

17. Youngers, *Violencia,* 2003, pp. 243 and 199; idem, "Peru Under Scrutiny: Human Rights and U.S. Drug Policy," *Wola Briefing Series: Issues in International Drug Policy*, issue brief no. 5, WOLA, 13 January 1992, pp. 17–19.

18. Gorriti, "Fujimori's Svengali."

19. The meeting is reported in an intelligence note, "Meeting on Drugs in the SIN," WOLA files. Other sources also make reference to it: "At least one National Intelligence Service meeting last year (September), apparently chaired by retired captain Vladimiro Montesinos, touched on the subject of pay-offs to the security forces," in *The Peru Report,* "Special Report on the Upper Huallaga," May 1992.

20. Gorriti, "Fujimori's Svengali."

21. U.S. embassy, Lima, to the State Department, "FY1993 Post Operating Plan (POP) for NAS Lima, Peru," 16 October 1992, p. 18.

22. Américo Zambrano, "Huamán Azcurra Entregó Equipos de Chuponeo a Embajada de EE UU," in *Correo,* Lima, 9 August 2002. The article also says that the CIA had used SIN equipment to spy on other countries' ambassadors in Lima.

23. Youngers, *Deconstructing,* p. 71.

24. Testimony before the Investigating Commission for Compliance with the Conclusions and Recommendations of the Five ex-Investigating Commissions on the Period of Government of ex-President Alberto Fujimori (known as the Herrera Commission), the Congress of the Republic (Peru), Second Legislative Session of 2002.

25. *TRC Report,* p. 760.

26. President of Peru, Supreme Decree 137-91-PCM, 26 September 1991.

27. Legislative Decree 749 modified article 5 of Law 24150, on the role of the political-military command in emergency zones, to include the elimination of drug trafficking among their objectives.

28. Resignation letter from Hernando de Soto, WOLA files.

29. Enrique Obando, "Las Relaciones Civiles Militares en Perú en la Década de los 90: Lecciones para el Futuro," in Martin Tanaka, ed., *Las Fuerzas Armadas en la Región Andina: ¿No Deliberantes o Actores Políticos?* (Lima: Comisión Andina de Juristas, 2001).

30. U.S. embassy, Lima, "Several Shades of Black," pp. 16–17.

31. U.S. embassy, Lima, cable to the State Department, "Montesinos: Rumors and Facts on a Powerful Behind-the-Scenes Player," 7 January 1992, p. 1. Lima embassy site.

32. Ricardo Soberón, "Armed Forces and the Drug War: Between Garrisons, Caletas, and Borders," *Democracy, Human Rights, and Militarism in the War on Drugs in Latin America* (Guatemala: TNI, Cedib, and Inforpress Centroamericana, April 1997).

33. Youngers, *Violencia,* p. 245.

34. President of Peru, Decree 25426.

35. *Newsweek*, "A Spy Mission Gone Wrong," 31 May 1993, p. 35.

36. U.S. embassy, Lima, to the State Department, "FY1993 POP," 16 October 1992, p. 3.

37. Decrees 25626 and 25635, 21 July 1992. *El Comando Operativo del Frente Interno* is the Operational Command of the Internal Front; the "internal front" refers to Peruvian territory."

38. Rospigliosi, *Montesinos,* p. 36.

39. Obando, "Las Relaciones Civiles Militares."

40. *Newsweek,* "Spy Mission," p. 35.

41. U.S. embassy, Lima, to the U.S. State Department, "Monthly Report on Narcotics Program Developments in Peru—January 1993," 9 March 1993, p. 2; and U.S. embassy, Lima, "April 1993," 1 June 1993, p. 12.

42. Communication with former U.S. official, 16 January 2004, here and following paragraph.

43. Cynthia McClintock and Fabian Vallas, *Cooperation at a Cost: The United States and Peru* (New York: Routledge, 2003), p. 125.

44. U.S. State Department, Bureau for International Narcotics and Law Enforcement, *International Narcotics Control Strategy Report (INCSR) 1996*, p. 102.

45. Operational Agreement between the Governments of Peru and the United States for the Drug Control Project, 28 August 1996.

46. *Caretas*, "Lo que Faltaba: Asesor Montesinos Recibe Bendición Gringa," 24 October 1996.

47. Cited in McClintock and Vallas, *Cooperation*, p. 123.

48. *Caretas*, "Lo que Faltaba."

49. Terry Allen, "CIA and Drugs, Our Man in Peru," *Covert Action Quarterly,* no. 59 (December 1996).

50. Information on Vaticano case from U.S. embassy, Lima, to the State Department, "Intelligence Chief Montesinos Accused of Protecting Drug Traffickers," 6 September 1996. Lima embassy website.

51. Cited in Mario Valderrama, "Las Cuestionables Alianzas del los Estados Unidos en el Tema Anti-Droga," Centro Peruano de Estudios Sociales, 14–15 June 2001, p. 6.

52. *Caretas,* "Lo que Faltaba." See also Allen, "CIA and Drugs."

53. Congress of the Peruvian Republic, statements made to the Herrera

Commission by the former chiefs of Dinandro, National Police Generals Luis Pérrigo Pérrigo and Denis del Castillo, 4 March 2003, and by Commander Marco Roldán Bazán, 18 March 2003.

54. Ibid., p. 34.
55. DEA, Report of Investigation, *Corrupt Officials*, 27 August 1996. NSA collection, "Fujimori's Rasputin."
56. Statements of Generals Perrigo and del Castillo and Cmdr. Roldán, Herrera Commission, March 2003.
57. U.S. embassy, Lima, to the State Department, "The 'SIN' Sponsors GP Senior-Level, Multi-Agency, Multi-Service Counternarcotics Strategy Briefing," 26 March 1997, p. 2.
58. Vladimiro Montesinos, transcription of video no. 1792. Participants: General Villanueva, Admiral Ibarcena, General Bello, 26 November 1999, Congress of the Republic, Second Legislative Session, 2000.
59. State Department cable, to All American Republic Diplomatic Posts, "INR Intelligence Briefs and Assessments," 1 August 1997, p. 4. Lima embassy website.
60. U.S. embassy, Lima, to the State Department, "The Slow-Motion Auto-Golpe That's Killing Peru's Democracy," 30 April 1998, p. 1.
61. *Gestión*, "Dennis Jett Critica a Bush por no Reanudar Vuelos de Interceptación Antidrogas," 14 January 2002.
62. U.S. embassy, Lima, to the State Department, "ONDCP Director Speaks Out and Montesinos Reacts," 15 May 1998, p. 5. Lima embassy website.
63. Youngers, *Deconstructing Democracy*, p. 71.
64. Senate Appropriations Committee, Subcommittee on Foreign Operations, *Senate Report on the Fiscal Year 2000 Foreign Operations Bill.*
65. *Gestión*, "McCaffrey Admite Deterioro en Lucha Antidroga al Testificar en Camara de Representantes de los Estados Unidos," 7 August 1999.
66. U.S. embassy, Lima, to the director of ONDCP, "The Montesinos Factor," 22 July 1999. NSA collection, "Montesinos: Blind Ambition."
67. *La República*, "McCaffrey no Quiso Hablar de Corrupcion en el SIN," 27 August 1999.
68. *INCSR 2003*, "South America," Peru statistics.
69. Youngers, *Violencia,* pp. 406–408.
70. Youngers, *Deconstructing Democracy*, p. 373.
71. U.S. Secretary of State to U.S. embassy, Lima, cable, "Guidance on Peru Policy," 20 September 2000, p. 2. NSA collection, "Montesinos: Blind Ambition."
72. Senate Committee on Foreign Relations, Subcommittee on Terrorism, Narcotics, and International Operations, report, *Drugs, Law Enforcement, and Foreign Policy* (also known as the Kerry report) (Washington, D.C.: U.S. Government Printing Office, 1989).
73. David W. Dent, *The Legacy of the Monroe Doctrine: A Reference Guide to U.S. Involvement in Latin America and the Caribbean,* "Panama" (Westport, Conn.: Greenwood, 1999).
74. Seymour M. Hersh, "U.S. Aides in '72 Weighed Killing Officer Who Now Leads Panama," *Special to The New York Times*, 13 June 1986.
75. Information on Guatemala can be found in: Kate Doyle, "The Guatemalan Military: What the U.S. Files Reveal," National Security Archive Electronic Briefing Book No. 32, June 2000; Susanne Jonas, "Dangerous Liaisons: The U.S. in Guatemala," in *Foreign Policy*, no. 103 (Carnegie Endowment for International Peace, Summer 1996); Jennifer G. Schirmer, *The Guatemalan Military Project: A*

Violence Called Democracy (Philadelphia: University of Pennsylvania Press, 1998), pp. 16–17, 36, and 169; and José Rubén Zamora, "Crimen Organizado, el Ejército y el Futuro del Pueblo Guatemalteco," *El Periódico*, 12 November 2002.

76. Vaticano testimony, cited in Obando.

77. Youngers, *Deconstructing Democracy*.

78. *Caretas*, "Donde Están los Capos?" 16 May 1996.

79. These were the Herrera Commission (2002–2003), the Waisman Commission (2000–2001), and the Townsend Commission (2001–2002).

80. Unless otherwise noted, the information here is from Vaticano's testimony to the Waisman Investigating Commission as cited in Obando, "Las Relaciones Civiles Militares," 2001, pp. 298–299.

81. *AgenciaPerú.com*, "Habla 'Vati,'" interview with Demetrio Chávez Peñaherrera (Vaticano), 6 February 2001.

82. Comisión Herrera, Congreso de la República, Segunda Legislatura Ordinaria del 2002, folio 3921.

83. Comisión Herrera, folio 3923.

84. Comisión Herrera, folios 3921–3923.

85. For an analysis of the complexities of the cases against Montesinos and other officials of the Fujimori regime, please see: Gustavo Goritti y Graciela Villasis, "Cómo juzgar a Montesinos," in *ideele*, no. 153 (March 2003).

86. *La República*, "Montesinos Representaba en Peru al Cartel de Tijuana de Mexico," 28 May 2003.

87. The International Consortium of Investigative Journalists, "U.S. Shrugged Off Corruption, Abuse in Service of Drug War (Peru)," in Special Report, *U.S. Military Aid to Latin America Linked to Human Rights Abuses*, Center for Public Integrity website, www.publicintegrity.org/report.aspx?aid=257&sid=100, 12 July 2001.

88. *Revista Cambio*, "El Hombre que Vio Llover Fusiles," Bogota, 16–22 December 2002; *La República*, "Narcotraficantes Brasilenos Dieron U.S.$8 Miliones para Tráfico de Armas a las FARC," 15 November 2002.

89. Comisión Herrera, folios 3408–3409.

90. Sharon Stevenson, "Peru Farmers Blame U.S. for Coca-Killing Fungus," *Miami Herald*, 2 June 1991. Accusations that the fungus had been introduced through aerial fumigation were never proven.

91. For more details, please see the excellent study by Theo Rocken et al., eds., *The Drug War in the Skies: The U.S. Air Bridge Denial Strategy* (Cochabamba: Transnational Institute, 1999).

92. *INCSR 1995* and *INCSR 1996*, "Peru."

93. Roncken et al., *Drug War*.

94. U.S. embassy, Lima, to State Department, "Despite Slight Increase in Coca Prices, Peru´s Upper Huallaga Valley Remains Severely Depressed," 20 September 1996, pp. 2, 6.

95. Herrera Commission, testimony of Juan Armando Gil Ruiz, former executive secretary of Contradrogas, session of 5 March 2003, pp. 9–11.

96. This paragraph and next: Herrera Commission, testimony of General (ret.) Ibsen del Castillo, former executive secretary of Contradrogas, session of 5 March 2003, pp. 9–11, 15.

97. Statements made by Nancy Obregón during negotiations between coca farmers of the Upper Huallaga Valley and Padre Abad with Devida officials, Lima, 11 July 2002.

98. A number of these accusations appear in Eric J. Lyman, "U.S. Accused of Creating Blight Killing Coca Plants and Harming Other Crops." Also, Stevenson, "Peru Farmers."

99. Supreme Decree 004-2000-MA, 24 March 2000.

100. For more detail on this period, see Isaías Rojas, "The Adventure of Zero Coca: Drug Control Policy and the Democratic Transition in Peru," *Drug War Monitor* briefing series, WOLA, February 2003.

101. Supreme Decree 009-2001-SA, 15 March 2001.

102. *INCSR 2001*, "Peru."

103. *Gestión*, "Programas de Cultivos Alternativos de Hojas de Coca Son un Fracaso Admite 'Zar' Antidrogas," 28 January 2002.

104. *INCSR 2001* and *2003*, "Peru."

105. Notes on coca farmers' negotiations: Valle del Monzón, Huánuco, 19 June 2002; Valle del Alto Huallaga, Tingo María, 28 June 2002; Valle del Río Apurímac, San Francisco, 29 June 2002.

106. Here and next paragraph, see Rojas, "Adventure."

107. Hamilton´s remarks are from the U.S. embassy, Lima, *Boletin Antidrogas*, no. 4, 17 July 2002.

108. Comisión Andina de Juristas, "Afirman que Erradicacion de Drogas es Más Rentable que Interdicción," in *Boletin Hoja Verde: Noticias andinas sobre control de drogas*, no. 25, 2nd half May 2002.

109. U.S. embassy, Lima, *Boletin Antidrogas*, no. 2, 2 May 2002.

110. *Gestión*, "Precio de Hoja de Coca Estaría a Punto de Alcanzar Su Record Histórico," 2 January 2002.

111. *Correo*, "Casa Blanca Ratifica Apoyo a Presidente," 27 July 2002.

112. Interview with U.S. embassy trade attaché Richard Brown in *El Comercio*, "Combate Contra las Drogas Debe Ser Eficiente y Exitoso," 15 August 2002.

113. U.S. embassy, Lima, "Nuevo Convenio."

114. *El Comercio*, "Combate."

115. For a description of "Bolivian-style" drug control, see Kathryn Ledebur, "Coca and Conflict in the Chapare," *Drug War Monitor* briefing series, WOLA, July 2002.

116. Information in this paragraph from U.S. embassy, Lima, "Autoeradicación y Desarrollo Alternativo avanzan con Éxito en la Selva," in *Boletin Antidrogas*, no. 7, October–November 2002.

117. Agreements were signed by fifty-one communities, and 1,300 hectares of coca were eradicated during the last four months of 2002. Pablo O'Brien, "Las Palomilladas del Indio Palomino," in *Caretas*, no. 1761, 27 February 2003; *La República*, "35 Mil Cocaleros Marcharán Hacia Lima," 27 February 2003.

118. *La República*, "Narcotraficantes y Terroristas Están Detrás de Protestas," 27 February 2003.

119. Author interview with Vicente Kitazono, mayor of Llochegua, Huanta Province, Ayacucho, August 2003.

120. Field notes, Ayacucho, July 2003.

121. *La República*, "Toledo Hace Autocritica y Lanza Ambicioso Paquete de Medidadas," 29 July 2003.

122. *La República*, "Hay Alianza Entre Sendero y los Narcotraficantes— Ministro de Defensa Loret de Mola: La Postura Official Sobre el Terrorismo," *Domingo* supplement, 6 July 2003; *La República*, "Narcoterrorismo Está en Fase Inicial en Peru," 30 June 2003; *La República*, "Sendero es un Peligro Inmediato," 23 June 2003.

123. *La República,* "Reactivarán 42 Bases Antisubversivas," 4 March 2004.

124. *La República*, "Sendero es un Peligro Inmediato."

125. *La República*, "Mas Severidad en la Lucha Antidrogas Piden a Peru, Bolivia, y Venezuela," 30 July 2003.

126. See Youngers, *Violencia Política*.

127. Youngers, *Deconstructing Democracy*, p. 69.

7

Ecuador:
Untangling the Drug War

Fredy Rivera Vélez

Although Ecuador is not considered a major drug-producing or drug-trafficking country, its proximity to Colombia and its location within the Andean source zone places it close to the center of the drug policy debate. Ecuador's participation in the U.S.-led drug control strategy, the presence of warring factions in neighboring Colombia, and the geostrategic vision of the country's security and defense forces have led to the "securitization" of the country—that is, a perceived threat to national security is used to justify military and police actions inimical to the rights and well-being of the population and to distract attention from the government's inability to govern and provide for its citizens.

The Colombian conflict has indeed had a major impact on Ecuador's northern border region. However, the response to that conflict, specifically Plan Colombia, has also had serious negative consequences. This comprehensive effort by the Colombian government to resolve that country's internal crisis was announced in late 1998. One year later, Bill Clinton's administration threw its support behind the military component of the initiative, and in July 2000 the U.S. Congress approved U.S.$1.3 billion in aid, 75 percent of which went to the Colombian armed forces and police. But the U.S.-backed Plan Colombia's consequences for neighboring countries were not fully considered. Aerial spraying of coca crops in Colombia with powerful herbicides has reportedly had effects within Ecuador, for example. Nongovernmental organizations have documented the destruction of crops and livestock, as well as health problems apparently linked to the fumigation. When the Colombian conflict or fumigation efforts intensify, refugees seek shelter and protection across the border in Ecuador, straining that country's already dismal economy and its rudimentary social services and infrastructure.

Both the U.S. and Colombian governments have called on Ecuador to beef up its security forces along the northern border, and the U.S. government has provided significant resources toward that end. Thousands of

Ecuador	
Population	12,600,000
GDP	U.S.$18.0 billion
GDP per capita	U.S.$1,396
Share of Income	
• Poorest 10 percent of population	0.7%
• Richest 10 percent of population	44.2%
• Ratio of income of richest 10% to poorest 10%	63.6 times
Percentage living in poverty (<$2/day)	52.3%
Percentage living in extreme poverty (<$1/day)	20.2%
Public perception of corruption among public officials and politicians (0=more, 10=less)	2.2

Sources: UNDP, *Human Development Report 2004;* World Bank, *Inequality in Latin America: Breaking with History?;* Transparency International, *Corruption Perceptions Index 2003.*
Notes: Population and GDP data from 2001; share of income data 2000; poverty data 1990–2001.

troops have been sent north. The Ecuadorian government has declared much of the northern border, which Ecuador's security and defense forces consider highly conflictive, to be a "reserve area" under military control. As a result, civil liberties are restricted, and human rights violations sometimes occur. In short, Plan Colombia and the militarization of the border region have contributed to the steady escalation of tensions in a region that already faced a myriad of deep-rooted socioeconomic problems.

A range of other issues has emerged from the drug control strategies adopted by Ecuador at the urging of the U.S. government. The military and police forces now compete for U.S. resources and have overlapping responsibilities. Harsh antidrug legislation raises concerns regarding due process and civil liberties. Lack of oversight, transparency, and accountability mechanisms impede the effective implementation of drug control policies.

Of particular concern, counterdrug policies are taking a toll on the functioning of democratic institutions—already far more fragile than those found in neighboring countries. Ecuador has been unable to establish adequate levels of good governance or to strengthen state institutions since its transition to democracy in 1979. The inability of the country's different political factions to find common ground on most issues is one of the principal reasons for Ecuador's recurring economic crises and the fragility of its public institutions.

Poorly planned and implemented structural adjustment programs and other economic measures have not led to economic growth or increased standards of living for the majority of the population. On the contrary, Ecuadorians in general have little faith that they will ever see improvements in their situation, given the country's high levels of social inequality, poverty, unemployment, marginalization, and exclusion, in addition to rampant corruption.

The country has been enmeshed in a series of economic problems that have made its governments extremely weak, made the political situation unpredictable, and limited Ecuador's ability to develop within a framework of human rights and democracy. Political institutions have lost most of their legitimacy. Ongoing political conflicts have contributed to the destabilization of the democratic system, with a temporary government taking office in 1997 and a coup d'état in 2000.

Yet U.S. policy toward Ecuador remains myopically focused on the drug issue and the Colombian conflict with little regard for the potentially destabilizing impact of those policies on such a fragile political system. It fails to recognize that the greatest threats to Ecuadorian security—and hence to U.S. interests—are persistent poverty and inequality, the failure to strengthen democratic institutions, and continued political instability.

• Ecuador's Roles in the Drug Trade

Ecuador does not produce enough cocaine or other illicit drugs to make it a regional or international security threat. Nevertheless, Ecuador has two roles in international drug trafficking. First, it is considered a transit route for drugs, a supplier of precursor chemicals and weapons used in the drug trade, and—though this has not been well documented—a minor haven for money laundering. Second, the Ecuadorian government has been a participant in the international drug war since the 1980s, when drug trafficking was first defined as a national security issue. Since then, issues related to drug control have gradually been making their way into Ecuadorian debates over social and public policy.

Virtually no coca leaf is grown in Ecuador. This has been the case since the seventeenth century, when the colonial government abolished production of coca for what, in Peru and Bolivia, became known as "traditional" uses. Coca use was never revived in Ecuador, and present-day Ecuadorian farmers have neither knowledge about nor a tradition of coca leaf cultivation.[1]

In addition, the process of colonizing the Ecuadorian jungle coincided with the oil boom of the 1970s, which stimulated the use of land for agriculture and ranching under state supervision. Population growth in the zone began in the early 1970s with the construction of the Trans-Ecuadorian Oil Pipeline and the construction of highways linking Quito to the northern border areas. The oil industry played a key role in shaping the current configuration of towns, socioeconomic relations, and exploitation of natural resources in the region.

Because of the strategic importance the Ecuadorian government placed on oil, this process was accompanied by a significant expansion of the military's role. A five-decade conflict with Peru meant that Ecuador's southern border was highly militarized, thereby impeding illegal coca production. All of these factors have so far prevented coca production from spreading into Ecuador across either border as it is eradicated in Bolivia, Colombia, and Peru.[2]

Since the 1990s, the U.S. State Department, which monitors coca production on an annual basis, has reported only tiny amounts of cultivation in Ecuador, all of which have been destroyed in joint police/military operations. Eighty hectares of coca were located in 1991, but no other production was reported until 2001, when 5.5 hectares were found in the northern province of Sucumbíos. Twenty hectares were reported in scattered northern border locations in 2002, and in 2003 some 5,000 individual plants were found in the same region. In relation to cocaine production, the State Department reported the discovery and destruction of "several" small cocaine refining laboratories in 2000, and four small labs in 2001, with no labs reported since then.[3]

As the State Department notes, although "the absence of significant cultivation and of processing laboratories suggests that drug production is not now a serious problem in Ecuador," the country is an important transit route for cocaine being shipped to international markets.[4] Total annual cocaine seizures have ranged from 1.72 metric tons in 2000 to 10.83 metric tons in 2001, averaging 6.78 metric tons a year for the period 1994–2003.[5] The drugs move in and out of the country via the Pan-American Highway or through seaports in Manta, Guayaquil, and Puerto Bolívar. Due to increased monitoring and control at the country's international airports, they are used to export only small amounts of drugs. Ecuador's northern region is also a source of precursor chemicals used by the drug industry in southern Colombia.

In 2000, the Ecuadorian government—facing a severe economic and banking crisis—did away with the local currency and made the U.S. dollar the official medium of exchange, a policy known as "dollarization."[6] The immediate impact of dollarization was a steep rise in the prices of most goods and services. The impact on the northern border region was particularly devastating. Before the change, products were cheaper on average in Ecuador than in neighboring countries, resulting in a booming contraband trade from Ecuador into Colombia. Many border families depended on such trade for their livelihood. As the flow of cheaper contraband goods was reversed, many Ecuadorians lost their primary or an important additional source of income. In short, dollarization contributed significantly to the already dismal economic situation faced by towns and communities along the northern border.

According to the U.S. State Department, dollarization has made Ecuador more attractive for money laundering, an activity already favored by Ecuador's proximity to Colombia and Peru.[7] Nevertheless, no serious investigations of the issue have taken place—only news articles that have not contained any hard evidence—making it impossible to estimate with any accuracy the extent of money laundering in the country.[8] In addition, Ecuador's banking laws guarantee confidentiality and limit access to information on financial movements, making it difficult to investigate the issue. Investigations of bank accounts must be done through extremely complicated judicial procedures that have proven to be ineffective and, due to endemic corruption, lack credibility. There do appear to be informal networks for money laundering that do not use the financial system, further complicating an objective analysis of the issue.

Drug Trafficking, Fumigation, and Plan Colombia

Another dimension of the problem is the coca-growing/cocaine-producing industry in southern Colombia and the presence of a mobile rural workforce on the Ecuadorian side of the border. Regional poverty levels of over 60 percent, lack of job opportunities, the recent crash in international coffee prices, and the generally weak farm economy along the border have forced Ecuadorians to temporarily cross into Colombia in search of jobs in Colombia's illicit drug industry.[9] In short, poverty pushes Ecuadorians into an illegal business.

In addition, the institutional presence of the national government is weak in the border areas, especially in the northern jungle region. Within this context of economic decay and governmental neglect, the initiation of the U.S. aid package for Plan Colombia in 2000 provoked new fears. A central component of the strategy was a significant increase in U.S. assistance for aerial spraying of coca crops in the department of Putumayo, Colombia. This in turn led to an intensification of the conflict in Colombia and the potential for significantly more refugees flowing over the border into Ecuador. Moreover, because the chemicals used in the spray program can drift some distance from the actual application site, Ecuadorians living along the border worried that the spraying would have serious consequences on their own environment and health.

In October 2000, the press reported that health problems in the Ecuadorian town of Mataje were being linked to fumigation carried out in

Colombia's Nariño Province; forty-four people in Mataje reportedly fell sick after the first spraying.[10] Several months later, 188 farmers from border communities presented a complaint to the Ecuadorian Human Rights Ombudsman's Office in Lago Agrio with details of crops that they said had been damaged by the spray and of animals that had died. They asked for an end to the aerial spraying. The document was forwarded to Quito, where it was shelved. Despite the reported impact on the country's domestic agricultural production and the severe losses claimed by small family farmers, no government authorities traveled to the area to investigate the complaints.[11]

U.S. officials have repeatedly claimed that the herbicide glyphosate and the other chemicals used in the spray program are safe (see Chapter 4). However, according to an investigation carried out by nongovernmental organizations, since December 2000 large areas of Ecuadorian farmland and wildlife and some residents have reportedly been affected by exposure to the chemicals. In the province of Sucumbíos, for example, the investigation found that more than half the fish in local fish farms had been killed and nearly half the local coffee crop had been harmed by the spraying. In addition to the destruction caused to crops and wildlife, aerial spraying in Colombia has reportedly resulted in skin rashes and other health problems in humans on the other side of the border that are difficult to diagnose and cure.

Spraying chemical or biological herbicides on drug crops from planes is now prohibited within Ecuadorian territory. Ecuadorian officials have also made a request to their Colombian counterparts that no aerial spraying occur within a margin of ten kilometers from their shared border. Through mid-2004, however, the Colombian government has refused to come to an agreement, and fumigation continues close to the border.

Ecuadorians are not in favor of their country getting dragged into the Colombian conflict. In a public opinion poll published in November 2002 by a local polling firm, 65 percent of the adult population in Quito and Guayaquil, the country's major cities, said that Colombia's problems of drug trafficking and guerrillas needed to be solved exclusively by Colombians.[12]

Nongovernmental organizations in Ecuador, mainly human rights and environmental groups, have focused on three issues linked to the war on drugs: fumigation and its harmful effects, the violence associated with Plan Colombia and the plan's repercussions on citizen security, and human rights violations by the Ecuadorian military and police forces along the northern border.

Ecuador is clearly immersed in the problems caused by Plan Colombia and U.S. regional security strategy. U.S. Ambassador Kristie Kenney has said that "Ecuador is involved in the Colombian conflict because the Colombia problem is regional and neighboring countries must help find a solution to the conflict. ... Ecuador is involved because drug traffickers and guerrillas move freely over the border, and there is a considerable flow of weapons and drugs."[13] U.S. rhetoric has concrete consequences. As documented below, U.S. military aid to Ecuador has increased significantly in recent years (Figure 7.1). Given the diplomatic and economic encouragement from Washington, Ecuador is taking on a much larger role than it has in the past in the war against drugs and in the regional security strategy being pushed by the United States.

In the wake of the September 11 terrorist attacks, the U.S. government has also pushed Ecuador to play a more active role in the global war on terrorism, at times provoking anger in Ecuador. The U.S. State Department's 2002 report *Patterns of Global Terrorism 2002* was viewed by many Ecuadorians as unfairly critical. "The government's weak financial controls, inadequate preparation of security personnel and widespread document fraud limit counter-terrorism efforts," it said, although it also recognized "the work of the [Ecuadorian] security forces in reducing the traffic of illegal weapons for Colombian terrorist groups and for closing border control posts at night."[14]

Security and Drug Policy under Lucio Gutiérrez

As a presidential candidate, Lucio Gutiérrez promised that he would develop an autonomous national security strategy, independent of U.S. policy

Figure 7.1   U.S. Aid to Ecuador, 1997–2005

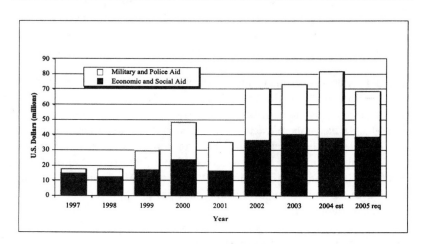

Source: Data from the U.S. State Department, Bureau for International Narcotics and Law Enforcement Affairs, *International Narcotics Control Strategy Report*, various years. Please see WOLA website, www.wola.org, for full listing.

toward Colombia. He also supported a negotiated settlement to the neighboring Colombian conflict. However, since his election in 2002, President Gutiérrez has changed his position on the issue, doing an about-face from his campaign promises once it became clear that U.S. economic assistance and other forms of support could be at stake. In a visit to Washington in February 2003, he embraced the U.S. strategy but at the same time attempted to downplay his turnaround by stating that Ecuador would play only a mediating role in the Colombian conflict.

This policy reversal began a new phase in the relationship between Quito and Washington, which had cooled during the administration of President Gustavo Noboa (2000–2003). The scant attention paid by the United States to Ecuador's requests for increased aid had led to numerous tensions between Washington and Noboa's administration, which were reflected in strong criticism of the United States by his foreign and defense ministers.[15] The accommodation with Gutiérrez opened the door to the possibility of increased U.S. economic assistance for Ecuador's northern border regions.

Colombian President Alvaro Uribe's militaristic approach to Plan Colombia has included establishing direct avenues of communication with Ecuador for coordination on specific security issues. In contrast to his predecessor's attempt to reach a negotiated settlement with the insurgents, Uribe has instead sought to establish the government's supremacy over the guerrillas by means of direct military confrontation.[16] Uribe's policies are also in line with the U.S. approach of intensifying fumigation and persuading neighboring countries to buy into the U.S. interpretation of the Colombian conflict as a regional problem.

U.S. Defense Secretary Donald Rumsfeld emphasized the regional approach during his visit to Bogotá in August 2003. After reiterating his support for Uribe's policies of "democratic security," Rumsfeld said "irregular Colombian groups are a threat to the entire region and, as such, must be confronted by all the countries in the area."[17] His statements were immediately echoed by the Colombian ambassador to Ecuador.

Security was the main topic of talks when Uribe paid a state visit to Ecuador three days later. Uribe and Gutiérrez signed a joint declaration in Quito that defined concrete actions for fighting drugs and improving border security. They also ratified an agreement for police cooperation and created a binational commission to draw up additional security measures.[18] This spirit of collaboration has continued. In March 2004, President Gutiérrez traveled to Colombia for more talks and photo opportunities with his Colombian counterpart.

• Drug Trafficking and Security

The war against drugs in Ecuador involves a number of actors and institutions. While the drug issue had a relatively minor place on the country's list of security concerns in the 1980s and early 1990s, it has grown in importance in recent years due to the implementation of Plan Colombia. This has affected Ecuador itself in several ways. The flow of additional resources into the police and security forces has altered priorities and increased competition. The use of the air force base at Manta by U.S. forces has become the subject of significant debate. And most important, the northern border area has been profoundly affected.

In the 1980s, the Ecuadorian government's policies showed a clear lack of understanding of the drug problem, with the country signing any and all agreements to combat drug consumption and trafficking. Ecuador faithfully followed the U.S. lead, generally accepting the thesis that linked guerrillas to drug trafficking. The link between terrorism and drug trafficking was not based on objective analysis or Ecuadorian reality but on ideology and the political needs of the country's leaders. This was particularly true during President León Febres Cordero's administration in the mid-1980s. Febres Cordero depended heavily on the military to shore up his administration, which lacked popular support and suffered numerous political and economic crises.[19]

When a short border war with Peru broke out in 1995, the question of the military's role in combating drug trafficking was temporarily eclipsed by concerns related to that conflict. A definitive solution to the border conflict was reached in 1998. Thereafter, renewed concerns about drug trafficking and increased levels of violence in Colombia refocused attention on the part of the Ecuadorian government, public policy institutions, and the military itself on the need to redefine the country's national security agenda and the roles of the armed forces and national police.

The Ecuadorian Military in National Security Policy

Ecuador's armed forces have played a much different role than that played by the military in many other Latin American countries. While the Ecuadorian armed forces have carried out coups, led military governments, and supported other disruptions of the constitutional order, they were not involved in the massive acts of corruption and human rights violations that characterized dictatorships in Argentina, Bolivia, Chile, Paraguay, and Uruguay during the 1970s and 1980s.

Ecuador's armed forces did incorporate the U.S. national security doctrine as one of the central pillars of their identity and decisionmaking processes. In contrast to other militaries in the region, however, the Ecuadorian military's nationalism, focus on national development, and close links to the civilian population have allowed it to cultivate a level of legitimacy and acceptance that is higher than that enjoyed by the Ecuadorian police or political parties—despite the military's repeated breaches of civilian rule. According to one survey published in 2003 by the armed forces, more than twice as many people trusted the military as trusted the police, which had the confidence of 38 percent and 18 percent of the population, respectively. Political parties were trusted by only 2.5 percent of those polled.[20]

Since the 1960s, the armed forces have emphasized the economic and social development of the nation. They have seen themselves as a modernizing force within a backward population that was falling behind in a demanding modern world.[21] Ecuador's 1978 constitution prioritized the role of the government in the economic and social spheres while highlighting the military's role in economic areas deemed strategically important. This allowed the Ecuadorian armed forces to wield great political influence.

The military's participation in national politics during times of crisis has been characterized by its role as arbitrator between civilian factions. Examples of this can be seen in the collapse of President Abdalá Bucaram's administration in 1997 and the fall of President Jamil Mahuad in 2000. Both presidents were accused of corruption, their economic decisions were unpopular, and their administrations were marked by political instability. In the case of Bucaram, the military gave its tacit endorsement to the congressional move to remove him from office. In that of Mahuad, his fall from power was the result of an alliance between sectors of the military and indigenous and other popular groups. Even as they took on the role of defenders of the rule of law, the armed forces made it clear that if they were ever faced with choosing between democracy and security, they would opt for the latter.[22]

In December 2002, the Ecuadorian armed forces put together a white paper for the National Defense Policy of Ecuador that laid out the need to rethink national security doctrine. The military is now facing new challenges that include reduced autonomy, budget cuts, and the need to build a stronger institutional image. Changes in border policy, now that the threat from Peru has been resolved, have also contributed to the need for a reassessment of defense policy and the military's role. One of the new national security issues included in the National Defense Policy is the illicit drug trade.

Given the history of the Ecuadorian military just described, it is not surprising that the Ecuadorian armed forces now see drug trafficking as a threat to national security. According to the Defense Ministry, the drug trade could violate the integrity of the state by mobilizing "a systematic series of elements that undercut the state's function, generating parallel structures that weaken the state's constitutional legitimacy."[23] This argument is linked to notions such as "narcoguerrillas," popularized by the

United States in the 1980s, revived in the 1990s by U.S. drug control agencies, and now implicit in post–September 11 antiterrorist rhetoric.[24] Such thinking has permeated the Ecuadorian security sector despite the absence of significant insurgent movements in the country, much less ones involved in the drug trade.

The picture becomes much clearer if the situation faced by the Ecuadorian military is seen within the context of the Colombian conflict. According to official military documents, the conflict in Colombia threatens Ecuadorian national security on a number of fronts, including increased flows of refugees and displaced persons, high levels of rural and urban violence along the border, criminal activities related to the presence of illegal armed groups, and organized crime. To confront these various threats, the priority for the Ecuadorian military is to implement a counterinsurgency strategy that deters Colombian guerrillas and paramilitary forces from bringing their war across the border.[25]

This perspective coincides with the U.S. emphasis on regional conflict. Tensions have surfaced, however, regarding some U.S. antidrug initiatives that are seen as threatening the country's sovereignty. Perhaps the best example is the issue of maritime interdiction. During an October 2002 visit to Ecuador, General James Hill, head of the U.S. Southern Command, proposed that Ecuador and the United States sign a maritime interdiction treaty. The head of Ecuador's joint chiefs of staff quickly rejected the idea, and the Defense Ministry publicly stated that Ecuador would not be part of a multinational maritime force.[26]

Military and Police Competition for U.S. Resources

Both the Ecuadorian military and the government—which has swung toward complacent acceptance of the U.S. strategy—have been eager to receive the increased U.S. economic assistance that U.S. counterdrug programs potentially provide. Ecuador received U.S.$20 million in 2001 from Plan Colombia supplementary funds as well as U.S.$1.2 million in international drug control assistance. The amount of International Narcotics Control (INC) aid from the State Department for Ecuador rose to more than U.S.$24 million in 2002 and approximately U.S.$31 million in 2003. For fiscal year 2004, Ecuador is slated to receive another U.S.$35 million for drug control and related efforts, and U.S.$26 million will be requested for FY2005.[27]

In February 2004, George W. Bush's administration announced that it was withholding U.S.$15 million in military assistance to Ecuador because the government would not sign a waiver granting U.S. military personnel immunity from the International Criminal Court, a condition mandated by the U.S. Congress for aid disbursements. Ambassador Kenney told the press, however, that the cut in assistance for FY2004 should not affect funding for the following year.[28]

The U.S. government pursues various objectives through its counter-drug assistance. These include helping the Ecuadorian military to defend the northern border, maintaining the U.S. base in Manta, and increasing the professional capacity of the Ecuadorian armed forces. Washington also works to improve the capacity of the Ecuadorian armed forces and government agencies to direct antiterrorism activities.

Despite the U.S. funding they receive, Ecuadorian armed forces have expressed certain reservations about their role in the antidrug strategy promoted by the U.S. government. The first concern is that they are being encouraged to take on a more proactive counterdrug role, especially along the northern border, that may exceed the armed forces' technical and operational capacity at a time when their overall budget is being reduced. Ecuador's Congress has approved cuts to the military budget estimated at 7 percent. This translates into a reduction in current salaries and pensions for retired officers and reduced resources for general spending, equipment maintenance, and the construction and equipping of new units along the Colombian border.[29] Yet according to one high-ranking officer, the armed forces need U.S.$50 million in equipment, technology, and special weapons to deal with the security issues on the northern border.[30]

A second concern is that the armed forces will be pressed to assume tasks historically assigned to the national police. The military is willing to establish interinstitutional communication channels and coordinate with the police to combat drugs, but loath to take on tasks that would require training soldiers in new areas such as fighting crime and relevant legal issues. Most important, the military fears having to operate among the population in ways that would tarnish its image and harm the good relations the armed forces have cultivated with the public over the years.

In addition, these added responsibilities have led to competition between the police and military forces for available resources; this has even prompted their respective intelligence services to investigate each other. Negotiations between the national police and international antidrug agencies have been carried out behind closed doors, and many international agreements on security issues have not been fully explained to the joint chiefs of staff. While there have been no public statements on the issue, interviews with members of the armed forces reflect jealousy and misgivings about efforts to provide increased resources to the national police and about the competition for funding that this has fueled between the forces.

The U.S. government is providing resources, equipment, and technical training to the Ecuadorian police to strengthen logistical capacities and interdiction efforts. From 2001 through 2003, the national police received approximately U.S.$17 million in law enforcement support. Aid to the police from the State Department's Bureau of International Narcotics and Law Enforcement (INL) was U.S.$1.2 million in FY2001 and rose dramatically thereafter, to U.S.$7.8 million in FY2002 and U.S.$8 million in FY2003. The FY2004 budget allocates U.S.$13 million in counterdrug aid to the police.[31]

In addition, 681 Ecuadorian military and police personnel received military training in 1999, provided either by the U.S. Defense Department or the U.S. State Department. The number jumped to 899 in 2001 and to 1,267 in 2002.[32] U.S. Special Forces participated in sixteen antidrug training missions in 1999 and twelve in 2000, mostly with Ecuadorian forces on the northern border.[33]

The training of local police forces by U.S. military personnel is particularly problematic. While the police clearly have a role to play in drug interdiction, local analysts question whether or not the police should be provided counterinsurgency or paramilitary-type training, which could undermine efforts to promote democratic civilian policing. Some fear that a militarization of the police is possible, further confusing the roles and mandates of the police as well as the armed forces. This is of particular concern given the poor track record of the Ecuadorian police with regard to human rights violations and corruption. As is the case in other countries, U.S. assistance is provided before mechanisms are established to ensure the accountability of local forces.

In fact, the security forces have shown a rapid decline in image, performance, and legitimacy as a result of both alleged and proven cases of corruption. During the first months of 2003, the police expelled a number of officers accused of taking bribes to falsify documents. In 2002 and 2003, other police officers were expelled from the force for links to drug trafficking.[34] In July, two former police commanders were arrested for embezzlement committed on the job.[35] The good reputation once enjoyed by the armed forces has also been damaged by a series of corruption cases involving military officers.

Members of the security forces, both military and police, are also accused of committing human rights violations, though compiling accurate statistics on complaints against police officers and soldiers is extremely difficult. As the U.S. State Department mentions in its 2002 annual human rights report on Ecuador, "During the year, the armed forces continued cooperating with the police in an occasional manner. Some police officers and soldiers continued to commit human rights abuses."[36]

The most recent reports by Amnesty International note the problem of human rights abuses committed by the police with impunity in Ecuador: "Concern remained that cases of human rights violations involving members of the security forces were not resolved promptly, impartially and independently. Many of these cases are brought before police courts where the vast majority of those accused of human rights violations are not convicted." Amnesty International has documented numerous cases of extrajudicial execution and torture in Ecuador in recent years.[37]

Manta Air Base: Focus of Attention and Debate

In November 1999, during the truncated administration of President Jamil Mahuad (1998–2000), Ecuador and the United States signed an agreement to allow U.S. forces to use the air force base in Manta as a forward operating location (FOL). This is one of four such sites that have been established in Latin America to carry out counterdrug detection and monitoring operations (see Chapter 2). These installations are owned by the host countries but provide unrestricted access to U.S. personnel and aircraft. The U.S. Air Force is in command of the FOL, and U.S. military forces and counterdrug personnel operate from the base. The FOL agreement with Ecuador permits the United States to make improvements to the airstrip and installations; U.S.$61.3 million was slated for these improvements. Work began in 2001, and the base was fully functional by late 2002.

The ten-year agreement was kept secret from the Ecuadorian Congress while negotiations over its terms were under way. Because it did not receive congressional approval as required in Ecuador for all international treaties, the agreement raised serious constitutional questions.[38]

Under the terms of the agreement, the "technical" operations carried out at Manta are kept secret from the Ecuadorian population for "security" reasons. For the United States, the agreement opens greater channels of cooperation with Ecuador in counterdrug efforts. Because of the base's geographic proximity to Colombia, it allows for easier surveillance of illegal activities there. Hence, it is intricately related to the implementation of Plan Colombia. Although there are no U.S. or Ecuadorian combat troops at the base, the information, air intelligence, and logistical support provided by the base to U.S. drug control agencies convey to Ecuador a certain responsibility for actions originating there.

Ecuadorian observers are concerned that Manta could become a strategic target of the warring factions in Colombia or—in the wake of September 11 and the subsequent U.S. war on terrorism—even a target of international terrorist networks. The expansion of the U.S. mission in Colombia after September 11 to include counterinsurgency as well as antidrug components raises concerns that what are now strictly antidrug operations at Manta may be expanded to include a broader mandate. This is difficult to monitor, however, because as noted, the agreement with the United States classifies as reserved all information related to operations or activities carried out by U.S. personnel on the base.

In addition, in 2000 an Ecuadorian congressional commission began investigating the activities of Dyncorp, a U.S.-based company contracted to provide administrative and other services to U.S. personnel working on the Manta base. Several human rights groups had denounced Dyncorp for allegedly employing mercenaries accused of committing human rights violations in other countries. This investigation came to a halt in 2002 when the roster of lawmakers changed, and no action has been taken by the new congress.

The presence of the U.S. FOL at the Manta base has also provoked heated debate in the communities surrounding the base. Supporters say the base has increased local tourism and trade and the use of local services, creating jobs and improving local economic conditions. Critics fear that the presence of U.S. soldiers is leading to increased prostitution and incidence of sexually transmitted diseases such as HIV. They also note increases in local prices because the soldiers have greater purchasing power compared to residents.

Activities on the base increased during the first months of 2003 with the transfer to Manta of Ecuadorian navy air units from Guayaquil and the south of the country. Following President Gutiérrez's visit to Washington in February 2003, Manta expanded its air operations to become the principal base for monitoring Ecuador's northern border. The former head of the joint chiefs of staff, General Oswaldo Jarrín, said that Manta "is the stepping off point for air-maritime exploration along the northern border."[39] This decision was made only a week after Gutiérrez declared Ecuador to be the U.S. government's greatest ally.

The debate over the military base at Manta is really over whether Ecuador should take part in the regional security strategy promoted by the United States and, more broadly, U.S. efforts to expand its sphere of influence into the Andes after the end of the Cold War.[40] Because Ecuador's political system is so fragile, the debate over Manta could lead to internal conflict that could compromise the agreement with the United States. This would make the country vulnerable to the system of punishments and rewards used by Washington in conducting its foreign policy.

• The Northern Border: Tension, Conflict, and Insecurity

There has long been social and cultural continuity in the region of Ecuador's 600-kilometer common border with Colombia, shown in Figure 7.2, with few notable differences between the populations on either side of the border. These populations have long-standing economic, cultural, and family ties that have helped define the nature of the bilateral relations between the two countries.

At the same time, economic changes along Ecuador's coast, in the highlands, and in the jungle have fueled constant migration to the border region. In the 1960s and 1970s, coffee and banana farming, cattle ranching,

Figure 7.2   Ecuador's Northern Border

and the start of oil production led to a process of colonization and regional development and to the region's greater integration into the Ecuadorian state, which has had a precarious presence along the border.

At one time it was thought that the Amazonian provinces of the border region could become major producers of coffee for the international market, but the poor quality of jungle soil and the lack of appropriate technology, along with international price fluctuations and competition from larger, higher-quality producers like Brazil, Colombia, and Vietnam, prevented this.[41] Bananas are today Ecuador's top-grossing agricultural export, but banana production in the border province of Esmeraldas was quickly eclipsed by that of other coastal provinces with better shipping infrastructure that were better able to plug into international markets. The highland province of Carchi has been affected by the economic problems in southern Colombia and by the downturn in trade linked to the 2000 dollarization of the Ecuadorian economy.

Overall, Ecuador has not registered any significant economic growth since the end of the 1980s. Oil income has not produced the effects anticipated by economic policymakers. In addition, cities and provinces in the border region have not received an equitable share of state resources, since power and economic decisionmaking are centralized in Quito and Guayaquil.

The economic situation in the northern border region has worsened in recent years. According to official government statistics published in 2003, the level of poverty in the border provinces was 59.6 percent in Carchi, 76 percent in Esmeraldas, 81.7 percent in Sucumbíos, and 82.7 percent in Orellana (to the south of eastern of Sucumbíos).[42] These revealing statistics show how precarious life is for the border population, especially for poor farmers who produce crops such as coffee, rice, cassava, and bananas, largely for family consumption. Very few peasant families plant other crops or raise livestock to complement their incomes. Some local residents work as farmhands on plantations that grow crops that have stable markets, but there is little other formal employment. The bulk of the population takes part in informal activities or illicit ones such as smuggling cooking gas.

Out of economic necessity, the border population has had to adapt to the opportunities offered by the proximity of the Colombian border—primarily job opportunities in the coca–cocaine industry—and the economic, political, and cultural dynamics of the region just across the border. The border population also had to adapt to the dynamics of the Colombian conflict, including the presence of armed groups: drug traffickers, right-wing paramilitary groups, and the Revolutionary Armed Forces of Colombia (FARC). In short, the proximity of the Colombian border has created unique conditions in the northern border region of Ecuador. National and local government officials must deal with a series of challenges and demands from the population, as well as with the security agendas of both Ecuador and Colombia. From the confluence of all these factors, this corner of Ecuador has been gradually heating up over the past few years.

The Humanitarian Corridor

The relationship between the movements of people caused by the implementation of Plan Colombia and the dynamics of Colombian armed groups, which have camps near Ecuadorian territory, are important elements for understanding the border situation. Social, economic, and political problems in the border region have worsened because of military and police measures that the Colombian government has implemented as part of Plan Colombia. The failure of peace talks between the FARC and the administration of former Colombian president Andrés Pastrana (1998–2002) and the efforts of the current president, Álvaro Uribe, to dismantle the drug production networks in southern Colombia have had negative repercussions in Ecuador.

Colombia's internal problems have sent refugees fleeing into neighboring countries, especially Ecuador. The Ecuadorian-Colombian border is now considered to be a kind of corridor for people trying to escape the Colombian conflict. Refugees and asylum-seekers go to towns along the border in search of physical safety, food, employment, and health care. However, neither the Ecuadorian government nor nongovernmental agencies operating in the area have the resources to meet these demands.

Likewise, the amount of financial assistance provided for alternative development by the U.S. Agency for International Development (USAID) has not been sufficient to strengthen the work of the Unit for Development of the North, the government agency in charge of managing resources for the border region. In fact, the border population's demands for social services far outstrip the operational capacities of this agency.[43]

According to census data collected in 2001 from 51,556 Colombians living in Ecuador, 10,052 of them entered Ecuador between 1998 and 2001. The largest number arrived in 1999, the year Plan Colombia first got under way.[44] Statistics from the Foreign Ministry's Office for Refugees also show that the number of people seeking refuge in Ecuador corresponds to the rhythms of the Colombian crisis: as either the armed conflict or fumigation intensifies, more Colombians seek refuge, often temporarily, in Ecuador. The number of asylum requests rose from 323 in 2000 to 6,244 in 2002.[45] Of the thousands of asylum requests each year to the Ecuadorian government, 98 percent are from Colombians. According to statistics provided by the Ministry of Foreign Relations, approximately 30 percent of those who requested asylum in recent years were denied, 30 percent were accepted, and an almost equal number did not pursue the request.[46]

The most pressing problems faced by Colombian immigrants in Ecuador relate to the weakness of the border economy. There are few jobs in the dollarized economy, where prices greatly exceed most people's buying power. Nearly half (49.5 percent) of Colombians in Ecuador live below the poverty line. In border areas the proportion soars to 60–90 percent, evidence that the situation is extremely difficult for Colombians coming to Ecuador in search of protection and refuge.[47]

This situation has strained the budgetary and technical capacities of humanitarian organizations working along the border as they confront growing demands for immediate assistance and public services. The Colombian refugees are poor when they arrive in Ecuador. The influx thus puts pressure on the already limited resources available to poor Ecuadorians living on the border.

The increased migration is undermining the region's traditionally harmonious social relations. There are recent reports that Colombians are being increasingly marginalized and that they are the targets of xenophobia, racism, and discrimination. "Colombian women are prostitutes" ... "they [Colombians] are taking our jobs" ... "the presence of Colombians only brings violence and crime" ... "they should be placed in special camps" ... and "the border should be closed and they should need visas to enter the country"—these are a few of the reactions interviewers collected from Ecuadorians living on the border.[48]

These perceptions are even more problematic when expressed by chamber of commerce representatives, police officers, immigration officials, or local government authorities. Ecuador has signed international conventions against racism, discrimination, exclusion, and related forms of intolerance within the framework of the United Nations. Ecuador is also signatory to international treaties that require compliance with the mandates of the United Nations High Commissioner for Refugees (UNHCR), whose office supervises and coordinates international actions to protect refugees around the world and helps alleviate the problems they face. Such international commitments mean that Ecuador is responsible for protecting the rights and well-being of refugees, including the right to request asylum.

Insecurity on the Border

The militarization of the border zone, far from helping to resolve problems, is complicating the situation by restricting a number of civil rights. Beginning in 2000, the armed forces began a systematic relocation of personnel and weapons from bases in the south to the northern border. This decision was based on the strategic plan of the joint chiefs of staff, which determined that the presence of irregular groups like the FARC on the northern border was a threat. The provinces of Carchi, Esmeraldas, and Sucumbíos experienced the greatest influx of military personnel, with the posting of sixteen detachments to monitor the Colombian border.[49] Joint military-police border patrols have also been stepped up.[50] According to local press reports, 1,267 Ecuadorian soldiers were trained by U.S. soldiers in 2002 on bases near the Colombian border.[51]

In April 2003, President Gutiérrez signed an executive decree establishing reserve areas where, for security reasons, the movement of people and vehicles from the border to twenty kilometers inland is restricted. The decree stipulates that border zones and reserve areas come under the armed forces' official war plan, and states that, in accordance with the National Security Law, these areas will be under the control of the armed forces and joint chiefs of staff. The National Security Law allows the military to maintain or change the status of temporary or permanent residents and to apply restrictions when, in the military's view, the situation merits. A new census is being planned as part of these activities to gather information on people living along the border.

The restrictions adopted by the Ecuadorian military in some cases contradict international resolutions adopted by the Andean Community of Nations. For example, Resolution 503 recognizes the free movement of peoples within Andean Community member nations. However, new restrictions mean that Colombians can no longer move freely into Ecuador, and their individual status in the country is subject to the will of the military.

The United States has announced it will dispatch all-terrain vehicles, helicopters, and small planes to the border region to support these security activities. In 2003, according to *Jane's Defense Weekly,* the United States donated "50 AM General M939 five-ton 6x6 tactical trucks and 100 High Mobility Multipurpose Wheeled Vehicles to the Ecuadorian Army. The estimated value of the vehicles is $5 million. They are expected to remain in service for a further 15 years."[52] This lot of equipment will most likely be put into service along the northern border, where 10,000 troops have been mobilized to augment control and security patrols.[53]

The greater military and police presence has increased tensions along the border and has had a negative impact on the cross-border commercial and cultural links that have existed for decades. However, the increased security presence has also been a response to high levels of crime and violence in the border provinces. According to statistics compiled by a non-governmental research center, the homicide rates in the border provinces are higher than the national average. In 2000, the once peaceful border province of Carchi registered a rate of 18.8 homicides for every 100,000 residents, as compared to a national average of about 15 homicides per 100,000 residents.[54]

Not only have crime and violence increased; they have also diversified. For example, no kidnappings were recorded in the country before 1993. By 1998 forty-two cases were reported, making it necessary to create specialized police antikidnapping units. Though accurate statistics are not available, the problem appears to be most serious in the border provinces. There is some evidence that Colombian armed groups (both guerrillas and common criminals) have extended their reach to Ecuador's border areas with threats and demands for *vacunas* (vaccines), payments against being kidnapped.

Human Rights on the Northern Border
As the security forces have been beefed up along the border, charges of abuse leveled against police and military officers have increased. Violations of human rights carried out by police officers and soldiers have included restrictions on free movement; arbitrary arrests; warrantless searches for precursor chemicals, weapons, and drugs; and threats or pressure directed against civic organizations that denounce abuses. Testimonies collected by human rights groups and academic researchers reveal the serious human rights problems faced by the local population.

Some statistics can be obtained at the local level, providing at least a partial picture. For example, in the border province of Sucumbíos, where the police force operates with U.S. resources, the human rights ombudsman's office has recorded nineteen complaints of abuse of authority filed against police officers.

The number of formal complaints made to public authorities, however, appears to be much smaller than the actual number of cases occurring, some of which are reported in the media. Fear of reprisals in an area of the country with such a weak state presence and where people can be located with relative ease discourages people from filing complaints. This contributes to ongoing impunity, as well as a lack of reliable statistical data.[55] When human rights organizations have filed complaints about abuses, formal legal investigations of the complaints get caught up in the rigid judicial bureaucracy (described below).

The situation is further complicated by the fact that the security forces maintain close links to the petroleum companies operating in the area. Both the armed forces and national police provide security services to the petroleum companies as one way of earning additional resources to offset their limited budgets.

Perceptions of Plan Colombia Among the Border Population
A 2002 survey conducted by a research institute in the border provinces of Sucumbíos, Carchi, Imbabura, Pichincha, and Esmeraldas reveals how the local population perceives Plan Colombia.[56] A full 89 percent of those polled said Plan Colombia is having a negative impact on Ecuador, in part because it has disrupted communications and commercial links. Those surveyed also said the central government is not supporting local initiatives or helping the region pull out of its economic crisis.

When asked about their perceptions of drug trafficking, 90 percent responded that Ecuador is not a drug-producing nation. Fifty-four percent said that Ecuador did not produce coca crops because this is not part of the local culture, but that in Ecuador some unemployed people do seek temporary work in Colombian coca fields for economic survival.

More than 90 percent said the drug business is dangerous for Ecuador, especially for the border region, because of the levels of violence that accompany it. But respondents also said that Ecuador's current antidrug policies have negative effects on innocent people. Along these same lines, those polled said the security forces are corrupt. This corruption means less protection for the population, making them, in turn, even more vulnerable to the violence generated by the drug trade. Some are subjected to increased persecution simply because they live on the border, yet officials do not take responsibility for harm caused to this segment of the population.

• Drugs and the Justice System
The pervasive sense of insecurity and vulnerability felt by many Ecuadorians along the border, as well as across the country more broadly, is

also directly related to the deficient administrative structures that character-
ize the Ecuadorian public sector and political system. Those who hold jobs
in the government bureaucracy, especially high-level, decisionmaking
posts, are caught up in a game of special interests. They dole out power
according to the institutional norms of a hierarchical, clientelistic, and pat-
rimonial political culture, subject to the prevailing political winds. The justice sector—crucial to any anti-drug-trafficking strategy—is no exception.

The legal norms for dealing with drug trafficking and drugs in Ecuador
are found in the constitution, the Narcotics and Psychotropic Substances
Law and its subsequent modifications,[57] the norms governing the attorney
general's office, and the legal statutes of the National Council for the
Control of Narcotics and Psychotropic Substances (known by its Spanish
acronym, CONSEP). The framework is conceptualized in the National
Strategy on Drugs and laid out in the National Plan 1999–2003. The
Narcotics and Psychotropic Substances Law, better known as Law 108, is
aimed at combating and eradicating production, supply, illicit use, and trafficking of narcotics and psychotropic substances. It establishes the legal
framework for control of specific drugs and precursor chemicals.[58]

At least on paper, CONSEP determines the country's drug policies and
carries out work in three areas: prevention, treatment, and rehabilitation;
control and oversight; and administration of seized property and technical
and legal assistance. However, the institutional structure dedicated to managing the numerous areas related to drug control is extremely complex, as
well as ineffective and inefficient. The situation is further complicated by
the role of the security forces in interdiction and other drug control efforts.
As a result of these factors, CONSEP has never had the leading role in
Ecuador's fight against drugs and lacks the political clout to manage the
various policies related to drug control. Rather, it functions as an umbrella
institution that channels information to the public and to international agencies concerned with drug control.

Apart from a public relations role, the major functions of CONSEP
include reducing demand for illicit substances, destroying seized drugs, and
managing assets seized from drug traffickers. Yet internal problems, procedural debates, and overlapping and poorly defined responsibilities keep the
agency from carrying out even these limited functions well. For example,
CONSEP's warehouses are weakly guarded, and it takes years for seized
drug shipments to be destroyed. Meanwhile, the stored drugs are vulnerable. According to one high-ranking CONSEP official interviewed in 2002,
"The Police Intelligence Department has information on possible plans by
Colombian drug traffickers to raid CONSEP warehouses." He added that
confiscated drug shipments are no safer in police stations—in 2001, an officer substituted flour for cocaine in the antidrug police warehouses in Quito
and then sold the drugs in bulk to drug traffickers.[59]

A range of obstacles prevents effective prosecutions in drug-trafficking cases. The prosecutor in Esmeraldas, for example, stated that a large number of trafficking cases are not tried because CONSEP has no office in the provincial capital, and the lab tests to identify illicit substances take longer than the ninety days the prosecution has to investigate. As a result, most evidence is not admissible and cannot be used in court proceedings.[60]

Impact of Law 108

The implementation of antidrug laws also raises concerns related to due process, fairness, and civil rights. The Ecuadorian government and Congress have largely followed the U.S. model, often at Washington's urging, of stiffening the sanctions for drug trafficking. As originally passed in 1991, Law 108 included a ten-year mandatory minimum jail sentence and a twenty-five-year maximum sentence for drug-related crimes. The minimum sentence was increased from ten to twelve years in 2003. The law does not differentiate between consumers, mules (those paid to carry or transport illegal drugs), small-time traffickers, and major traffickers. Anyone convicted, regardless of the crime, must serve at least a ten-year sentence. Revisions to the law in 1997 now allow judges to take into account extenuating circumstances, such as age, terminal illness, and good behavior.

Moreover, the twenty-five-year maximum sentence is greater than that mandated for other serious crimes, such as murder, which carries a maximum sentence of only sixteen years. In other words, a small-time trafficker can receive a longer sentence than a convicted killer. This disproportionality in sentencing practices reflects the rushed and irrational manner in which the sentencing regime for drug-related crimes was designed.

In 1997, the possession of drugs for personal consumption was decriminalized: one can no longer be arrested for possession of small amounts of drugs. But for the first six years that the drug law was in effect, the justice system had no way to distinguish between personal drug consumption and actual drug trafficking. The revisions to the law are also problematic, as the specific amount of drugs deemed for personal use is not specified. Hence, "what might be an amount for personal use to one judge is enough for another judge to convict someone for trafficking."[61]

Another problem with drug cases is that judges often base their decisions on police reports alone. These often include confessions obtained through pressure and torture and leave little room for the presumption of innocence. The lack of due process guarantees and the low standards of proof used to declare a defendant guilty have led some lawyers to complain that their clients in fact have to prove their innocence in order to avoid conviction.[62]

Antidrug cases are processed without following procedural guarantees established in the constitution, article 24, part 7, which stipulates the presumption of innocence in all legal proceedings. Part 3 of the same article states that "the laws will establish a proportionality between the crime and the sentence."

All the same, the number of those detained and tried on drug charges has been much greater than the number of those actually convicted. In 2000, 157 people were sentenced on drug-trafficking charges, only 24 percent of those arrested on such charges. In 2001, 272 people were sentenced, representing 30 percent of those arrested. On possession charges, 192 people were sentenced in 2000 and another 272 in 2002, representing 23 and 26 percent, respectively, of those arrested.[63]

One factor contributing to this disparity has been the fact that time limits are set for preventive detention. According to Ecuadorian law, detainees must be released if they are neither tried nor sentenced within one year of arrest. Judicial inefficiency benefits some in this situation. In addition, wealthy individuals arrested on drug-trafficking charges can, via bribes, remain in prison past the time limit and then obtain their freedom based on this technicality, thus avoiding prosecution. General concern about the way in which alleged criminals had turned this time limit into a judicial loophole forced its elimination in 2002, with the reform of the criminal procedure code. If the judge deems there is sufficient evidence, he or she can now legally hold the accused behind bars until the trial is held, thereby eliminating the opportunity to intentionally delay the process.[64]

The number of people detained on drug-trafficking charges has remained relatively steady since 2000. According to data from the National Social Rehabilitation Bureau, 2,538 people were detained on drug-related charges in 2002, 31 percent of the total detained on all charges that year. The numbers are not much different from 2000, when 2,844 people were arrested, or 2001, when the number was 2,505.[65] There are two possible reasons for this. The first is that the agencies in charge of controlling, monitoring, and combating drug trafficking are ineffective because of the institutional problems enumerated above. A second, and perhaps more likely, reason is that the national police may have to meet a kind of unspoken quota of annual arrests for drug trafficking to ensure continued U.S. support.

It is also clear that the Ecuadorian population has little faith in the justice system. Surveys conducted in 2001 found that 85 percent of Ecuadorians mistrusted the courts. In the cities of Quito and Guayaquil, where the largest part of the judicial structure is concentrated, the lack of trust is particularly high. Polls show that 53 percent of residents believe that the courts function poorly because of corruption, 14 percent because they are not impartial.

The country's penitentiary system is one of the government institutions that has deteriorated the most. The deplorable conditions suffered by inmates—both men and women—have worsened as a result of the expanding prison population. There were 8,723 inmates in Ecuador's prisons in 2002, including 7,925 men and 798 women. Of the inmates jailed on drug charges, 70 percent were women, and 46 percent of these women were Colombian. Only 27 percent of the male prisoners jailed on drug charges were Colombian. The number of foreigners serving time in Ecuadorian prisons in 2002 rose by 39 percent with respect to the previous year.[66] Scarce resources and poor management prevent the government from providing for the basic needs of the prison population.

In contrast to the growing amount of U.S. assistance to Ecuador's military and police forces, very little U.S. aid is provided to strengthen and improve the country's justice sector. In FY2003, in addition to the counterdrug aid described previously, Ecuador received U.S.$46 million in U.S. economic support. Of that, only about U.S.$3.5 million was designated for USAID justice-sector programs.[67] Some Ecuadorian officials complain that U.S. counterdrug assistance is disproportionately skewed toward the security forces to the detriment of the justice sector and drug treatment and prevention programs.[68]

Accountability and Transparency

As vital components of democratic procedure and effective governance, accountability and transparency are crucial to effective policy implementation. However, as noted previously, U.S. assistance is being provided even though there are no mechanisms in place to ensure the accountability of those who receive U.S. funding, nor are the operations of recipient organizations transparent. The main question is whether or not Ecuador's democratic system and political class are capable of establishing adequate mechanisms for management, accountability, and transparency in government institutions.

There is rarely any congressional or public debate in Ecuador about political accountability or about how drug control policies affect the public, much less discussion about mechanisms that would allow the public to monitor these policies. Indeed, congressional oversight of drug policy is extremely limited. Congress does not see the issue as part of the political debate, and the few discussions that have taken place on the issue generally have been related to corruption scandals involving high-ranking government officials. None of the opposition blocs in the Ecuadorian Congress has taken up the cause of oversight of the diverse agencies involved in national security issues, including drug policy.

The August 2003 discovery that a shipment of Ecuadorian army weapons had been diverted to the FARC potentially set the stage for an investigation. However, the military responded with complete silence, despite loud calls from the public and sectors of the justice system for the armed forces to clarify what had happened.[69] As of mid-2004, it remained unclear whether the arms had been stolen or internal corruption was involved. Only one member of congress attempted to investigate the case, and the military was continuing to attempt to have his parliamentary immunity rescinded; they have accused him of offending their institutional honor.

A review of Ecuador's antidrug legislation and its institutional structures shows that accountability procedures are nonexistent or ambiguous at best.[70] Internal government control mechanisms are confusing. The institutions that are charged with supervising the antidrug agencies, such as the congress, know little of the agencies' work. The situation is further complicated by the involvement of the military, which historically operates with little or no effective civilian oversight or control.

Finally, lack of coordination on drug policy among the various government offices and agencies involved further muddies the water. Bureaucratic infighting, turf battles, and unwillingness to share information hamper effective policy coordination, as does general administrative inefficiency and corruption. To date, the government has not designed measures and procedures that are capable of coordinating the numerous activities carried out by the country's security forces. The government ministry that should oversee issues related to the police forces and internal domestic order fails to guide policy implementation. Of particular concern, this ministry often appears to be out of the loop in direct negotiations for aid between the national police and U.S. antidrug agencies. At the least, civilian officials should be empowered by Washington to design, oversee, and implement counterdrug policies.

The lack of oversight means that Ecuadorian drug control efforts, and U.S. support for them, take place within a structure without the basic checks and balances needed for democratic processes to function.

• Conclusion

Defining drug trafficking as a national security threat—along with the deployment of armed forces that this implies—are producing a process of securitization of human relations in Ecuador as a whole and in the border region in particular. Securitization is eroding legal protections established for both individuals and institutions and undermining already fragile human rights, especially those of people living in the northern border region.

Ecuador has increased its participation in Plan Colombia, the regional security strategy promoted by the U.S. government. This has led to the presence of U.S. troops at Manta, the supply of technical equipment and financial resources to a number of police agencies, new measures of control exercised over the general population, negative environmental and health effects from aerial spraying, and human rights abuses.

As a result of Plan Colombia, the border provinces are experiencing new social problems that could overwhelm the mechanisms of public order. Particular attention should be paid to the economic and social needs of the civilian population living in the northern border region. Economic resources must be allocated to ensure that basic needs are met and public services provided.

The central government's lack of control over some agencies and its failure to put into place mechanisms to make these agencies accountable to the general public further frustrates effective policy implementation. Specific mechanisms for institutional oversight of the antidrug agencies within the security forces have yet to be created.

Moreover, restrictions on access to information—counterdrug efforts are classified as a national security concern—limit the ability of civil society organizations to monitor and to evaluate drug control activities. The creation and strengthening of social networks that can pressure government authorities and political parties for transparency on drug control efforts are indispensable. In addition, open debate on security issues, especially those linked to drug trafficking, is urgently needed.

U.S.-supported drug control programs and assistance have produced conflict within the military and police. The armed forces question some interdiction policies pursued by Washington that could jeopardize Ecuadorian national sovereignty. The existence and distribution of resources have led to interinstitutional jealousies as the police receive a greater share of money and technical resources to carry out tasks that are strengthening and militarizing them. Ecuadorian analysts point to the growing role of the military in domestic drug enforcement operations, as well as the training of local police forces by U.S. military troops, as further confusing the roles and missions of these two institutions. Moreover, they point out that such efforts run counter to the process of democratic institution-building needed in the country.

The judiciary has also been affected by the war on drugs and urgently requires modernization. One needed reform would give the National Judiciary Council greater power to investigate and to hand down sanctions, especially in drug-trafficking cases where a judge's actions are not transparent. Impunity must be overcome: military and police forces that commit human rights violations—as well as any other crimes—should be tried and sanctioned accordingly. The use of military and police tribunals to handle such cases internally limits the actions of civilian courts, distorting the role of the judicial branch and further weakening Ecuador's fragile democracy.

Especially since President Gutiérrez assumed office, Ecuador's policies on drug trafficking are increasingly defined by what has lately been called the Washington-Bogotá axis. That is, the consolidation of a security system involving the United States and Ecuador is fundamentally affected by the dynamics of the Colombian conflict, where insurgency, terrorism, and drug trafficking are closely intertwined. In short, Ecuador is viewed through the lens of Colombia. This distorts the national security agenda and diverts attention from the country's most pressing problems: economic malaise, weak governance institutions, and growing political instability.

Finally, with all these issues in mind, it should be remembered that Ecuador's president made a number of election promises. He pledged that he would not align the country with the U.S. security strategy, that he would increase citizen security while respecting human rights, that he would promote transparency in public management and strengthen the fight against corruption, and that he would implement policies for a more equitable distribution of wealth. Though his actions and those of his government to date raise doubts that any of these promises will be kept, his fellow citizens can continue to remind the president that they expect him to meet the challenges he set for himself and the nation.

• Notes

The author wishes to thank Jorge Núñez Vega for his support and assistance in carrying out the research for this chapter.

1. Fredy Rivera, "Campesinado y Narcotráfico," in *Revista Ecuador Debate*, no. 22, CAAP, Quito, 1991, p. 30.

2. Salomón Cuesta, *Putumayo, la Frontera de las Fronteras* (Quito: Fundación de Investigaciones Andino Amazónicas [FIAAM], Abya Yala, 1998), p. 42.

3. U.S. State Department, Bureau of International Narcotics and Law Enforcement (INL), *International Narcotics Control Strategy Report (INCSR) 2000, 2001, 2002, 2003*, "South America."

4. *INCSR 2003*, "South America."

5. *INCSR 2003*, "Ecuador Statistics 1994–2003."

6. Fander Falconi and Hugo Jacome, "La Invitada Indiscreta de la Dolarización: La Competitividad," in *Revista Sociedad y Economía*, no. 3, Universidad del Valle, Cali (October 2002).

7. *INCSR 2003, Volume 2: Money Laundering and Financial Crimes*, "Country Reports, Ecuador."

8. *El Comercio*, "5000 Cuentas Son Sospechosas de Lavado de Dinero en el País," Quito, 18 September 2002.

9. Instituto Nacional de Estadísticas y Censos (INEC), *VI Censo de Población y Vivienda*, Quito, November 2001.

10. *El Comercio*, "Efectos de fumigaciones," Quito, 12 January 2001.

11. Here and following paragraph: Acción Ecológica et al., Misión de Verificación, *Impactos en Ecuador de las Fumigaciones Realizadas en el Putumayo dentro del Plan Colombia*, report, October 2002. The number of fish mentioned in the next paragraph was calculated on the basis of the fish farms belonging to families in the border zones and is therefore approximate.

12. Social Studies and Public Opinion Institute (IESOP), report, Quito, 9 November 2002.

13. *El Comercio*, "Ecuador Está Involucrado en Conflicto," 17 May 2003.

14. U.S. State Department, *Patterns of Global Terrorism 2002*, "Western Hemisphere Overview."

15. *El Comercio*, "El Gobierno Contesto con una Fuerte Crítica a los Estados Unidos," 26 May 2002; and "Unda Propone un Sistema de Defensa Continental," 7 November 2002.

16. D. Román Ortiz, "La Estrategia Contrainsurgente del Presidente Álvaro Uribe: ¿Fórmula para la Victoria o Receta para una Crisis?" unpublished manuscript, Real Instituto Elcano, España, February 2003.

17. *El Comercio*, "El Problema de Colombia es Regional," 22 August 2003; and *Servicio Informativo Alai-amlatina*, "Uribe por un Mayor Involucramiento del Ecuador en Conflicto Colombiano," 22 August 2003.

18. *Diario Hoy*, "Colombia Gana Más con el Acuerdo," y "Gutiérrez Debe Aclarar Acuerdo Bilateral," 24 August 2003.

19. Adrián Bonilla, "Política Internacional y Narcotráfico: Acercamiento al Caso Ecuatoriano," in *Narcotráfico y Deuda Externa: las Plagas de América* (Quito: Caap, Cecca, Cerg, Ciudad, 1990); and Alexei Paez, "La Inserción Ecuatoriana en la Dinámica Andina del Narcotráfico," in *La Economía Política del Narcotráfico: el Caso Ecuatoriano*, Bruce Bagley and Adrián Bonilla, eds. (Quito: North-South Center, University of Miami, and Flacso/Ecuador, 1991).

20. Ministerio de Defensa Nacional, *Revista de las Fuerzas Armadas de Ecuador 2003*, no. 135, Quito, May 2003, p. 76.

21. Fernando Bustamante, "Fuerzas Armadas, Democracia, y Ciudadanía: Una Reflexión Preliminar," in *Fuerzas Armadas: Desarrollo y Democracia*, Abya-Yala, CELA, Academia de Guerra de la Fuerza Terrestre (Quito: ILDIS, 1995).

22. Fredy Rivera, "Democracia Minimalista y Fantasmas Castrenses en el Ecuador Contemporáneo," in *Las Fuerzas Armadas en la Región Andina. ¿No deliberantes o actores políticos?* Martín Tanaka, ed. (Lima: Comisión Andina de Juristas [CAJ] y la Embajada de Finlandia, 2001).

23. Ministerio de Defensa Nacional, Política de Defensa Nacional, 2002.

24. The White House, *The National Security Strategy of the United States of America*, September 2002, www.whitehouse.gov/nsc/nss.html.

25. Ministerio de Defensa Nacional, *Política de Seguridad para la Frontera Norte*, internal document, February 2002.

26. *Diario Hoy*, "Ecuador No Será Parte de Fuerza Multinacional," 17 October 2002.

27. USAID, Congressional Budget Justification, FY2004, Latin American and Caribbean Overview, Ecuador. Please note that Ecuador has also received both military and economic aid that is not INC aid; please see Ecuador aid chart on the WOLA website for details, www.wola.org.

28. *World-AP*, Latin America, "U.S. to Cut U.S.$15M in Aid to Ecuador," 2 February 2004.

29. Ministerio de Defensa Nacional, *Revista*, May 2003.

30. Information here and in the following two paragraphs is from author interviews with several military officers who wished to remain unnamed, February–March 2003.

31. INL, *FY2004 Budget Justification*, "Andean Counterdrug Initiative," June 2003.

32. Adam Isacson, "La Asistencia Estadounidense a la Seguridad en los Países

de la Región Andina," in *Colombia Internacional*, no. 49–50, Centro de Estudios Internacionales de la Universidad de los Andes (Bogotá, 2001); and Defense and State Departments, *Foreign Military Training in Fiscal Years 2002 and 2003, Joint Report to Congress*, respectively (for the two years).

33. César Montufar, "El Ecuador Entre la Iniciativa Andina y el Plan Colombia: Del Enfoque de los Efectos a una Perspectiva de Regionalización," in *Turbulencia en los Andes y Plan Colombia*, C. Montúfar and T. Whitfield, eds. (Quito: Universidad Andina Simón Bolívar, Corporación Editora Nacional, 2003), p. 226.

34. For example, see *El Comercio*, "El Jefe Antidrogas Preso en Santo Domingo," 28 August 2003.

35. *El Comercio*, "Dos ex Comandantes de Policía en Prisión," 14 June 2003.

36. U.S. State Department, *Country Reports on Human Rights Practices 2002*, "Ecuador."

37. Amnesty International, *Amnesty International Report 2002*, "Ecuador" (covering January–December 2001).

38. Montufar, "El Ecuador."

39. Author interview with General (ret.) Oswaldo Jarrín, 6 April 2004.

40. Juan Gabriel Tokatlian, "Colombia, el Plan Colombia, y la Región Andina ¿Imposición o Concertación?" in *Revista Nueva Sociedad*, no. 173 (Caracas, 2001).

41. See data from the most recent agricultural survey, conducted in 2000, from Farm Information Service of the Agriculture and Livestock Ministry of Ecuador (SICA), Proyecto SICA/MAG, in "Historia e Importancia del Café en Ecuador," which can be found on the SICA website, www.sica.gov.ec.

42. Integrated System of Social Indicators of Ecuador, (Sistema Integrado de Indicadores Sociales del Ecuador, SIISE), versión 3.5, Quito, 2003.

43. Observatorio de la Cooperación al Desarrollo en Ecuador, *Boletín* 3, July 2003, p. 11.

44. INEC, *VI Censo*, November 2001.

45. Ministerio de Relaciones Exteriores, Oficina de Refugiados.

46. Information provided to author by the Ministry of Foreign Relations, March 2004.

47. Salomón Cuesta and Fredy Rivera, "Perfiles y Percepciones del Refugio Colombiano en Ecuador," FLACSO/Ecuador, investigation document no. 1 (Quito, 2003).

48. Ibid.

49. *El Comercio*, "16 Bases Militares Cercan el Norte," 14 March 2003.

50. *El Comercio*, "Los Militares y los Policías Inician el Patrullaje en Carchi," 24 February 2003. The joint activities include training in the adequate treatment of criminals and detainees.

51. *El Comercio*, "1,267 Soldados Entrenados por EEUU," 30 July 2003.

52. Jane's Defence Weekly 39, no. 28, (23 July 2003), p. 8.

53. *El Comercio*, "El Control en la Frontera Norte Se Amplia," 3 May 2003.

54. Edison Palomeque, *Diagnóstico sobre Seguridad Ciudadana en Ecuador* (Quito: Flacso/Ecuador–PAHO/WHO, 2002). The average homicide rate was 15.1 per 100,000 inhabitants in 1998 and 14.8 in 1999.

55. Interview with an official of the Human Rights Office (Defensoría del Pueblo) in Sucumbíos Province, February 2003.

56. All information on the poll is from Claudio Gallardo, report: "Encuesta Sobre la Percepción de los Ecuatorianos Sobre Seguridad y Plan Colombia," January 2003. The survey covered all the border provinces, with a sample of 800 people.

57. The Political Constitution of the Republic was published in the Official Register (Registro Oficial/RO) no. 1, 11 August 1998. The drug law (La Ley de Sustancias Estupefacientes y Psicotrópicas), its regulations, and its reforms can be found in RO no. 523, 17 September 1990, and later modifications in RO no. 637, 7 March 1991 and RO no. 173, 15 October 1997, respectively.

58. "Estrategia Nacional para Enfrentar las Drogas: Plan Nacional 1999–2003." See www.consep.gov.ec/plan.htm for the executive summary of Ecuador's National Plan for Drug Prevention and Control; also, the OAS Progress Report in Drug Control at www.oas.org/main/main.asp?sLang=E&sLink=www.cicad.oas.org.

59. This information and that immediately following are from an interview with a CONSEP official who wished to remain anonymous, Quito, December 2002.

60. Author interview with provincial prosecutor in Esmeraldas, February 2003.

61. Sandra Edwards, "Illicit Drug Control Policies and Prisons: The Human Cost," Washington Office on Latin America *Special Update*, November 2003. www.wola.org/publications/ddhr_ecuador_memo4.pdf.

62. Ibid.

63. The Organization of American States (OAS), Interamerican Drug Abuse Control Commission (CICAD), Progress Report in Drug Control, Multilateral Evaluation Mechanism (MEM), 1999, 2000, 2001, and 2002.

64. For additional information see Edwards, *The Human Cost.*

65. Dirección Nacional de Rehabilitación Social, "Boletín Estadístico 2002."

66. Ibid., p. 43.

67. U.S. Agency for International Development, *Congressional Budget Justification 2004, Latin America and the Caribbean,* "Ecuador," p. 12.

68. Edwards, *The Human Cost,* p. 8.

69. *El Comercio,* "Las FFAA Ponen Bajo Llave el Juicio por el Robo de las Ametralladoras," 4 September 2003.

70. See CONSEP's website for Ecuador's legislation and CONSEP's structure; also the Progress Report in Drug Control, MEM, CICAD.

8

Mexico:
The Militarization Trap

Laurie Freeman and Jorge Luis Sierra

M exico has historically been a producer of marijuana and heroin destined for U.S. markets. The first drug networks were family-based
groups that smuggled drugs and other contraband across the U.S. border.
The landscape changed drastically in the mid-1980s, when a major U.S.
interdiction effort shut down Florida as an entry point for Colombian
cocaine. Colombian traffickers turned to Mexico, with its porous 2,000-
mile border with the United States, and began working with their Mexican
counterparts to supply U.S. demand. Enriched and emboldened by the
lucrative cocaine trade, the Mexican cartels grew in sophistication and
power to corrupt. They escalated their violence, leaving a trail of intimidation, terror, and bloodshed.

Mexico's growing importance in the drug trade triggered a number of
U.S policies toward Mexico intended to invigorate that country's ability to
disrupt and to dismantle drug-trafficking organizations. Although these
policies have not had a discernible impact on the amount of drugs entering
the United States via Mexico, they have become obstacles to consolidating
democracy, protecting human rights, and establishing civilian oversight of
the military in Mexico. The United States supported the creation of elite
and "corruption-free" antidrug units in Mexico's security forces, but so far
the track record of these units suggests that they cannot be completely inoc-
ulated against corruption. Their creation has diverted effort and attention
from more comprehensive reform.

With U.S. encouragement, Mexico has given military personnel an
increasing role in the federal police forces and prosecutors' offices. When
this trend began, U.S. and Mexican authorities claimed it was a temporary
solution to the problems of police and prosecutorial corruption and inepti-
tude. More than a decade later, however, today the military is entrenched in
this role and shows no signs of withdrawing. The armed forces have themselves taken on growing and more public drug control responsibilities. U.S.
military assistance has helped make this possible by providing the Mexican

263

Mexico	
Population	100,500,000
GDP	U.S.$617.8 billion
GDP per capita	U.S.$6,214
Share of Income	
• Poorest 10 percent of population	1.0%
• Richest 10 percent of population	43.1%
• Ratio of income of richest 10% to poorest 10%	45.0 times
Percentage living in poverty (<$2/day)	24.3%
Percentage living in extreme poverty (<$1/day)	8.0%
Public perception of corruption among public officials and politicians (0=more, 10=less)	3.6

Sources: UNDP, *Human Development Report 2004;* World Bank, *Inequality in Latin America: Breaking with History?;* Transparency International, *Corruption Perceptions Index 2003.*

Notes: Population and GDP data from 2001; share of income data 2000; poverty data 1990–2001.

military with training and equipment. As a result, the Mexican military has gained political influence and has seen its autonomy reinforced, thus altering its traditional subordination to civilian control.

Mexican police and soldiers have committed grave human rights violations during drug control efforts, and few are ever prosecuted for these crimes. In some cases, abusive soldiers or police have been the beneficiaries of U.S. training or other assistance. In other cases, the U.S. government has turned a blind eye toward human rights violations in the interest of obtaining drug-related information.

More than any other country studied in this volume, Mexico has a unique relationship with the United States that has complicated both nations' responses to the drastic escalation of drug trafficking and drug-related violence and corruption in Mexico. Their intertwined histories, societies, and economies have made the U.S. counterdrug relationship with Mexico complex and fraught with tension.

U.S. and Mexican leaders often declare that they have no bilateral relationship more important than that with each other. Yet U.S.-Mexican relations have been marked by distrust and occasional conflict since 1846, when the United States declared war on Mexico and the countries fought bitterly for two years. When the war ended, half of Mexico's territory had been lost to—or, in the Mexican view, stolen by—the United States. Since then, Mexico has been extremely sensitive to issues of sovereignty and any perception that the United States might be meddling in its affairs. The Mexican military saw the United States as its natural enemy, and Mexico's defense was oriented northward to protect the nation from any future U.S. invasion. The drug war opened the door for the Pentagon to engage with this untrusting neighbor. "It is a miracle this relationship exists, given Mexican nationalism," according to one U.S. official.[1]

Promoting free trade has long been the number-one U.S. policy priority regarding Mexico. Although Mexico in the 1980s and 1990s was marked by widespread electoral fraud and official corruption, the main thrust of U.S. policy was to secure the economic reforms necessary for the signing of the North American Free Trade Agreement (NAFTA). Currently, thanks to NAFTA, Mexico is the second-largest U.S. trading partner, to the tune of about U.S.$260 billion every year. Every day, more than 250,000 vehicles cross into the United States from Mexico.[2] U.S. trade policy with Mexico has torn down barriers to the free flow of goods. Yet at the same time, U.S. counterdrug policy seeks to stop the flow of a particular type of goods— illicit drugs—for which there is heavy U.S. demand. The United States is simultaneously and paradoxically trying to create what has been called "a borderless economy and a barricaded border."[3]

The relationship between these interdependent neighbors reached some of its all-time lows as a result of anger and frustration over the drug issue. Twice, in 1969 and 1985, the U.S. government essentially shut down the U.S.-Mexico border in counterdrug-related actions. Mexico refused to receive U.S. drug control assistance for several years during the 1990s, and even after aid began flowing again, Mexico unceremoniously returned seventy-two U.S.-donated helicopters. At about that time, the U.S. Congress came close to decertifying Mexico as a drug ally, a move that would have cut off economic assistance to, and triggered trade sanctions against, an important trading partner.

Since President Vicente Fox took office in December 2000, however, previous friction over the drug-trafficking issue has largely evaporated from U.S.-Mexican relations. Efforts during the Fox administration's first three years led to the arrest of 22,000 people on drug crimes, including dozens of kingpins, among them some of the most wanted and feared.[4] Tijuana cartel leader Benjamín Arellano Félix was arrested in March 2002 by Mexican special forces soldiers in what was described by the U.S. State Department as "the most significant arrest ever of a wanted drug trafficker in Mexico." Special army units netted top figures from all the other major cartels as well, including the Gulf cartel's Osiel Cárdenas, captured after a wild shootout in the streets of Matamoros. These aggressive Mexican efforts have pleased the United States enormously, leading drug czar John Walters to exclaim that "Mexico is going farther [in antidrug efforts] than any other nation, including the United States."[5] At first glance, U.S. and Mexican drug control policies finally appear to be paying off.

Yet even the State Department admits that

> in spite of these successes, Mexico remains the major transit country for cocaine entering the United States. Approximately 65 percent of cocaine reaching the United States passes through Mexico and waters off the Pacific and Gulf coasts. ... Additionally, Mexican traffickers figure prominently in the distribution of drugs, particularly cocaine, heroin, methamphetamine, and marijuana in U.S. markets.[6]

In short, the arrests of key traffickers have failed to make a significant dent in the flow of illicit drugs over the U.S.-Mexico border.

• Human Rights and the Security Forces in Mexico

Unlike most of Latin America's other main drug-producing or trafficking nations, Mexico is neither at war nor in serious social turmoil; nor is it emerging from a period in which the military played a predominant role. Even so, the military is involved in counterinsurgency efforts, primarily in the southern states of Chiapas and Guerrero, to combat guerrilla groups that surfaced in the 1990s. The Mexican military has remained largely under civilian control and has had relatively little involvement in politics and public affairs, though there are fears that this may be eroding, partly as a result of increased military participation in drug control.

At the same time, Mexico's unique political system has long fostered serious human rights abuses by both the military and the police. In the wake of the Mexican Revolution of 1910–1920, Mexico remained a formal democracy and elections were held, but the party that was eventually called the Institutional Revolutionary Party (Partido Revolucionario Institucional, PRI) kept control of the government for seventy years. One-party rule severely crippled Mexico's civilian institutions, breeding a culture of authoritarianism and impunity. Power was concentrated in the executive branch, with the president exercising near-total control over every aspect of government. The legislature and judiciary existed to affirm and uphold the president's actions and thus did not develop into full-fledged, independent actors capable of checking the executive's excessive power.

When the PRI could not maintain its grip on political power through the cooptation of political opponents or tight control of the media, it resorted to electoral manipulation, outright fraud, and violent repression. From the late 1960s to early 1980s, the Mexican military, police, and intelligence services conducted counterinsurgency campaigns against dissidents and left-wing guerrillas that resulted in torture, forced disappearances, and several massacres.[7] The U.S. government ignored these "dirty war" tactics, as well as electoral fraud that kept the PRI in power, satisfied that the PRI guaranteed stability in an important Latin American ally—and next-door neighbor—during the Cold War.

In particular, the United States tended to ignore corrupt and abusive practices on the part of the Mexican intelligence services because they were anticommunist allies.[8] The Federal Security Directorate (Dirección Federal de Seguridad, DFS), one of the lead agencies in Mexico's campaign against political dissidents and guerrillas, was deeply involved in organized crime and drug trafficking, even issuing police badges to drug traffickers and other criminals so they could carry out their activities without fear of arrest. Top DFS officials were themselves crime bosses. DFS director Miguel Nazar Haro, implicated in a number of forced disappearances, was indicted by the Federal Bureau of Investigation (FBI) in 1982 for orchestrating a theft ring that moved cars out of the United States into Mexico. The FBI was told not to pursue the indictment against him because he was a valuable intelligence asset.[9]

In this context, the Mexican justice system evolved not to establish the rule of law but to preserve the power of the powerful—from local political bosses all the way to the president. Police and intelligence agents spied on, harassed, and intimidated political opponents; in return for their services, they were allowed to engage in lucrative criminal activities without fear of punishment. Police were essentially the private security forces of the elite and had little reason to develop the technical skills needed to conduct professional investigations based on solid evidence. When called on to solve crimes, they often resorted to threats or torture to obtain confessions from suspects or convenient scapegoats. Police relied on *madrinas*—thugs hired as police backup or to serve as freelance policemen themselves. Impunity for these acts led to an "array of abuses that have become an institutionalized part of Mexican society…, especially in Mexico's efforts to curb narcotics trafficking."[10]

Police often resort to human rights violations in their attempts to investigate crimes. The most common is arbitrary arrest. Authorities generally claim to have arrested suspects in flagrante delicto (in the act of a crime). In Mexico, the legal definition of what is in flagrante is so broad that it may apply up to three days after the commission of a crime, as long as a witness identifies the suspect. With such broad sway, it is easy for police and soldiers to detain people without a warrant, and judges rarely question their accounts. Many of the complaints made about arbitrary detention are for drug-related offenses.[11]

Torture continues to be widespread, although its use has declined in recent years. The UN Committee Against Torture issued a report on Mexico in 2003 concluding that torture is not the result of "exceptional situations or occasional excesses by police agents" but is "habitual and is used systematically as a resource in criminal investigations." Methods include beatings, electric shocks, simulated executions, suffocation with plastic bags, and deprivation of food and water. Torture is used to obtain information or confessions.[12]

The Mexican Military

Mexico is the Latin American country with the longest record of military subordination to civilian rule—a situation that can be characterized as "civilian, but not necessarily democratic, control" of the Mexican armed forces.[13] At the same time, the Mexican military is considered one of the most closed and secretive in Latin America. In exchange for the Mexican military staying out of politics, PRI granted the military almost complete internal autonomy and placed it beyond public scrutiny or even legislative oversight. Mexico's Congress exerts little real control over military budgets. The military is responsible for making its own decisions about its size and about weapons and equipment purchases, budgets, and contracts. Circumventing civilian oversight, the defense minister comes from within the military.[14] Prior to the Fox administration, defense ministers did not appear at congressional oversight hearings. According to Luis Astorga, an expert on drug trafficking, "There are no counterweights to the military. All the decisions—the who, when, where, and why—shouldn't be left in their hands. They leave a lot in the shadows."[15]

Military courts have broad jurisdiction to handle offenses against military discipline as well as any crimes committed by military personnel on duty, even when those crimes are committed against civilians. These courts are not transparent or accountable to civilian authorities. Military justice officials are legally prohibited from making documents from judicial proceedings public.[16] As a result, the military justice system has often been used as a protective shield for soldiers implicated in human rights violations or as a weapon against military personnel who advocate for change within the institution.

Although the military has remained subordinate to civilian control, it has been brought into civilian spheres and roles as a result of presidential orders. At various times, Mexican presidents have called on military personnel to serve in top police and prosecutorial posts, especially those responsible for combating drugs, with the hope that the famed discipline of the army would act as an antidote to corruption. The military accepted out of loyalty to a system that granted it complete internal autonomy and with an eye to securing a role for itself in the post–Cold War security environment. In 1995, Mexico's military was officially given a role in public security decisionmaking and policymaking as a member of the National Public

Security Council. The Mexican Congress did not contest the implications of this decision—only a small minority expressed concerns about its possible dangers—and it was upheld in March 1996, when the Mexican Supreme Court determined that the armed forces may intervene in public security matters as long as civilian authorities request it.

Compared to the police, the military has a generally positive public image. In one poll carried out by a Mexican newspaper, 53 percent of respondents said they had confidence in the Mexican army compared to only 32 percent for the police.[17] Much of the public's respect for the military comes from its robust disaster-response mission. Whenever a hurricane strikes or a volcano erupts or a river floods, it is the military that can be counted on to deliver supplies and shepherd people to safety.

The military also has a reputation for being more disciplined and less corrupt than the police—a perception that may derive from the fact that the military has been so shielded from public scrutiny. After all, military corruption scandals are legion: soldiers protecting a drug flight gunned down federal police in Veracruz in 1991; a general offered an official U.S.$1 million a month to go easy on the Tijuana cartel; and General Jesús Gutiérrez Rebollo, once considered by U.S. officials to be a man of "absolute integrity" as Mexico's drug czar scored major victories against one cartel as a favor to its rivals.[18] Lack of oversight and accountability has permitted and possibly even fostered corruption, and the extent to which it has pervaded the institution is probably underestimated as a result.

The Mexican Justice System

Understanding why Mexico's human rights problems persist requires an examination of the criminal justice system, which does not adequately safeguard against abuse; on the contrary, it often provides incentives for illegal arrest and torture. Nor does it hold human rights violators accountable.

In Mexico's criminal justice system, trials consist of a series of hearings where evidence is presented in written form, confessions are the "queen of evidence" (and often the only evidence), and the accused are not guaranteed access to legal counsel. Prosecutors exercise a monopoly over the criminal process, and judges do not play an active role. In fact, judges are often absent from the proceedings, taking the prosecution's case at face value and issuing guilty verdicts in 90 percent of cases. The judicial branch's lack of independence leaves judges "vulnerable to pressure from the executive branch, including prosecutors, to convict based on tainted confessions" or to allow the wealthy and well-connected to evade justice.[19] (In early 2004, Fox proposed justice reforms aimed at correcting some of these faults; at the time this chapter was written it seemed unlikely that Mexico's Congress would pass the proposal.)

In a similar fashion, the criminal justice system has overlooked and even encouraged abuses by the Mexican military as the military's public security and law enforcement role has grown. The military is technically prohibited from arresting or investigating criminal suspects, but the fact that civilian prosecutors and judges accept "evidence" gathered by soldiers during illegal detention and torture, turning a blind eye to clear signs of human rights violations and improper procedure, creates incentives for the military to do police work.

When soldiers are accused of human rights violations against civilians, impunity is the general outcome. During the administration of Ernesto Zedillo (1994–2000), military attorney general Rafael Macedo de la Concha (now serving as Fox's attorney general) received numerous credible reports of torture and other human rights violations committed by members of the military, several documented by the government's own National Human Rights Commission (Comisión Nacional de los Derechos Humanos, or CNDH). There is no evidence that the allegations were seriously investigated or prosecuted. The UN special rapporteur on torture noted, "Military personnel appear to be immune from civilian justice and generally protected by military justice."[20]

Although the PRI's "perfect dictatorship" ended with the election of opposition presidential candidate Vicente Fox in July 2000, the process of democratic reform has proceeded in fits and starts. The weaknesses and flaws of Mexico's institutions, particularly the criminal justice system, are proving difficult to overcome, and so the police and military continue to commit human rights violations with little fear of punishment. No efforts to make the military more transparent or accountable are in view, particularly because Fox feels indebted to the military for accepting the PRI's defeat and thereby giving stability to the political transition after the 2000 elections. According to Raúl Benítez, an expert on the Mexican military, "This attitude of subordination and loyalty ... gives the armed forces great benefits, [particularly] the power to 'influence the possibility that they will not be affected as institutions' in the event of national security or defense policy reform."[21]

• U.S.-Mexican Drug Control Policy

Mexico has historically been a producer of marijuana and opium. Cultivation of both crops occurs in the Sierra Madre Mountains of northwestern states such as Sinaloa and Chihuahua, as well as in Guerrero to the south (see Figure 8.1), all of which have substantial populations living in rural poverty. The Mexican army has spent more than a half-century in its permanent eradication campaign, trekking through remote mountain fields to hack down illicit crops.

Equally historic are the trafficking networks established to smuggle drugs and other contraband from Mexico into the United States. These net-

Figure 8.1   Mexican Opium Cultivation Areas, 1999

Opium poppy
growing regions

Source: Drug Enforcement Administration, *The Mexican Heroin Trade*, DEA-20014, April 2000.

works experienced a dramatic growth in power and sophistication in the mid-1980s, when Colombian traffickers, stymied by U.S. interdiction efforts in Florida and the Caribbean, sought Mexican services to traffic cocaine across the U.S.-Mexico border. Cocaine rapidly transformed the drug landscape in Mexico. The old marijuana smugglers became part of a complex, hemisphere-wide network of drug traffickers.

As drug-trafficking activity increased in Mexico, traffickers resorted to previously unknown levels of bribery and violence. In November 1984, former defense minister Juan Arévalo Gardoqui was implicated in the Buffalo Ranch—an enormous marijuana plantation of twelve square kilometers employing 12,000 people—owned by major kingpin Rafael Caro Quintero. In February 1985, Enrique "Kiki" Camarena Salazar, an agent of the U.S. Drug Enforcement Administration (DEA) who was investigating police ties to the Buffalo Ranch, was kidnapped, tortured, and murdered. Two days after Camarena's disappearance, Caro Quintero fled the city of Guadalajara in a private airplane after a brief, and presumably staged, exchange of gunfire with police.[22]

Camarena's murder brought tensions between the two countries to a head. Collusion between drug traffickers and the Mexican police was already well known to the United States, but this was the first time that Mexican corruption had led to the death of a U.S. agent. U.S. drug control officials acted swiftly and forcefully to identify those responsible. As they did so, they became aware that Mexican drug traffickers were being given cover by a vast network reaching the highest levels of government. Mexico and the United States plunged headfirst into a crisis of confidence.

Beginning in 1986, the United States reacted with an antidrug strategy that would have a deep and long-term impact in Mexico. This strategy consisted of three overall policies. First, in a search for trustworthy police partners, the United States supported efforts to purge, disband, and restructure corrupt police forces; helped create vetted units within these forces; and provided training, equipment, and infrastructure support to federal police agencies. Second, U.S. officials sought a larger counterdrug role for the Mexican military. Finally, Congress imposed the requirement that drug production or transit nations, including Mexico, be certified annually as cooperating with U.S. drug control efforts (described in Appendix 1). These policies taken together reinforced the military approach, provided incentives for abusive practices, and caused serious tension and conflict between the U.S. and Mexican governments.

Building Trustworthy Police Partners

> *There is not one single law enforcement institution in Mexico with whom DEA has an entirely trusting relationship.*
> —DEA administrator Thomas Constantine, 1997[23]

When DEA chief Thomas Constantine uttered those damning words at a 1997 congressional hearing on Mexico, more than ten years had passed since the Camarena murder. In that time, U.S. drug control agencies had undertaken a range of efforts, all unsuccessful, to create trustworthy police counterparts. In Mexico, the DEA can collect intelligence about the drug trade, but it is not empowered to arrest traffickers or to seize shipments. For that it must depend on the Mexican police.

Among the various police forces in Mexico, only the federal police can intervene directly in drug control efforts because drug trafficking is codified as a federal crime.[24] The Federal Preventive Police (Policía Federal Preventiva, PFP) is responsible for public order and security; it exists, in essence, to prevent crimes from occurring. Operating under the Public Security Ministry, the PFP is allowed to detain suspects caught in the act of a crime. They also gather intelligence on a range of federal crimes but do not investigate or serve arrest warrants. After a drug crime is committed, responsibility to investigate and arrest suspects pursuant to a judicially issued warrant falls to the Federal Investigations Agency (Agencia Federal de Investigaciones, AFI), formerly known as the Federal Judicial Police (Policía Judicial Federal).[25] The AFI works for the attorney general's office (Procuraduría General de la República, PGR), akin to the FBI working under the U.S. Justice Department.

The PGR is technically Mexico's lead drug control agency, with responsibilities for eradicating illicit crops, interdicting drug shipments, and investigating and prosecuting drug offenders. The PGR has a helicopter fleet for aerial eradication, but it carries out only about 25 percent of all eradication efforts, with the military performing the remaining 75 percent on the ground. The PGR, in coordination with the military, also establishes checkpoints, maritime patrols, and aerial surveillance to detect and to interdict drug trafficking.

Though in recent years the Mexican military has received the bulk of U.S. counterdrug aid, the United States also supports a variety of counterdrug programs for the Mexican attorney general's office (Figure 8.2 shows overall U.S. aid to Mexico). Since the mid-1980s, the focus of this assistance has largely been to build up the PGR's helicopter fleet for aerial crop eradication and interdiction efforts, to train thousands of police and prosecutors, to enhance the PGR's intelligence capabilities, and to improve

Figure 8.2   U.S. Aid to Mexico, 1997–2005

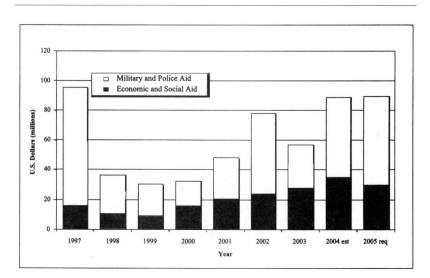

Source: Data from the U.S. State Department, Bureau for International Narcotics and Law Enforcement Affairs, *International Narcotics Control Strategy Report*, various years. Please see WOLA website, www.wola.org, for full listing.

money-laundering controls and investigations; and to provide equipment, computers, and infrastructure. U.S. law enforcement agents are working ever more closely with the Mexican police to share information, conduct investigations, and prepare prosecutions for drug cases. (The U.S. government also provides some training and assistance to the Federal Preventive Police.)

In response to the crisis of confidence, at first the U.S. government seemed satisfied that a wholesale purge of corrupt police forces would make important inroads in the fight against corruption. After the Camarena murder in 1985, intense U.S. pressure forced Attorney General Sergio García Ramírez to dismiss numerous DFS agents for their links to drug trafficking and later to disband the DFS entirely. Several years later, under President Carlos Salinas de Gortari (1988–1994), there was an attempt to purge and restructure the attorney general's office because of rampant corruption and human rights abuse, especially in the counterdrug brigade of the Federal Judicial Police. The purge was precipitated by the murder of human rights attorney Norma Corona by brigade agents in cahoots with drug traffickers. Every successive president has purged and restructured the PGR on at least one occasion. President Zedillo implemented several such rounds, including the dismissal of nearly 1,000 federal police and prosecutors in 1996, though few were actually prosecuted for corruption, and several hundred were later reinstated by the courts.

As corruption continued unabated, the United States encouraged the Mexican government to create special counterdrug units within the PGR. In 1988 President Salinas formed the Center for Drug Control Planning (Cendro), the PGR's drug intelligence analysis center, and in 1992 he created the National Institute to Combat Drugs (Instituto Nacional para el Combate a las Drogas, or INCD), roughly styled after the DEA.[26] The INCD was disbanded in the wake of allegations that its director, General Jesús Gutiérrez Rebollo, was on the payroll of the Juárez cartel. It was replaced by a new agency, the Special Prosecutor for Crimes Against Health (Fiscalía Especial para Atención a Delitos Contra la Salud, FEADS). The FEADS employed scores of former INCD agents after subjecting them to a vetting process in which the DEA and FBI played a central role.[27] U.S. funds also provided technical support for the new agency. But in its turn, the FEADS was disbanded in 2003 after agents were discovered to be extorting drug traffickers.

As corruption continued to frustrate U.S. efforts to cooperate with Mexican law enforcement agencies, the DEA sought to identify and train counterparts within the Mexican attorney general's office and Federal Judicial Police to work in Sensitive Investigative Units (SIUs).[28] The SIU program's purpose is to create, train, and support a team of trustworthy investigators who are subjected to a "rigorous selection and vetting process" consisting of U.S.-administered criminal background checks, urine testing, and polygraph tests.[29] U.S. agents can share sensitive information only with these "supervetted" counterparts.

U.S. officials had high hopes for the SIU program, believing that it would lead to "a new era of successful investigations between the U.S. and Mexican Governments."[30] Yet not long after the SIU program began, U.S. officials discovered "significant drug-related corruption" among SIU agents that caused "great concern about the long-term prospects for success."

Five years later, however, U.S. law enforcement agents characterized the SIU program as a success. According to the DEA, it "has proven to be an extremely effective approach in conducting high-level international narcotics investigations" by allowing DEA agents to "work hand-in-hand with trustworthy foreign law enforcement officials."[31] But there are few concrete examples of SIU successes; most arrests of major drug traffickers have been carried out by the military.

Under President Fox, U.S. training and support for the Mexican police continues, and has actually increased, as the Mexican government has become more receptive to receiving new kinds of assistance from the United States. The DEA and FBI have seized on training as a way to build important relationships with their counterparts. During 2002, more than 6,200 Mexican law enforcement personnel attended more than 120 U.S.-sponsored training courses.[32]

Although the DEA is the lead U.S. drug control agency in Mexico, in 1994, the FBI was authorized to work on international drug investigations, known as Resolution Six investigations. Mexico is the FBI's largest of three Resolution Six programs, with nine agents assigned to drug investigations in 2003, and training is a large part of the program. From February to May 2003 alone, the FBI's Resolution Six agents trained slightly fewer than 800 Mexican police. An average of 1,000 law enforcement officials every year are now trained by the FBI in interview and interrogation techniques, crime scene investigations and evidence recovery, crisis management, ethics and anticorruption, media relations, police street survival, and tactical operations.[33]

The Fox administration disbanded the Federal Judicial Police force and replaced it with the Federal Investigations Agency, styled, at least in name, after the FBI. The AFI was intended to be a more professional and effective investigative police force with clear personnel procedures and command structures, internal controls, and compartmentalized intelligence and operational arms in order to curb corruption.[34] Like its predecessor, the AFI falls under the attorney general's office, the PGR, and is responsible for investigating all federal crimes, including drug trafficking. The United States has supported the PGR's housecleaning efforts, which resulted in the firing or suspension of about 2,600 federal agents; the U.S. government has also provided assistance for the development of PGR's internal affairs division.[35] Fox also shut down the FEADS drug control agency after its corruption scandal. And in 2003 the attorney general's office was itself restructured once more, combining responsibility for all organized crime investigations under a single department.

The United States is for the first time actively involved in institutional development of the PGR and AFI rather than just emphasizing eradication, seizures, and arrests or building special units. One U.S. official remarked that even though drug seizures and arrests have decreased since Fox took office, "We're less concerned by that than [we would have been] ten years ago because the clear lion's share of Mexico's efforts is on developing institutions and investigations. ... We can't accomplish [our] goals without becoming institution builders."[36]

According to a State Department official responsible for counterdrug programs in Mexico, institutional reforms of the AFI and PGR under Fox have been deep-rooted and fundamental. U.S. officials believe these efforts stand a chance of breaking the cycle of corruption that has plagued all previous attempts to create trustworthy police partners.

But it is not clear that the Fox administration is attacking the structural problems that lead to corruption or even prosecuting corrupt cops for their crimes. Despite repeated requests, the PGR could not provide the authors with information on the number of federal police and prosecutors charged with drug crimes. As of September 2003, only nine PGR officials had been charged out of the more than 1,000 PGR personnel sanctioned in some way (suspension, fine, dismissal, etc.) for violating laws governing the responsibilities of public servants.[37] Many agents from the disbanded Federal Judicial Police were incorporated into the AFI, both to make up for the shortage of trained police when the agency was formed, and because the courts ruled there were insufficient grounds to dismiss them for corruption.

In some cases, corrupt cops are detained but later freed for lack of evidence. For example, in April 2002 federal police detained forty-two law enforcement officials from Baja California, including Tijuana's police chief and a top prosecutor, under suspicion of links to the Arellano Félix cartel. The arrests received considerable national and international press coverage and favorable commentary by U.S. officials. However, almost all of those arrested were released within a few days, and only ten ended up facing charges.[38]

Militarization of Counterdrug Efforts

> *Now the military is making arrests and carrying out investigations. Drug suspects are being arrested and interrogated by the military before they're handed over to civilian authorities. Establishing these precedents risks the democracy that we're building.*
> —Sigrid Arzt, expert on drug control policy, Mexico City, 2002[39]

In 1986, President Ronald Reagan elevated drug trafficking to the status of national security threat and ordered the Defense Department to take on a larger role in counterdrug efforts. Mexico soon followed his lead. In 1987, President Miguel de la Madrid (1982–1988) declared drug trafficking a national security issue, which opened the door for the militarization of drug control efforts. While the army had been involved in manual crop eradication involving some 20,000–30,000 troops a day since the 1940s, casting drug trafficking in national security terms led to the expansion of the military's counterdrug mission to embrace law enforcement and intelligence tasks as well.[40]

The militarization of counterdrug efforts involves two separate but interrelated phenomena: the expansion of the antidrug role of the military as an institution into domestic law enforcement responsibilities; and the appointment of military personnel (whether active duty, on leave, or retired) to posts inside civilian law enforcement institutions such as the police and attorney general's office.

The United States was an eager participant in the militarization of Mexico's counterdrug policy, prompting and supporting it every step of the way. U.S. officials encouraged Mexico to use the military to fight drugs for two basic reasons. First, the military was seen as the only institution with the manpower, resources, and equipment to counter the threat of well-armed and wealthy traffickers. Second, by 1986 Mexican law enforcement agencies had been thoroughly discredited by their links to drug traffickers, and the U.S. government saw the military as a less corrupt counterpart.

During de la Madrid's administration, the U.S. Central Intelligence Agency (CIA) helped the Mexican military form an elite team of about fifty soldiers intended to strike more effectively against drug traffickers. Mexican law enforcement officials were not told of the plan, effectively undercutting any possible civilian oversight. The elite team botched their first three operations—in one, they raided a residential neighborhood to apprehend a marijuana trafficker but ended up killing four people—so the program was shut down.[41]

Salinas was the first Mexican president to directly include the armed forces in counterdrug decisionmaking bodies. The INCD had an executive coordinating group that included representation from the defense and the navy ministries, as well as various civilian ministries. Salinas also created military rapid deployment units to combat drug trafficking and to neutralize the outbreaks of armed insurgency in the southern part of the country.

In the mid-1990s, the CIA again began providing training, equipment, and operational support to an elite team of Mexican soldiers, forming a special intelligence unit called the Center for Antinarcotics Investigations. This unit is responsible for developing the intelligence that is used to identify top drug traffickers and for designing strategies for dismantling drug cartels.

The military's role intensifies under Zedillo. In 1995, during the first year of the Zedillo administration, militarization of counterdrug efforts intensified. Zedillo placed the armed forces on the front lines of the drug war. His administration developed the Chihuahua Pilot Project, which replaced 120 Federal Judicial Police assigned to the Chihuahua offices of the attorney general's office with members of the army on loan from the defense ministry. The pilot project was soon extended to all the PGR's regional offices in areas with high levels of drug-trafficking activity. The Federal Judicial Police was soon filled with troops and high-ranking military officials, and military personnel were placed in charge of the Cendro, the PGR's intelligence center. Zedillo also created the National Public Security Council and, for the first time ever, gave the defense and naval ministries a role in decisionmaking and policymaking on domestic public security issues, including but not limited to drug control efforts.

The Chihuahua Pilot Project began to show signs of failure almost immediately. Within a few months, a number of members of the regional PGR office in Chihuahua, all of them military personnel on leave, were accused of having links to the Juárez cartel.[42] Despite this, the replacement of police by military personnel on leave was soon extended throughout the country. Division general Jesús Gutiérrez Rebollo was named director of the PGR's National Institute to Combat Drugs, roughly equivalent to the DEA. During the first three years of Zedillo's government, military personnel entered the ranks of the majority of the federal, state and municipal police forces in thirty out of Mexico's thirty-two states (including the Federal District).[43] The military began participating in public security councils replicated at the state levels as well and provided training to police forces throughout the country.[44] The line between police and military was effectively erased when Zedillo created the Federal Preventive Police in 1999, incorporating about half of its original agents from the military police.

To keep pace with these changes, the Ministry of Defense issued the Azteca Directive and the General Plan to Combat Drug Trafficking, establishing the military's permanent campaign against drug trafficking with programs to eradicate drug crops, confiscate illegal drugs, and combat organized crime. The Ministry of Defense reorganized its territorial structure in order to better respond to drug-trafficking threats. The military also provided support to civilian law enforcement officials in counterdrug and other crime control efforts through its participation in "mixed operations forces" *(bases de operaciones mixtas)* throughout the country. These forces paired soldiers with state and federal police and prosecutors, providing military backup to civilian law enforcement personnel in operations to combat crime.

At the same time Zedillo was giving the military responsibilities in drug control policymaking and law enforcement, the U.S. government began a concerted effort to train and equip the Mexican military for counterdrug tasks. In October 1995, Defense Secretary William Perry visited Mexico to seek closer ties with that country's military in the first-ever visit of a U.S. defense secretary to Mexico. Perry was reportedly alarmed by the lack of military-to-military relations and used counterdrug cooperation to reach his goal of improving relations. As a result of his visit, Mexico agreed to accept U.S. counterdrug assistance (from 1993 to 1995, Mexico funded its antidrug efforts on its own, refusing U.S. aid). Mexico and the United States also agreed to establish a bilateral working group for military issues that would include counterdrug cooperation.[45]

Perry's visit cemented the common counterdrug mission, and training became the heart of bilateral military relations. In 1996 the Pentagon devised a program to form, train, and equip Air-Mobile Special Forces Groups (Grupos Aeromóviles de Fuerzas Especiales, GAFEs). These special Mexican army units were to serve as "combat-ready shock troops to attack drug cartels."[46] The U.S. government trained thousands of Mexican soldiers at U.S. military academies in courses such as helicopter assault tactics, explosives, rural and urban warfare, drug interdiction, and operational intelligence gathering and planning. After the GAFE training program officially ended in late 1998, the U.S. government began training Mexican counterdrug amphibious units within the army (Grupos Anfíbios de Fuerzas Especiales, GANFEs), as well as the Mexican marines and navy. These programs are funded primarily through the Pentagon's budget and therefore subject to little U.S. civilian oversight.[47]

To equip the new counterdrug army units, the U.S. government sold and donated equipment to the Mexican military, including a gift of seventy-three UH-1H helicopters and components. The U.S. General Accounting Office criticized the Pentagon for some of these transactions, finding that "the effectiveness and usefulness of some equipment provided or sold to Mexico is limited."[48] The problems were evident in 1999 when the Mexican military returned all of the donated helicopters except for one that had crashed. The Mexican military was frustrated by the Vietnam-era equipment, which could not fly high enough to be effective at locating some illicit crops, as well as by a lack of spare parts to keep the helicopters in the air. (The U.S. military countered that the helicopters were being overused.) Mexico also bristled at U.S.-imposed restrictions limiting the helicopters' use to counterdrug efforts.[49]

Meanwhile, U.S.-trained and equipped GAFEs were deployed throughout Mexico to investigate and apprehend drug traffickers, particularly in Jalisco State and along the U.S.-Mexico border. The government increasingly relied on GAFEs in the wake of police corruption scandals in 1997 and 1998. The State Department's top drug control official, discussing the widespread corruption in the Mexican attorney general's office, stated that, "In the shorter-term, the Government of Mexico will use small, elite law enforcement and military counterdrug units … to attack key trafficking organizations and to handle sensitive information or investigations."[50]

The U.S. military took advantage of the counterdrug mission to promote closer relations with the Mexican military. Training became a way to engage with the institution itself and with thousands of Mexican military personnel. According to the White House's Office of National Drug Control Policy (ONDCP), one of the successes of U.S.-Mexican counterdrug efforts was that the two countries went from a "virtually nonexistent" military-to-military relationship to the formation of a bilateral military working group.[51]

However, one expert on the Mexican armed forces notes that U.S. training has not necessarily made the Mexican military less distrustful of the U.S. military. He argues that the biggest impact of U.S. training has been its influence on the design of military education programs in Mexico.[52] Despite its historic distrust of the U.S. military, the Mexican military embraced these training opportunities out of admiration for U.S. military education and profound dissatisfaction with its own system.

Between 1981 and 1995, Mexico sent a total of 1,488 personnel to U.S. military academies.[53] In 1997 and again in 1998, more than 1,000 GAFEs were trained in the United States—surpassing in two years the number of soldiers who had been trained in the previous fifteen.[54] For two consecutive years, the School of the Americas trained more soldiers from Mexico than from anywhere else in the hemisphere: 305 in 1997 and 219 in 1998. During that period, hundreds of Mexican troops were trained at the Inter-American Air Force Academy (141 in 1996, 260 in 1997, and 336 in 1998). When the GAFE training program ended in FY1998, absolute training numbers dropped—ranging from a low of 564 in 2000 to 857 in 2001.

The training was funded by a variety of U.S. budgets, both through the traditional security assistance programs paid for by the State Department and through the Pentagon's authority to use its own budget to train and equip foreign militaries for counterdrug purposes. Mexico became the top Latin American recipient of International Military Education and Training (IMET) assistance for four consecutive years (FY1996–FY1999) and continues to figure among the top three. IMET is administered by the State Department.

In fact, training funded through the Defense Department outpaced that funded by the State Department. Mexico was the top recipient of assistance (for training and equipment) through the Pentagon's counterdrug account in 1997 and 1998 and was the number-two recipient of Pentagon counterdrug funding in the following three years.

Fox follows Zedillo's lead. The Fox administration has continued the two interrelated policies of directly enlisting the armed forces in drug control efforts and filling civilian justice institutions with military personnel. Before Fox took office, his justice advisers were proposing a "strategy of gradually demilitarizing the police forces."[55] In response, the U.S. drug czar "warned Fox not to move too quickly in eliminating the role of the Mexican military in the drug war," saying, "until you have other institutions and ways of going about it, be careful of what you do."[56] Fox heeded the U.S. drug czar's advice, increasing the military's presence in federal police agencies. Many analysts believe Fox acquiesced in order to get the historically prickly drug control issue off the bilateral agenda so the two countries could concentrate on trade and migration. To overwhelming U.S. approval, Fox named a top military official, a brigadier general and former military prosecutor, Rafael Macedo de la Concha, as his attorney general. Experts have noted that, technically, the attorney general is subordinate to the defense minister, because although he is temporarily on leave he is still a member of the military and, as such, subject to the defense minister's authority.[57]

Once General Macedo became the nation's attorney general, he gave a number of military officers important strategic, intelligence, and operational positions in the attorney general's office, the PGR. The newspaper *Reforma* reported that as of November 2002 there were at least 227 military officers in the PGR, with twenty of them heading up important bureaus overseeing intelligence, eradication, interdiction, and seized assets. In all, 107 members of the military were assigned to the FEADS drug control agency (since dissolved), forty-two to the federal police, eight to the drug intelligence center Cendro, and seventy others to a range of other divisions and units.[58] U.S. officials regard the inclusion of military personnel in the PGR as positive, believing that military structure and discipline would be a good influence on reform efforts.

Although the presence of military personnel in the Federal Preventive Police was supposed to be temporary, lasting only until enough new civilian agents could be selected and trained, the number of soldiers within the PFP has actually increased during the Fox administration. Between September 2001 and June 2002, an additional 826 military personnel were brought into the Federal Support Forces (Fuerzas Federales de Apoyo, FFA), the PFP's operational arm, which is composed entirely of military police and members of the navy. Eight entire army units have been transferred to the PFP, as well as 1,600 members of several navy battalions.[59] Top positions in the PFP are also held by military officers: the FFA is led by a general, and the PFP as a whole is led by a retired brigadier general.

The Fox administration has also given the army a direct role in efforts to dismantle drug-trafficking organizations by having it track cartel bosses and stage commando operations to detain them. Special forces battalions and the second and seventh sections of the defense ministry—the sections responsible for military intelligence and military operations, respectively— are investigating the cartels' leadership structures and apprehending king- pins, tasks formerly carried out by the federal police.

Under General Macedo, much greater coordination exists between the PGR and military structures. Army special forces provide backup to the PGR or even carry out major arrests themselves. One high-ranking antidrug official attributed the Fox administration's successful captures of drug kingpins to the PGR's close coordination with the army. "We've been working with them for five years, getting closer each year. It's been like an engagement, and I think we're married now. This year is the honeymoon of our marriage."[60] According to that official, a special antidrug military intel- ligence unit works hand-in-glove with the PGR to investigate and arrest drug traffickers. The unit is unwilling to have its role known publicly.

According to the State Department, during the Fox administration the Mexican military has "aggressively sought out training and assistance to improve its counterdrug capabilities. ... The Mexican military services have requested additional types of training and have shown greater interest in use of U.S. Mobile Training Teams [MTTs] to provide training for large groups at lower costs."[61] Training was expected to top 1,000 troops in 2003, and most of the training continues to be paid for by the Pentagon.[62] Because of Mexico's historic concerns about sovereignty and its ingrained distrust of the U.S. military, Mexican military personnel are almost entirely trained in the United States (as opposed to troops from other Latin American countries, who receive substantial U.S. training at home). The Mexican government had shied away from allowing MTTs to train troops on Mexican soil until the late 1990s.

The consequences of militarization. Now, says drug control expert Sigrid Arzt, the military is "entrenched, and new venues of modernization and professionalization were opened up to them as a result of their involve- ment" in drug control, and "it opened up doors for them—training, resources, increased budgets every year."[63] Mexican officials no longer dis- cuss militarization as a temporary, short-term measure. According to President Fox, the military

> will continue in this task as long as [the drug trade] represents a threat to national security, to the health of young people, and to the tranquility of families. They will do it as long as it is necessary to destroy the criminal networks that attack the health of our young people, [and] they will do it in harmony and coordination with all the institutions responsible for com- bating [drug trafficking].[64]

Meanwhile, the military's participation in drug control efforts has exposed the institution to the corrupting forces of drug trafficking. Since 1997, three generals have been convicted of drug trafficking—former drug czar Gutiérrez Rebollo, as well as Francisco Quirós Hermosillo and Arturo Acosta Chaparro, architects of the military's dirty war on leftist insurgents in the 1970s. Between 1995 and 2000, more than 150 soldiers and officers were tried for drug-related crimes.[65] During the Fox administration, between thirteen and twenty-six members of the army and air force have been tried and sentenced for drug trafficking (the information provided by the Ministry of Defense varies).[66]

The U.S. government's efforts to establish trusted military counterdrug units have also been frustrated by corruption. GAFE soldiers assigned to counterdrug duties at the Mexico City airport in 1997 were caught accepting bribes from drug traffickers and migrant smugglers.[67] Deserters from GAFE units deployed to Mexico's northern border are currently using their high-tech skills to aid the Gulf cartel.[68]

DEA deputy administrator Donnie Marshall told Congress in 1998 that "in order to overcome the problem of widespread corruption in law enforcement, the Mexican Government replaced civilian authorities with military officers. Recent experience has shown that military officers, once exposed to the extraordinary opportunities for corruption, are equally susceptible as civilians."[69] Nevertheless, U.S. policy continues to promote an active counterdrug role for the military.

The Mexican military does not provide a specific accounting of the money it spends on counterdrug efforts.[70] The United States has not established oversight mechanisms for its training programs with the Mexican military. To secure Mexican participation in the special forces training program, U.S. officials agreed that they would not monitor the performance of recipient groups. As a result, "there [was] little oversight of how the training and intelligence is used in Mexico by a military with a long history of corruption, much of it drug-related, and human rights abuses."[71]

Through training, the United States encouraged a policing role for the Mexican military. Courses were provided to Mexican officers in "how to use their weapons in support of police, as opposed to using them in standard military ways."[72] The purpose of the training, according to the Pentagon official in charge of counterdrug operations at the time, was to teach Mexican soldiers "how to search vehicles, boats, and buildings. They will learn not only how to conduct a proper search, but also how to protect a crime scene.... We hope they will emerge from this with enhanced skill so they can help the police enforce the law in Mexico."[73]

U.S. officials downplay the armed forces' involvement, and some deny that they are playing such a large law enforcement role.[74] However, one

DEA intelligence report cites the Mexican military as one of the DEA's law enforcement counterparts, explaining: "The Mexican military ... plays a major role in Mexico's counterdrug efforts. In recent years, the military has been tasked with ... investigating and arresting drug traffickers."[75]

The military has historically been responsible for about three-fourths of eradication. Since Fox took office, however, the military has also become responsible for a large majority of drug seizures and a growing percentage of drug arrests. This trend is clearly reflected in the statistics shown in Figure 8.3. In 1993, the army carried out 3 percent of drug-related arrests in Mexico. Ten years later, the army's share of arrests rose to 28 percent. Likewise, whereas the military was responsible for only a small percentage of cocaine seizures in the early 1990s, the military made 94 percent of cocaine seizures in 2003.[76] These dramatic increases demonstrate that the Mexican armed forces, more than just supporting the PGR in counterdrug efforts, have taken over investigations and intelligence gathering of trafficking networks, as well as the operations to disrupt them.

Certification

> I keep a look at the scoreboard. As high as 50 to 70 percent of all narcotics comes through and from Mexico.... I liken certifying Mexico as a

Figure 8.3   Participation of the Mexican Armed Forces in Drug Control Efforts, 1990–2003

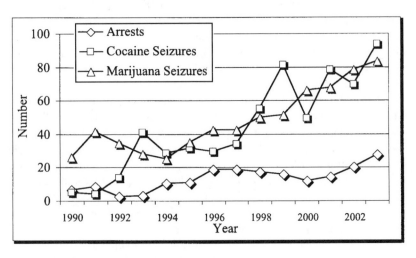

Source: Office of the President of Mexico, *Tercer Informe de Gobierno del C. Presidente Vicente Fox Quesada* (Mexico City: September 2003), Statistical Annex, p. 469.

cooperative partner in our war against drugs to giving a special tax exemption to Al Capone during Prohibition to sell booze. Nothing personal against Mexico. It is not working. American cities are busting at the seams with narcotics. Mr. Speaker, if we are going to have a war on drugs, we cannot do it with the Peace Corps. It is time to start fighting.
—U.S. Representative James Traficant (D-Ohio), 1997[77]

Enacted by Congress in 1986, the certification law required the president to certify by March 1 of every year that major drug-producing and trafficking nations (the "majors") were cooperating fully with U.S. counterdrug measures; Congress had thirty days to overturn any decision with which it did not agree. Countries that were decertified faced a range of punishments: a cutoff of all economic assistance (with the exception of counterdrug and humanitarian aid), automatic denial of loans from multilateral banks, and discretionary trade sanctions, such as the removal of trade preferences and the suspension of import quotas. These punishments could be waived in the interests of U.S. national security, but that did not remove the sting of humiliation for having received a failing grade from Washington.

The annual certification ritual gave members of Congress an easy way to look tough on drugs while casting blame for the nation's drug problems beyond U.S. borders. Yet the policy was not without harmful consequences. It instituted a scorecard approach to U.S. international drug control policy, rewarding countries for arrests and seizures without questioning the overall efficacy of those measures (i.e., if fewer drugs were entering the United States) or the context in which they were carried out. It drove military involvement in counterdrug efforts. And it provided a forum for insulting and alienating sovereign nations.

The approach also reinforced some abusive practices. For example, to demonstrate President Salinas's political will to fight drug trafficking, his administration drastically increased the number of arrests on drug crimes, filling Mexican prisons with small-time traffickers and those who had been subject to dubious arrests. U.S. officials praised this aggressive effort and years later—even after the Salinas administration had been disgraced as one of Mexico's most corrupt—held up these arrest statistics as an enviable achievement. Later, when total arrests dropped, the lower numbers were frequently cited in congressional debate in both the House and Senate as a criticism of Mexico and of President Bill Clinton's decision to certify Mexico in 1997 and 1998.[78]

Similarly, U.S. authorities used the certification process to push for legal reforms. At a March 1996 hearing, DEA administrator Thomas Constantine described Mexico as lacking the "sophisticated law enforcement structure necessary" to combat the drug cartels: "Just consider that, in Mexico, wiretaps are currently illegal, conspiracy laws do not exist, police cannot use confidential informants, there is no witness protection program, and money laundering is not a criminal offense."[79] The Mexican Congress was not long in passing an organized crime bill granting federal police and prosecutors these investigative powers.

Yet basic, fundamental justice reforms—ensuring presumption of innocence, making procedures more transparent, guaranteeing access to counsel—were never a U.S. policy priority. Although there is nothing inherently wrong with giving police the power to wiretap, use informants, or conduct surveillance—in fact, these tools are necessary in order to conduct investigations into organized crime—these should exist only if adequate safeguards are in place to ensure they are not used unfairly. Because Mexico does not have an independent judiciary capable of withstanding political pressures, it cannot serve as an effective check on possible excesses by the police or prosecutors.

The certification debate also became the basis for pushing the Mexican military into a greater counterdrug role.[80] Even members of Congress who supported fully certifying Mexico used the process to encourage continued support for the Mexican military in the drug war. In 1998 Senator Strom Thurmond argued:

> If we decertify Mexico, the problem will not go away but will only be exacerbated. The progress that Mexico has made thus far, albeit modest, will come to a standstill. With the assistance of the Department of Defense (DOD), Mexico has countered extensive drug-related official corruption with unprecedented reform efforts.... It is of vital importance that the DOD continue to provide assistance to the Mexican military to combat drugs.[81]

Other members of Congress supported decertification with a national security waiver—they wanted to punish Mexico yet keep military aid flowing. Representative Benjamin Gilman argued in 1997 that if the United States chose to decertify Mexico, it should ensure that the president is able to "continue United States assistance to Mexico, particularly military assistance, which is likely our last best hope down there."[82]

Certification became an annual exercise in Mexico-bashing, as members of Congress roundly denounced Mexico's lack of progress in combating drugs and related corruption. The process consistently produced tensions and conflict between the United States and Mexico, eroding the sense of common purpose and partnership necessary for effective counterdrug cooperation and closing the political space for bilateral dialogue on important issues such as improving human rights.

Throughout Latin America, the certification process was seen as hypocritical bullying by Uncle Sam—how did the largest drug-consuming nation in the world dare judge everyone else on their drug control efforts? Mexico especially resented the policy as an affront to its sovereignty.

President Zedillo called the certification process an offense and suggested that the United States be subjected to the same review. Overturning the unilateral certification process was a priority for the Fox administration. During President Fox's official state visit to the United States in September 2001, he urged Congress to suspend the drug certification requirements as a gesture of faith in the new government, arguing that "trust requires that one partner not be judged unilaterally by the other." Because Fox's new government represented a break from the PRI's long record of corruption, Washington was willing to "avoid an early confrontation" with the new government and give it a chance to develop effective bilateral counterdrug programs.[83] President George W. Bush signaled his commitment "to replace the annual counternarcotics certification regime with new measures designed to enhance international cooperation in this area."[84]

The certification process was modified, although not completely repealed as Mexico had hoped. Under the original law, the president had to certify that each of the majors was fully cooperating with U.S. antidrug efforts, creating a situation where countries had to jump through hoops to earn a positive rating. The reform reversed that burden of proof, requiring the president to decertify only those countries that "failed demonstrably, during the previous 12 months, to make substantial efforts" to adhere to their international counterdrug obligations.[85] In other words, countries would be automatically certified unless their antidrug efforts were resoundingly poor. Reforming the process also removed the thirty-day window for Congress to overturn the president's decision, eliminating Congress's role in a procedure often used to bash Mexico for failing to live up to U.S. expectations. In addition, the process was changed so that an international (and not U.S.) standard was used to evaluate the efforts of drug-producing and trafficking nations.

• Impact on Human Rights

The links between U.S. counterdrug policy and Mexico's human rights problems and fragile democracy are difficult to disentangle. Mexico had a dismal human rights record long before U.S. drug control policy took hold, and Mexican presidents have frequently experimented with militarizing police and law enforcement institutions, often in response to their own citizens' clamor for a tough-on-crime approach. Yet by fueling the Mexican military's intrusion into police work, by supporting police units and forces that are not transparent or accountable, and by applying a scorecard approach to drug control, U.S. drug control policies have adversely affected Mexico's human rights situation.

The State Department itself has recognized that "the police and military were accused of committing serious human rights violations as they carried out the Government's efforts to combat drug cartels."[86] In the

1970s, as part of Operation Condor, the Mexican government sent 10,000 soldiers and police to a poverty-stricken region in northern Mexico plagued by drug production and leftist insurgency. Hundreds of peasants were arrested, tortured, and jailed, but not a single big drug trafficker was captured.[87] During the Salinas administration, a U.S.-supported counterdrug brigade within the judicial police was implicated in the worst reports of torture and killing, including the Norma Corona assassination. The elite brigade was composed of many police officers that had previously served in earlier repressive police units.[88] During Zedillo's term, antidrug police and soldiers were responsible for scores of forced disappearances in drug-trafficking centers such as Juárez and Culiacán. In some cases the police and soldiers had been hired by traffickers to eliminate enemies; in other cases they had arrested, interrogated, and presumably tortured the victims before they disappeared.[89] Abuses committed by soldiers and police during counterdrug operations continue under the Fox administration.

Alarming allegations of torture and corruption surfaced within the Federal Investigations Agency as well. Only six months after AFI's creation, detainee Guillermo Vélez Mendoza was killed while in the custody of AFI agents. After the National Human Rights Commission determined that Vélez died as a result of torture, the agent implicated in his death was arrested, but he escaped after being released on bail.[90] By the end of the year, no AFI agent was being held accountable for Vélez's death.[91] The practice of using *madrinas* has not disappeared with the AFI. In June 2002, a man arrested on drug charges was shot to death in an AFI holding cell. The alleged murderer was a former member of the army's special forces and worked as a *madrina* for AFI agents. Several months later, *madrinas* killed a woman when they accompanied AFI agents on an arrest in Sinaloa in January 2003. They had broken into the home of a suspected drug criminal in order to arrest him—without a warrant—and in the firefight that ensued his sister was killed and his mother injured. It has also been alleged that AFI agents in Nuevo Laredo were involved in a number of disappearances.

The context in which drug law enforcement occurs allows it to be used as a weapon by local political bosses against opponents. Human rights organizations have documented that the criminal justice system is "used as a means of political control by corrupt local officials in drug producing areas. Peasants who grow marijuana and other banned crops are at the mercy of officials who engage in selective enforcement of drug laws and raid and arrest anyone who engages in dissent."[92]

Although lower than in previous years, drug-related arrests in Mexico since 1995 have hovered at around 10,000 a year, and about 90 percent of those accused of drug crimes are found guilty. Those imprisoned tend to come from the poorest sectors of society. In 2001, about three-fourths of the approximately 20,000 people convicted on federal charges (including more than 9,000 for drug crimes) had only an elementary or middle-school education, and more than half were farmers or day laborers.[93] According to the CNDH, nearly one-third of the indigenous prisoners in Mexico in 2001 were in prison for federal crimes, overwhelmingly drug related.[94] Mexico's indigenous population is the poorest, most marginalized, and most vulnerable to abuses by drug traffickers, the police and military, and the justice system. "The majority of these indigenous prisoners are used by organized crime to transport drugs," stated a CNDH official. "Faced with hunger, poor quality lands, without resources to cultivate, and left out of development efforts, indigenous people accept or are forced to transport drugs. They have to find some way to survive."[95]

Although the Fox administration has made an effort to target more high-level traffickers, the vast majority of people imprisoned on drug charges continue to be from the lowest rungs of the drug trade. Of the nearly 19,000 people arrested for drug crimes between December 2000 and April 2003, 98 percent were growers or low-level dealers.[96]

The Mexican military has committed a range of human rights violations in the context of antidrug efforts, as soldiers patrol mountain regions and border areas to eradicate and intercept illegal drugs. Human rights organizations have documented scores of cases in recent years, including illegal arrests, secret and prolonged detention, torture, rape, extrajudicial execution, and fabrication of evidence.[97] The military often attempts to refute these allegations through outright denials or false arrest and medical reports. In Fox's first six months in office, the CNDH received eighty complaints by civilians against military personnel, fifty-four of them related to antidrug operations, as well as twenty-six complaints by members of the military against their superiors.[98]

Only agents of the AFI are authorized to carry out arrest warrants for drug crimes, but soldiers can make arrests if they catch someone in the act.[99] In the first six months of 2003, the military arrested 914 alleged drug criminals, nearly one-third of all drug-related arrests during that period. This is a substantial share for an institution that is not legally empowered to conduct criminal investigations and that can carry out arrests only in what should be considered exceptional situations (i.e., without a warrant).[100]

Soldiers have taken advantage of the in flagrante provision to arrest people they consider suspicious but who have not been caught in the act of a crime. After being arrested, detainees have been held for a prolonged time in military custody while evidence is gathered, often through the use of coercion or torture to elicit a confession. Once this evidence has been obtained, the military transfers the detainees to the custody of the civilian authorities.

Soldiers have also committed extrajudicial executions. Between 1996 and 2000, soldiers taking part in antidrug operations were implicated in at least fourteen extrajudicial executions.[101] In some of the cases, the victims died as a result of torture. In others, they were shot by soldiers on drug patrol in rural communities and left to bleed to death. The military often denied its involvement or attempted to justify the executions by claiming that the victims were drug traffickers.[102]

Civilian authorities have reinforced, and even encouraged, the army's abusive actions by validating evidence gathered through torture and by ignoring clear signs of human rights violations and improper procedure. This has occurred even in cases where their own forensic doctors detected torture. The CNDH documented one such case from May 1996 in which a man was illegally detained by soldiers in Guadalajara, taken to a military base, interrogated about drug trafficking, and tortured until he lost consciousness. Four days after his arrest, soldiers took him to the police, claiming they had just arrested him in the act of a crime. Although a government physician certified evidence of torture, which should have invalidated the confession that was the basis of the charges against him, civilian authorities charged him with drug crimes. Eight similar cases from Guadalajara during the same period were documented by the CNDH, with civilian authorities charging suspected criminals on the basis of confessions extracted by soldiers through the use of torture.

The military often provides backup for civilian police, and sometimes police even ask soldiers to carry out tasks. In one case from February 2002, AFI agents asked the Mexican military to locate a particular criminal defense attorney who was implicated in a drug case and to bring him in for questioning. Military police organized an operation to detain him after he made a prison visit to one of his clients. As the target was driving away from the prison, a group of nonuniformed soldiers attempted to stop his vehicle. When he did not heed their orders they opened fire on the car, forcing it off the road and killing one of the passengers inside. The soldiers detained the lawyer (without a warrant) and brought him to the civilian authorities for questioning, leaving his companion to bleed to death.[103]

Sending the army into rural regions for counterdrug operations can also serve as cover for counterinsurgency efforts. Since the 1990s, the Mexican army has maintained a large presence in Guerrero, a region known for poverty, illicit crop cultivation, and opposition movements, both peaceful and armed. Civil society organizations active in regions affected by drug trafficking have long suspected that they were subjects of military surveillance. Organizations in Chihuahua had their suspicions confirmed by a

Defense Ministry document outlining a plan for establishing antidrug working groups that

> will adopt the measures necessary to obtain information on the existence of armed groups, subversive activities, unjustifiable presence of foreigners, organizations, proselytizing by priests or leaders of religious sects, ecological groups, political propaganda, [and] the presence and activities of bands or gangs of criminals.[104]

Soldiers have conducted counterdrug sweeps that target local activists and intimidate communities where they suspect insurgent activities. According to Human Rights Watch,

> The counterinsurgency mindset appears to be reproduced in the army's approach to the drug war, as officers rely on ... their perceived political allies for information about who to target in their operations. In this way, ... *caciques*—or political bosses—are able to bring the firepower of the army to bear upon their political opponents by denouncing them as guerrillas or drug traffickers.[105]

Illustrative of this danger is the case of environmental activists Rodolfo Montiel and Teodoro Cabrera. Their campaign against logging angered local *caciques*, who then denounced them as drug traffickers to regional military commanders. The men were illegally arrested by soldiers who tortured them into confessing to trumped-up drug and gun charges. Both men were convicted; Amnesty International declared them prisoners of conscience. Despite that, their case is listed as one of the "important convictions"—along with that of Colima cartel kingpin Adán Amezcua Contreras—in a document highlighting the Zedillo administration's major antidrug accomplishments.[106]

Impunity for human rights violations committed by the military is a serious problem. Most cases are not investigated; those investigated are rarely prosecuted; and the few convictions for human rights abuse that have been reached came after years of national and international pressure. The military justice system has jurisdiction over cases in which military personnel are blamed for abuses against civilians. Military courts are not transparent or accountable to civilian authorities or victims, and military justice officials are legally prohibited from making documents from judicial proceedings public. Even soldiers seconded to police forces like the PFP remain under military jurisdiction if they commit human rights violations against civilians while on police duty.[107]

• The U.S. Government's Human Rights Obligations

Under a U.S. law known as the Leahy Amendment, no member or unit of a foreign security force that is credibly alleged to have committed a human rights violation may receive U.S. training. Furthermore, no unit of a foreign security force can receive equipment or other assistance if any of its members is suspected of human rights abuse, unless the government is taking steps toward bringing that person to justice.

U.S. embassy officials in Mexico in charge of human rights and drug control programs state that they vet all proposed police and military trainees for alleged involvement in human rights violations.[108] However, human rights groups monitoring Leahy Amendment implementation in Mexico say it is not clear that the embassy is doing adequate human rights vetting of the police personnel and units that are receiving U.S. assistance. The embassy database that keeps track of human rights violations is seriously incomplete.[109] One human rights organization submitted information to the embassy on more than sixty well-documented cases of human rights abuse by the Mexican military, yet only a few had been registered in the database. Embassy officials reported that they had never asked the military for information about judicial actions against soldiers implicated in abuse. Given this lax oversight, and considering the thousands of soldiers and police that have been trained or have benefited from U.S. assistance, it is possible that some abusive agents received U.S. training or other assistance.

The United States has provided training to members of the Mexican military who have gone on to commit human rights violations. In December 1997, a group of heavily armed Mexican special forces soldiers kidnapped twenty young men in Ocotlán, Jalisco, brutally torturing them and killing one. Six of the implicated officers had received U.S. training as part of the GAFE training program.[110]

U.S. officials have also sought to use evidence that was obtained through torture. In one case reported by the *New York Times*, an agent from the Bureau of Alcohol, Tobacco, and Firearms (ATF) interrogated Alejandro Hodoyan Palacios, a Tijuana cartel enforcer suspected of murdering a Mexican antidrug prosecutor. Hodoyan had been arrested by the Mexican military and subjected to torture during his incommunicado detention; when the ATF agent met with Hodoyan, the latter was blindfolded and shackled to a bed in a military barracks. The DEA also had a chance to debrief the suspect and "eagerly accepted the offer as a rare chance to cooperate with the Mexican military and improve their relations" with drug czar Gutiérrez Rebollo.[111] The U.S. government indicted Hodoyan for drug crimes, even though the evidence against him had been "gathered with methods that would not be permitted under American law."[112] U.S. prosecutors found themselves in the position of defending the quality of Mexico's evidence.

The U.S. government has even hailed some abusive investigations as evidence of Mexico's commitment to the war on drugs. For example, in

October 2002, military authorities held hundreds of soldiers incommunicado to investigate reports that they were protecting drug traffickers. Military police and prosecutors, aided by army special forces groups, threatened, beat, and tortured soldiers in order to obtain information and confessions. The Mexican government's National Human Rights Commission documented that several soldiers bore physical evidence of torture such as bruised stomachs, backs, and testicles.[113] Thirteen soldiers were eventually charged with drug crimes, and the entire battalion was disbanded. The State Department pointed to the prosecutions as a success in the war on drugs, citing the effort as an example of how "Mexican leaders worked energetically to detect and punish corruption among law enforcement officials and military personnel."[114] But the use of torture raises questions about the validity of the charges.

U.S. agents have themselves been involved in extrajudicial action on Mexican territory. In 1990, the DEA organized a secret operation to apprehend a Mexican citizen allegedly involved in the Camarena murder. Using a tactic known as "irregular rendition," DEA agents, frustrated by corruption and the lack of cooperation from their Mexican counterparts, hired a man to kidnap Humberto Álvarez Machain and bring him to the United States for prosecution. This incident reinforced the impression that law enforcement agents may flout the law if their illegal actions ultimately result in the arrest and prosecution of suspected traffickers. It also aggravated tensions in the bilateral relationship, as Mexico had very real grievances about violations of its sovereignty.

In a more recent case, agents at the U.S. Bureau of Immigration and Customs Enforcement (ICE) kept a Juárez cartel hit man as a paid informant despite knowing of his participation in the murders of at least twelve suspected drug traffickers. This man's activities, and ICE's knowledge of them, came to light after he organized an assassination attempt against two DEA agents living in Juárez in January 2004. Perhaps to deflect attention from himself, the informant helped U.S. agents capture a prominent Juárez cartel member, which in turn led to the discovery of a clandestine graveyard in the backyard of a former Chihuahua state police officer's home where the bodies of the twelve suspected drug traffickers were buried.

According to U.S. and Mexican officials, one of the victims had been killed several months earlier by the informant, whose ICE handlers had been notified ahead of time and listened in on an open cellphone line as he tortured and murdered the man; the agency later altered an internal memorandum in an effort to cover up the informant's role in the killing.[115] By continuing its relationship with the informant despite knowledge of his responsibility for torture and murder, U.S. officials signaled that such illegal and unethical practices were an acceptable price to pay for information about drug trafficking.

• Conclusion

U.S. drug control policies in Mexico have not had a discernible impact on the amount of drugs entering the United States, yet they are hindering democratic reforms and respect for human rights. Adequate and effective mechanisms for the supervision, control, and accountability of the police and military do not exist. Human rights violations committed during drug control operations go unpunished. With U.S. encouragement and material assistance, Mexico has increased the role of its military in the fight against drugs and relegated civilians to a lower level of participation. Tactical successes against major kingpins will likely result in a continued role for the military in counterdrug policing.

The fact that Mexican police officials are corrupt and incapable of successfully confronting drug-related crime poses a dilemma. Although not consistent with democratic practice, temporarily employing the military to do police duty is an understandable choice in the absence of other immediate options. Yet in Mexico the military was given what has become a permanent and important role in counterdrug and public security operations and policymaking. A first, partial attempt at police reform did not even occur until the Federal Investigations Agency was created in 2001. U.S. officials acknowledge that Mexico is now investing more energy in the difficult process of institutional reform.

Giving the military responsibilities for civilian drug control, even if such measures are intended to be temporary, poses a threat to democratization. Mexico is undergoing a transition to democracy, but the rules for civil-military relations are not being rewritten. The Mexican military's increased antidrug responsibilities have given it greater autonomy precisely at a time when its role and powers should be curtailed and supervised, putting Mexico in the position of having a powerful, unchecked, and unaccountable military at the helm of major government initiatives. There is also the danger that the military will come to expect a permanent seat in civilian institutions and policymaking arenas. One Mexican expert argues,

> The more civilian leadership relies on the military to carry out politicized, internal police functions, the more the military itself expects to have a voice in political decision making, and equally important, the more society, including future civilian and military leaders, defines intervention as a legitimate military activity.[116]

Involving the Mexican military in counterdrug law enforcement has also created opportunities for some of its members to involve themselves in corruption and criminal activities, as mentioned earlier.

The United States should promote the establishment of clear legal divisions between military and police roles in Mexico modeled after Posse Comitatus, the U.S. law forbidding U.S. troops from making arrests or conducting searches or seizures within U.S. territory that would eliminate military participation in law enforcement. U.S. drug control programs that take advantage of the absence of such legislation in Mexico and encourage the involvement of the military in domestic law enforcement prevent this democratic principle from taking root. Efforts to remove the military from domestic police work would be consistent with recommendations by the UN special rapporteurs on torture, extrajudicial executions, and the independence of judges and lawyers, as well as the UN High Commissioner for Human Rights. All have called on Mexico to "achieve a demilitarization of society and avoid delegating to the armed forces the task of maintaining public order and fighting crime."[117] At the very least, civilian officials should regain and maintain control over the design and implementation of drug control policies.

Police reform and professionalization is a necessary precondition for more effective counterdrug operations. Since Fox took office, there appears to be a shift in U.S. training and institutional support for the federal police and attorney general's office that may represent an important break from efforts to create special "incorruptible" units. However, the emphasis continues to be largely on training police in ethics and investigative techniques. These are undeniably important values and skills, but their impact will not be felt unless the police and attorney general's office are more transparent and accountable. As one police expert noted:

> Training may be a good start, but it is nowhere near sufficient to create effective, democratic policing. If the institutions police enter upon leaving the police academy are corrupt, and the organizational dynamics of everyday police practice reinforce corruption and impunity, then a commitment to the rule of law will rest on shaky institutional ground. Real reform must change the structures of police accountability and enforce genuine oversight of policing by democratic institutions.[118]

In other words, all fundamental police reform hinges on transparency and accountability. Internal affairs divisions are not enough. Police forces must be made transparent and accountable to outside monitors. Corrupt and abusive cops must be brought to justice, not simply dismissed or fined.

Comprehensive police reform in Mexico is not something that U.S. policy can accomplish alone—domestic political will is key. But U.S. antidrug policy should send the message that it supports broad-based police and justice reforms in addition to efforts to impart specialized skills.

To complement police reform efforts, the U.S. government should support efforts to reform Mexico's justice system. A strong and effective justice system will not only discourage abuses by the military and the police but also ensure that those who are convicted of drug and other crimes are in fact guilty. The United Nations, the Organization of American States, and

Mexican and international human rights organizations have developed specific recommendations for improving the public defender system, strengthening the role of judges, removing structural incentives for torture and arbitrary arrest, and ensuring the presumption of innocence. Strong judicial and legislative institutions are the best ways to balance the power of the military, guarantee human rights and due process, and ultimately strengthen democracy.

Finally, U.S. drug control policy cannot continue to ignore the role poverty plays in drug cultivation. Viewed from certain angles, Mexico is an economic powerhouse: it is the world's ninth-largest economy and the second-largest U.S. trading partner. However, Mexico's impressive economic growth since the mid-1980s has not benefited the majority of Mexicans. More than half of Mexico's 100 million people are so poor they cannot meet their own basic needs. Twenty-four million Mexicans, most of them in rural areas, are considered "extremely poor"—so impoverished they are unable to adequately feed themselves. For the one-fourth of Mexico's population in such desperate conditions, harvesting marijuana and poppy crops is one of the only means of survival.

• Notes

1. *Wall Street Journal,* "Military Coup: Mexican Army Takes Greater Public Role as Democracy Grows. From Drug Lords to Lice, It Tackles the Problems Other Institutions Can't," 31 January 2000.

2. Rebecca Jannol, Deborah Meyers, and Maia Jachimowicz, "U.S.-Canada-Mexico Fact Sheet on Trade and Migration" (Migration Policy Institute, Washington, D.C., November 2003).

3. Peter Andreas, "U.S.-Mexico Drug Control in the Age of Free Trade," *Borderlines* 8, no. 4 (April 2000): 1–4. Available on Interhemispheric Resource Center website, www.americaspolicy.org/borderlines/PDFs/bl66.pdf.

4. Statistic cited by Deputy Attorney General José Luis Santiago Vasconcelos on the weekly radio program *Fox Contigo,* broadcast by Mexico's Office of the President, 11 October 2003, www.foxcontigo.presidencia.gob.mx/estenografica.php?H_C_Y=2003&H_C_M=10&H_C_D=11.

5. *St. Paul Pioneer Press,* "U.S. Drug Czar Lauds Mexico's Efforts," 14 August 2002, p. A7.

6. U.S. State Department, Bureau for International Narcotics and Law Enforcement Affairs (INL), *International Narcotics Control Strategy Report (INCSR) 2002,* "Canada, Mexico, and Central America" (Washington, D.C.: INL, March 2003).

7. Kate Doyle, "Human Rights and the Dirty War in Mexico," National Security Archive, 11 May 2003.

8. Sergio Aguayo Quezada, "Los Usos, Abusos, y Retos de la Seguridad Nacional Mexicana 1946–1990," in *En Busca de la Seguridad Perdida: Aproximaciones a la Seguridad Nacional Mexicana,* Sergio Aguayo Quezada and Bruce Michael Bagley, eds. (Mexico City: Siglo XXI Editores, 1990).

9. Information on the DFS from Jonathan Marshall, "CIA Assets and the Rise of the Guadalajara Connection," in *War on Drugs: Studies in the Failure of U.S.*

Narcotics Policy, Alfred W. McCoy and Alan A. Block, eds. (Boulder: Westview, 1992), pp. 200–203. See also Tim Golden, "Mexico and Drugs: Was U.S. Napping?" *New York Times*, 11 July 1997.

10. Human Rights Watch, *Human Rights in Mexico: A Policy of Impunity* (New York: Human Rights Watch, 1 June 1990). See also Lawyers Committee for Human Rights and Miguel Agustín Pro Juárez Human Rights Center, *Legalized Injustice: Mexican Criminal Procedure and Human Rights* (New York: Lawyers Committee for Human Rights, 2001). Please note: as of February 2004 LCHR's name was changed to Human Rights First.

11. United Nations Working Group on Arbitrary Detention, *Civil and Political Rights, Including the Question of Torture and Detention: Report of the Working Group on Arbitrary Detention on its Visit to Mexico*, UN Doc. E/CN.4/2003/8/Add.3 (17 December 2002), executive summary and para. 42.

12. United Nations Committee Against Torture, *Report on Mexico Produced by the Committee Under Article 20 of the Convention, and Reply from the Government of Mexico*, UN Doc. CAT/C/75 (26 May 2003), paras. 143 and 218.

13. Martin Edwin Anderson, "Civil-Military Relations and Internal Security in Mexico: The Undone Reform," in *The Challenge of Institutional Reform in Mexico*, Riordan Roett, ed. (Boulder: Lynne Rienner Publishers, 1995).

14. In Mexico, the Defense Ministry (Secretaría de la Defensa Nacional) is responsible for the army (the air force is a part of the army), while the Naval Ministry (Secretaría de la Marina) is responsible for the navy and marines.

15. WOLA interview with Luis Astorga, Mexico City, 4 November 2002.

16. Courts-martial are open to the public, and they have been in certain prominent cases, but victims of human rights abuses perpetrated by the military continue to be denied the right to participate in judicial proceedings or even to have access to information about them. Human Rights Watch, *Military Injustice: Mexico's Failure to Punish Army Abuses* (New York: Human Rights Watch, December 2001), p. 21.

17. U.S. Information Agency, *Briefing Paper*, no. B-82-97 (Washington, D.C.: USIA, 20 October 1997).

18. *Los Angeles Times*, "General Gutierrez to Head Up Mexico's War Against Drugs," 6 December 1997.

19. LCHR and Pro, *Legalized Injustice*. For more information on the Mexican justice system, see United Nations Economic and Social Council, *Civil and Political Rights, Including the Questions of: Independence of the Judiciary, Administration of Justice, Impunity*, UN Doc. E/CN.4/2002/72/Add.1 (24 January 2002).

20. United Nations Economic and Social Council, *Question of the Human Rights of All Persons Subjected to any Form of Detention or Imprisonment, in Particular: Torture and other Cruel, Inhuman, or Degrading Treatment or Punishment*, UN Doc. E/CN.4/1998/38/Add.2 (14 January 1998), para. 86.

21. Raúl Benítez Manaut, "México: Doctrina, Historia, y Relaciones Cívico-Militares a Inicios del Siglo XXI," in *Democracias Frágiles: Las Relaciones Civiles-Militares en el Mundo Iberoamericano* (Madrid: Instituto Universitario General Gutiérrez Mellado, 2004).

22. According to the DEA, one of the PJF's commanders spoke privately with the drug dealer and then let him get away. As an additional measure of protection, Caro Quintero carried an official DFS badge. U.S. Justice Department, Drug Enforcement Administration, *A Tradition of Excellence: The History of the DEA from 1973 to 1998*, "The Murder of DEA Special Agent Enrique Camarena" (Washington, D.C., April 1999).

23. Quoted in Carla Anne Robbins, "U.S. DEA Chief Blasts Mexicans on

Drug Efforts," *Wall Street Journal*, 26 February 1997, p. A13. See also U.S. Senate, Foreign Relations Committee testimony of Thomas A. Constantine, Administrator, Drug Enforcement Administration, *Mexico and the Southwest Border Initiative* Hearing, 12 March 1997. Available on DEA website: www.dea.gov/pubs/cngrtest/ ct970312.htm.

24. All of Mexico's states have separate preventive and investigative police forces, and a majority of municipalities have their own preventive police forces as well. These police forces are not authorized to investigate drug offenses, although they may arrest suspects caught in the act of a drug-related crime.

25. Although they were called "judicial" police, the PJF (as of 2001 the AFI) was not a part of the judiciary.

26. Government of Mexico, *Drug Control in Mexico, National Program 1989–1994: Progress and Results* (Mexico City: Procuraduría General de la República, 1992).

27. *Washington Post*, "Mexico Scraps Corrupted Drug Agency," 1 May 1997, p. A25; *INCSR 1997*, "Drug Enforcement Administration" (Washington, D.C.: March 1998).

28. U.S. General Accounting Office, *Drug Control: DEA's Strategies and Operations in the 1990s, GAO/GGD-99-108* (Washington, D.C.: July 1999), pp. 56–59.

29. DEA, *Response to Questions Submitted by José Serrano, Ranking Member of the Subcommittee for the Departments of Commerce, Justice, State, the Judiciary, and Related Agencies of the House Appropriations Committee* (Washington, D.C., June 2003).

30. All information contained in this paragraph is drawn from U.S. Senate, Caucus on International Narcotics Control, testimony of Thomas A. Constantine, Administrator, Drug Enforcement Administration, U.S. Justice Department, *Drug Trafficking in Mexico*, 24 February 1999, www.dea.gov/pubs/cngrtest/ct022499. htm.

31. DEA, *Response to Questions Submitted by Ranking Member José Serrano*, June 2003.

32. *INCSR 2002*, "Canada, Mexico, and Central America."

33. WOLA interview with FBI official, U.S. Embassy, Mexico City, 14 May 2003.

34. Government of Mexico, *Primer Informe de Labores* (Mexico City: Procuraduría General de la República, 1 September 2001).

35. *Dallas Morning News*, "Mexico's Attorney General Is Restructuring Ranks of Law Enforcement," 26 June 2003.

36. Quotes in this and the following paragraph from WOLA interview with Elizabeth Carroll, Senior Program Analyst, Office of the Americas Program, INL, 9 December 2003.

37. Government of Mexico, *Tercer Informe de Gobierno del C. Presidente Vicente Fox Quesada* (Mexico City: Office of the President of Mexico, 1 September 2003).

38. *San Diego Union-Tribune*, "After a Lull, Violence Resumes," 16 February 2003.

39. WOLA interview with Sigrid Arzt, expert on drug control policies at the Centro de Investigaciones y Docencia Económica, Mexico City, 18 November 2002.

40. This does not include the number of members of the navy involved in

counterdrug operations. The Defense Ministry claims that "approximately 30,000 men" are involved in counterdrug campaigns (eradication and other).

41. Information on this and the CIA elite teams is from *New York Times*, "Dangerous Allies: U.S. Helps Mexico's Army Take Big Anti-Drug Role," 29 December 1997.

42. Alejandro Gutiérrez, "La Militarización en Chihuahua No Dio Resultados: El Grupo Conjunto de la Defensa y la PGR Se Disolvió sin Poder Desintegrar al Cártel de Juárez," *Semanario Proceso*, no. 1038, 22 September 1996, pp. 26–27.

43. Raúl Benítez Manaut, "La Contención de los Grupos Armados, el Narcotráfico y el Crimen Organizado en México: El Rol de las Fuerzas Armadas," paper presented to the Mexico Project Workshop on Organized Crime and Democratic Governability in Mexico and the United States, sponsored by Georgetown University and the Iberoamericana University, Washington, D.C., 14–15 July 1997, pp. 44–45.

44. Government of Mexico, chapter 1 in *IV Informe de Gobierno del Presidente Ernesto Zedillo Ponce de León* (Mexico City: Presidencia de la República, December 1998), p. 15.

45. U.S. White House, Office of National Drug Control Policy (ONDCP), *Report to Congress Volume 1*, "U.S.-Mexico Counterdrug Cooperation" (Washington, D.C.: ONDCP, September 1997).

46. *Washington Post*, "Elite Anti-Drug Troops Investigated in Mexico," 9 September 1998.

47. Adam Isacson and Joy Olson, *Just the Facts: A Civilian's Guide to U.S. Defense and Security Assistance to Latin America and the Caribbean* (Washington, D.C.: Latin America Working Group and the Center for International Policy, 1999), pp. 87–91.

48. U.S. House of Representatives, Government Reform and Oversight Committee, Subcommittee on National Security, International Affairs, and Criminal Justice, *and* U.S. Senate, Caucus on International Narcotics Control, testimony of Benjamin F. Nelson, Director, International Relations and Trade Issues, National Security and International Affairs Division, U.S. General Accounting Office (GAO), *Drug Control—Status of Counternarcotics Efforts in Mexico, GAO/T-NSIAD-98-129*, hearing, 18 March 1998.

49. Isacson and Olson, *Just the Facts*, pp. 87–91.

50. Testimony of Rand Beers, Acting Assistant Secretary of State, INL, in GAO, *Drug Control*, hearing, 18 March 1998.

51. ONDCP, "U.S.-Mexico Counterdrug Cooperation."

52. Roderic Ai Camp, "Mexico's Armed Forces, Marching to a Democratic Tune?" in *The Dilemma of Mexican Politics in Transition*, Kevin Middlebrook, ed. (London: Institute of Latin American Studies, University of London, forthcoming, 2004).

53. A list of Mexican military officers who received courses in U.S. military schools was produced by the U.S. Defense Department in response to a 1995 Freedom of Information Act request made by the newspaper *Reforma*.

54. Information in this and next paragraph from Isacson and Olson, *Just the Facts*. The authors were unable to find public information on the number of Mexican soldiers trained in 1996.

55. "Presentación de Exposición de Conceptos Fundamentales," proposal for justice reform by President-elect Vicente Fox's Justice and Security Transition Team, Mexico City, 31 July 2002. WOLA files.

56. *Copley News Service*, "U.S. Drug Czar Warns New Mexican President on Anti-Drug Strategy," 12 October 2000.

57. Sigrid Arzt, "La Militarización de la Procuraduría General de la República: Riesgos para la Democracia Mexicana," paper commissioned by the Center for U.S.-Mexican Studies Project on Reforming the Administration of Justice in Mexico, Berkeley, 15 May 2003, repositories.cdlib.org/usmex/prajm/arzt/.

58. *Reforma*, "Amparan Seguridad 23 Mil 969 Elementos," 24 November 2002.

59. Ibid.

60. Author interview with Mexican antidrug official, Mexico City, 29 April 2002.

61. *INCSR 2002*, "Canada, Mexico, and Central America."

62. U.S. Defense and State Departments, *Foreign Military Training in Fiscal Years 2002 and 2003, Volume 1* (Washington, D.C.: U.S. State Department, Bureau of Political-Military Affairs, May 2003).

63. WOLA interview with Sigrid Arzt, Mexico City, 18 November 2002.

64. Vicente Fox Quesada, *Palabras del Presidente Vicente Fox Quesada durante la Ceremonia Conmemorativa del Día del Ejército*, Temamatla, Estado de Mexico, 19 February 2003, www.presidencia.gob.mx/?Art=4525&Orden=Leer.

65. International Consortium of Investigative Journalists, "U.S.-Trained Forces Linked to Human Rights Abuses," Mexico section, in *U.S. Military Aid to Latin America Linked to Human Rights Abuses* (Washington, D.C.: Center for Public Integrity, 12 July 2001), www.publicintegrity.org/report.aspx?aid=256&sid=100.

66. See the defense ministry's responses to questions submitted under Mexico's Freedom of Information Act on 13 June 2003, 24 June 2003, and 28 August 2003, www.sedena.gob.mx/index4.html.

67. *Washington Post*, "Elite Anti-Drug Troops," 9 September 1998.

68. *El Norte de Ciudad Juarez*, "Forman Cártel de Droga Desertores del Ejército," 11 October 2003.

69. Testimony of Donnie Marshall, Acting Deputy Administrator, DEA, in GAO, *Drug Control*, 18 March 1998.

70. In a response to a request under the Freedom of Information law (dated 5 November 2003), the defense ministry stated, "Specific accounting of the counternarcotics budget is not available because the military carries it out simultaneously with a variety of missions," www.sedena.gob.mx/index4.html.

71. *Washington Post*, "Mexican Drug Force is U.S.-Bred," 26 February 1998.

72. Quoted in Eric L. Olson, "The Evolving Role of Mexico's Military in Public Security and Antinarcotics Programs," WOLA, May 1996, p. 5.

73. *Washington Post*, "Mexican Drug Force is U.S.-Bred," 26 February 1998.

74. WOLA interview with defense attaché, U.S. embassy, Mexico City, 13 August 2003.

75. DEA, *Mexico Country Profile for 2003* (Washington, D.C., November 2003).

76. Data for the chart is taken from Office of the President of Mexico, *Tercer Informe de Gobierno del C. Presidente Vicente Fox Quesada* (Mexico City: September 2003), Statistical Annex, p. 469.

77. U.S. House of Representatives, *Congressional Record*, statement of Representative James Traficant, "Disapproval of Determination of President Regarding Mexico," HJ Res 58, 13 March 1997.

78. Representatives Burton, Barton, and Hamilton all referred to Mexico's decrease in arrests during their arguments to decertify Mexico. See *Congressional Record-House*, 13 March 1997. See also *Congressional Record–Senate*, statement of Senator Diane Feinstein, "Mexico Foreign Aid Disapproval Resolution," S2638, SJ Res 42, 26 March 1998.

79. U.S. Senate, Banking, Housing, and Urban Affairs Committee, testimony of Thomas A. Constantine, Administrator, DEA, *Drug Trafficking in Mexico,* hearing, 28 March 1996. Available at www.dea.gov/pubs/cngrtest/ct960328.htm.

80. In one debate about Mexico, Representative Peter Goss declared that "many applauded when Mexico mobilized its military in the war on drugs, including myself." See *Congressional Record–House*, 13 March 1997.

81. Statement of Senator Strom Thurmond, *Congressional Record–Senate*, 26 March 1998.

82. Statement of Representative Benjamin Gilman, *Congressional Record–House*, 13 March 1997.

83. K. Larry Storrs, *Mexican Drug Certification Issues: U.S. Congressional Action, 1986–2001* (Washington, D.C.: Congressional Research Service, 8 January 2002).

84. All direct quotes in this paragraph are ibid.

85. U.S. Congress, 22 USC 2291j-1, *Foreign Relations Authorization Act 2002–2003 (PL 107-228)*, sec. 706. International Drug Control Certification Procedures, 30 September 2002.

86. U.S. State Department, Bureau of Democracy, Human Rights, and Labor, "Mexico," *Country Reports on Human Rights Practices–2002*, 31 March 2003.

87. Luis Astorga, *Drug Trafficking in Mexico: A First General Assessment*, Management of Social Transformations (MOST) Discussion Paper 36 (Paris: UNESCO, 1999).

88. Human Rights Watch, *Human Rights in Mexico*, pp. 11–16.

89. *New York Times*, "A Toll of 'Disappearances' in Mexico's War on Drugs," 7 October 1997.

90. Government of Mexico, *Recomendación 12/2002 a la Procuraduría General de la República sobre el caso del homicidio del señor Guillermo Vélez Mendoza* (Mexico City: National Human Rights Commission, 14 May 2002).

91. U.S. State Department, *Country Reports 2002*, "Mexico."

92. Human Rights Watch, *Human Rights in Mexico*, p. 30.

93. Government of Mexico, *Estadísticas Judiciales en Materia Penal,* Cuaderno No. 10 (Mexico City: Instituto Nacional de Estadística, Geografía, e Informática, 2003), Chart 2.6.2, p. 478.

94. *La Jornada*, "Acusados de Delitos Federales, un Tercio de los 7 Mil 809 Indígenas Presos: CNDH," 12 February 2001.

95. Information in this paragraph from *La Jornada*, "Acusados de Delitos Federales, un Tercio de los 7 Mil 809 Indígenas Presos: CNDH," 12 February 2001.

96. Sigrid Arzt, "Militarización de la Procuraduría."

97. See Laurie Freeman, *Troubling Patterns: The Mexican Military and the War on Drugs* (Washington, D.C.: Latin America Working Group, September 2002). See also Human Rights Watch, *Military Injustice: Mexico's Failure to Punish Army Abuses* (New York: Human Rights Watch, December 2001). See also Reuters, "Peasants in Rural Mexico Claim Army Brutality," 17 November 2003.

98. *La Jornada*, "Apoyan Procuradores el Retiro del Ejército de Tareas Antinarco," 4 May 2001.

99. Government of Mexico, *Constitución Política de los Estados Unidos Mexicanos*, chapter 1 on Individual Guarantees, articles 16 and 21.

100. Government of Mexico, *Tercer Informe de Gobierno*, Statistical Annex, p. 478.

101. This figure does not include executions that occurred in other contexts (including counterinsurgency), for example, the killing of eleven people in El Charco, Guerrero, in 1998. Many other cases go unreported.

102. Freeman, *Troubling Patterns*, p. 11.

103. National Human Rights Commission, *Recomendación 15/2003* (Mexico City: April 2003).

104. Government of Mexico, *Orden General de Operaciones FTA 2000 del 33 Batallón de Infantería del Ejército* (Mexico City: Secretaría de la Defensa Nacional, 21 February 2000).

105. Human Rights Watch, *Military Injustice*.

106. Procuraduría General de la República, *Cuatro Años en la Procuraduría General de la República* (Mexico City: November 2000).

107. *Reforma*, "Juzgarán Militares a Soldados de PFP," 16 August 2002.

108. WOLA interview with Alberto Rodríguez and Karen Saskahana, U.S. embassy, Human Rights and Narcotics Affairs Section (NAS) officials, Mexico City, 13 August 2002.

109. Freeman, *Troubling Patterns*.

110. *La Jornada*, "Admite el Pentágono que Adiestró a 6 Militares Mexicanos Violadores de Derechos Humanos," 28 June 1998.

111. *New York Times*, "Mexican Tale: Drugs, Crime, Torture, and the U.S.," 18 August 1997.

112. *New York Times*, "U.S.-Mexico Drug War: 2 Systems Collide," 23 July 1997.

113. Government of Mexico, *Recomendación 16/2003 a la Procuraduría General de Justicia Militar sobre el caso de los integrantes del 65o. Batallón de Infantería en Guamuchil, Sinaloa* (Mexico City: National Human Rights Commission, 22 April 2003).

114. *INCSR 2002*, "Canada, Mexico, and Central America."

115. See stories by Alfredo Corchado of the *Dallas Morning News*, "Officials Allege Cover-Up in Drug Suspect's Slaying," 13 May 2004; "Inquiry in Drug Slayings Turns to 4 U.S. Agents," 17 July 2004; and "Latest Killing, Possible Cartel Link Worry El Paso," 2 September 2004.

116. Roderic Ai Camp, *Generals in the Palacio: The Military in Modern Mexico* (New York: Oxford University Press, 1992).

117. United Nations Special Rapporteur on extrajudicial, summary, or arbitrary executions, *Report of Ms. Asma Jahangir, Submitted Pursuant to Commission on Human Rights Resolution 1999/35, Visit to Mexico*, UN Doc. E/CN.4/2000/3/Add.3 (25 November 1999). See also United Nations High Commissioner for Human Rights, *Diagnóstico Sobre la Situación de los Derechos Humanos en México* (Mexico: United Nations, 2003).

118. Diane E. Davis, "Law Enforcement in Mexico City: Not Yet Under Control," *NACLA Report on the Americas* 37, no. 2 (September/October 2003).

9

The Caribbean: The "Third Border" and the War on Drugs

Jorge Rodríguez Beruff and Gerardo Cordero

The U.S. government's antidrug strategy defines the Caribbean region as a "transit zone," an extensive and problematic border that must be controlled to keep drugs away from U.S. shores. The notion of a transit zone implies that drugs pass directly through the region from the production zone to the consumption zone and that the flow of drugs could be stopped by turning the border into a kind of shield. At its most extreme, this would involve the impossible task of building a "Caribbean barrier" against illicit drugs, using police and military controls.

This approach overlooks the complexities of the region as well as those of the drug trade. The Caribbean is characterized by its vast geographic area, by its heterogeneity, and by the varied effects of the drug problem on the many nations and territories that form the region. Puerto Rico is one of the primary transportation hubs for illicit drugs in the Caribbean. U.S. drug control officials generally refer to the island as if it were not a U.S. territory; its borders are viewed as part of the barrier, when in fact there is a free flow of people and goods between Puerto Rico and the United States.[1] Perhaps most important, the Caribbean is far from being simply a transit zone; drug use and drug-related violence and corruption have proliferated within the region. In other words, for the people of the Caribbean, the primary question is not how to stop the flow of drugs through their countries but rather how to address the very real problems stemming from drug consumption and trafficking.

As in the United States, national leaders in the Caribbean, alarmed by the growing drug problem, have placed increasing emphasis on antidrug policies. As a result of joint U.S.-Caribbean efforts, over the course of the 1990s a complex legal, institutional, and financial framework for drug control, with an emphasis on interdiction and law enforcement, took shape in the Caribbean. However, two points of contention have emerged. One is the U.S. military presence in the region and the role of the military in counterdrug efforts. The other is how national security threats to the region are defined and addressed.

The antidrug mission came to dominate the U.S. regional security agenda in the 1990s. U.S. drug control policies served to strengthen and redefine the role of security forces throughout the Caribbean at a time when internal and external threats associated with the Cold War were declining. Caribbean security forces vary in size and capacity, but the majority are small, are meagerly financed, and operate mainly as police forces. Many Caribbean countries feared that the drug war agenda could give the U.S. military an unduly large role and too much influence over their own smaller forces. What is more, despite the already confused roles and missions of the local forces, U.S. policymakers encouraged greater participation for them in domestic law enforcement activities.

Following the U.S. withdrawal from the Panama Canal Zone in 1999, the U.S. military expanded its reach across other Central American countries and the Caribbean, most notably in Puerto Rico, largely within the framework of the antidrug mission. Even as this process bolstered the U.S. military presence in the region, a variety of military assistance and training programs and joint operations provided mechanisms for increasing U.S. military influence over regional counterparts. Many Caribbean analysts view the predominant role assigned to the U.S. Southern Command (Southcom) in U.S. strategic thinking about the region (see Chapter 2), along with the subordination of local forces to Southcom, as undermining the role of civilian governments in defining and shaping their own national security policies.

Meanwhile, criticism of the militarized approach to the drug issue has emerged, particularly in the English-speaking Caribbean nations. Critics have proposed alternative antidrug policies that emphasize socioeconomic issues and allow for increased attention to the serious social, health, and trade problems caused by drug trafficking. An alternative perspective based on the concept of "multidimensional security" has taken shape in international forums, particularly those of the Caribbean Community and Common Market (Caricom). According to this approach, security cannot be understood only in military terms; on the contrary, economic, political, social, and cultural factors must all be taken into account, as they may pose a threat to national security if they are ignored. This suggests that the drug problem should be dealt with as a social and economic problem, not simply a law enforcement and military matter. In short, it calls for shifting the emphasis of current policies to place greater emphasis on socioeconomic solutions.

The concept of multidimensional security and other alternative approaches to the war on drugs may start attracting more attention as evidence mounts that the current approach, with its emphasis on interdiction, repression, and militarization, is failing. No evidence exists of a significant, sustainable reduction in the quantity of drugs flowing through the

Caribbean. Indeed, many believe that the problems associated with drug trafficking and consumption in the Caribbean have worsened in many respects.

Puerto Rico is an especially relevant case because the island is both a key point on one of the most important routes in the drug trade and the largest market for illicit drugs in the region. As a U.S. territory, it followed Washington's hard-line approach to the war on drugs during the 1990s. That policy has led to serious civil rights issues, while at the same time, drug trafficking and consumption, and the high levels of violence associated with them, remain chronic problems. When it comes to the drug trade, Puerto Rico appears to have undertaken Sisyphus's impossible task.

The ineffectiveness of existing drug control policies has enhanced the relevance of alternative approaches that move away from an overemphasis on repression, interdiction, and law enforcement. In Puerto Rico, for example, growing support for a public health approach to the drug issue was reflected in the policies adopted by the government of Governor Sila María Calderon, elected in 2000. An open discussion of such alternatives is vital to the development of policies that are both effective and compatible with democratic practices and values.

Recent developments in the region may provide even more space for advocates of alternatives. In the case of Puerto Rico, popular protests against naval exercises and a live firing range forced the U.S. Navy to leave Vieques, a small island off Puerto Rico's northeastern shore. The last naval installation, Roosevelt Roads Naval Station, officially closed at the end of March 2004, leaving the army's Fort Buchanan near the capital city of San Juan as the lone active-duty U.S. military installation in Puerto Rico.[2] In broader terms, U.S. military resources have moved from the Caribbean to other parts of the world now considered more strategic in the wake of the September 11 attacks that catapulted international terrorism to the top of the list of U.S. security concerns. The Caribbean has clearly been bumped farther down the U.S. national security agenda as the new antiterrorism campaign has been superimposed on the antidrug campaign that previously prevailed in the region. As they have in relation to the drug issue, some Caribbean leaders have expressed concerns about the way in which the antiterrorism agenda is defined. They continue to put forward the idea that poverty and economic malaise are the principal threats to security and stability along what U.S. Secretary of State Colin Powell has called the "third border" of the United States (the other two being Canada and Mexico).

• Frontier in the War on Drugs

The Caribbean region is characterized by its vastness and diversity, including hundreds of islands spread across 3 million square kilometers of ocean. It is hard to generalize about the islands of the Caribbean; they differ widely in terms of size, culture, political institutions, and populations. The definition of the region used in U.S. drug control policy statements also includes nations in the Caribbean corridor that are not technically located in the Caribbean Sea, such as the Bahamas and Turks and Caicos, as well as mainland countries such as Suriname. To simplify analysis, the definition of the Caribbean used in this chapter is that used in the U.S. documents. It includes the Caribbean island states and territories, as well as the Bahamas, Turks and Caicos, Suriname, Guyana, and French Guiana. Belize is not included; although it is often considered a Caribbean country because English is one of its official languages, it is more closely linked to the drug trade in Central America.

The Caribbean has been an important theater in the U.S. war on drugs since at least the end of the 1980s. The U.S. government considers the Caribbean to be a transit zone for drugs originating in the Andean source countries, principally Bolivia, Colombia, and Peru. The Caribbean corridor is distinguished from the more important Mexico and Central America corridor, which is managed by Mexican drug cartels. Although traditionally the Caribbean has been a transit zone for cocaine, a growing supply of Colombian-produced heroin is also now being transshipped to the U.S. market.

As a transit zone, the Caribbean has the peculiar position of sharing borders with the United States, France, England, and the Netherlands (and, by extension, the entire European Union), since all of these countries still have some kind of sovereignty over Caribbean territories acquired during the colonial era. Great Britain controls the Cayman Islands, Anguilla, the British Virgin Islands, Montserrat, and Turks and Caicos. France has control over French Guiana, the north of St. Martin, Martinique, and Guadeloupe. The Netherlands still governs the south of St. Martin, Saba, St. Eustace, Aruba, and Curaçao. Puerto Rico and the U.S. Virgin Islands are both dependencies of the United States, the first as a commonwealth, the second as a territory under the jurisdiction of the Interior Department.

Technically speaking, drugs arriving in these territories do not have to leave the Caribbean before reaching the United States or the European Union. U.S. drug control officials, however, do tend to distinguish between the U.S. mainland, which is considered the destination zone, and the U.S. Caribbean territories, considered part of the transit zone.

Although there are obvious difficulties in quantifying an illegal and clandestine industry like the drug trade, various official sources have estimated the proportion of cocaine that moves through the Caribbean to reach the U.S. market. These estimates have ranged from 20 percent to 48 percent of the cocaine for sale in the United States.[3]

During congressional testimony in 2001 the director of the U.S. Drug

Enforcement Administration (DEA), Donnie Marshall, said that 31 percent of cocaine reaching the United States was trafficked through the Caribbean, while 66 percent came through the Mexico and Central America corridor and 3 percent arrived directly from South America.[4] Marshall also said that 30 percent of the drugs entering Europe from Latin America pass through the Caribbean.

By contrast, a report by the Caribbean Regional Office of the United Nations Office on Drugs and Crime (UNODC) stated that the Mexico and Central America and Caribbean corridors had accounted for similar levels of transit activity in 2001.[5] The office estimated that 160 metric tons of cocaine entered the United States directly from the Caribbean in 2001, down from 500 metric tons in the early 1980s. This is explained in the report as being due to decreased use of that drug in the United States (declining from 660 to 250 metric tons from 1989 to 2001).

Within the Caribbean itself, there are three principal trafficking routes (Figure 9.1). The first goes from western Colombia to Central America and Mexico via maritime routes, passing through the Caribbean's western waters. From Mexico, drugs move across the land border into the United States. The second originates in eastern Colombia and travels toward Jamaica before heading toward the enormous archipelago formed by the Bahamas and Turks and Caicos, moving through the straits lying between

Figure 9.1   Major Cocaine Routes in the Caribbean, 2003

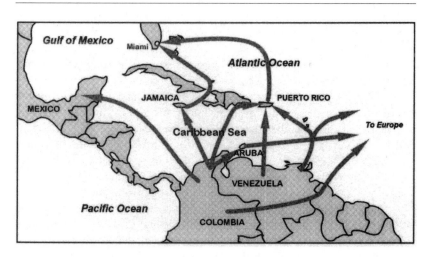

Source: Adapted by Linda Hess Miller from United Nations Office on Drugs and Crime, Caribbean Regional Office, *Caribbean Drug Trends 2001–2002*, Bridgetown, Barbados, February 2003.

Cuba and Haiti before reaching Florida. In the third route, the drugs come into Puerto Rico from Hispaniola (the island shared by Haiti and the Dominican Republic) to the west and from the Lesser Antilles to the east, then are shipped by various means to the continental United States. This last route is also an important source for cocaine being trafficked to Europe.[6]

There are diverse opinions as to the relative importance of these routes, and it should be stressed that the ranking can change very quickly. One of the characteristics of drug trafficking in the transit zones is the traffickers' ability to adapt to interdiction efforts on one route by finding alternate ones.

The route through the Bahamas, long used by pirates and smugglers, has geographic advantages for moving illicit drugs into Florida. This sparsely populated archipelago has twenty-nine islands, 661 keys, and 2,378 rock outcrops scattered over a vast area of sea only a short distance from the U.S. mainland.[7] Previously, a principal trafficking route to the Bahamas was by air from South America or by boat from Jamaica. To eliminate this route, the Bahamas and Turks and Caicos Operation was launched in 1982 as a combined effort of the U.S. DEA, State Department, Defense Department, Coast Guard, and Customs, as well as Bahamian authorities.[8] According to the DEA, increased U.S. collaboration with the Bahamas in the 1980s and early 1990s led to a huge increase in drug seizures.[9]

A parallel set of actions was aimed at the route across the U.S. border with Mexico. In 1990 the White House Office of National Drug Control Policy designated this border as a High Intensity Drug Trafficking Area, and Operation Alliance, an effort to coordinate the drug control work of U.S. federal, state, and local law enforcement agencies in the area, was launched. These agencies worked with Joint Task Force (JTF) 6, a U.S. military unit formed the previous year at Fort Bliss in El Paso, Texas, to back up antidrug efforts inside the United States.

Cuba's 6,500-strong border patrol, which is under the control of the Interior Ministry, has also played an important role in intercepting drug shipments.[10] U.S. officials' comments on Cuban antidrug efforts have generally been positive. A 2001 DEA report on the Caribbean, for instance, stated that Cuba is not a principal source of drugs or transit point for drugs into the United States; it is not involved in money laundering; nor is it a source of precursor chemicals for drug-trafficking organizations. The report highlights the cooperation between the Cuban Interior Ministry and the U.S. Coast Guard.[11] Contacts between the U.S. and Cuban governments in the war on drugs have tended to be ad hoc, although the opening of a Coast Guard liaison office in the U.S. Interests Section in Havana in 2001 seemed to point to the possibility of greater collaboration.

In its 2003 report on international drug control, however, the U.S. State

Department criticized the Cuban government for dedicating insufficient resources to interdiction. In the previous year's report, it had expressed concern about Cuba's deteriorating capacity to keep up the antidrug effort, stating that "Cuba's decaying infrastructure, declining operations budgets and sporadic fuel shortages have hampered enforcement efforts."[12] The U.S.-Cuban collaboration in drug control efforts cannot be evaluated, however, without taking into account the U.S. economic embargo of the island and other policies that have interfered with more effective coordination in the fight against drugs.

In any case, the massive outlays of civilian and military resources along the Mexico border and in the Bahamas, combined with measures adopted by the Cuban government to control drug trafficking, most likely produced the shift in the 1990s toward trafficking routes through Hispaniola, Puerto Rico, and the Eastern Caribbean.[13]

A report from the U.S. General Accounting Office (GAO) in April 1996 claimed that Puerto Rico had become the principal transshipment point for cocaine moving through the Eastern Caribbean to the U.S. mainland. It stated that "U.S. drug officials believe that after 1993 traffickers moved some of their activities from the Bahamas to Puerto Rico because U.S. interdiction efforts in the Bahamas had increased the risk to traffickers."[14] The GAO report included a map prepared by the Defense Department that showed nearly all the Eastern Caribbean routes emptying into Puerto Rico and the Virgin Islands.

This evaluation was repeated in testimony in mid-2000 by the commander of the Atlantic Area Coast Guard, Vice Admiral John E. Skhor. He listed the most problematic countries as follows: "In the Caribbean Transit Zone, the highest threat region is Puerto Rico, followed by Haiti, then Jamaica, and the Western Caribbean." He added that his primary counterdrug focus in 2000 would be Puerto Rico, since half of all cocaine entering the United States in 1999 moved through the Caribbean, and half of that had gone through Puerto Rico.[15]

According to the U.S. State Department's drug control report for 2003, however, "Jamaica [was] the preferred Caribbean transshipment point for South American cocaine en route to the United States." The report said that 110 tons of cocaine, 70 percent of which was destined for the United States and the rest for Europe, passed through the island's territory in 2003.[16] Criminal activity in Jamaica reached such high levels that in May 2003 the head of the Jamaica Defense Force, Vice Admiral Hardley Lewin, told the local press that transnational criminal activities, including drug trafficking, were a threat to his country's democracy and way of life.[17] Of particular concern was the growth of gangs, known locally as posses and yardies, and the dramatic increase in levels of urban violence.[18]

The Bahamas and the Dominican Republic were also named in the

State Department's 2003 report as major transit points for South American drugs en route to the United States, and Haiti was called a "key conduit." In Haiti, the report noted, "the road ahead is obstructed by the politicization and corruption of the police and judiciary, and further obscured at this time by social disorder and political violence."[19]

The State Department has no official role inside the United States or its territories. Its drug control reports therefore do not provide a separate country evaluation for Puerto Rico, despite the tendency of U.S. drug control officials to view Puerto Rico as distinct from the mainland. The report from the UNODC's Caribbean Regional Office for 2001 and 2002, however, stated that "since the early 1990s, Puerto Rico has remained the largest hub for cocaine in the Caribbean" and that trafficking through the Lesser Antilles to Puerto Rico had intensified.[20] In sum, available information points to an increase in drug trafficking through Jamaica and a continued role for Puerto Rico as a key entry point for drugs headed to the United States.

The idea of defining the Caribbean as a transit zone within the U.S. drug control strategy reflects the emphasis on interdiction and the goal of stopping drugs before they enter the country's mainland. It suggests that borders can be turned into shields or barriers against the flow of drugs. In the mid-1980s it was proposed that a blockade created by the DEA, Customs, and the U.S. Coast Guard would effectively stop 95 percent of drugs destined for the United States.[21] An official report on the antidrug actions of the Atlantic Command in the Caribbean carried the revealing title "Caribbean Barrier."[22]

The transit zone concept, however, masks the complexity of the drug trade in the Caribbean. It downplays the negative, and sometimes devastating, impact of drugs on the region's societies and governments. The region is linked to numerous aspects of the illicit drug business, including consumption, production, money laundering, government corruption, trafficking in small weapons, organized crime, and internal violence. Consumption is increasingly a problem: some part of the drug supply is not just in transit but remains in and is used in the region. The business affects state policies, the economy, public health, and communities more broadly. In short, people in the Caribbean are less concerned that their territory is used for the transshipment of drugs than they are about the multiple negative effects that the illicit drug trade has on their societies and daily lives.

• Counterdrug Law Enforcement Efforts

Concern over the growing impact of the Caribbean drug trade did not stem solely from the United States. It also came from regional leaders who began to see drug trafficking as an important threat to governance and the rule of law. Cuba tightened drug control policies after a 1989 drug-trafficking scandal in the Interior Ministry led to the firing-squad execution of General Arnaldo Ochoa.[23] Beginning in the early 1990s, the increase in the number of murders and serious crimes in Puerto Rico, the apparent inability of the police to exercise control over problematic urban areas, and the media's fascination with violence provoked an authentic panic; political forces took advantage of this climate of fear to push through hard-line drug control policies there. A similar process took place in the Dominican Republic.

While the principal concerns of Caribbean leaders were the appearance of drug mafias and the rising levels of internal violence associated with the drug trade, problems such as corruption, arms trafficking, and an increase in drug consumption also provoked alarm. A 1992 report by the West Indian Commission stated that "nothing poses greater threats to civil society in Caricom countries than the drug problem and nothing exemplifies the powerlessness of regional Governments more."[24] At a 1995 Caricom summit, regional leaders reiterated that drug trafficking was the main security threat facing their countries. Similar concerns were voiced by England, France, and the Netherlands, the European powers with Caribbean territories.

As a result, a complex legal, institutional, and financial framework that emphasized interdiction and law enforcement took shape in the Caribbean in the 1990s.[25] The majority of Caribbean nations eventually signed the 1988 Vienna Convention that updated and strengthened the UN accords that have long been the legal foundation of international drug control efforts. The UNODC has an extremely active regional office located in Barbados with programs throughout the Caribbean.

On a separate front, the United States began pushing for modernization of its treaties with the region. The Caribbean states signed the International Convention Against Corruption, as well as agreeing to new Mutual Legal Assistance Treaties, extradition treaties, and agreements allowing overflights by U.S. planes. New maritime agreements included shiprider provisions that allow U.S. vessels to engage in search-and-seizure activities in a given country's waters as long as an official from that country is on board to authorize the operation. Caribbean nations agreed to take part in the Caribbean Financial Action Task Force (CFATF), a regional subgroup of the Financial Action Task Force on Money Laundering (FATF) formed by the G7, leading economic powers, in 1989. CFATF now has twenty-five members. The Egmont Group, established in 1995, coordinates the work of the Financial Intelligence Units of countries around the world.[26] Many Caribbean countries passed laws against money laundering and the transport and illegal sale of precursor chemicals and agreed to allow properties and other holdings of accused drug traffickers to be seized.[27]

In fact, money laundering through the many offshore financial centers

(OFCs) that exist in the Caribbean became one of the top issues in the 1990s. The CFATF calculated that in 2000 U.S.$60 billion, of a total of between U.S.$300 billion and U.S.$500 billion moved worldwide by drug traffickers, was laundered through the Caribbean.[28] The OFCs in Aruba, the Cayman Islands, and the Netherlands Antilles were first on the list of alleged money laundering centers, followed by Antigua and Barbuda, the Bahamas, Montserrat, and St. Vincent and the Grenadines.[29] Dominica, Grenada, and St. Vincent had been on the FATF's blacklist of countries that had not been cooperating fully to combat money laundering between 2000 and 2003, but all were removed from the list in 2003.[30] During the 1990s, the Organization of American States (OAS) had a mission of experts on money laundering in the Caribbean working on the issue.

The Caribbean Law Enforcement Council was created to promote coordination on issues involving customs. In the Eastern Caribbean, the DEA and the U.S. Defense Department helped establish the civil-military Caribbean Law Enforcement-Intelligence Committee that meets once a month in San Juan, Puerto Rico. A regional DEA office was created in 1995, also based in San Juan, where the number of DEA agents nearly doubled in the 1990s. In addition, a new office was opened in Trinidad and Tobago, while yet other offices expanded. One of the programs most often mentioned by the DEA as an effective antidrug instrument is the Unified Caribbean On-Line Network, which allows thirty-six countries to share intelligence information electronically.

The State Department, through its Bureau of International Narcotics and Law Enforcement Affairs (INL), channels funds to individual countries for drug control. The INL also contributes to the UN's International Drug Control Program, the Inter-American Drug Abuse Control Commission of the OAS, and the Financial Action Task Force, and it helped fund the creation of the Financial Intelligence Units.[31] Nevertheless, the bulk of the State Department's funds go to the so-called drug-producing countries (Bolivia, Colombia, and Peru). Only a small part of the assistance makes it to the Caribbean, as can be seen in Table 9.1.

The Caribbean countries currently receiving the most INC aid are the Bahamas and Jamaica (each around U.S.$1 million to U.S.$1.5 million per year). Other nations such as the Dominican Republic, Haiti, and Trinidad and Tobago share funding from the State Department's Caribbean Country Assistance program. In FY2002, this program's budget was almost U.S.$4 million, but the request for FY2004 was down to just U.S.$1 million.[32]

• The Military and the Antidrug Fight

Despite this apparent cooperation on several fronts, significant differences have emerged between Washington and many Caribbean states regarding the role of the military in counterdrug activities. Over the course of the

Table 9.1   U.S. International Narcotics Control (INC) Aid, 1997–2005, Andes Versus the Caribbean (millions of U.S. dollars)

Type of INC Aid	Andes	Caribbean
INC Military and Police Aid	3,049.38	30.18
INC Economic and Social Aid	1,490.95	29.91
Total	4,540.33	60.09

Source: U.S. State Department, Bureau for International Narcotics Law Enforcement Affairs, various years. The countries included in the Caribbean are the Bahamas, the Dominican Republic, Guyana, Haiti, Jamaica, Suriname, Trinidad and Tobago, and the Eastern Caribbean (Antigua and Barbuda, Barbados, Dominica, Grenada, St. Kitts and Nevis, St. Lucia, St. Vincent and the Grenadines). The Andes column includes Bolivia, Colombia, and Peru only.

1990s, regional leaders confronted with growing problems of drug abuse and drug-related violence placed increasing emphasis on the serious social, health, and economic problems caused by the drug trade. They called for a multidimensional security approach, described in greater detail below, that would give them greater flexibility to set policies and to allocate resources. Moreover, many Caribbean countries feared that the drug war agenda would give U.S. military forces undue influence over their own small and poorly funded security forces.

The U.S. Congress gave the Defense Department a lead role in counterdrug efforts, a role ultimately embraced by Southcom. Southcom has a broad range of mechanisms—including military aid and training programs and its own significant presence in the region—that it can use to promote its drug control agenda with regional security forces. With the threat of the Cold War gone, Southcom has contributed to an overall redefinition of the mission of local security and military forces, as it has pushed these forces to become directly involved in drug interdiction and law enforcement.[33] A U.S. military officer complained in 1999 about the obvious contradiction— that a country legally blocked from using its armed forces for law enforcement at home promotes this activity for foreign militaries:

> We have a long-standing law codified almost 150 years ago, Posse Comitatus, that precludes the military from exercising police power against our own citizens. Why then do we persist with a foreign and national security policy that encourages, even demands at times, that Latin American countries utilize their militaries in counterdrug operations against their own citizens?[34]

The U.S. security agenda for the Caribbean, dominated by Cold War policies until the 1980s, began to shift as a result of radical geopolitical changes in that decade. These included the failure of the Marxist New

Jewel Movement in Grenada (capped by the 1983 U.S. military occupation); the subsequent crisis of other left-wing movements in the English-speaking Caribbean; the end of the conflicts in Central America; and perhaps most important, the disappearance of the Soviet Union and the collapse of the socialist-communist bloc. These developments also had, to varying degrees, negative political and economic repercussions for Cuba, seen as the main U.S. antagonist in the region.

By the end of the 1980s, the lack of looming communist threats led to the refocusing of U.S. attention on new, nontraditional concerns. The general consensus that then developed among military and civilian leaders in the United States was that the principal threats emanating from the Caribbean were illegal immigration and drug trafficking. The idea was to redefine security policies to ensure that these threats would not affect the United States.[35]

In a 1989 book emphasizing "new threats," former Southcom commander General Paul Gorman called for creating a unified U.S. command for the Caribbean that would have as its main missions fighting the drug trade and controlling the movement of weapons and subversives.[36] At that time all the maritime and land zones in the Caribbean fell under the jurisdiction of the Atlantic Command, except for the Dominican Republic, which traditionally fell under Southcom. General Gorman based his call to place the entire Caribbean under one unified command largely on the increasing participation of the U.S. armed forces in drug control. His view apparently played a key role in the eventual decision to have Southcom replace the Atlantic Command in overseeing the Caribbean. The crux of Gorman's argument was that the post–Cold War mission required the military to close the gaps that had resulted from the division of Latin America and the Caribbean between two separate commands.

The Atlantic Command, based in Norfolk, Virginia, with significant installations in Puerto Rico, was predominantly a naval command. Although Southcom had control only over the Dominican Republic, this was strategically important because the country has the largest security forces in the Caribbean after Cuba. In sum, the Atlantic Command was in charge of pursuing drug control policies on the military front in most of the Caribbean during the first half of the 1990s, while Southcom did the same in the Dominican Republic.

The U.S. administration's decision under Ronald Reagan to send 6,000 U.S. troops to Grenada in 1983 had noticeably increased the U.S. military presence in the region. Shortly thereafter, the United States helped sponsor the creation of a seven-member Regional Security System (RSS) in the Eastern Caribbean, which included Grenada as well as Barbados, Antigua and Barbuda, Dominica, St. Kitts and Nevis, St. Lucia, and St. Vincent and the Grenadines. Security forces in the other English-speaking countries of Caricom were also strengthened.

The Atlantic Command was in charge of developing and supporting this RSS, coordinating Caribbean security forces through joint exercises, and sponsoring the regional forum known as the Caribbean Island Security Conference, among other efforts. In 1989, the U.S. military created three joint task forces to advance the antidrug fight. The Atlantic Command had control over both Joint Task Force 6, which operated along the border with Mexico, and JTF-4, based in Key West, Florida, with jurisdiction over the entire Caribbean. The Atlantic Command also introduced changes in the regional electronic surveillance system with construction of the system known as Relocatable Over-the-Horizon Radar (ROTHR).[37]

In July 1997, Southcom became a unified command for all the territories in Latin America and the Caribbean, with the exception of Mexico. By that time, Southcom's drug control mission had already become a top priority. Its other most important mission was to guarantee strong relationships with the armed forces in the region.[38]

The Post-Panama Military Structure

The transfer of control over the Panama Canal to that nation in 1999 resulted in the relocation of U.S. military infrastructure and activities. It also was accompanied by other changes. Though the removal of U.S. military personnel and facilities from Panama meant a short-term reduction in some counterdrug efforts, over the long term it allowed the U.S. military to extend its military presence in the Caribbean.

Southcom moved its general headquarters to Miami. Its operational component, U.S. Army South, with 1,800 soldiers, was moved from Panama to Puerto Rico (and relocated once again in 2003 to San Antonio, Texas).[39] Given the loss of access to Howard Air Force Base in Panama, where U.S. counterdrug surveillance flights had been based, some Air Force activities were also transferred to Puerto Rico.[40] Many of these air operations included "support of U.S. troops and the Drug Enforcement Administration"[41] and were intended to provide aerial surveillance of Colombia and the rest of the Andean region. The military command also set up new air bases known as forward operating locations, two of which were located on Aruba and Curaçao in the Netherlands Antilles.[42]

Intelligence structures used in the antidrug effort were restructured with the merger of the two Joint Interagency Task Forces (JIATF): JIATF-South in Panama, and JIATF-East in Key West. According to Southcom, JIATF-East "is an interagency organization designed to facilitate coordination of military counterdrug efforts in the Source and Transit zones."[43] The combined JIATF uses information provided by the ROTHR system to coordinate operations for intercepting drug boats in the Caribbean.

The ROTHR system took up tasks previously carried out by the Caribbean Basin Radar Network (CBRN). At the height of its activity, CBRN had seventeen radars operated by the U.S. Air Force in ten Caribbean countries, 1,000 employees, and an annual budget of U.S.$200 million. According to an Air Force officer who worked on the system, CBRN was "one of the most intense radar nets ever configured."[44] This system was reduced in scope in the mid-1990s and now operates in only six countries, one of which is Colombia.[45]

The new ROTHR technology was projected to be cheaper and more effective than the CBRN system. The ROTHRs in Virginia and Texas, which cover nearly the entire Caribbean, came on line in April 1993 and September 1995, respectively. In 1999, ROTHR operations got under way in Puerto Rico, covering a large swath of South America. The receptor component is located at Fort Allen in Ponce and the transmitter on Vieques. Because of strong protests by residents of Valle de Lajas, the site originally intended for the transmitter, Vieques was chosen instead.

The original purpose of ROTHR, according to manufacturer Raytheon, was "to provide early warning of strikes against aircraft carrier task forces"; the company claimed that it would also be effective in detecting drug shipments.[46] Nevertheless, the GAO later reported that the "modernization" of the electronic detection mechanisms had effectively downgraded surveillance capacity.[47] As noted by one former U.S. military officer: "The deployment of ground based radar ... was severely reduced by the Fall of 1994 closure of the Caribbean Radar Network Program.... The decision was decried as tactically unsound, and ... a breach of faith among Caribbean nations opposed to drug trafficking."[48]

Critics of the ROTHR in Puerto Rico pointed out that its technology was obviously unsuited for drug surveillance. Notably, it cannot detect wood or fiberglass boats, the principal means of transporting drugs. According to a high-ranking Coast Guard officer, "About 90 percent of the cocaine flow moves by maritime means, and in the Caribbean over 80 percent of the time the traffickers' choice of conveyance is by 'go-fasts'—typically 30 to 50-foot, multiengine boats which carry 50 to 1,500 kilograms of cocaine each trip."[49]

However, it has been difficult to evaluate the ROTHR system in more detail because it is operated with a high degree of secrecy. Only recently has information on the system's questionable effectiveness come to light through data provided by the U.S. Navy to the Puerto Rican government's Office of Drug Control. According to this source, in 2001 the three radars detected less than 1 percent of the cocaine estimated to pass through the Caribbean. These data also confirm ROTHR's inefficacy in detecting surface vessels such as go-fast boats. During the three-year period from 2000 to 2002, information from the radars helped intercept only four boats in the region. The system also proved ineffective over the same period in detecting small planes used to transport drugs; only twenty-seven were intercepted.[50]

Despite the criticism, the Navy has decided to keep the system. Perhaps, despite the system's relative ineffectiveness, it is simply the least expensive option.[51] However, while ROTHR's purpose is ostensibly counterdrug surveillance, it is not publicly known whether it is performing other functions as well. The secrecy in which the ROTHRs operate makes it difficult, if not impossible, to evaluate the decisionmaking about its operations.

Another important aspect of the U.S. military presence in the region is Socsouth, the unified command of Southcom's special operations unit, which includes U.S. Special Forces from the Army, Navy, and Air Force.[52] Socsouth facilities were located at Roosevelt Roads Naval Base in Puerto Rico from 1999 until late 2003 and subsequently moved to the U.S. mainland. Officials said the move would not affect the command's mission, which included on-site training of regional military forces in antidrug operations.[53] Before the move, the command carried out more than 200 operations annually, with an average of forty-two missions in sixteen countries at any given time. It is made up of 350 soldiers and has several C-130 transport planes and antidrug Orion P-3C patrol units at its disposal.

Southcom's Naval Command also moved to Roosevelt Roads at the end of 1999. Unlike the naval units that had been in Panama and which fell under the Atlantic Command, this new unit fell under Southcom. Its first commander was Vice Admiral Kevin Green, who was put in charge of dealing with the controversy regarding the U.S. live firing range in Vieques.[54] This command, which was relocated to the continental United States in 2004 in the aftermath of the Vieques protests, organizes the Navy's Unitas combined maneuvers with other naval forces in Latin America and the Caribbean. Counterdrug operations are a principal mission for the Naval Command, which "oversees U.S. naval forces participating in drug enforcement operations."[55]

Other Mechanisms of U.S. Military Influence
In addition to the direct U.S. military presence in the region, the already asymmetrical military relationship is also influenced by joint exercises, military assistance programs, and weapons sales. Joint exercises with Caribbean militaries and security forces are an important mechanism used by Southcom to maintain and strengthen its military-to-military ties. Since 1995, Southcom has not carried out bilateral exercises in the region, preferring a multilateral approach. The most important multilateral exercises are the Tradewinds and New Horizons exercises.

Socsouth and the U.S. Coast Guard are in charge of the annual Tradewinds exercises. Forces from Antigua and Barbuda, the Bahamas, Barbados, Belize, Canada, Dominica, the Dominican Republic, Great Britain, Grenada, Guyana, Haiti, Jamaica, the Netherlands Antilles, St. Kitts and Nevis, St. Lucia, St. Vincent and the Grenadines, and Trinidad and Tobago all have participated. The operation works not only to improve coordination in drug control but also to "establish sanctions, embargo or blockade; collect information on theater strategic situation; conduct security assistance activities; provide humanitarian assistance; and assist in restoration of order."[56]

New Horizons, by contrast, consists of engineering exercises in which U.S. units participate in the construction of infrastructure and provide services to the civilian population. General James T. Hill, commander of Southcom, reported to Congress in April 2004:

> Last year the New Horizon exercises completed 31 engineer projects consisting of schools, medical clinics, wells, and rudimentary road construction and repair. The 70 humanitarian medical deployments treated more than 300,000 patients.... Panama, Belize, Dominican Republic, Grenada, and St. Kitts will host New Horizons exercises [in 2004].[57]

Other mechanisms of military influence include authorizations for direct commercial arms sales, as well as programs such as Excess Defense Articles, Foreign Military Financing, and Foreign Military Sales. The Defense Department also channels drug control assistance to the Caribbean. Training activities include Joint Combined Exchange Training (JCET) and the more traditional International Military Education and Training (IMET) and expanded IMET (see Chapter 2 and Appendix 1). Many JCET training missions are carried out in the Caribbean. In 2001 and 2002, 688 students were trained in twelve JCET antidrug training missions carried out with Caribbean security forces and paid for with Section 1004 monies.[58] It is not known how many other JCETs took place in those years because information about JCETs funded by the Special Forces budget is classified. In 2002, more than 400 Caribbean students participated in the IMET program.[59]

The Dominican Republic has historically been the primary beneficiary of U.S. military aid and training programs in the region. As a result, its military has a strong relationship with Southcom. The Dominican Republic's decision to send troops to Iraq—the only Caribbean nation to do so—is evidence of these strong military ties. The other principal participants in the IMET program in recent years have been Jamaica and the Eastern Caribbean nations.[60]

Two other programs merit mention. The Law Enforcement Detachment (LEDET) program was set up so that U.S. Navy ships could take part in antidrug operations. Under it, Coast Guard personnel—authorized to carry out law enforcement activities—are placed on navy ships and even vessels from other countries. In 1988, the U.S Congress voted that there should be LEDET personnel on all ships in or passing through areas of drug interdiction, including the Caribbean. By the year 2000, LEDET personnel on Navy ships were credited with nabbing 51 percent of the drugs seized by the Coast Guard in the Caribbean and the Pacific.[61]

In addition, there are the shiprider agreements, mentioned earlier, that most Caribbean countries have signed with the United States. These agreements have sparked controversy because of their implications for national sovereignty. Opponents charge that they dangerously weaken national control over territories and maritime zones. The United States, however, has attempted to expand the Caribbean model for the shiprider agreements to Central and South America and recently proposed that Cuba accept a similar arrangement. The U.S. position in its most extreme form was stated in 1996 by Elliot Abrams, who had been a high-ranking official in the Reagan administration (1981–1989) and later served in the George W. Bush administration. In what came to be known as the Abrams doctrine, he argued that U.S. security concerns "in our proverbial back yard" might require Caribbean nations to relinquish their sovereignty in the area of national security to allow the United States to assume "its role as the ultimate guarantor of peace, stability, and, nowadays, democracy" in the Caribbean.[62]

Caribbean Security Forces and Southcom

Caribbean security forces span a wide range in terms of size and capacity. The Royal Bahamas Defense Force consists of a small coast guard and air unit. The tiny Eastern Caribbean countries of St. Kitts and Nevis, Grenada, Dominica, and St. Vincent, all members of the Regional Security System, do not have armed forces but depend on eighty-member Special Service Units and some limited coast guard resources. The Antigua and Barbuda Defense Force is slightly larger at 115 members. Barbados, the Eastern Caribbean nation that is home to the Regional Security System, has a considerably larger force, consisting of the 850-member Barbados Defense Force and a 100-member coast guard. On the South American mainland, Guyana, which has an extensive territory and border disputes with Venezuela, has 1,800 soldiers in the Guyana Defense Force, while Suriname, a former Dutch colony, has 2,000 troops. The largest militaries in the English-speaking Caribbean are found in Jamaica and in Trinidad and Tobago. The Jamaica Defense Force has 2,500 members, and there are 190 in the coast guard and 140 in an air unit. The Trinidad and Tobago Defense Force has a 2,300-member infantry, an 800-member coast guard, and a 50-member air force.[63]

In the Spanish-speaking Caribbean, the Dominican Republic has approximately 24,500 troops under arms. The only Caribbean country with a substantial military force is Cuba, but it has been reducing the size of its military since the end of Soviet economic and military subsidies forced Havana to begin cutting the military's size and budget after 1989.[64] Cuba's military budget dropped from 9.6 percent of gross national product in 1985 to 2.8 percent in 1995. By 2001 it had reduced its military to an estimated 46,000 troops. There are an additional 70,000 young people with military training in the Youth Work Army. Cuba's antidrug missions are coordinated by the Interior Ministry, in a structure separate from the Revolutionary Armed Forces, even though both come under the same military command. The Interior Ministry's interdiction efforts are largely carried out by a border patrol unit.[65]

Because of significant asymmetries between the United States and Caribbean nations and the small size and minimal resources of most of the latter's security forces, the impact of U.S. military aid programs in the Caribbean is far greater than that of similar programs in larger Latin American countries. This brings into question not only the autonomy of the small security forces in Caribbean nations but also the ability of political leaders and civil society to move alternative proposals forward.

The situation is further complicated by the corrosive effect of drug money on security institutions. Researchers Humberto García and Gloria Vega summarize the problems as follows: "The models and level of penetration of drug trafficking in the Caribbean can take various forms, but corruption of the security forces is a common denominator."[66]

In addition to the heterogeneity of the region's security forces described above, two other special characteristics of the Caribbean affect the relationship between Southcom and the region's military and security forces. First, the majority of the Caribbean's small security forces operate mainly as police. Second, a number of the Caribbean islands are not independent states but rather territories belonging to one of three NATO allies of the United States.

Despite these differences, Southcom has followed the same model used in Latin America. It has encouraged Caribbean security forces to become involved in the antidrug fight and to carry out law enforcement tasks that would be illegal in the United States, heightening the existing confusion between military and police roles. Of particular note is the creation of drug control agencies controlled directly by the armed forces. This has further eroded the distinction between military and police tasks and has reinforced the tendency of Caribbean security forces to gear their efforts toward internal security and control of the population.

The clearest example is the Dominican Republic. The Dominican military is in charge of the National Directorate for Drug Control (Dirección

Nacional de Control de Drogas, or DNCD), and all of the DNCD directors have been high-ranking military officers (three army generals, two vice admirals, and one air force general).[67] In 2002 the Dominican military created the Unified Special Forces Command, made up of elite units of the different military branches and the police, to reinforce patrolling along the border zone. Major General Carlos Díaz Morfa stated that "border control belongs to the National Army."[68] Added to this was the decision of Southcom to send soldiers to the Dominican-Haitian border in fifteen groups of 900 soldiers each to participate in joint military exercises.[69] The presence of such a large number of U.S. soldiers in the Dominican Republic was a new development and most likely reflected security concerns regarding neighboring Haiti.

Although DNCD documents talk about the National Police as a force independent of the military, the relationship between the military and police forces is symbiotic. This is reflected not only in the practice of naming military officers to run the National Police but also in other forms of collaboration that bring into question the autonomy and civilian character of the police. One recent study states that clear limits between the police and the military do not exist. Another highlighted recent progress made by the Dominican military in democratizing the institution but added the caveat that police tasks continue to be an area reserved for military control.[70]

There are important additional factors in the Dominican case. The growing role of the armed forces in controlling the border with Haiti has to do in part with concerns about drug trafficking and illegal immigration. Haiti's inability to exercise control of its national territory and the impunity with which drug traffickers operate, at times with the open complicity of police officers, led Haiti to be labeled a "narcostate." Dominican DNCD authorities interviewed for this study (before the ouster of President Jean-Bertrand Aristide in February 2004) used this term to describe Haiti, noting that drugs cross the border by land, sea, and air.

Nevertheless, the largest illicit drug seizures in the Dominican Republic occur not along the border with Haiti but in the capital, along the east coast where tourist resorts are located, and in the southern provinces such as San Pedro de Macorís and La Romana.[71] The largest drug busts in these provinces have happened in La Altagracia, which is the spot on the island closest to Puerto Rico. Drug seizures in places closer to Haiti, such as Dajabón on the border and Santiago and Puerto Plata in the north-central Dominican Republic, are relatively small. Some Dominican politicians allege that, as happened in Haiti, the drug trade has penetrated the upper echelons of the Dominican government, including the judiciary and political parties.

• The Caribbean Response: Multidimensional Security

As noted, the significant U.S. military presence in the region and the role assigned to local security forces have provoked concern across the Caribbean. Moreover, there is a fundamental difference in perspective, arising from contrary understandings of the principal security threats to the region and how to address them.

A summit held in Bridgetown, Barbados, in May 1997, attended by President Bill Clinton and Caribbean leaders, served to reaffirm regional cooperation in the war on drugs. It also highlighted regional perceptions that the U.S. strategy was inadequate and increasingly unilateral. The summit produced the Bridgetown Declaration of Principles and a Plan of Action. The plan contained two basic components, one dealing with trade, development, finances, and the environment while the other focused on justice and security issues.[72] The fourth point of the Bridgetown Declaration of Principles recognized an "inextricable link between trade, economic development, security and prosperity in our societies."[73]

Leaders from the Caricom nations expressed dismay that drug control strategy was not linked in any real way to measures that would deal with the region's deteriorating economic situation. They complained that the United States gave low priority to the region's economic and trade issues in contrast to the high priority assigned to drugs and illegal immigration. The Caribbean leaders' primary concerns at the Bridgetown summit included the impact of the North American Free Trade Agreement; reduction in direct foreign investment; social consequences of structural adjustment policies and other neoliberal measures; U.S. support for Central American producers in what was known as the banana war; and the channeling of U.S. economic assistance to other regions, such as Eastern Europe, that were considered a higher priority in the post–Cold War context.[74] They pointed out that the majority of the agreements signed by the United States and Caribbean countries in the 1990s dealt with security and not economic or trade issues.[75]

The U.S. approach to the war on drugs is also perceived as damaging to the sovereignty of the Caribbean's independent nations. New international treaties related to financial controls, deportations, and maritime pacts, particularly shiprider agreements, have evoked resistance from some countries, including Jamaica and Barbados.

In 1998, the prime minister of St. Kitts and Nevis summarized the Caribbean perspective when he said, "Washington must not see everything within the crucible of narcotics. There are other social problems that exist in the Caribbean, and a lot of these social problems, to some extent, the United States can help and has not helped."[76]

Some of the hesitations Caribbean nations had expressed at the Bridgetown summit about U.S. drug control policy, such as the opposition of Barbados and Jamaica to shiprider agreements, were overcome during later negotiations by U.S. promises of economic assistance. However, the Clinton administration failed to deliver on these promises.[77]

Since then, the differences in focus between the Caricom nations and the United States on how to define and deal with security issues in the region have continued to surface when there are opportunities to express them. In 2001, the Caribbean position was presented in a number of international forums using the concept of *multidimensionalism*, put forward as an alternative to the U.S. emphasis on military participation in the drug war. According to this multidimensional approach, security cannot be treated as a military concern only. Economic, political, social, and cultural factors must all be taken into account, as they may pose a threat to national security if ignored. Within the context of the drug war, this concept calls for shifting the emphasis of current policies to place greater stress on socioeconomic solutions.

In June 2001, Caricom leaders meeting in Nassau, the Bahamas, created the Regional Working Group on Crime and Security. This working group, headed by Lancelot Selman of Trinidad and Tobago, included representatives from each member state as well as from the Regional Security System, the Caribbean Association of Police Commissioners, the University of the West Indies, and the regional subsecretariats of Caricom and the Organization of Eastern Caribbean States. Caricom established the framework of the working group in the following terms: "Security threats, concerns and other challenges in the hemispheric context are multi-dimensional in nature and scope. ... The traditional ways of meeting the challenges [need] to be expanded to encompass new non-traditional threats, which include political, economic, social, health and environmental aspects."[78] The working group submitted more than 100 recommendations to the twenty-third meeting of Caricom leaders, held in July 2002.[79]

The issue of multidimensionalism in regional security also was addressed at the thirty-second general assembly of the OAS, held in Barbados in June 2002, and at the October 2002 meeting in Washington, D.C., of the OAS Committee on Hemispheric Security. In an article titled "Multi-Dimensional vs. Military Security," Norman Girvan, a well-known Jamaican economist and secretary general of the Association of Caribbean States, commented on the speech given by Barbados prime minister Owen Arthur at the Barbados meeting:

> He asserted that a meaningful definition of security cannot be limited to traditional military operations, but must adopt an integrated approach that addresses the conditions creating social instability such as HIV/AIDS, illegal arms and drug trafficking, trans-national crime, ecological disasters and the poverty that afflicts some 70 million people in the hemisphere.[80]

Guyana's ambassador to Washington, Odeen Ismael, used similar terms, again highlighting the contrast between the concept of multidimensionalism and the military approach to security and the drug war.[81] The multidimensional concept of security, finally, was incorporated into the Declaration on Security in the Americas adopted at the OAS Special Conference on Security held in Mexico in October 2003.[82]

• Puerto Rico: Problems in the Laboratory

In many ways, Puerto Rico can be considered a laboratory for U.S. drug control policy in the Caribbean. The Puerto Rican situation illustrates the complex issues encompassed by the concept of multidimensional security. All U.S. federal agencies, including security agencies, operate on the island as if it were part of the continental United States, and U.S. federal drug control laws are applied. Puerto Rico's growing importance in cocaine trafficking during the 1990s attracted the attention of Washington and stimulated an increase in resources dedicated to the antidrug fight throughout that decade. In addition, the Puerto Rican government, in close collaboration with the U.S. federal government, implemented a policy known as the "iron fist against drugs and crime."

Yet the approach used in the war on drugs in Puerto Rico has not produced results that demonstrate the effectiveness of current policies. Although the United States has experimented with diverse measures in Puerto Rico since the 1980s, there is no evidence of a significant, sustainable reduction in the quantity of drugs flowing across its borders. At the same time, internal problems related to drug trafficking and consumption have worsened. Given that the approach being used in Puerto Rico is the model promoted by the United States for the rest of the Caribbean, the implications of the Puerto Rican "laboratory" go well beyond its own shores.

The Puerto Rican government promised an all-out assault on drugs and criminal gangs. Its policies included much tougher treatment of criminals; more money, equipment, and personnel for security forces, particularly the police; new prisons; and greater collaboration with federal agencies. Between 1992 and 1998 the budget and manpower of the police force nearly doubled. Municipal police forces were increased. Antidrug laws were stiffened (continuing a process that began in the 1980s) and new, privatized prisons were constructed. The budgets for drug prevention and rehabilitation, however, continued to be miniscule compared to resources for the security forces.

Federal agencies operating on the island, mainly the DEA, Customs, and the Coast Guard, were also reinforced. The number of agents nearly doubled over the course of the 1990s. In 1994, Puerto Rico and the U.S. Virgin Islands were declared a High Intensity Drug Trafficking Area, which meant access to additional federal resources.

The most visible example of the militarization of the drug war in the 1990s was the use of the National Guard, a military force, in raids conducted in housing projects to root out gangs and drug trafficking. The period from 1993 to 1995 saw the greatest number of raids on these extremely poor neighborhoods. The operations, conducted jointly by local police and federal agents, led to a significant increase in complaints of police abuse and other violations of civil rights filed with Puerto Rico's Civil Rights Commission. In 1993, the commission reported that:

> The patterns of police abuse and brutality reflected in the complaints show that the victims are usually young men with few economic resources. In addition, the victims are usually accused of crimes such as the "obstruction of justice," "disturbing the peace," or "aggression," among others.[83]

Nevertheless, it soon became evident that the government did not have sufficient resources to go into all of the most problematic housing projects, much less sustain a presence for an extended period of time. Nor did the proposed Quality of Life Council, which was to be implemented by a number of civilian agencies after the occupations, ever really get off the ground. By 1997 or 1998, plans for the council were basically abandoned.

Ironically, the highest annual number of murders recorded in Puerto Rico—1,039 in 1994—took place during the period in which the iron-fist plan was most vigorously applied. Police reluctance to admit this situation led to the police reporting fewer murders than those recorded by the government's Institute of Forensic Sciences, a discrepancy unprecedented in Puerto Rican history. In total, from 1990 to 2000 the police had reported 761 murders fewer than the institute reported, with the greatest underreporting coming during the preelectoral period.[84]

The death of seventeen-year-old Anthony Hernández on January 1, 2000, in the Monte Park housing project was emblematic of the excesses that occurred during the continuing police raids. According to witnesses, the teen, who was popular in his community, was killed by the police who then placed a rifle in his hands. Another youth, fourteen years old, was shot and wounded during the same operation. A report by the local bar association's Commission on Human and Constitutional Rights contained dramatic testimonies from the raid and concluded that the identification of "high-crime zones" and "dangerous individuals" had resulted in "a class-based interpretation and application of criminal law, worsening the class divisions in Puerto Rico."[85]

The number of deaths from drug overdoses, one of the most reliable indicators of consumption levels, also began to increase, reaching alarming levels by 2001 (Figure 9.2).[86] Drug trafficking through Puerto Rico also continued at a high level, another indication of the failure of the iron-fisted approach despite the efforts of federal agencies.[87]

Figure 9.2   Deaths from Overdoses in Puerto Rico

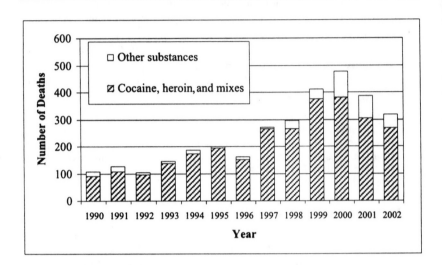

Source: Instituto de Ciencias Forenses de Puerto Rico, "Muertes por Intoxicación con Drogas, 1990–2002."

This inability to meet the expectations created by the antidrug and anti-crime strategy was one of the factors that led to the defeat of the New Progressive Party in the November 2000 elections and the victory of Sila María Calderon. In her government plan, Puerto Rico for the 21st Century, the new governor emphasized the revitalization of poor neighborhoods, identified as Special Communities, and made a commitment to improve infrastructure and the standard of living in general.

With respect to antidrug policies, Calderon's principal project centered on the creation of the Office for Drug Control (OCD), with a mission including coordination of antidrug efforts with the police superintendent and other government agencies. The idea of putting a single authority in charge of coordinating drug control efforts was copied from the U.S. White House's Office of National Drug Control Policy. Former U.S. drug czar Barry McCaffrey was brought in as an adviser to local politicians. When local civic groups opposed the concept of appointing a powerful drug czar to head up the new Puerto Rican office, the government abandoned the idea, though the office itself was maintained. The OCD is the link to the federal antidrug agencies operating in the Caribbean region. Under its second director, Luis Guillermo Santana, the OCD developed a drug control program that, for the first time, took a public health approach and put less emphasis on repressive law enforcement tactics.[88] This approach had been advocated for years by civil society groups.

Critics, however, noted that there were not enough resources assigned to the plan and that the police continued to violate civil rights. Police raids using military tactics continued in some communities, as did complaints of abuses, albeit with less frequency than in the early 1990s.[89]

One case involved occupation of San Juan's oldest slum, the La Perla neighborhood, on September 13, 2002, which sparked a loud outcry from human rights organizations. The operation came after drug dealers spoke openly on television of their burgeoning client lists and showed samples of what they had for sale. Although the National Guard did not participate, local residents questioned the paramilitary tactics used by the police, who remained in La Perla until October. The operation included raids and searches that critics denounced as illegal.[90] The characterization of the government's approach as the "criminalization of poverty," and intimations that the rule of law did not seem to apply in some urban areas, became common in the media and among the general public.

The fledgling OCD, with only fifteen employees, faces a truly overwhelming task. There were an estimated 200,000 Puerto Rican drug addicts in 2002, and the OCD director estimated that about 178,000 of them needed inpatient treatment in clinics. Many of Puerto Rico's homeless people—there are 6,000 in San Juan alone—are chronic addicts. Drug consumption appears to have increased dramatically since the beginning of the 1990s. In 1990 there were 144 deaths from overdoses, and in 1995 there were 194. By 2000 the number had jumped to 477, with the majority of victims young people between the ages of eighteen and thirty-eight. In addition, 1,500 new cases of AIDS are reported annually, 77 percent of them linked to drug use.

In 1998, officials estimated that there were 500 locations where drugs were sold. The number is believed to have doubled over the next five years.[91] In May 2003, the governor reported that police estimates put the number of drug sale locations at 1,600. This means that drugs are being sold in every barrio and even in middle-class neighborhoods. While the murder rate has dropped from the levels reached in the mid-1990s, it is still three times the U.S. national average. It surpasses the rates in Washington, D.C., Detroit, and Chicago, which have vied for the title of murder capital of the United States from year to year.[92] It ranks sixth worldwide in murders per capita.[93] These dramatic statistics do not indicate success for the policies adopted in Puerto Rico, which are being applied throughout the Caribbean. In short, there are serious problems in the Caribbean laboratory.

The existence of an enormous internal market, numerous organizations supplying drugs, and networks of corruption involving police officers and

Table 9.2   Seizures of Cocaine and Cannabis in Puerto Rico, 1997–2001 (kilograms)

	1997	1998	1999	2000	2001
Cocaine	15,153	10,344	9,977	5,416	2,831
Cannabis	1,337	1,285	12,605	1,982	24

Source: UNODC, Caribbean Regional Office, *Caribbean Drug Trends 2001–2002,* Bridgetown, Barbados, February 2003, Annex I–II, pp. 27–28.

local authorities complicates any effort to stop the flow of drugs through Puerto Rico to the United States. Two important drug-trafficking routes— the one through the Lesser Antilles and the other through Hispaniola—converge in Puerto Rico. Moreover, Puerto Rico cannot be characterized solely as a transit zone because it is also a small-scale drug producer. Between August and October 2003, the police acted in eleven cases of hydroponic marijuana growing. Marijuana was found in both rural and urban zones in six municipalities, and some of the growers used extremely sophisticated techniques.[94]

The most recent data on drug interceptions in Puerto Rico are not encouraging. The statistics offered by the regional UN Office on Drugs and Crime show a decrease in drug seizures (Table 9.2). These results call into question not only the rhetoric used in the war on drugs but also the effectiveness of the measures applied in Puerto Rico, the principal U.S. territory in the region. Federal officials have said that the decrease in drug seizures is the result of trafficking routes moving farther to the west, but this claim has not been confirmed.

Given the failure of drug control policies to date, many public health experts and civil society advocates in Puerto Rico are calling for a fundamental shift in drug policy toward a harm reduction approach, as originally proposed by the Calderon government. They call for a move away from defining the complex problems of drug trafficking and consumption as national security issues or police problems to be dealt with mainly by the armed forces and other state security agencies. Rather, they say, notwithstanding the serious consequences of the problem for public security, a more effective response requires defining drugs primarily as a public health issue to be dealt with by civilian authorities.

• New Security Developments

Recent events have provided more impetus for supporters of alternate policies. Two factors have lead to a reconfiguration of the U.S. military presence and role in Puerto Rico and the Caribbean more broadly. First, protests against the naval exercises in Vieques forced Navy operations, and then most other U.S. military operations, off the island. Second, as a result of the September 11 terrorist attacks, U.S. military resources have moved from the Caribbean to other parts of the world now considered more strategic.

The closing of the Vieques practice range led to the permanent deactivation of the Atlantic Fleet Weapons Training Facility at the Roosevelt Roads Naval Base. This in turn led to the decision to close Roosevelt Roads, once the largest U.S. naval base outside the mainland.[95] The special operations forces of Socsouth that had been stationed at Roosevelt Roads were moved to various mainland locales, and the Socsouth command moved to Homestead Air Base in Florida in March 2004.[96] Usarso (U.S. Army South), the command responsible for all Army operations in Southcom, had already pulled out of Puerto Rico in 2003.

The closing of Roosevelt Roads and other military facilities in Puerto Rico marks the end of a long era that began during World War II. This era had been characterized by the presence of large military bases and high-profile activities by the U.S. Armed Forces, particularly the Navy. At the same time, the intensive use of National Guard personnel in military operations as part of the war against terrorism in the Middle East and Central Asia makes it unlikely that they will be available for counterdrug police functions anytime in the near future.

The transfer of Puerto Rico from Southcom to the new Northern Command (Northcom) is yet another signal of the restructuring of Puerto Rico's traditional military role. Northcom was created in 2002 in response to September 11 the previous year, with its main mission to "protect the homeland."[97] The new command structure broke the geographic coherence that had been achieved under Southcom since 1997. Puerto Rico and the U.S. Virgin Islands, as well as Mexico and the Gulf of Mexico, are included in Northcom's area of responsibility. Northcom's two missions are to "dissuade, prevent and defeat threats to the United States, its territories and its interests," and to "provide military assistance to civilian authorities, including consequence management operations" within its area of responsibility. Drug control is not specifically mentioned in the Northcom mission statements.[98] The creation of Northcom most likely signifies a new emphasis on antiterrorism measures. It remains to be seen what the impact will be on the U.S. Caribbean territories or, in particular, how much of a priority will be given to antidrug operations.

Some regional leaders perceive the new antiterrorism agenda as simply being superimposed on the drug war in the Caribbean, exacerbating the tensions described previously without taking into account the highly dubious results counterdrug efforts have achieved to date. The Caribbean nations have questioned this change in security agenda made by U.S. fiat.

Announcing the Special Security Concerns of Small Island States meeting to be held in January 2003, Ellsworth John, St. Vincent's ambassador to the OAS, stated that the issues of poverty and unemployment were "weighing heavy on our governments." This he contrasted with the central U.S. focus on discussing antiterrorism actions.[99] During the meeting John added that "we cannot place all our resources and all our energy into terrorism," because if the issue of poverty were left off the agenda, "we can expect our citizens to rebel."[100] Nonetheless, at the same meeting the U.S. assistant deputy secretary of state for the Western Hemisphere, Thomas Shannon, called for a new antiterrorism agenda focusing on three central issues: airport security, border control, and greater intelligence capacity.

There are elements of both continuity and change in the antidrug and antiterrorism agendas. Both strategies define the Caribbean as a U.S. border that is difficult to close to security threats. In one sense, both agendas put forward the idea of a "widened border" that covers the entire region and is intended to serve as a barrier to entry into the United States. This vision is expressed in the concept of the third border put forth by Secretary of State Colin Powell at the Caricom meeting in Nassau in February 2002,[101] as well as earlier in the Abrams doctrine. Both agendas also share goals such as strengthening intelligence and monitoring capacities, control of borders and illegal immigration, and participation of military forces in law enforcement functions.

In his testimony before Congress on March 24, 2004, General James Hill, Southcom's commander, cited both agendas, stating, "The primary challenges in the Caribbean come from narcotrafficking, terrorism, document fraud, and corruption. ... Many countries [are] unable to police fully their sovereign territory, resulting in porous borders and coastlines and ungoverned spaces."[102]

Nevertheless, the two agendas differ in how they define the enemy and in their identification of vulnerabilities and security problems, among other issues. For example, significant attention is now paid to Islamic groups in the Caribbean, such as Jamaat Al Muslimeen and the Islamic Front of Trinidad and Tobago.[103] The antiterrorism agenda in the Caribbean has stressed air security, safety for U.S. tourists traveling abroad, and border control, focusing more on the movement of people and weapons than on contraband.

An additional consequence is that the Caribbean region has declined in priority on the U.S. national security agenda. An evaluation of national security risks within the context of the war on terrorism carried out by the Defense Intelligence Agency barely makes reference to Latin America and the Caribbean. Its description of "global terrorism" refers to the FARC in Colombia but makes clear that the real concern is the Al-Qaeda network. There is a mention of "international crimes" that includes Colombia. More generally, the author highlights "major concern ... over the growing link between terrorism and organized crime, especially the prospect that criminal groups will use their established networks to traffic in nuclear, biological, and chemical weapons, and to facilitate movement of terrorist operatives."[104] Apart from this implication of a threat from drug traffickers, this document has not a single mention of drug trafficking as an important security threat to the United States.

This shift appears to be affecting how resources are assigned as well as the level of the Pentagon's participation in counterdrug activities in the Caribbean. As noted by one journalist:

> Once the United States began its war against terrorism, the anti-drug fight was affected in that the military forces have withdrawn a great deal of their support and resources from the federal agencies in charge of the eradication of drug trafficking. ... In addition, the federal government has reassigned resources earmarked for anti-drug agencies to the armed forces for actions in Afghanistan and possibly Iraq.[105]

It remains to be seen how, in the long run, these changes will affect the U.S. military's approach to the Caribbean and how military-security relations will adapt.

• Conclusion

U.S. drug control policy toward the Caribbean has failed to achieve even minimal objectives. Not only is the drug trade as deeply rooted as ever in the area; related violence and illicit drug consumption are on the rise.

Changing U.S. priorities could, however, provide an opportunity for new policy approaches across the region. As the United States turns its attention elsewhere, the Caribbean and other countries may be given the flexibility they need to develop integrated alternative policies that take into account the complex socioeconomic challenges they face. It is vital that the spectrum of public debate be broadened, that is, democratized. Government resources should not be used to delegitimize alternative or critical positions, as has been the practice of the U.S. drug control bureaucracy.

The Caribbean requires a civilian-led approach to the drug problem. This would allow for the adoption of policies in tune with the region that could act as a counterbalance to policies imposed by the United States. Subordinating Caribbean security forces to Southcom or Northcom does not constitute a system of regional security. On the contrary, it undermines the role of civilian governments and tends to exclude Caribbean societies from participating in security issues.

Caribbean security forces, however small and poorly funded, have a role to play in any antidrug policy. Nevertheless, giving the armed forces operational control over what should be civilian-led police actions, as in the

Dominican Republic, does not promote democratic institutionality. Current counterdrug policies have tended to increase the prominence of the military and security forces, blurring the line between civilian and military roles. It is vital that the U.S. military revise its approach to the region's security forces to ensure full adherence to the democratic model in which the armed forces are subordinated to civilian control. It must do the same with regard to the new antiterrorism agenda.

The United States will not be able to keep its territory free from problems originating in the Caribbean as long as serious economic and political instability persists in the region. Washington's policy toward the area it sees as a third border continues to be reactive, short-term, and centered on the immediate security concerns posed by drugs and, now, terrorism. Meanwhile, Caribbean leaders, instead of seeing the problem as one of constructing barriers, are seeking long-term policies that can bring prosperity, stability, and integration to the region.

• Notes

1. The United States took control of Puerto Rico after the Spanish-American War. In 1952 the island became a U.S. commonwealth—neither a state of the union nor an independent nation, but a territory of the United States. Washington controls Puerto Rico's laws, courts, customs, immigration, defense, foreign relations, and trade. In addition, Puerto Ricans are U.S. citizens and can travel freely between Puerto Rico and the fifty states.

2. Miami Herald.com, "U.S. Navy Base Closure Affects 'A Lot Of People,'" 23 February 2004; Associated Press, "Navy Closes Its Last Base in Puerto Rico," 1 April 2004; U.S. House of Representatives, House Armed Services Committee, testimony of General James T. Hill, United States Army Commander, Southcom, before the House Armed Services Committee, United States House of Representatives, 24 March 2004.

3. The estimate of 20 percent is mentioned in U.S. State Department, Bureau for International Narcotics and Law Enforcement Affairs (INL), *International Narcotics Control Strategy Report (INCSR) 1996* (Washington, D.C.: March 1997), pp. 121–124. The estimate of 48 percent comes from the United Nations Office on Drugs and Crime (UNODC), Caribbean Regional Office, *Caribbean Drug Trends 2001–2002* (Bridgetown, Barbados: UNODC, February 2003), p. 4.

4. U.S. Senate, Caucus on International Narcotics Control, testimony by Donnie R. Marshall, administrator, Drug Enforcement Administration, U.S. Justice Department, *Drug Trafficking in the Transit Zone,* hearing, Senate Caucus on International Narcotics Control, 15 May 2001.

5. United Nations Office on Drugs and Crime, Caribbean Regional Office, *Caribbean Drug Trends 2001–2002*, Bridgetown, Barbados, February 2003, pp. 3–5.

6. Ibid., "Major Cocaine Routes in the Caribbean," map, p. 6. Cocaine moving to Europe through the Caribbean (not including that which only flies over the Caribbean) rose from 15 metric tons in 1991 to 53 metric tons in 2001.

7. Michael Craton, chapter 1 in *A History of the Bahamas* (Waterloo, Canada: San Salvador Press, 1986).

8. INL, *FY2003 Congressional Budget Justification (CBJ)* (Washington, D.C.: May 2002).

9. U.S. Senate, testimony by Donnie R. Marshall, 15 May 2001.

10. The Economist Intelligence Unit (EIU), *Cuba: Country Profile* (London: EIU/The Economist, 2002).

11. U.S. Justice Department, Drug Enforcement Administration (DEA), Office of Strategic Intelligence, Strategic Intelligence Section, South America/Caribbean Strategic Intelligence Unit, *The Drug Trade in the Caribbean: A Threat Assessment* (Washington, D.C.: September 2003), www.dea.gov/pubs/intel/03014/03014.html.

12. INL, *INCSR 2003*, "The Caribbean."

13. DEA, *The Drug Trade in the Caribbean*, pp. 12–13.

14. U.S. General Accounting Office (GAO), *U.S. Interdiction Efforts in the Caribbean Decline* (Washington, D.C.: GAO, April 1996), GAO-NSIAD-96-119.

15. U.S. Senate, Committee on the Judiciary, Subcommittee on Criminal Justice Oversight, testimony of Vice Admiral John E. Skhor, commander, Coast Guard Atlantic Area, *The Drug Smuggling Problem in the Caribbean*, hearing, 9 May 2000.

16. INL, *INCSR 2003*, "The Caribbean."

17. *Jamaica Gleaner*, "Democracy Under Threat from Drug Trade," 6 May 2003. The author thanks David E. Lewis for sending him this text.

18. See Humberto García Muñiz and Gloria Vega Rodríguez, *La Ayuda Militar como Negocio, Estados Unidos y el Caribe* (San Juan: Ediciones Callejón, 2002), pp. 281–289.

19. *INCSR 2003*, "The Caribbean." Embattled Haitian president Jean-Bertrand Aristide went into exile on 29 February 2004, the day before the State Department report was officially released in Washington.

20. UNODC, *Caribbean Drug Trends 2001–2002*, p. 8.

21. Captain (ret.) John E. La Couture, "Isn't It Time to Declare War on the Drug Invaders?" *U.S. Naval Institute Proceedings* (December 1986), pp. 84–85.

22. Captain (ret.) Alexander G. Monroe, USNR, *Caribbean Barrier: U.S. Atlantic Command Support of Counterdrug Operations, 1989–1997* (Norfolk, Va.: U.S. Joint Forces Command, December 2000).

23. The official book documenting the case was subtitled "The End of the Cuba Connection." Government of Cuba, *Case 1/1989* (Havana: Editorial José Martí, 1989).

24. *Report of the West Indian Commission: Time for Action* (Kingston: University of the West Indies, 1992), p. 343.

25. For a general and optimistic discussion of these measures, see Ivelaw L. Griffith, "Caribbean Geonarcotics," chapter 5 in *Caribbean Security on the Eve of the 21st Century* (Washington, D.C.: National Defense University, Institute for National Defense Studies, October 1996).

26. For a list of countries with operational FIUs, see the Egmont Group website, www.egmontgroup.org.

27. For information on these treaties and laws, see Appendix 3 in DEA, *The Drug Trade in the Caribbean*.

28. Anthony T. Bryan, "Transnational Organized Crime: The Caribbean Context" (working paper no. 1, commissioned by the Dante B. Fascell North-South Center, University of Miami, October 2000), p. 5. See also Anthony Maingot, "Rank and Share in the Corruption Game: The Situation of Small States" (paper presented at the CFAFT Conference, 2000).

29. See the table of Caribbean money-laundering centers in 1995 in Griffith, *Caribbean Security*, p. 45.

30. Financial Action Task Force, *Annual Review of Non-Cooperative Countries or Territories* (Paris: FATF Secretariat, OECD), 20 June 2003.

31. INL, *FY2004 CBJ, Global Programs.* For FY2002–2004, INL provided U.S.$25.4 million to UNDCP and U.S.$15.8 million to CICAD.

32. INL, *INL Program and Policy Guide*, May 2001, Appendix A; *INCSR 2003*, "The Caribbean"; and *FY2004 CBJ.*

33. For a discussion of Posse Comitatus and the Caribbean, see Appendix 1 in this volume; and Humberto García, "Algunas Notas Sobre las Tendencias Actuales de la Ley *Posse Comitatus* en los Estados Unidos y Su Impacto en el Caribe," in *Fronteras en Conflicto, Guerra Contra las Drogas, Militarización, y Democracia en el Caribe, Puerto Rico y Vieques*, Jorge Rodríguez Beruff and Humberto García Muñiz, eds. (San Juan: Red de Geopolítica, 1999), pp. 119–132.

34. Major Daniel L. Whitten, USAF, "Perspective on the Military Involvement in the War on Drugs—Is There a Better Way?" research report submitted in partial fulfillment of graduation requirements at Air Command and Staff College, Maxwell Air Force Base, Alabama, April 1999, (AV/ACSC/227/1999-04), pp. 6, 17.

35. This transition is discussed in Jorge Rodríguez Beruff and Humberto García Muñiz, *Security Problems and Policies in the Post–Cold War Caribbean* (Houndmills, Basingstoke, Hampshire, UK: Macmillan, 1996).

36. General Paul F. Gorman, "Defining a Long-Term U.S. Strategy for the Caribbean Region," in *Security in the Americas*, Georges A. Fauriol, ed. (Washington, D.C.: National Defense University Press, 1989), p. 351.

37. Ibid., p. 351.

38. See "U.S. Southern Command" on the Center for International Policy (CIP) website, www.ciponline.org/facts/dodsc.htm. For a more detailed discussion see Chapter 2 in this volume.

39. For a general discussion of special operations forces, see U.S. General Accounting Office, *Special Operations Forces: Force Structure and Readiness Issues, GAO/NSIAD-94-105* (Washington, D.C.: 24 March 1994). See also testimony of General James T. Hill, U.S. Army Commander, Southcom, 24 March 2004.

40. Jorge Rodríguez Beruff, "Guerra Contra las Drogas, Militarización, y Democracia," pp. 92–94.

41. See "Coronet Oak" at Globalsecurity.org/military/ops/coronet_oak.htm.

42. See "Forward Operating Locations" at www.ciponline.org/facts/fol.htm; and the Transnational Institute, "Forward Operating Locations in Latin America: Transcending Drug Control," *TNI Drugs & Conflict Debate Paper* 8, September 2003, www.tni.org/pubs/index.htm.

43. "U.S. Southern Command," globalsecurity.org/military/agency/dod/southcom.htm.

44. Whitten, "Perspective," p. 20.

45. See "Counter-Drug Radar Sites," www.ciponline.org/facts/radar.htm.

46. *Journal of Aerospace and Defense Industry News*, "Raytheon Awarded Navy Radar Operation, Maintenance Contract," 13 August 1999.

47. GAO, *U.S. Interdiction Efforts*, pp. 14–15.

48. Monroe, *Caribbean Barrier*, pp. 55–56.

49. Testimony of Vice Admiral Skhor, 9 May 2000.

50. U.S. Navy information provided by the Drug Control Office of the Government of Puerto Rico, in *El Vocero*, "Disminuye Efectividad Radar ROHTR," 13 January 2002, p. 5.

51. "Although this radar system provides a larger area of coverage footprint than microwave radars, it has less probability to detect an air event and is not as accurate in vectoring in interceptions as microwave radars." GAO, *Drug Control: U.S. Interdiction Efforts in the Caribbean Decline* (Washington, D.C.: GAO, April 1996), GAO-NSIAD-96-119, p. 16.

52. See CIP, "U.S. Southern Command"; and globalsecurity.org/military/ agency/dod/socsouth.htm.

53. *Navy Newsstand*, "Special Operations Units to Leave Roosevelt Roads, Mission Unaffected," 29 August 2003.

54. Information in this paragraph from Alejandro Torres Rivera, "El Surgimiento de USNAVSO y Su Relación con el AFWTF," manuscript, 27 January 2002, pp. 3 and 9.

55. globalsecurity.org/military/agency/navy/navso.htm.

56. Please see CIP website, ciponline.org/facts/trad.htm.

57. General James T. Hill, testimony, 24 March 2004.

58. The figures are available on the CIP website, ciponline.org/facts/sof.htm.

59. García y Vega, *La Ayuda Militar,* figure 7.3, p. 156; U.S. State Department, Bureau of Political-Military Affairs, *Foreign Military Training and DoD Engagement Activities of Interest, Volume 1,* U.S. Department of Defense and U.S. Department of State Joint Report to Congress, released March 2002.

60. García y Vega, chapter 7 and the figures appearing on pp. 145–160. See also CIP, www.ciponline.org/facts/imet.htm.

61. Michael Shelton, "The Forward Edge of Drug Interdiction: LEDETs Extend the Long Arm of Maritime Law Enforcement," in *Seapower Magazine* (September 2001). See also Whitten, "Perspective," April 1999.

62. Elliot Abrams, "The Shiprider Solution: Policing the Caribbean," *National Interest* (Spring 1996). Available on the Ethics and Public Policy Center website, www.cppc.org/publications/pubID.1970/pub_detail.asp.

63. The data come from various Economist Intelligence Unit (EIU) 2002 *Country Profiles* and from U.S. Library of Congress *Country Profiles.* Figures on Guyana are from Dion Phillips, "The Military in Guyana," in *Soldados y ciudadanos en el Caribe* (Santo Domingo: FLACSO, 2002), p. 165.

64. U.S. Defense Intelligence Agency, report, "The Cuban Threat to U.S. National Security," 18 November 1997, www.defenselink.mil/pubs/cubarpt.htm.

65. For statistics on the Cuban Armed Forces see EIU, *Country Profile: Cuba,* 2002.

66. García and Vega, *La Ayuda Militar,* p. 281.

67. The DNCD is listed among the forces represented on the home page of the State Secretariat of the Armed Forces of the Dominican Republic, www.secffaa.mil.do/.

68. Elia Ruiz Matuk, *Hoy Digital,* 4 January 2003.

69. Manuel Jiménez, *Hoy Digital,* 4 January 2003.

70. John Gitlitz and Paul Chevigny, "Crisis and Reform: The Police in the Dominican Republic," *WOLA Citizen Security Monitor* (November 2002): p. 13; and Wilfredo Lozano, "Los Militares y la Política en República Dominicana: De la Muerte de Trujillo al Fin del Siglo XX," in *Soldados y Ciudadanos,* p. 151.

71. Authors' interview with DNCD officials, 12 February 2003. Drug seizure statistics by province are from DNCD. See also *El Caribe* (Dominican Republic), "La Marihuana: Reina de las Drogas en 2002," 12 February 2003, p. 2.

72. For two opposing accounts of the Bridgetown summit see Ivelaw L. Griffith, "The Caribbean Security Landscape: A Reality Check," *Caribbean Affairs* (Last Quarter 1997): 35–46; and Sue Smith, "'We Will Not Grovel,' Drugs and

Jamaican Sovereignty" (speech at the Caribbean Studies Association Conference, Antigua, May 1998).

73. Caribbean/U.S. Summit, "Bridgetown Declaration of Principles: Partnership for Prosperity and Security in the Caribbean," Bridgetown, Barbados, 10 May 1997, www.caricom.org/usccs.htm.

74. The Caribbean debate about the relationship between the economic situation and antidrug policies is detailed in Ivelaw L. Griffith, *The Political Economy of Drugs in the Caribbean* (London: Macmillan, 2000).

75. Humberto García Muñiz, "Los Estados Unidos y el Caribe a Fin de Siglo XX: Transiciones Económicas y Militares en Conflicto," in *Fronteras en Conflicto,* table 1, p. 29.

76. *Miami Herald,* "U.S. Relations with the Caribbean Under Strain," 27 October 1998.

77. García Muñiz, *Fronteras en Conflicto,* p. 26.

78. Caricom Secretariat, "Crime and Security," 25 June 2002.

79. *Jamaica Observer,* "Caricom Security Ministers Call for Co-operation on Crime," 20 June 2002.

80. Norman Girvan, "Multidimensional vs. Military Security," www.acs-aec.org/column/index38.htm.

81. For the proposal of a diplomat based on this concept, see "Approaches on Security in the Caribbean Region," statement by Ambassador Odeen Ishmael at the Meeting of the Committee on Hemispheric Security of the OAS, Washington, D.C., 29 October 2002.

82. OAS, *Declaration on Security in the Americas,* Special Conference on Security, Mexico City, 27–28 October 2003, OEA/Ser.K/XXXVIII, CES/DEC.1/03 rev. 1, 28 October 2003.

83. Informe Anual de la Comisión de Derechos Civiles 1992–1993, San Juan, Puerto Rico, 1993, p. 13.

84. Figures obtained by author from the Puerto Rican police.

85. Colegio de Abogados, "Informe de la Comisión de Derechos Humanos y Constitucionales del Colegio de Abogados sobre la Comunidad de Monte Park," San Juan, n.d. [early 2000].

86. Instituto de Ciencias Forenses de Puerto Rico, "Muertes por Intoxicación con Drogas, 1990–2002," 17 December 2002.

87. This is analyzed in more detail in chapter 2 in Rodríguez and García, *Fronteras en Conflictos.*

88. The plan was signed by Governor Calderón on 5 January 2003. See also *El Nuevo Día,* "Vistas Públicas Sobre el Plan Antidrogas," 4 November 2002, p. 41.

89. Comisión de Derechos Civiles, *Informe Anual, 2001–2002* (San Juan: CDC, 2003), pp. 9–13.

90. *El Nuevo Día,* "Operativo en La Perla," 14 September 2002, p. 45.

91. *El Nuevo Día,* "Estiman en 500 los Puntos Fijos de Drogas," 20 March 1998, p. 12.

92. Matthew Hay Brown, "Puerto Rico's Homicide Rate Climbing," *Morning Call,* Allentown, Pa., 5 January 2004, pg. A.1.

93. *Primera Hora,* "Soluciones Contra el Crimen, Informe Pone el Dedo en la Llaga," 13 November 2003, p. 10.

94. See, for example, *El Nuevo Día,* "Descubierto un Cultivo de Marihuana," 26 September 2003, p. 43.

95. See *El Nuevo Día,* "Ceiba y Su Base Naval," 12 November 2003, p. 94, and "No es Desquite el Cierre," 26 September 2003, p. 10.

96. Associated Press, "U.S. Special Ops-South HQ Moves to Fla.," *New York Times*, 19 November 2003.

97. Information on Northcom appears at www.northcom.mil.

98. See www.northcom.mil/index.cfm?fuseaction=news.factsheets# usnorthcom.

99. *Barbados Daily Nation*, "St. Vincent to Host Security Meeting," 30 December 2002.

100. Associated Press, "Caribbean Leaders Discuss Cooperation to Counter Terrorist Threats," ABC News, 10 January 2003.

101. Colin Powell, "The United States and the Caribbean," Embassy of the United States, Caracas, Venezuela, press release, 14 February 2002, embajadausa.org.ve/wwwh1648.html. The column "The United States and the Caribbean: Trade, Democracy and Development," by Secretary of State Colin Powell, appeared 10 February 2002 in *Diario las Americas*.

102. Testimony of General James T. Hill, U.S. Army Commander, Southcom, 24 March 2004.

103. Latin America Newsletters, "Special Reports: Latin America and the U.S. 'War on Terror,'" London, May 2003, p. 23. See also *El Nuevo Herald*, "Grupos Terroristas Islámicos se Apoyan en América Latina," 4 June 2003.

104. Vice Admiral Lowell E. Jacoby, USN, Director, Defense Intelligence Agency, Statement for the Record, Senate Select Committee on Intelligence, "Current and Projected National Security Threats to the United States," 11 February 2003.

105. *El Vocero*, "Menor Esfuerzo en la Lucha Antidrogas," 13 January 2003.

10

The Collateral Damage of the U.S. War on Drugs: Conclusions and Recommendations

Coletta A. Youngers

The fundamental objective of U.S. international drug policy is to reduce the supply of illicit drugs. The theory is that this will drive up the price and reduce demand as fewer people are able or willing to pay the cost to get high. Available evidence clearly indicates, however, that this supply-side policy has had no significant impact on the availability and price of illicit drugs in the United States. Since the 1980s, prices of illegal drugs have steadily declined, and supply remains abundant. Fluctuations in drug use appear to be unrelated to either indicator. In short, a significant gap exists between the U.S. government's drug policy goals and objectives and what has actually been achieved since the drug war was first launched in the early 1970s.

Those advocating the supply-side approach to drug control argue that the problems related to illegal drug production and consumption would be even worse without the international counterdrug programs currently in place. If these programs were abandoned, they say, the situation would deteriorate and illicit drugs would be even more readily available. In short, even a marginal impact resulting from these efforts is better than none. What is missing from this line of reasoning, however, is a frank assessment of the collateral damage caused by supply-side efforts and whether this harm outweighs the unproven positive impact of current programs, which is likely to be marginal at best. As the studies presented in this volume collectively show, the collateral damage of U.S. policy is extensive. Its negative impact on the people and countries where the U.S. war on drugs is being waged is being felt across the hemisphere.

The harm caused by the drug trade itself, and the violence it generates, are also extensive. Drug trafficking breeds criminality, exacerbates criminal and political violence, and fuels armed groups. It greatly increases problems of citizen security, public order, and ultimately law enforcement. Across the region, drug-trafficking-related corruption has further weakened national and local governments, judiciaries, and police forces.

339

Cocaine production damages the environment, and its profits distort local economies.

Illicit drug use, once considered a problem of the global north, is now rampant across the region. A particularly perverse effect is that those who get involved in local drug-trafficking networks are often paid in drugs rather than cash. They in turn sell the drugs on local streets, stimulating new markets and illicit drug consumption. Violent crime associated with the drug trade escalates accordingly. This is particularly true in transit zones. For example, since the late 1980s, Puerto Rico has gone from exceptionally low to extremely high rates of drug abuse. The social fabric, particularly in poor urban areas where both drug use and drug-related violence tend to be highest, is torn apart.

The question remains, however, whether the drug war strategy works to counteract such disintegration or instead aggravates it by further undermining local institutions. The primary focus of our investigation was to evaluate the impact of U.S. international drug policy on democracy and human rights trends in Latin America and the Caribbean. Though that impact varies significantly by country and by region, the case studies included in this volume point to similar conclusions: U.S. drug control policies have contributed to confusing military and law enforcement functions, militarizing local police forces, and bringing the military into a domestic law enforcement role. They have thus strengthened military forces at the expense of civilian authorities. They have exacerbated ongoing human rights problems and generated significant social conflict and even political instability. And they have led to the adoption of harsh antidrug legislation that more often than not fails to comply with minimal due process standards. Moreover, U.S. counterdrug policies and programs have failed to incorporate mechanisms to ensure transparency and accountability. Even when drug policy officials have acknowledged the damage caused by current policies, they have dismissed it as an unintended consequence of a top-priority mission.

Drug control policies are carried out in coordination between the United States and Latin American and Caribbean governments, often with input from the relevant bodies of the United Nations and Organization of American States (OAS). Sometimes the programs are collaborative in nature. More often, however, the U.S. government uses its economic and diplomatic leverage to ensure cooperation, making use in particular of the annual certification process (see Appendix 1). Because of their dependence on economic aid and desire for trade agreements, many countries find themselves obliged to adopt policies and programs supported by Washington.

Not all U.S.-backed programs have negative effects. Some are bearing fruit, particularly those financed by the U.S. Agency for International

Development (USAID) to promote democratic development, institutional reform, and the rule of law. U.S. economic assistance programs are increasingly shortchanged but remain important. Law enforcement efforts aimed at capturing drug kingpins and dismantling the upper echelons of criminal networks are both more appropriate and more effective than indiscriminate measures. Likewise, efforts to control money laundering, the proliferation of small weapons, and the flow of precursor chemicals target the drug trade without generating collateral damage. Most of these programs, however, tend to receive far fewer resources than those that do have harmful consequences.

Domestic politics fuels what has become a failed and misguided policy. U.S. drug control policies are designed in Washington with an eye toward winning votes at election time and obtaining short-term results that can be used to justify budgets and personnel. Politicians continue to believe that appearing tough on drugs sits better with their constituents than acknowledging the failure of policies in which the U.S. taxpayers have invested billions of dollars. As contributor Adam Isacson notes, "Telling people what really needs to be done—alleviating poverty, treating addicts, helping neighboring states create conditions for a legal economy to flourish—takes courageous leadership." Instead, leaders have played on public fears, turning a public health issue into an all-out war on addictive substances and those who supply them. In short, U.S. counterdrug policies are more often than not designed to address domestic concerns and interests, regardless of the social, political, and economic consequences on the ground or their true effectiveness in reducing consumption.

Government officials point to the hectares of coca eradicated, the number of cocaine labs destroyed, the number of people arrested, and the amount of illicit drugs seized to show success. This ensures continued resources at a time when many agencies face budget cuts. Such body count–type statistics may indeed make for good public relations and convey a sense of action, but they shed no light on whether the tactics being used actually translate into progress toward achieving basic policy goals. The standards commonly used for measuring the effectiveness of international drug policy are, simply put, off the mark.

Serious evaluation of current policies and open-minded debate could lead to an alternative policy that is both more effective and more humane. Such a policy should begin from the premise that, while controlling illicit drug abuse is a legitimate and important goal, drugs will be produced as long as there is demand. The goal should therefore be to reduce the demand as well as the damage that illicit drugs cause to individuals and society. Policymakers should seek to minimize the negative consequences at home and abroad of illicit drug production and use and the strategies designed to curtail them.

• Principal Conclusions and Recommendations

Drug trafficking and drug abuse present clear challenges to governments and communities across the Western Hemisphere. Coordinated law enforcement that is police-led (as opposed to military-led) is needed to confront any transnational crime. Our study, however, points to serious concerns with regard to the many ways in which U.S. international drug control policy is undermining democracy and democratic development. These areas of concern include: the expansion of the role of military forces in drug control efforts; inappropriate roles assigned to police forces; human rights violations; restrictions on civil liberties; the fostering of political instability; undermining local decisionmaking; lack of transparency and accountability; and abuses resulting from forced eradication of crops used in drug production.

The following sections summarize conclusions from our study on each of these topics, as well as current recommendations for alternative policy options.

The Role of the Military

As the crack cocaine epidemic intensified in the United States and police-led law enforcement failed to make a dent in the burgeoning illicit drug trade, politicians in Washington sought a greater role for the U.S and Latin American military forces in confronting the firepower of drug traffickers. Congress gave the Pentagon the leading role in the detection and monitoring of illicit drugs coming into the United States and granted it the authority to use its budget to train and equip foreign security forces for drug control purposes. As a result, the Defense Department developed counterdrug aid and training programs for police as well as military forces across the region. These programs legally circumvent traditional congressional oversight and monitoring requirements, not to mention the State Department's roles in determining the nature and content of foreign aid and in overseeing its delivery.

The increasing reliance on military forces to play a lead role in combating the illicit drug trade set off alarms for civilian leaders across the region. The experiences of military coups, other forms of political intervention, and, perhaps most disturbing, massive human rights violations committed in the name of combating internal "subversion" have been all too recent. In providing the resources, training, and doctrinal justification for militaries to play a significant role in domestic counterdrug operations, the U.S. government was viewed as legitimating Latin American security forces in yet another internal security role, now directed at new enemies. And it did so even though sufficient mechanisms for civilian control, transparency, and accountability were—and remain—sorely lacking.

Although many in the U.S. Defense Department objected to the role being thrust upon them, in the post–Cold War environment the drug war became the vehicle for maintaining and in some cases expanding both the Pentagon's presence and its military-to-military relations with Latin American and Caribbean counterparts. Perhaps the best example of the latter is Mexico, where the U.S. military had no significant relationship with its Mexican counterpart before initiating joint counterdrug efforts. In many cases, local militaries themselves initially resisted being pulled into the drug war but were encouraged by the opportunity to obtain U.S. resources and training.

The expanding U.S. military presence is most obvious in Colombia, but it is evident in other areas studied as well. Following the U.S. withdrawal from the Panama Canal Zone in 1999, significant numbers of U.S. troops and infrastructure were relocated to Puerto Rico. In Ecuador, El Salvador, Aruba, and Curaçao the United States has established forward operating locations (now called cooperative security locations), that is, bases leased to the U.S. military for antidrug detection and monitoring missions.

Military forces do have a role to play in detecting and monitoring the flow of illicit drugs. Their involvement in border, aerial, and maritime interdiction efforts fits clearly into the military's traditional mission. Provided that these programs are carried out under the direction of civilian leaders, with appropriate oversight and transparency and human rights safeguards, they do not hinder democratic development. Military involvement in counterdrug activities also has to be coordinated with the law enforcement authorities ultimately responsible for carrying out arrests and domestic drug control efforts. However, through its drug policy, the United States has promoted the insertion of Latin American military forces into domestic law enforcement and internal security operations.

In every country studied that receives significant U.S. counterdrug assistance, U.S. support was instrumental in bringing the military into a domestic law enforcement role and has created a confusion of roles and conflicts between military and police forces. In Mexico and Ecuador, military and police personnel carry out joint operations. Often military forces are brought in to maintain public order when conflicts erupt over coca eradication policies, as often happens in the Bolivian Chapare.

A related problem is U.S. military training of countries' police forces. Such training goes directly against efforts across the region during the 1980s and 1990s to bring police forces under civilian control. Moreover, funding for this training is largely provided by the U.S. Defense Department budget and hence circumvents congressional oversight and human rights safeguards. Of particular concern, in 2002 U.S. Special

Forces provided light infantry training to police in Colombia, Ecuador, and Peru. U.S. Special Forces' training of Guatemalan forces in 2001 took place at a time when the U.S. Congress had suspended almost all other U.S. training for the Guatemalan military and when the counterdrug police was under scrutiny for corruption.

Responsibility for the design, implementation, and oversight of drug policy should lie with civilian authorities in each country. Yet off the record, officials in such countries as Peru, Bolivia, and Ecuador complain that local counterdrug forces report first to the U.S. embassy and that civilian authorities are often kept out of the loop. Moreover, military and police forces often negotiate directly with Washington on aid and training packages with little civilian government input. In some countries, military and police officials have been named to head key civilian counterdrug agencies. Mexico provides the most striking example: military personnel (whether active duty, on leave, or retired) have taken charge of key posts in the police forces and the attorney general's office. Upon assuming office, President Vicente Fox named a brigadier general, Rafael Macedo de la Concha, as his attorney general.

Even when countries take such initiatives on their own accord, as in Mexico, the U.S. government praises rather than questions the confusion of military and law enforcement roles. In discussing Latin America's crime problem, General James Hill, commander of U.S. Southern Command, further blurred the picture, claiming that efforts to address crime fall "precisely on a seam between law enforcement and military operations. Latin American leaders need to resolve this jurisdictional responsibility issue to promote cooperation among their police and military forces."[1] He failed to mention, however, that the Posse Comitatus Act in the United States has historically prohibited the U.S. military from engaging in most domestic law enforcement. Nonetheless, General Hill is essentially asking other militaries to perform functions that would be illegal in his own country.

The confidential nature of counterdrug programs can further exacerbate problems of lack of civilian oversight and impunity within military forces, thereby contributing to the proliferation of corruption when military personnel are brought into more direct contact with the drug trade. Peru provides a case in point. At the urging of U.S. officials, in the early 1990s President Alberto Fujimori brought the armed forces into a key counterdrug role. The result was rampant personal and institutionalized corruption, the magnitude of which only came to light once the Fujimori government collapsed. Dozens of generals and other high-level military and police officials are now awaiting trial on corruption, drug trafficking, and human rights charges.

Policy Recommendations

- No branch of the U.S. government, including the Defense Department, should provide assistance, training, or any other support to military forces for domestic drug enforcement efforts.
- The U.S. military should not train local police forces. Training of local police by U.S. Special Forces is particularly problematic and should be suspended immediately.
- The U.S. government, through its counterdrug policy as well as its interaction with regional militaries, should promote the principle of Posse Comitatus.
- All authority for foreign military training and assistance should be returned to the State Department, which should have sole responsibility for overseeing such programs in order to ensure that they fit within overarching U.S. foreign policy objectives and come under established oversight procedures.

The Role of the Police

Confronting criminal networks, be they drug traffickers, smugglers, or others, is primarily a law enforcement task—and that task is formidable in Latin America and the Caribbean today. The World Health Organization rates Latin America and Africa as the world's most violent regions, as determined by statistics on homicides.[2] As citizen security concerns grow, local communities and federal governments look to the police—and sometimes military forces—to impose tough law-and-order measures. In some cases citizens take the situation into their own hands, occasionally leading to horrific acts of violence, such as lynching criminals who are caught red-handed.

In this context, it is easy to understand why governments resort to harsh and repressive law enforcement measures. However, experience with such practices to date indicates that the short-term successes sometimes obtained are rarely sustainable. Ultimately, police forces—as well as judiciaries—must be fundamentally reformed for the rule of law to take root. All too often, in the face of crime and violence, long-term developmental reform issues are given a backseat to short-term, hard-line policing tactics. A better balance must be sought between the two approaches.

Simply shifting drug control resources from military to police forces does not provide an immediate answer, as police forces across the region remain abusive and corrupt and have also at times taken on disturbing paramilitary characteristics. As just noted, through the drug war, the United States has trained local police forces in counterinsurgency and other techniques not appropriate for effective and democratic civilian policing. For example, the light infantry training provided by U.S. Special Forces to local police includes "small unit tactics such as evasion, maneuver and ambushing; squad and platoon tactics ... and combat in difficult terrains like jungles."[3]

U.S. counterdrug policy, particularly military training of police forces, runs directly counter to national efforts to civilianize and professionalize these forces. Lessons learned in recent postconflict situations of developing democratic policing include the importance of effective oversight, accountability, and transparency; respect for human rights; demilitarizing police forces in terms of command structures and roles; and responsiveness to the communities they serve. Often U.S. counterdrug police assistance programs seek short-term gains to the detriment of the long-term reform efforts necessary for reducing corruption and strengthening effective policing. U.S. drug policy will be served best in the long run through the promotion of reformed, democratic, and accountable police forces.

For example, in an effort to circumvent corruption, the U.S. government often creates specialized investigative units that primarily carry out investigations of drug-trafficking networks. The strategy is to vet participating officers and focus intensive training on a specific group that can then be isolated from the rest of the force to prevent sensitive information from leaking out. In short, specialized units are designed to be protected from the broader vices of the police force as a whole. These units by their very nature are secretive and are rarely held accountable. Like other antidrug units, they often report to U.S. rather than local civilian authorities. Although specialized units have had some tactical successes, experience also shows that these units cannot be immunized against corruption and are frequently disbanded and replaced with yet other units. The problems with this approach are documented at length in the chapter on Mexico.

The focus on short-term targets also leads to a body-count mentality, as local forces strive to beef up the numbers of hectares of coca or poppy eradicated and the numbers of arrests in order to show progress to Washington. Such statistics, however, do not necessarily reflect any meaningful impact on the drug trade itself.

Some ongoing law enforcement efforts are paying off and deserve continued or increased support. The Justice Department's International Criminal Investigative Training Assistance Program, for example, promotes police reform and efforts to build sound policing skills and investigative capacity within local forces. The U.S. Bureau of Alcohol, Tobacco, and Firearms is tasked with helping to reduce the flow of small arms in the region. Given the increase in armed crime and violence throughout the region, and the close relationship between illicit drugs and weapons trafficking, greater attention and resources to stemming the flow of weapons could bring concrete benefits to local communities and law enforcement officials. The U.S. government also provides important assistance to local authorities in their efforts to stop precursor chemicals (needed to produce cocaine) from entering drug-producing countries or being diverted from licit to illicit use, as well as in developing and enforcing regulations and procedures for banks and other financial institutions in order to prevent drug trafficking–related money laundering. U.S. efforts to prevent money laundering in the United States are also effective in targeting big drug traffickers overseas and their corruption networks.

Policy Recommendations

- U.S. police assistance should be oriented toward police reform efforts, with special attention paid to issues of transparency, effective oversight and accountability, and respect for human rights.
- Local police forces should not receive U.S. military training.
- Rather than create specialized units per se, the U.S. government should continue to provide specialized training and skills to units that are accountable to local civilian authorities.
- U.S. counterdrug police assistance that is oriented toward strengthening the capacity of local forces to carry out sound criminal investigations should continue.
- More U.S. resources should be dedicated to significantly reducing the illegal arms trade in Latin America and to stemming the flow of precursor chemicals.
- The use of short-term statistical indicators, such as crops eradicated or arrest numbers, should not be used to evaluate drug policy effectiveness.

Human Rights Violations

In order to further its drug control policy, the U.S. government has forged alliances with military and police forces with questionable and even deplorable human rights records. Though sometimes the human rights problem is recognized, training and assistance are usually provided to recipient governments and security forces even before they have shown clear signs of political will to alter past patterns of abuse. Moreover, successive U.S. administrations have, at different times, downplayed or misrepresented human rights situations in order to obtain congressional support for counterdrug assistance. In some cases, the U.S. government is still supporting forces with a history of human rights violations and impunity. In others, U.S. policy directly results in human rights abuses.

The overall numbers of extrajudicial executions and forced disappearances have declined markedly across the region. Yet few countries have carried out effective prosecutions of human rights violators, and even those that pursued "truth" are now confronting renewed demands for "justice," as in Argentina and Chile. The underlying problems that fostered human rights violations to begin with—including lack of civilian control over military forces, patterns of military impunity, and weak judiciaries—remain largely in place today. U.S. drug policy is therefore being carried out in countries without adequate mechanisms either to provide human rights protections or to ensure prosecution of violators.

In this volume, human rights violations on a lesser scale are discussed with reference to counterdrug operations in Ecuador, Mexico, and Puerto Rico. More detailed presentations of the link between U.S. international drug control policy and human rights violations are provided in the chapters on Colombia and Bolivia.

Colombia is the primary recipient of U.S. counterdrug military aid and training in the hemisphere. Yet it is also the country with one of the worst human rights situations. Violations of international humanitarian law, including massacres, executions, and indiscriminate attacks that affect civilian noncombatants, are routinely committed by the illegal armed actors, guerrillas as well as right-wing paramilitary groups. Impunity for those responsible for the abuses, especially within the armed forces, is nearly absolute. Collusion between right-wing paramilitary groups—many of which are implicated in drug trafficking—and members of the security forces continues with disturbing frequency. Human rights groups have long argued that ending impunity and severing paramilitary-military ties should be necessary preconditions for the provision of U.S. military assistance and support. Nevertheless, U.S. military support to Colombia grew steadily over the second half of the 1990s, culminating in the U.S.$1.3 billion aid package known as Plan Colombia, and it continues unabated.

In Bolivia, U.S.-backed counterdrug efforts have resulted in human rights violations perpetrated by local security forces against coca farmers in the Chapare region. Although current abuses pale in comparison to the executions and disappearances carried out under some of Bolivia's military dictators, a disturbing pattern of killings, mistreatment, and abuse of the local population prevails in the Chapare. Moreover, the primary victims are not drug traffickers but poor farmers who eke out a subsistence-level living through coca production. Efforts to meet U.S. coca eradication targets have led to significant social conflict and violence. Between 1997 and 2004, thirty-three coca growers and twenty-seven police and military personnel were killed; 567 coca growers and 135 military and police were injured.[4]

Peru presents a somewhat different scenario. In that country, the U.S. government provided antidrug aid to the national intelligence service, despite growing evidence of its involvement in death squad activity and the significant setbacks to democracy that it helped orchestrate. Peru's de facto drug czar, Vladimiro Montesinos, had a working relationship with the U.S. Central Intelligence Agency and received important political backing from key U.S. officials. Montesinos, however, appears to have amassed a multi-million-dollar fortune through drug-related and other forms of corruption, including the sale of arms to Colombia's FARC. In short, he was working at cross-purposes with the stated aims of U.S. drug policy.

U.S. foreign policy—counterdrug policy included—should be guided by human rights norms and principles. In the final analysis, it is morally wrong and ultimately counterproductive to provide U.S. assistance to any military or police force that operates outside the boundaries of the rule of law.

Concern about the impact of U.S. security assistance on human rights led members of Congress to place strict human rights conditions on the provision of U.S. counterdrug and other forms of security assistance. The Leahy Amendment, named after its sponsor, Senator Patrick Leahy of Vermont, stipulates that no U.S. security assistance can be provided to foreign military or police units implicated in human rights violations unless effective measures are being taken to bring the case to justice. First passed in 1997, the Leahy Amendment has also been included in subsequent foreign aid appropriations legislation, and defense appropriations legislation now has a version of it as well. This legislation has been helpful in raising the profile of human rights issues with U.S. embassies and the U.S. military, and in some cases this has resulted in significantly closer scrutiny of the human rights record of recipient forces.

Yet the amendment itself has only been invoked in a handful of cases, and its application is uneven. In some countries, U.S. embassies have failed to put into place even minimal procedures for vetting units for individuals implicated in human rights violations. In the case of Bolivia, sufficient documentation exists in numerous cases that would justify the application of the Leahy Amendment, yet this has not happened. Nor do embassy officials object publicly when Bolivian military and police officials implicated in atrocities are promoted. In Mexico, human rights monitors claim that the embassy database that keeps track of human rights violations is seriously incomplete.

Policy Recommendations

- Counterdrug activities carried out by the U.S. government and regional governments should be guided by the human rights standards established in the jurisprudence of the inter-American system.
- The Leahy Amendment should be vigorously upheld. The U.S. government should not provide any form of assistance to security forces that violate human rights and fail to bring alleged human rights violators to justice.
- The vetting procedures that need to be put in place to effectively

implement the Leahy Amendment should be thorough and serious. In addition, after-training tracking could be incorporated to monitor whether or not those who receive training go on to commit human rights abuses or become involved in acts of corruption.

- The Leahy Amendment remains an unfunded mandate; sufficient resources should be earmarked to encourage its effective implementation.
- A thorough investigation should be initiated by the U.S. Congress into U.S. drug policy in Peru over the course of the 1990s, the alliances made and deals struck, and whether that policy served or in fact undermined U.S. counterdrug and broader foreign policy goals.

Restrictions on Civil Liberties

U.S. drug policy has also promoted the adoption of harsh antidrug laws that are at odds with basic international norms and standards of due process and undermine already tenuous civil liberties. In almost every country studied, such laws have been approved, often creating either courts or procedures that greatly limit due process guarantees, such as the presumption of innocence, the right to an adequate defense, and that the punishment be commensurate with the gravity of the crime. Such legislation is often modeled directly on U.S. laws; other times it goes even farther as local officials seek to impress Washington with their zeal.

Both Ecuador and Bolivia adopted U.S.-backed legislation in which the burden of proof for conviction of drug offenders was so low that local human rights lawyers complained that defendants were forced to prove their own innocence. As in the United States, harsh mandatory minimum sentencing laws have also spread across the region. In Ecuador, the law mandates a ten-year minimum jail sentence and a twenty-five-year maximum sentence for drug-related crimes. The law does not differentiate between mules (those who are paid to carry drugs), small-time traffickers, and drug kingpins—all are subject to the ten-year minimum.

Antidrug legislation, including these mandatory minimum sentencing laws and the use of numerical quotas for arrests, have filled the prisons of countries across the region with low-level offenders, even innocent people, who have little access to adequate legal defense. In some countries, only a small percentage of those arrested are actually convicted, whereas in others conviction rates are astoundingly high. Pervasive corruption and weak judiciaries mean that major drug traffickers are rarely sanctioned. And when they are, they often benefit from far more acceptable prison conditions, as they have the resources to purchase a range of amenities.

USAID provides economic and technical support to local judiciaries. However, U.S. justice-sector support has sometimes included different programs working at cross-purposes. For example, the U.S. government supported the Bolivian antidrug courts described above. Yet USAID also provided economic and technical assistance for a penal code reform that eliminated some of the most egregious problems with the antidrug law. Justice-sector reform efforts are essential in order to guarantee respect for civil liberties and due process and to ensure that those who are guilty of serious crimes are effectively prosecuted. USAID, the World Bank, and the Inter-American Development Bank all support rule of law programs that assist local reform efforts, seek to increase access of the poor to the justice sector, and provide training and professional development. Past experience has shown that the political will for reform on the part of recipient governments is crucial, as is the role of civil society organizations in maintaining momentum for reform and in providing valuable input into the process.

Policy Recommendations

- U.S. and Latin American drug laws should be brought into compliance with international standards of due process and respect for human rights. U.S. counterdrug assistance should respect due process standards and reinforce the rule of law in criminal cases.
- Mandatory minimum sentences should be eliminated; sentences imposed should correspond to the gravity of the crimes committed. Major drug traffickers should face extended sentences; those at the lowest end of the drug-trafficking chain should indeed be sanctioned, but on a different scale.
- More U.S. attention and assistance needs to be given to promoting justice-sector reform and institutional strengthening across the region, with particular attention to civil liberties and due process issues.

Fostering Political Instability

It is in the interest of the United States to have stable democratic governments in its hemisphere. Yet U.S. international drug control policies can have a profoundly destabilizing effect, economically as well as politically. Even when significant social conflict and political instability is generated by the implementation of drug policy, more often than not U.S. policymakers fail to adjust the policy to the realities—and consequences—on the ground. Particularly in the convulsive Andean region, U.S. drug policy may in fact be destabilizing democracies that are already quite fragile.

It has already contributed to the fall of one government in Bolivia. At key moments when former President Gonzalo Sánchez de Lozada's government attempted to negotiate with coca growers, the United States objected, ultimately forcing the suspension of negotiations and undermining possibilities for resolving the ongoing conflict. Continued U.S. pressure on Sánchez de Lozada to meet counterdrug targets, in spite of widespread social upheaval, generated further protest and unrest. Local opposition to U.S.-backed drug policies—fueled in part by the view of many Bolivians that these were contributing to the country's economic malaise—became an important factor in the downfall of the Sánchez de Lozada government in October 2003.

In Peru, U.S.-backed coca eradication policies are generating significant social unrest in coca-growing regions, contributing to widespread protests and popular opposition to Alejandro Toledo's administration. U.S. insistence that Peru meet coca eradication targets and beef up the presence of its security forces in coca-growing areas could also fuel political violence. In the mid-1980s, Shining Path grew rapidly as a result of forced eradication programs by portraying itself as the people's protector against government abuse and the destruction of livelihoods. Only a dramatic shift in Peruvian policy in the late 1980s—away from eradication and toward community development—resulted in Shining Path beginning to lose ground. Ultimately, peasant farmers drove the rebels from their rural strongholds.

Today, coca farmers continue to reject Shining Path; however, U.S. rhetoric criminalizes coca growers as "narcofarmers" and statements by U.S. officials blur the line between coca farmers, drug traffickers, and insurgents. For example, in July 2003 U.S. drug czar John Walters complained that coca cultivation had increased in Peru and that the Peruvian government needed to be more aggressive to prevent actions by those that "look for alternative means to produce drugs and carry out terrorism."[5] The elimination of the distinction between farmers, drug traffickers, and terrorists could potentially fuel a new round of political violence in Peru's coca-growing regions.

The use of "narcoterrorist" rhetoric in coca-producing countries identifies small coca farmers as military threats and suggests that they are somehow related to global terrorist networks. It also paints them as criminals, rather than valid interlocutors, so that any efforts to seek dialogue and common ground are cast as illegitimate. This in turn marginalizes significant sectors of the population and creates a situation in which conflict and violence are almost inevitable. The political consequences of ignoring significant sectors of society could be explosive.

In Bolivia, the United States appears to be creating a terrorist threat where one does not exist. U.S. officials point to a potential for terrorism and are providing equipment and training for the Bolivian army's new counterterrorism unit. To date, however, no evidence has emerged linking Bolivian social movements to either international terrorists or to Colombian or Peruvian insurgents. U.S. officials also warn of the consequences of continued political success for the Bolivian coca growers' movement. Their statements to this effect can backfire. Coca grower leader Evo Morales nearly won the 2002 presidential election after the U.S. ambassador to Bolivia publicly voiced opposition to him. In March 2004, General Hill warned that "we could find ourselves faced with a narcostate that supports the uncontrolled cultivation of coca" and called for close U.S. scrutiny of Bolivia.[6]

In the wake of September 11, both the drug war and the Latin American region have lost political ground in Washington. The attention of policymakers has shifted to the terrorism threat and to other parts of the world; Latin America and the Caribbean have moved to the bottom of the U.S. foreign policy agenda. In response, officials in charge of U.S. policy toward the region have sought attention and resources by lumping a myriad of issues in the counterterrorism—and narcoterrorist—basket. Many U.S. officials and policymakers now refer to all illicit transborder activities as terrorist threats, including drug production and trafficking, illegal migration, arms trafficking, and money laundering. It is certainly possible that illicit transborder activities could be used to support terrorism, but Latin America is not the Middle East. Defining all of these problems as terrorist threats is unhelpful and potentially destabilizing. Taking the fervor over antiterrorism a step farther is the U.S. Southern Command, which has now taken to calling drugs a "weapon of mass destruction."[7] This rhetoric encourages hysteria and the notion that the United States, through its drug policy toward Latin America, must protect itself at any cost against this evil product emanating from the region.

Policy Recommendations

- The U.S. government should show greater flexibility with regard to the counterdrug policies adopted by governments in the region, taking into account the socioeconomic and political situation on the ground. Deepening democracy and stability should be prioritized over short-term counterdrug gains.
- The current challenge for U.S. policymakers is to stop seeing the region through the counterterrorism lens, which distorts the view of real problems and threats in the region.
- The "narcoterrorist" rhetoric that has come to dominate current U.S. drug control policy should cease.
- Small farmers who produce crops for illicit drug production should not be stigmatized as "narcofarmers" but rather treated as valid interlocutors.

Undermining National Governments' Decisionmaking

U.S. drug control policy is undermining democratic developments in the region in other ways as well. Latin American countries have a long history of wide economic and social disparities. Systems of governance have been elitist and clientelistic, with a very small segment of the population holding most of the wealth and power. Legislatures are weak and often ineffective, and political power is concentrated in the executive branch. There is little capacity for citizen involvement in the policymaking process or effective accountability mechanisms for those in office. These are not problems caused by U.S. drug policy; however, that policy is often carried out in ways that reinforce these negative features of the political and socioeconomic status quo. The way in which counterdrug policies are pursued by Washington, moreover, is in itself undemocratic and often circumvents legislative oversight and public debate in the countries affected.

Through its diplomatic and economic leverage, the United States has all too often dictated the counterdrug policies adopted by countries across the hemisphere, often over the objections of important sectors of government and civil society, and at times draining scarce resources from other national priorities. In every country studied that receives significant U.S. counterdrug assistance, drug policies and programs are negotiated by U.S. officials directly with a small group of local political elites, in addition to local military and police forces. There is little role for legislative oversight, public debate, and engagement with civil society actors.

U.S. policymakers urge other countries to make changes in their law enforcement structures, antidrug laws, judicial systems, and public health and rural development policies. U.S. economic and technical assistance is provided to implement such changes and can be denied if countries fail to conform to U.S. strategy. Following his 2002 election, Ecuadorian president Lucio Gutiérrez did an about-face on his positions on national security policy. When it became clear that U.S. diplomatic and economic support was at stake, he shifted from supporting a negotiated settlement to the neighboring Colombian conflict and promising to develop an autonomous national security strategy, independent of U.S. policy, to embracing the U.S.-backed Plan Colombia.

As noted, some countries, particularly in the Andean region, choose to cooperate with U.S. counterdrug policies to avoid economic, trade, or other sanctions. Decisionmakers rarely involve the legislative branch, much less the population, in substantive debate on the issue. Sometimes, constitutionally mandated legislative approval processes are purposefully avoided. For example, the United States and Ecuador signed an agreement to establish the forward operating location in Manta without first seeking the congressional approval mandated by the country's constitution. In some countries, drug laws modeled on those in the United States are presented to legislatures for rubberstamp approval. Of all of the Latin American and Caribbean countries studied, not one had evidence of serious legislative oversight of counterdrug policy.

One of the most powerful sticks used by Washington is the certification process, which denies U.S. aid and trade benefits to countries viewed as not doing their part to combat illicit drugs. Recent legislative changes have made the process somewhat less offensive. Fundamentally, however, these changes have failed to alter the approach of having an annual scorecard, on which the largest consumer of illicit drugs in the world grades the progress of other countries in seeking to limit its supply.

U.S. trade benefits to the Andean region are also now directly linked to achieving coca eradication and other counterdrug goals, as explicitly stated in the Andean Trade Preference and Drug Eradication Act. This stands in stark contrast to the previous free trade agreement between the United States and Andean countries (more aptly named the Andean Trade Preference Act) and to the preferential trade agreement that the European Union has with Andean nations. Though the latter is also seen as a means of helping countries reduce economic dependence on the drug trade, trade benefits with the European Union are not contingent on meeting specific antidrug targets.

Concern with the animosity generated by the U.S. certification process led the OAS to develop its own Multilateral Evaluation Mechanism (MEM), which many countries see as a more palatable alternative. It is a transparent process—information provided by countries for MEM evaluation is public and easily obtained.[8] While the MEM process also has its pitfalls, it does provide a multilateral approach to a multilateral issue. The Inter-American Drug Abuse Control Commission, the OAS's drug control agency, also provides a multilateral forum for discussing and debating drug control policies. Though often dominated by Washington, it too offers a space for developing sound policies.

For a multilateral approach to succeed, Latin American and Caribbean leaders need to seek unity around common concerns and alternative approaches. In various regional forums, some Caribbean leaders have united in calling for antidrug policies that place greater emphasis on socioeconomic issues and for increased attention to the serious social and health problems caused by the drug trade in the so-called transit zone. They argue that the drug problem should not be viewed through a traditional national security lens, leading to exclusively military and law enforcement solutions. On the contrary, while law enforcement efforts are clearly needed, equal weight must be given to the economic and social underpinnings of the drug trade.

Within the United Nations, an informal coalition of like-minded countries has emerged seeking to open up debate within the UN system.[9] A

Latin American coalition of countries willing to debate alternative policies would find echo with these countries at the level of the UN and could contribute significantly to the development of a more humane and effective approach in the region.

Policy Recommendations

- The annual certification process should be eliminated; more carrot and less stick is needed in U.S. drug policy.
- U.S. trade agreements should be delinked from explicit counterdrug objectives, in particular coca and poppy eradication targets.
- U.S. drug policy should, ultimately, be a multilateral effort coordinated through the UN and the OAS and in close collaboration with other donor countries, particularly the European Union.
- The formation of an informal coalition of like-minded countries in Latin America and the Caribbean would provide an important forum for debating drug policy alternatives.

Transparency and Accountability Issues

While governments receiving U.S. aid are often characterized by a lack of transparency and effective oversight, many U.S. counterdrug assistance programs also evade scrutiny. Dozens of government agencies and programs are involved in illicit drug control efforts, which makes determining expenditures and monitoring programs difficult. Information on military and police programs is particularly hard to obtain. In 2003 the U.S. Congress dropped its requirement for the Defense Department to report on expenditures related to training and equipping foreign security forces. Since September 11, information on Special Forces training, which is significant in Latin America, has mostly been classified.

Inadequate reporting on U.S. military and police assistance and training programs undercuts both the transparency of and accountability for U.S. efforts when they fail to meet their desired objectives or generate negative consequences. Both congressional monitoring and the ability of civil society organizations to evaluate U.S.-backed programs are essential to ensuring the efficient and effective use of resources. They are also necessary to ensure that any funding furthers U.S. policy objectives and that such assistance is not used in a way that is detrimental to the promotion of human rights, the rule of law, and democratic principles.

U.S. legislative oversight of certain drug control programs is problematic and is particularly ineffective with regard to Defense Department and Drug Enforcement Administration (DEA) programs. Apart from mandating the Foreign Military Training Report, which provides annual data on U.S. military training of foreign troops, the relevant congressional committees have failed to conduct public hearings to evaluate the effectiveness of Pentagon counterdrug efforts in any serious way. Likewise, while DEA officials are often called to testify on drug-trafficking trends and the like, meaningful evaluation of the success or failure of DEA's efforts in a given country or more broadly is sorely lacking. Monitoring U.S. police assistance programs and the content of those programs is particularly difficult. No systematic reporting requirements exist, and agencies such as the DEA often refuse to provide even the most basic information.

The first official public criticism of the DEA occurred in 2003, when the federal Office of Management and Budget (OMB) published a scathing critique as part of its Performance Assessment Rating Tool review process. OMB gave the DEA a "results not demonstrated" rating, finding that "DEA is unable to demonstrate its progress in reducing the availability of illegal drugs" in the United States. OMB also gave the Coast Guard a "results not demonstrated" rating for its drug interdiction efforts, pointing out that there is "no clear link between the annual goal of total amount of drugs seized and the long-term goal of reduction in use."[10] OMB's concerns, however, have yet to be taken up seriously in Congress.

If the ability of civil society groups to monitor U.S. drug policy is difficult in the United States, it is next to impossible in Latin America and the Caribbean. Very little information is made available to local civil society actors by either regional governments or U.S. embassies on the nuts and bolts of U.S. assistance and local operations. And as noted, public debate on drug policies is not only discouraged but at times actively thwarted.

These problems are compounded by pervasive corruption, which leads local actors to avoid implementing or supporting more effective mechanisms of control or oversight. Corruption is a common theme in all of the countries and regions studied, running to different degrees through civilian and military governmental institutions. The presence of corruption within a government means that neither elected nor appointed officials can be counted on to perform their duties as disinterested public servants—judges may be bought off, the police may allow criminals to operate in return for bribes, political parties may buy votes, and decisionmakers may promote policies and laws in return for financial reward. Rarely do corruption cases result in prosecution, and journalists who investigate cases of official corruption are routinely harassed and even killed.

Transparency International and other nongovernmental organizations are contributing significantly to generating public debate and awareness of the corruption issue. The United States has supported anticorruption and transparency promotion programs through USAID. Though it remains extremely difficult to make headway against the vast amounts of money generated by drug trafficking, anticorruption programs are an important step in the right direction.

Policy Recommendations

- The U.S. Congress should ensure that the administration provides comprehensive and detailed reporting on U.S. military and police assistance and training programs. The Foreign Military Training Report requirement should be maintained in the law. In addition, Congress should require a single, comprehensive annual report on all police assistance, including information on courses, units trained, and trainees, compiling information from all U.S. agencies involved in police training.
- Regular public congressional hearings should be held to evaluate Pentagon and DEA antidrug efforts, with testimony by independent experts.
- The U.S. Congress could also undertake a serious study of the stated objectives of U.S. drug control agencies, listed each year in the White House's National Drug Control Strategy Report, and examine what has actually been achieved.
- Greater efforts should be undertaken in the region by U.S. embassies to reach out to local nongovernmental and other civil society organizations in order to provide more information and seek more input into the process of making drug policy.
- The administration should continue to use its diplomatic leverage to discourage official corruption and support USAID's programs to combat corruption and to promote transparency on the ground.

Crop Eradication and Alternative Development Programs

This volume presents powerful evidence that forced coca eradication efforts are futile in the long run. In every case studied, short-term gains have been quickly reversed. Crop eradication efforts have stimulated production in new areas (the so-called balloon effect). Production has also shifted due to changes in the drug-trafficking industry. In the cases of Bolivia, Peru, and Colombia, forced eradication efforts have outpaced the development of economic alternatives for families dependent on coca production for their livelihood. As a result, farmers seek out new areas for planting or replant where their coca was eradicated; a short-term victory creates even greater challenges for the long term as coca production spreads. Moreover, the costs are high: forced eradication efforts, and in particular aerial fumigation, often have dire consequences, generating social unrest, instability, and violence.

The only country in the region that currently allows aerial fumigation is Colombia. In 2002 and 2003, there were numerous official and unofficial reports indicating that fumigation has caused significant damage to legal crops (including subsistence food crops), pasture, fish, livestock, and agricultural development projects. Residents in areas that are sprayed report being frequently exposed to the spray mixture and suffering a variety of ailments as a result. (Similar complaints have been lodged from border areas of Ecuador also affected by the spraying in Colombia.) Concerns have also been raised about the impact that widespread spraying may have on Colombia's fragile tropical ecosystems. Yet to date, no serious, independent scientific study of the impact of aerial fumigation has been carried out. Finally, aerial eradication contributes significantly to displacement of populations from the regions affected. One human rights group estimates that in 2001 and 2002 alone fumigation in Colombia led to the displacement of more than 75,000 people nationwide.[11] Some flee to Ecuador; most join the ranks of Colombia's internally displaced.

Poverty, poor conditions for sustainable agricultural production, and the growing of crops for illicit drugs go hand-in-glove. Coca and poppy cultivation regions are characterized by a lack of infrastructure and poor accessibility, and this remoteness makes access to markets for alternative agricultural products extremely difficult. Farmers generally lack access to credit and technical support; the presence of state agencies is often quite limited. Most small producers grow food crops for subsistence and coca or poppy as their only source of cash income. Nonagricultural income opportunities, if they exist at all, are very limited.

Promoting integrated economic development in these areas is not impossible; however, the term "crop substitution" is used less and less frequently. As donors come to recognize that simply replacing coca with another crop or product is usually not economically viable, they increasingly talk of sustainable, and equitable, development that will slowly reduce farmers' dependence on coca cultivation by creating the conditions for improved agriculture, employment, and income generation more broadly. The most effective strategies combine agricultural development with off-farm employment opportunities. Many donors also recognize the importance of the participatory approach to development, which builds on farmers' existing knowledge and leads to projects that are more appropriate for local conditions, making local buy-in much more likely. This is necessary for effective project implementation as well as for ensuring continuity after the donors have left.

Increasingly, international donors are explicitly recognizing that simultaneous forced eradication and alternative development efforts are incompatible. The repressive nature of the former greatly limits, or hinders altogether, the cooperation needed for the latter. Although no United Nations agency is involved in forced eradication efforts, significant discussion has taken place within the UN on the relationship between alternative development and forced eradication. One UN document notes: "In areas where alternative development programs have not created viable alternative income opportunities, the application of forced eradication might endanger the success of alternative development programs." It also affirms that in low-income rural areas "alternative development is more sustainable and socially and economically more appropriate than forced eradication."[12]

The German government's foreign aid agency, GTZ, which has played a leading role in the UN debate, points out that when poverty is the root cause of production, then repressive eradication measures are inappropriate and counterproductive:

> Alternative development initiatives should be free of deadlines and the precondition of total eradication of drug crops prior to the availability of viable alternatives. A more flexible and gradual reduction of drug crop production must be allowed to avoid problems related to economic and social suffering. Today many communities are forced to hasten the eradication process without viable alternatives, which has resulted in aggravated poverty and migration. Accordingly, drug crop reduction must be voluntary and development assistance offered without preconditions on area reductions.[13]

Based on its extensive experience working in coca-growing regions of the Andes, GTZ concludes that even though substituting the safety net that coca production provides may take time, that approach—without the threat of eradication—"is the only manner to achieve a sustainable reduction in drug crop cultivation."[14] When dealing with small-scale coca production, eradication targets (defined within a participatory process) can be set and met only when other sources of income are put in place. Development experts also point out that repressive measures against coca producers raise the price of coca leaf on the market, which in turn stimulates new cultivation.[15]

Incorporating sound development practice and this new thinking implies a fundamental shift in U.S. policy. It implies developing a new and more equitable relationship with families involved in coca and poppy production, accepting them as legitimate partners in development efforts, and removing the threat of forced eradication. It also implies investing more resources in economic development, particularly in rural sectors, and recognizing the need for local governments to have greater economic decisionmaking ability. Finally, strengthening democratic institutions at the local level is essential to ensuring the sustainability of development efforts in poor rural areas.

Two significant steps should be taken to reduce the harm caused by current drug control policies. First, cultivation of coca for traditional uses should not result in criminal sanctions, as is currently the case in Bolivia and Peru, where coca cultivation for traditional use is legal. Second, coca and poppy production by small producers should be decriminalized; rather than viewed as criminals, small growers should be defined as "economic victims that have become 'addicted' to illicit crops for survival."[16] In other words, international drug control policies must take into account the right of all people to dignity and an adequate livelihood, as established in article 11 of the International Covenant on Economic, Social, and Cultural Rights. Such thinking is echoed by the UN Development Programme (UNDP): its 2003 Human Development Report points to the need in Colombia to "avoid treating peasants as criminals."[17]

Innovative discussion is beginning among some European government officials and drug policy analysts as to how this approach—what some call a "pro-poor drug control policy"[18]—could be implemented in practice. It takes as its starting point the principle that all individuals have a right to a life with dignity and hence should not be deprived of their only income source. Determining the income level below which families' livelihoods must be sustained must be decided at the local level. While more study is needed on how this approach could be implemented in practice, it is a step in the direction of creating a more humane, and ultimately effective, drug policy.

Policy Recommendations

- The U.S. government should adopt a "pro-poor" drug control policy, integrating the lessons learned by GTZ, UNDP, and other international donors in its approach to development assistance.
- Aerial and other forms of forced eradication should be eliminated, as should coca and poppy eradication targets.
- Coca and poppy production by small, subsistence-level producers should be decriminalized.
- Forced eradication more broadly should be replaced with voluntary crop reduction efforts carried out in accordance with the local population and only when viable alternatives for income generation exist.
- U.S. economic support and technical assistance for economic development, particularly in rural areas, should be increased significantly across Latin America and the Caribbean.

• Toward an Alternative Policy

Putting into place a pro-poor drug control policy requires giving greater flexibility and decisionmaking power to local actors. Specifically, Latin America and the Caribbean countries need the flexibility to develop their own policy approach—without the threat of certification or other sanctions hanging over their heads. While far from perfect, international monitoring should take place through the UN and OAS systems. Likewise, in the United States, local and state governments need the flexibility to experiment with alternatives in order to deal with skyrocketing prison costs, unmet demand for treatment, and related problems. Across the Western Hemisphere, civil society groups, local politicians, the media, and the public at large should be encouraged to participate in a meaningful debate on how to best approach the very real problems of illicit drug production, trafficking, and consumption and the violence that they generate.

Opening up the debate and taking up a broader range of issues for discussion at home as well as abroad are fundamental first steps forward. Successive U.S. administrations, as well as some other governments, have tended to dismiss discussion of alternatives. Those voicing alternative viewpoints are often portrayed as morally wrong or stigmatized as promoting the legalization of drugs. Such claims mask both the failure of current policies and the harm that they are causing. They also fail to take into account accumulated evidence-based research that does not back current policy. As one former British government official commented, "There is now a large body of evidence that shows you aren't going to bring rates of use down through harsh penalties ... the evidence is overwhelming."[19]

New Standards of Measure

An open-minded debate would likely lead to a shift in thinking at numerous levels. Ultimately a new mentality is required, one that recognizes that the problem of drug abuse and its related violence in the United States is homegrown and hence must be primarily addressed domestically. Once that is accepted, it leads to questions about the ways in which international drug control policies are evaluated at present. Success should not be determined by how many hectares of coca or poppy are eliminated, how many drug labs are destroyed, or how many individuals involved in the drug production train are put behind bars. Yet these numbers are put forward every year to justify the continued or increased use of U.S. taxpayer dollars for ongoing programs. These statistics may help explain how policy is being implemented; they do not provide evidence of the impact that the policy is having on the availability and dangerous use of illicit drugs per se.

Other standards of measurement should be prioritized in determining policy success or failure. At a minimum, they should focus on the price, availability, and purity of illicit drugs on U.S. city streets—where, as noted in the introduction, several decades of the U.S. war on drugs have failed to have a significant or sustainable impact. Better yet, the primary standards of measure should relate to reducing consumption levels, including among hard-core users; the incidence of HIV/AIDS and other health-related diseases among the user population; rates of drug-related crime; and levels of violence in communities where drug abuse is prevalent.

Following the same reasoning, drug policy goals should be recast in public health terms and seek to reduce the harm caused by illicit drugs. This approach implies reorienting strategies to focus on developing effective treatment and education programs, including treatment upon demand, HIV/AIDS programs, realistic prevention strategies, and community development. These strategies should be guided by evidence-based research and practical, community-based experience.

Focusing on the demand side of the drug policy equation is also more cost effective and a better use of taxpayer dollars. A 1994 study by the RAND Corporation found that money spent on treatment has a far better payoff than that spent on interdiction, as recently noted in the *Miami Herald*: "Investing $34 million in treatment reduces cocaine use as much as spending $783 million for foreign source country programs ... or $366 million for interdiction."[20]

Mitigating the Harm Caused by Drug Abuse

A realistic assessment of current policies would recognize that completely eliminating illicit drug demand or production is simply not achievable. Illicit drug use is not going to disappear. As the U.S. and other governments battle cocaine, heroin, and marijuana production, synthetic drugs are posing an increasing danger to today's youth. These tend to be relatively easy to produce and have no geographical constraints for their production—a good basement will often do. Similarly, economic incentives ensure that production of cocaine, heroin, and marijuana will continue to meet demand, even if the costs are high for those caught in the law enforcement web. The challenge, therefore, is to mitigate the harm caused by drugs to individuals and society.

A similar harm-reduction approach can be applied to international policies. This means seeking to reduce the harm or negative consequences caused by illicit drug production and the policies intended to eradicate it, including efforts to decrease the crime and violence associated with both the drug trade and some counterdrug efforts.

A constructive middle ground lies between the drug hawks—those advocating no-tolerance, supply-side strategies—and the drug legalizers. Such an approach recognizes that illicit drug control is a legitimate goal; the question is what path to take to achieve it. It also recognizes that despite the limitations of the supply-side approach, borders cannot simply be opened up and left uncontrolled. Detection, monitoring, and interdiction efforts are necessary. Likewise, drug trafficking, growing crime rates, and increasing citizen insecurity are felt by people and communities across the hemisphere. Sound law enforcement efforts and effective prosecutions of those engaged in illicit activities are needed to maintain order and to provide a sense of security, particularly in the poor communities that tend to be the most affected by crime and violence. The issues, rather, are the framework within which interdiction and law enforcement efforts are carried out and, of particular importance, how resources are allocated.

Illicit drug use is largely a demand-driven phenomenon. U.S. policymakers must recognize that they cannot solve the problems of drug abuse and drug-related violence in the United States by sending soldiers and guns to Bolivia, Colombia, or any other producer country. Nor will meeting short-term drug policy objectives—such as coca eradication, arrest, and drug confiscation targets—lead to long-term progress in stemming the flow of illicit drugs over U.S. borders, as is evident from decades of investment into supply-side efforts.

Supporting Latin American Governments and Communities
This is not to say, however, that the United States should not help its Latin American neighbors. On the contrary, it is in the broader U.S. interest to aid other countries in the Western Hemisphere as they address the deep-rooted problems that allow drug trafficking to flourish, along with the violence and other problems caused by drug production and trafficking.

However, a fundamental shift is needed in U.S. resource allocation overseas, from military- and police-oriented programs to equitable economic and democratic development. In short, the U.S. government needs to substantially increase the assistance it provides for economic development and income generation programs. The U.S. government should work with multilateral development banks, national governments, and local communities to develop comprehensive poverty reduction strategies and to ensure debt relief for the poorest nations to free up scarce government resources.

Particular attention needs to be paid to rural communities, which often get short shrift in today's development models. While the right approach must be determined at the local level, rural poverty alleviation strategies can include land reform, access to credit and other forms of technical assistance, and infrastructure development. In addition, subsidies for rural producers in order to protect food security are often essential, along with import tariffs to provide incentives for local agricultural production.

Similarly, institution-building and reform efforts merit far more resources and attention from the U.S. government. Respect for human rights, the rule of law, and good governance are all essential ingredients for an effective counterdrug policy. Promoting justice-sector reform—grounded in respect for and protection of human rights and civil liberties—is fundamental to both establishing the rule of law and carrying out transnational law enforcement efforts. In addition to rule of law programs, USAID is engaged in a range of democracy promotion activities that could provide the framework for more ambitious efforts.

USAID's justice-sector programs are not without their critics. In some cases, technically oriented programs overlook the need to change people's attitudes and practices. Improved efficiency is not necessarily accompanied by greater justice. Likewise, a 2003 study of USAID democracy promotion efforts in six countries by the U.S. General Accounting Office details the difficulties of implementing and sustaining institutional reforms and points to the need for more effective evaluation and learning processes on the part of USAID.[21]

Nonetheless, these programs are a step in the right direction. USAID's democracy promotion efforts include promoting justice-sector reform, enhancing legislative effectiveness, building local governance at the municipal level, increasing citizen participation in political processes, combating corruption, promoting human rights, and ensuring free and fair elections. Similar programs are supported by the World Bank, the Inter-American Development Bank, and a range of nongovernmental organizations. These efforts speak directly to the deficiencies in current U.S. international drug control policy.

It is in the U.S. interest to build a more equitable partnership with its Latin American neighbors, allowing local views to inform the U.S. policy-making process. If that were to happen, it would become evident that promoting poverty elimination and democratic development should be the centerpiece of U.S. foreign policy toward Latin America and the Caribbean. Striving to achieve those goals would, in the long run, be more effective than current policy in curbing illicit drug production and trafficking and their devastating impacts throughout the Western Hemisphere.

Building such partnerships, along with fundamental policy reform and rethinking, is needed to develop a more humane and effective drug control policy to the benefit of people, communities, and governments across the hemisphere.

• Notes

Co-editor Eileen Rosin contributed significantly to this chapter. While it is based on the research carried out by chapter contributors, the views expressed are those of the editors and the Washington Office on Latin America. Other WOLA staff also provided assistance, including Laurie Freeman, Joy Olson, Kimberly Stanton, and John Walsh.

1. U.S. House of Representatives, House Armed Services Committee, testimony of General James T. Hill, United States Army Commander, Southcom, before the House Armed Services Committee, United States House of Representatives, 24 March 2004, p. 3.

2. World Health Organization, *World Report on Violence and Health* (Geneva: WHO, 2002), p. 7.

3. Description of training from WOLA/CIP interview with U.S. Southern Command, June 2002.

4. Chapare Human Rights Ombudsman's Office, January 2004.

5. *La República*, "Mas Severidad en la Lucha Antidrogas Piden a Peru, Bolivia, y Venezuela," 30 July 2003.

6. Hill testimony, 24 March 2004, p. 5.

7. *United Press International*, "DOD Wants More Forces for Colombia," 21 March 2004.

8. See the OAS website, www.oas.org/main/main.asp?sLang=E&sLink= www.cicad.oas.org.

9. For additional information on the UN drug control system see Martin Jelsma and Pien Metaal, *Drug War Monitor*, "Cracks in the Vienna Consensus: The UN Drug Control Debate," WOLA, January 2004.

10. U.S. Office of Management and Budget, *Performance and Management Assessments FY2004*, Programs: "Drug Enforcement Administration" and "Drug Interdiction."

11. Cited in Latin American Working Group, "Going to Extremes: The U.S.-Funded Aerial Eradication Program in Colombia," March 2004, endnote no. 182.

12. United Nations, "Action Plan on International Cooperation on the Eradication of Illicit Drug Crops and on Alternative Development," General Assembly Special Session (UNGASS) on Drugs, A/RES/S-20/4 (New York: 10 June 1998).

13. GTZ, "Drugs and Conflict," discussion paper by the GTZ Drugs and Development Programme, September 2003, p. 23, www.gtz.de/drogen/download/ english/publications/drugs_conflict.pdf.

14. GTZ, *Drugs and Poverty: The Contribution of Development-Oriented Drug Control to Poverty Reduction*, a cooperative study of the Drugs and Development Programme (ADE) and the Poverty Reduction Project of GTZ, June 2003, p. 19.

15. GTZ, *Drugs and Poverty*, p. 27.

16. Martin Jelsma, "Revising and Integrating Drug Policies at the National and International Level: How Can Drug Reform Be Achieved?" paper presented at the Wilton Park Conference on Drug Policies and Their Impact, 27 March 2002, www.tni.org/archives/jelsma/wilton.htm.

17. Quoted in *Reuters MSNBC*, "Colombia Needs 'New Deal' from U.S. on Drugs," 10 September 2003.

18. GTZ, *Drugs and Poverty*, p. 26.

19. Quoted in *The Independent*, "How I Lost My Drugs War," 30 March 2004. Mike Trace was deputy drug czar in Great Britain (1997–2000).

20. Dan Christman and John Heimann, "Andean Policy Falls Short of Region's Needs," *Miami Herald*, 31 March 2004.

21. U.S. General Accounting Office, *U.S. Democracy Programs in Six Latin American Countries Have Yielded Modest Results*, GAO-03-358, 18 March 2003.

Appendix I

An Overview of U.S. Laws and Agencies
Related to International Drug Control Efforts

T racing the flow of U.S. funds used to pay for the drug war in Latin America is a complicated task. These funds come from a wide variety of budgetary sources, and a bewildering array of federal departments and agencies is involved in overseeing and spending these funds. The names of many of these entities have changed over time, as have their mandates, responsibilities, and relationships to each other. Adding to the confusion, the State Department is the principal agency responsible for disbursing military aid—although the Pentagon's role in that process has been growing— and conversely, the Pentagon conducts counterdrug police training.

• U.S. Laws

Foreign Assistance Act (FAA)
Counterdrug aid is part of the overall U.S. foreign assistance process. In 1961, in an effort to rationalize, provide legislative oversight, and exert civilian control over proliferating aid efforts in the post–Cold War environment, the U.S. Congress passed the Foreign Assistance Act (FAA). FAA made foreign aid part of the annual budget process, as one of thirteen appropriations bills that Congress must debate and approve each year to pay for all federal government operations.

FAA *authorizes* the U.S. government to provide certain types of foreign assistance; the annual foreign operations appropriations bill actually *allocates* resources to specific countries and programs.

The main drug-related items of the FAA are: (1) security assistance and (2) International Narcotics Control (INC) assistance.

The information contained in this appendix was drawn primarily from research conducted by Laurie Freeman, Adam Isacson, Lora Lumpe, and Rachel Neild.

- *Security Assistance*: The FAA authorizes the State Department to set policy, control budgeting, and prioritize recipient countries for the Defense Department's military assistance activities. Types of security assistance include the International Military Education and Training (IMET), Anti-Terrorism Assistance (ATA), and Foreign Military Financing (FMF) programs, which fund transfers of equipment, services, and some training to foreign governments.
- *International Narcotics Control*: Section 481 authorizes the State Department to disburse INC assistance. These monies fund military and police assistance for interdiction and eradication, as well as economic and social aid, including alternative development programs in drug-producing areas and judicial reform programs (see the section below on the State Department's Bureau for International Narcotics and Law Enforcement Affairs).

Other kinds of aid authorized include Economic Support Funds (ESF), which are cash transfers to foreign treasuries; Development Assistance (DA), development projects managed by the U.S. Agency for International Development; Food for Peace, distribution of food in coordination with the Department of Agriculture; and the Peace Corps. In FY2004, Latin American and Caribbean countries received an estimated U.S.$938 million in economic and social aid from these four programs combined. Most countries receive at least as much economic as military aid, if not more—except for Colombia, where nearly five out of every six dollars goes to the military and police.

For drug source and transit countries, a large share of the economic and social aid they receive comes from INC funds, usually in the form of alternative development programs (encouraging farmers to grow legal crops) or democracy/rule of law programs (to strengthen civilian institutions such as judiciaries, prosecutors, investigators, legislatures, and local governments). The overwhelming majority of these programs are carried out by third parties, usually private companies or nonprofit organizations that bid for contracts to deliver assistance.

Aid authorized pursuant to the FAA is subject to several human rights and democracy conditions. Two of the best known are Section 502B, which sought to ban aid to abusive militaries, and Section 660, which banned assistance to foreign police forces. However, vague definitions and the approval of numerous exceptions (such as allowing police training for drug control) have rendered these restrictions virtually toothless.

The FAA is also subject to extensive reporting requirements on how aid is spent. First and foremost is the annual budget justification document, submitted by the president to Congress, which details the dollar value of all foreign assistance, by category and by country, provided by the United States to foreign countries and international organizations. There are also congressionally mandated reports on arms sales and transfers, the use of private contractors in Colombia, and foreign military training, among many others.

Since 1997, military aid and training have been subject to an additional human rights condition known as the Leahy Amendment (see below).

Section 660 of the FAA (ban on police training and assistance). Section 660 of the FAA prohibits the use of security assistance funds to train foreign police forces. While often perceived as an overarching ban on U.S. police training and assistance, Section 660, in reality, applies only to activities funded through the FAA. It has never affected the use of the separately authorized and appropriated budgets of the Justice, Defense, Treasury, or Transportation Departments for training or otherwise assisting foreign law enforcement officials.

An early exemption to Section 660 allowed the use of foreign aid monies for counterdrug activities.

In addition, a further series of amendments beginning in 1981 created a long list of exemptions, including permission for U.S. police training in Haiti during the regime of Jean-Claude Duvalier and antiterror police training. The president was given the authority to provide assistance when necessary to ensure U.S. national security, as well as in cases when it is "inadvisable to specify the nature of the use of such funds." Even before the most recent amendments to Section 660, in 1992, the U.S. General Accounting Office was able to identify 125 countries that received police training financed by U.S. taxpayers despite the legislative ban.

National Defense Authorization Act

Traditionally, the Defense Department has not been permitted to use its own budget to provide foreign military assistance without State Department supervision, except for joint exercises, seminars and conferences, and other training deployments whose ostensible primary purpose is to train U.S. personnel or maintain channels of military-to-military contact.

However, in 1988 Congress included a provision in the National Defense Authorization Act (NDAA), making the Pentagon the *single lead agency* for detecting and monitoring illegal drugs transiting to the United States by air or sea (Title 10, section 124, U.S. Code). Three years later, in Section 1004 of the 1991 NDAA, Congress gave the Pentagon the authority to use its budget to carry out these new responsibilities.

The NDAA *authorizes* the U.S. military to carry out certain responsibilities; the annual defense appropriations bill actually *allocates* resources to specific programs.

Section 1004. Section 1004 of the 1991 NDAA and its subsequent renewals (1995, 1999, and 2002, the latest two as Section 1021; all are referred to as "Section 1004") allow the Defense Department to use its own budget to provide counterdrug assistance to foreign security forces without State Department involvement. It does not allow the Pentagon to give away weapons or most types of equipment—this still must occur within the authority of the FAA.

Under this authority, the Defense Department may use its enormous budget to pay for such drug interdiction operations as radar sites, surveillance flights, naval and Coast Guard maritime patrols, and intelligence gathering throughout Latin America and the Caribbean. It authorizes the presence of U.S. military personnel on counterdrug missions in the region.

This authority allowed the Pentagon to establish a parallel foreign aid program outside the constraints of the Foreign Assistance Act. Section 1004 is now one of the largest sources of military and police assistance to Latin America and the Caribbean, totaling more than U.S.$270 million in aid in 2001. Two-thirds of all U.S. military training for Latin America is now paid for through the defense budget, representing a significant shift in how military training programs are funded.

Section 1004 funding is administered by the deputy assistant secretary of defense for counternarcotics and is managed on the ground by U.S. Southern Command.

Section 1004 is not subject to the human rights and democracy conditions of the FAA or similar provisions in the annual foreign aid appropriations bills. The only legal condition prohibiting the provision of Section 1004 assistance is a weaker version of the Leahy Amendment (which appears in the annual defense appropriations bill) restricting training for units of foreign security forces that have abused human rights unless "all necessary corrective steps" are taken.

Until 2001, there were no significant reporting requirements with respect to how the Pentagon spent its budget under Section 1004–authorized programs. The 2001 and 2002 NDAAs required the secretary of defense to submit a report to the congressional armed services committees detailing the Defense Department's counterdrug assistance to foreign governments. The report included the amount and types of country assistance provided and a description of the types of counterdrug activities carried out. However, the report was eliminated from the 2003 and 2004 NDAAs. The Defense Department considers much congressionally mandated reporting to be burdensome.

Section 1033. In 1998 Congress approved a second, smaller antidrug military assistance program in the NDAA. Section 1033 (also renewed, currently through 2006) established a five-year program to help the navies and police of Colombia and Peru to interdict drugs on rivers. The program was renewed and modified in the 2004 NDAA. In its new form, the law removed the word "riverine"—thus making it a catch-all counterdrug assistance program—and expands it to eight countries worldwide, among them Bolivia, Colombia, and Ecuador.

Like Section 1004, Section 1033 is not subject to congressionally mandated human rights safeguards or reporting requirements, but it is subject to the Leahy Amendment.

Leahy Amendment

The Leahy Amendment is a provision within foreign operations and defense appropriations legislation that prohibits U.S. assistance to individuals and units of foreign security forces that violate human rights with impunity. Its name comes from its principal sponsor, U.S. Senator Patrick Leahy (D-Vermont). Under this law, no unit of a foreign security force that is credibly alleged to have committed a human rights violation may receive U.S. training or aid.

The Leahy Amendment has appeared in appropriations legislation since 1997, when it was part of the Foreign Operations Appropriations Act (Public Law 104-208). Initially, the law applied only to the State Department's INC program, but its jurisdiction has now expanded to include all security assistance programs funded by the foreign operations appropriations bill, as well as to all training programs funded by the Defense Department appropriations bill. The Leahy Amendment must be renewed in both bills every year (appropriations bills are passed annually).

The Leahy Amendment, as it appears in the 2004 Foreign Operations Appropriations bill (Section 553 of Public Law 108-199), states that funds may not be provided to units that have committed "gross violations" of human rights unless:

> the Secretary [of State] determines and reports to the Committees on Appropriations that the government of such country is taking effective measures to bring the responsible members of the security forces unit to justice: ...
>
> In the event that funds are withheld from any unit pursuant to this section, the Secretary of State shall promptly inform the foreign government of the basis for such action and shall, to the maximum extent practicable, assist the foreign government in taking effective measures to bring the responsible members of the security forces to justice.

In other words, this version of the Leahy Amendment applies to training and assistance (such as weapons grants). In addition, it not only bars abusive units from receiving assistance but also is meant to confront the phenomenon of impunity by encouraging foreign governments to prosecute abusive members of the police or military as an incentive to get aid flowing again. It also instructs the secretary of state to work with the foreign governments to see that effective measures are taken to bring those responsible for human rights abuses to justice.

The version of the Leahy Amendment in the 2004 Defense Appropriations Act (Section 8077, Public Law 108-87) is much more limited. It covers training only (not weapons or other assistance) and has no strong or precise language encouraging foreign governments to bring human rights violators to justice; instead it simply asks that "corrective steps" be taken.

Drug Certification

Enacted by Congress in 1986, certification (the restriction on aid to countries failing to meet antidrug goals) required the president to certify by March 1 of every year that major drug-producing and transit nations (the "majors") were cooperating fully with U.S. counterdrug measures; Congress had thirty days to overturn any decision with which it did not agree.

Decertified countries faced a range of punishments: a cutoff of all economic assistance (with the exception of counterdrug and humanitarian aid); automatic denial of loans from multilateral banks; and discretionary trade sanctions such as the removal of trade preferences and the suspension of import quotas. These punishments could be waived in the interests of U.S. national security, but that did not remove the sting of humiliation for having received a failing grade by Washington.

In 2002 Congress modified the certification process. Under the original law, the president had to certify that each of the majors was fully cooperating with U.S. antidrug efforts in order for them to earn a positive rating. The Foreign Relations Authorization Act 2002–2003 reversed that burden of proof, requiring the president to decertify only those countries that "failed demonstrably, during the previous 12 months, to make substantial efforts" to adhere to its international counterdrug obligations. In other words, countries would be automatically certified, unless their antidrug efforts were resoundingly poor. In addition, the process was changed so that an international (and not U.S.) standard was used to evaluate the efforts of drug-producing and transit nations.

Posse Comitatus Act

The Posse Comitatus Act (Title 18, Section 1385, U.S. Code) forbids U.S. troops from carrying out crime-fighting and most other internal police roles such as making arrests or conducting searches or seizures. Passed in 1878 in the aftermath of the U.S. Civil War, the law states: "Whoever, except in cases under circumstances expressly authorized by the Constitution or Act of Congress, willfully uses any part of the Army or the Air Force as a posse comitatus or otherwise to execute the laws shall be fined under this title or imprisoned not more than two years, or both."

The rationale is that the purpose of a military should be limited to defending violent threats to the state through the use of overwhelming force. Unless organized as an opposition army, a nation's own citizens never meet this definition and thus should not be subject to arrest or interrogation by soldiers.

According to U.S. Northern Command's website, the Posse Comitatus Act

> has come to symbolize the separation of civilian affairs from military influence. [The law] generally prohibits U.S. military personnel from interdicting vehicles, vessels and aircraft; conducting surveillance, searches, pursuit and seizures; or making arrests on behalf of civilian law enforcement authorities. Prohibiting direct military involvement in law enforcement is in keeping with long-standing U.S. law and policy limiting the military's role in domestic affairs.

The U.S. military does play an episodic internal security role in emergencies, such as natural disasters, riots, and the September 11 terrorist attacks. Another exception is Joint Task Force 6, a U.S. military unit based at Fort Bliss in El Paso, Texas, that was formed to back up antidrug efforts inside the United States.

U.S. Agencies

Bureau for International Narcotics and Law Enforcement Affairs, U.S. State Department

The State Department's Bureau of International Narcotics and Law Enforcement Affairs (INL) is the key hub of U.S. drug control efforts abroad. It is responsible for formulating and implementing international drug control policy at the State Department and for coordinating the drug control activities of all U.S. agencies overseas. The INL also manages foreign assistance provided by the International Narcotics Control (INC) program.

INC is one of the most versatile programs in the entire FAA. It funds military and police assistance for interdiction and eradication—including high-priced helicopters and other lethal equipment and training—as well as economic and social aid, including alternative development programs in drug-producing areas, judicial reform programs, human rights support, and even emergency humanitarian assistance for victims of Colombia's conflict.

Despite the Pentagon's growing role in providing counterdrug security assistance, INC remains the principal source of military and police assistance to Latin America, contributing about 60 percent of all such aid between 1997 and 2002. INC also made up most of the large 2000 outlay known as Plan Colombia and all of its successor efforts, known since 2002 as the Andean Regional Initiative or Andean Counterdrug Initiative. The INL even maintains its own air wing—a fleet of small planes and helicopters used mainly for drug eradication missions, especially fumigation in Colombia.

By the late 1990s, INC had become a main channel for economic and social aid to the region as well. Between 1997 and 2002, INC assistance accounted for more than one-fifth of dollars spent in development and humanitarian aid to the hemisphere. Most INC economic assistance goes to alternative development, institution building, administration of justice, human rights, and emergency relief programs. Funds for these programs are normally passed to the U.S. Agency for International Development (USAID), which administers them just like other official development assistance. Occasionally funding is passed to another agency, as in the case of judicial reform efforts managed by the U.S. Department of Justice.

The INL publishes the annual *International Narcotics Control Strategy Report,* in which it reviews the status and advances made by countries during the year and U.S. funding, support, and coordination.

White House Office of National Drug Control Policy

Since 1989 the White House Office of National Drug Control Policy (ONDCP), known colloquially as the office of the drug czar, has stood atop the aid decisionmaking process, at least on paper. The office is responsible for setting overall drug control policy, both foreign and domestic. However, the drug czar has little authority over actual drug control spending by federal departments and agencies. Nor does the drug czar appoint or remove officials with counterdrug responsibilities in other agencies; he or she can only make recommendations to the president.

ONDCP's overarching goal is to reduce illicit drug consumption in the United States as well as the drug-related violence that often accompanies it. Its annual National Drug Control Strategy divides the overall strategy among five general goals, of which two are relevant to foreign assistance. Goal 4 is to "Shield America's air, land, and sea frontiers from the drug threat"; and Goal 5 is to "Break foreign and domestic drug sources of supply."

The ONDCP prepares an annual budget on federal drug control spending but does not exert control over it—the budget document merely describes what is being spent by various agencies. Traditionally, about two-thirds of the federal antidrug budget has been spent on *supply reduction*— domestic and international law enforcement (antidrug spending by the military, police, prosecutors, judiciaries, and prisons). The remaining one-third goes to *demand reduction* efforts such as education, prevention, and treatment. Domestic law enforcement has always been the largest single component of the budget, usually hovering around 25 percent of the total drug control budget.[1]

The FY2004 budget moved some spending categories out of the national drug control budget, notably funds for the prosecution and incarceration of drug offenders. The new system gave the impression that the percentage of drug control money going to law enforcement was reduced in comparison to that for treatment and prevention.[2] However, the numbers may be misleading—the money for these law enforcement activities is still budgeted and spent but is no longer reflected in the National Drug Control Budget. The FY2005 budget is similarly structured.

U.S. Agency for International Development

USAID is the main U.S. agency responsible for offering development assistance in countries around the world. Created by executive order in 1961, USAID is an independent federal government agency that receives overall foreign policy guidance from the secretary of state. It funds projects that fall under several broad categories: economic growth, agriculture, trade promotion, global health, democracy, conflict prevention, and humanitarian assistance.

In Latin America and the Caribbean, USAID supports a number of initiatives that have counterdrug objectives, mainly alternative development projects designed to help farmers switch to legal crops. In addition, USAID carries out democracy promotion activities that, for example, provide support to legislatures and local governments and promote improved administration of justice. Some funding for these counterdrug-related programs comes directly from INC.

Department of Defense

The U.S Department of Defense (DOD) is the single lead federal agency for the detection and monitoring of aerial and maritime movement of illegal drugs toward the United States. There are several offices within DOD that have a role in formulating DOD policy with regard to drug control.

- *The undersecretary of defense for policy* develops, coordinates, and oversees national security and defense policy, including the implementation of drug control policy for DOD's counterdrug mission; defense security assistance; and special operations and low-intensity conflict activities (including counterdrug operations).
- *The office of the deputy assistant secretary of defense for counternarcotics,* part of the assistant secretary of defense for special

operations and low-intensity conflict, is the focal point for DOD's counterdrug efforts, which include intelligence; interdiction; investigations (to support domestic and foreign law enforcement activities engaged in arrests, prosecutions, and seizures); research and development; and assistance to state and local law enforcement entities with counterdrug activities. These programs are carried out by the Combatant Commands (such as Southcom, Northcom, and the Special Operations Command) and the Defense Intelligence Agency.

- *The assistant secretary of defense for international security affairs* manages regional and bilateral defense relations with foreign governments, coordinates policy matters for foreign military sales, international military education and training, and other security assistance programs; and develops, negotiates, implements, and monitors defense cooperation agreements with foreign countries on military facilities, basing rights, access and propositioning, operating rights, personnel exchange programs, and arrangements with foreign governments governing the status of U.S. forces in their territory and of their defense personnel in the United States.

U.S. Southern Command

Southcom is one of five regional commands coordinating U.S. military activities throughout the world. It is responsible for U.S. security and military operations in all of Latin America and the Caribbean except Mexico. Southcom incorporates units from all branches of the armed services (Army, Navy, Air Force, Marines), with a separate subcommand for special operations forces.

Southcom manages military advisory and assistance groups (Milgroups) in U.S. embassies throughout the region, some of which maintain offices within host-country defense ministries. Milgroups carry out aid programs and arms sales, choose students for U.S. military training, encourage their counterparts to buy U.S. weapons, and organize military exercises. Many of the Defense Department's requests for specific military aid initiatives originate with Southcom, which usually develops them after close consultation with recipient-country defense and military leaders.

Southcom seeks to stop the flow of drugs using radar and overflights, as well as naval and Coast Guard patrols. In the territorial waters of countries that have signed bilateral agreements, Southcom assets have a limited ability to pursue, board, and search suspected smuggling craft.

U.S. Northern Command

Northcom, established in 2002 and headquartered at Peterson Air Force Base in Colorado Springs, Colorado, is responsible for military activities relating to the continental United States, Alaska, Canada, Mexico, and the surrounding water out to approximately 500 nautical miles. It also includes the Gulf of Mexico, Puerto Rico, and the U.S. Virgin Islands.

Northcom has two overall missions: (1) to defend against threats to the nation and its interests within Northcom's area of responsibility; and (2) to provide military assistance to civil authorities for disaster relief, counter-drug, and "consequence management" (i.e., after the use of a weapon of mass destruction), if such emergencies exceed the capabilities of civil authorities.

U.S. Coast Guard

The U.S. Coast Guard (USCG) is the lead federal agency for maritime drug interdiction and shares lead responsibility for air interdiction on maritime routes with the U.S. Customs Service. It has the unique distinction of being both the fifth U.S. military service and a law enforcement agency. Part of the Transportation Department for thirty-five years, it was merged into the new Department for Homeland Security in 2003.

The Coast Guard's counterdrug mission is to reduce the supply of drugs from the source by denying smugglers the use of air and maritime routes in the *transit zone*, a six-million-square-mile area that includes the Caribbean, Gulf of Mexico, and Eastern Pacific. The Coast Guard tracks, interdicts, and apprehends vessels and aircraft smuggling cocaine and mari-juana into the United States via maritime routes.

The Coast Guard deploys cutters and aircraft off South America and in the Caribbean and Pacific transit zones in support of its counterdrug role. It conducts frequent combined operations with military and law enforcement organizations from many of the countries in the Caribbean.

To facilitate the Coast Guard's counterdrug enforcement authority throughout the region, the U.S. government seeks bilateral maritime coun-terdrug agreements. The model agreement proposes giving the Coast Guard the authority to: board and search vessels claiming the flag of a signatory nation; pursue suspect vessels into sovereign coastal waters with permis-sion to stop, board, and search; and conduct overflights of sovereign air-space in support of counterdrug operations. Not all states are willing to relinquish their sovereignty in all of these areas, and in such cases more limited bilateral agreements are achieved. By April 2004, the U.S. govern-ment had signed and implemented bilateral maritime counterdrug agree-ments with twenty-one drug transit zone governments.

In addition, the Coast Guard assists in the development and strengthen-ing of foreign maritime law enforcement, such as the Haitian Coast Guard and the Panamanian National Maritime Service. With funding from the INL, the U.S. Coast Guard trained more than 300 foreign law enforcement agents in maritime law enforcement in 2001.

Intelligence Agencies

U.S. military and intelligence agency personnel offer another type of assistance that is powerful yet difficult to quantify: sensitive intelligence about suspected drug-trafficking activity. Agents of the Central Intelligence Agency (CIA), Defense Intelligence Agency (DIA), and Drug Enforcement Administration share satellite and reconnaissance imagery, signals intercepts, and human intelligence related to drug trafficking with their counterparts throughout the region. (Section 1004 authorizes the U.S. military to do the same.)

In 1989, the CIA established its Counter-Narcotics Center and announced that it would commit one-fourth of its efforts in Latin America to drug control. These efforts have included paying for some training of foreign security forces and the gathering of intelligence about drug-trafficking targets. While very little unclassified information is available, the intelligence community, particularly the CIA's Directorate of Operations, is a likely source of significant amounts of antidrug aid to foreign military and police forces. CIA imaging and reconnaissance data have proven essential for estimating levels of illicit crop cultivation and drug production, as well as locating suspected drug-trafficking flights.

Drug Enforcement Administration

The DEA, part of the Justice Department, is the only U.S. government agency that concentrates solely on counterdrug operations, though only 10 percent of the DEA operations are international.

It is the principal federal agency responsible for coordinating drug enforcement intelligence overseas and conducting drug law enforcement operations, but in some cases it shares jurisdiction with the FBI and/or CIA. The DEA receives significant portions of its funding for international operations from the State Department's INC budget.

In 1976, the DEA had a budget of just under U.S.$200 million, and of its 2,117 agents, 228 were stationed overseas in thirty-three countries. Including supplementary funding from other agencies (principally INC), the overall DEA budget request for FY2005 totaled nearly U.S.$1.8 billion. During the 1990s, the DEA expanded its overseas presence; as of 2002, the DEA had 38 offices located in twenty-four countries in Latin America and the Caribbean.[3] In 1996, Congress appropriated nearly U.S.$60 million dollars to expand DEA investigations primarily in Latin America; this supplementary budget has increased to about U.S.$104 million for FY2004.

As of 2003, the DEA had 680 intelligence analysts worldwide gathering drug-related intelligence, and it runs the Joint Information Coordination Centers program, which provides equipment and training to more than twenty countries, primarily in Central and South America and the

Caribbean. These are modeled after and linked to the DEA's El Paso Intelligence Center.

The DEA cannot legally conduct investigations or make arrests abroad and must work with local partners that have the legal standing to do so. During bilateral investigations, DEA agents work closely with local counterparts—developing sources of information, interviewing witnesses, working undercover, assisting in surveillance efforts, photographic reconnaissance, and overflights, and providing forensic analysis—with the aim of producing indictments and prosecutions in either the host country, the United States, or a third nation.

Police training is considered by the DEA to be a key tool for improving the capabilities of the DEA's local partners. The DEA provides extensive training to foreign police through its International Training Section in Quantico, Virginia, and through teams of instructors who provide training on site in foreign countries. In several countries the DEA has set up special vetted units within foreign police forces as a way of enhancing their trustworthiness. The DEA also coordinates and cooperates with foreign governments in other programs designed to reduce the availability of illicit drugs, such as crop eradication and substitution.

Following the attacks of September 11, 2001, the DEA shifted some of its emphasis toward "narcoterrorism," defined by the DEA as a "subset of terrorism," or

> terrorist groups, or associated individuals, participat[ing] directly or indirectly in the cultivation, manufacture, transportation or distribution of controlled substances and the monies derived from these activities. Further, narcoterrorism may be characterized by the participation of groups or associated individuals in taxing, providing security for, or otherwise aiding or abetting drug trafficking endeavors in an effort to further, or fund, terrorist activities.[4]

The DEA has no regularly scheduled evaluations of program performance. Its Office of Inspections does conduct reviews of each field office to ensure compliance with DEA procedures and policies (evidence handling, time and attendance, security procedures, etc.), but it is not an evaluation of program performance. The judiciary committees in the House and Senate bear primary responsibility for oversight of DEA programs (both domestic and international).

Federal Bureau of Investigation

The FBI's mandate authorizes it to investigate all federal criminal violations that have not been specifically assigned by Congress to another federal agency. The FBI's investigative functions fall into the categories of civil rights, counterterrorism, foreign counterintelligence, organized crime/ drugs, violent crimes and major offenders, and financial crime.

The FBI has had an overseas presence for more than sixty years. Historically, this foreign presence has been restricted to a few countries in which agents attached to the embassies (legal attachés, or LEGATs) functioned largely as facilitators of investigative inquiries between the United States and the host country. The FBI tends to focus on activities that have some link to domestic cases.

Because of its responsibility for fighting organized crime, the FBI staked out a role in drug-trafficking investigations and has concurrent status with the DEA. FBI involvement in antidrug cases mushroomed in the 1980s and 1990s. In January 1981, no FBI agents were assigned to drug control investigations; by August 1993, 1,700 agents and 1,900 support personnel were conducting antidrug work domestically and internationally.

In 1994 the FBI was authorized to work on international drug investigations, known as Resolution Six investigations. The FBI has three Resolution Six programs—Mexico, Colombia, and Thailand. In 1996, the Congress approved an FBI plan for doubling the number of FBI LEGAT offices from twenty-three to forty-six over four years. Currently there are forty-five LEGAT offices and four suboffices, and the FBI is working in fifty-two countries. In Latin America, LEGATs are based in Argentina, Barbados, Brazil, Chile, Colombia, the Dominican Republic, Mexico, Panama, and Venezuela. The expansion was motivated by the need to provide support for American law enforcement, but in Latin America it increasingly focused on drug control missions.

In some countries, the FBI trains local law enforcement in interrogation techniques, crime scene investigations and evidence recovery, crisis management, ethics and anticorruption, tactical operations, and other skills. There is no comprehensive annual report on FBI training.

After September 11, the FBI announced that it was reorganizing the bureau to more effectively deal with the threat of terrorism. Part of this plan included transferring about 500 agents from criminal investigations to terrorism prevention; 400 of those agents came from the narcotics division. Prior to the 2001 attacks, more than twice as many FBI agents were assigned to fighting drugs (2,500) than fighting terrorism (1,151). However, investigating and prosecuting drug traffickers continues to be an FBI priority. According to the ONDCP, the FBI remained committed to targeting major drug-trafficking organizations and their financial infrastructure despite its post–September 11 reorganization. On its website, the FBI asserts that its participation in counterdrug efforts is important and does not duplicate the efforts of other agencies because "while other law enforcement organizations seek to disrupt drug-trafficking organizations, the dismantlement of major international and national drug-trafficking organizations is an area of FBI expertise and core competency. Dismantlement means the targeted organization is permanently rendered incapable of being involved in the distribution of drugs" because the organization's leaders have been completely incapacitated, its financial base thoroughly destroyed, and its drug supply connection and networks irreparably disrupted.

U.S. Customs Service

Part of the Treasury Department, Customs is the primary agency responsible for preventing the import and export of contraband to the United States, including interdicting illegal drugs, and has attachés in embassies and consulates in five countries in Latin America.[5] The Customs Service investigates drug-smuggling organizations overseas and assists foreign border agencies in interdiction efforts through training, intelligence cooperation, and the provision of equipment.

Bureau of Alcohol, Tobacco, and Firearms

The Bureau of Alcohol, Tobacco, and Firearms (ATF), also part of the Treasury Department, began to have a role in counterdrug programs when it became apparent that firearms originating in the United States were frequently used by international drug traffickers. In 1974 it implemented the International Traffic in Arms Initiative, designed to foster close cooperation with foreign governments in order to enforce U.S. federal firearms laws, to gather intelligence regarding the dynamics of international firearm trafficking, and to offer assistance to foreign law enforcement regarding U.S. illegal trafficking of U.S.-origin weapons. The ATF has country offices in Mexico and Colombia to assist in identifying the sources of illegally trafficked firearms and provide training to increase local law enforcement capacity to trace illicit firearms. The ATF has also conducted regional workshops on investigating firearms trafficking.

Private Contractors

Private companies (or contractors) carry out routine—and sometimes risky—military missions. Though not government employees, private companies doing government contract work have played a rapidly growing and controversial role in the drug war. The State and Defense Departments argue that hiring private companies is more cost-effective than using active-duty military personnel whom they claim are already thinly stretched on other missions worldwide. They also cite a lack of trained pilots, mechanics, and other skilled personnel among the region's security forces.

According to the State Department's April 2003 *Report on Certain Counternarcotics Activities* in Colombia, sixteen different companies were working under contract to the State and Defense Departments in Colombia in 2002, as shown in Table A1.1.

Table A1.1   Contractors Operating in Colombia, 2002

Company	Functions	Cost of Contract
DynCorp	Pilots, maintenance technicians, and logistic support to Army Counterdrug Brigades and Police aerial eradication program	$79,200,000
	A wide variety of personal services	$4,875,017
	UH-60 Blackhawk Night Vision Goggle (NVG) instructor pilot support	$1,292,000
Lockheed-Martin	Maintenance and support of Black Hawk helicopters	$2,128,663
	Installation of force protection systems	$3,525,077
	Maintenance, logistic, and other technical personnel, spare and repair parts for Police Air Service aircraft	$3,133,431
	Logistics support for four C-130B and two C-130H heavy transport planes	$4,216,748
	UH-60 Blackhawk instructor pilot support	$813,000
	Huey II instructor pilot support	$3,600,000
	UH-1H and Huey II instructor pilot support	$1,700,000
	UH-1H and Huey II Flight Simulators	$7,500,000
ARINC	Maintenance and logistics support for Police C-26 aircraft	$1,146,826
	Training and logistic support for aircraft for the Air Bridge Denial Program	$3,557,929
	Fuel systems upgrades at six Police Airfields	$1,549,309
	Improve the counterdrug operational capabilities of the Air Force	$11,000,000
TRW	Radar data processing and display system and voice communications system	$4,300,000
Matcom	Coordinate activities between the U.S. and Colombia Air Force	$120,000
Cambridge Communications	Move radar equipment from Leticia to Tres Esquinas	$450,000
Virginia Electronic Systems	Install value added equipment in boats purchased for Colombia	$150,000
Air Park Sales and Service	Aircraft radio and equipment upgrades (Navy); program and aircraft technical support (Air Force)	$1,100,000
Integrated AeroSystems	Inspection, acceptance, and ferry flights of Schweizer SA 2-37B aircraft	$560,000
	Overhaul of LANAS aircraft	$50,000
	Tail wheel transition training for pilots and copilots of FAC AC-47 aircraft	$35,000
Northrop Grumman California Microwave Systems	Operate an airborne system to counter illicit drug trafficking	$8,600,000
Alion	Improve the Colombian government's capability to collect and process intelligence	$20,000
The Rendon Group	Multiple echelon counterdrug public communications capability	$2,400,000
ACS Defense	Logistic support to USG personnel and operational assets	$517,035
	Senior counterdrug logistician	$237,811
INS	Logistic support to USG personnel and operational assets	$196,000
Science Applications International Corp.	Imagery Analysis	$255,335
ManTech	Database connectivity	$2,146,692
Total		$150,380,000

Source: Report to Congress, "Certain Counternarcotics Activities in Colombia," submitted to the Congress by the Secretary of State, 14 April 2003. Available on CIP website www.ciponline.org/colombia/03041401.htm.

• **Notes**

1. U.S. White House, Office of National Drug Control Policy, *National Drug Control Strategy FY2005*, "FY2005 Budget Summary," March 2004.

2. Drug Policy Alliance, "'Fuzzy Math' in New ONDCP Report," 12 February 2003, www.lindesmith.org/news/pressroom/pressrelease/pr021203.cfm.

3. U.S. Justice Department, Drug Enforcement Administration, "Domestic and Foreign Offices," www.dea.gov/agency/domestic.htm#foreign.

4. U.S. House of Representatives, Committee on International Relations, statement of DEA administrator Asa Hutchinson at the hearing, "International Global Terrorism: Its Links with Illicit Drugs as Illustrated by the IRA and Other Groups in Colombia" (Washington, D.C.: U.S. Government Printing Office, 24 April 2002), Serial No. 107–87, available on www.c.house.gov/international_relations/107/78947.pdf.

5. Caracas, Venezuela; Bogotá, Colombia; Hermosilla, Mexico City, Monterrey, and Tijuana, Mexico; Montevideo, Uruguay; and Panama City, Panama, U.S. Customs Service, "Attachés—Our Representatives Abroad," *U.S. Customs Today*, August 2001, www.cbp.gov/xp/CustomsToday/2001/August/custoday_attache.xml.

Appendix 2

Funding and Staffing for DEA Programs in Latin America, 1998–2004

Table A2.1   Funding (in thousands of U.S. dollars)

Country	1998	1999	2000	2001	2002	2003 est	2004 est
Belize	590	906	824	1,014	1,286	1,339	1,367
Costa Rica	1,637	1,816	1,665	1,733	1,828	1,903	1,941
El Salvador	634	778	983	1,136	1,075	1,119	1,141
Guatemala	1,559	1,745	1,493	1,661	1,661	1,729	1,763
Honduras	752	754	647	806	788	820	836
Mexico	13,658	15,986	17,520	16,713	18,203	18,949	19,316
Nicaragua	400	1,704	883	1,116	971	1,011	1,031
Panama	1,416	1,595	1,473	1,544	1,770	1,843	1,879
Subtotal Central America & Mexico	20,646	25,284	25,488	25,723	27,582	28,713	29,274
Argentina	2,311	2,200	1,928	2,483	2,605	2,712	2,766
Bolivia	20,226	19,821	19,095	17,724	17,425	18,139	18,502
Brazil	4,377	4,256	3,654	5,412	5,235	5,450	5,559
Chile	1,260	922	979	1,171	1,321	1,375	1,403
Colombia	14,065	17,661	15,667	22,128	21,457	22,337	22,784
Ecuador	2,234	3,146	3,500	4,006	3,831	3,988	4,068
Paraguay	595	726	1,016	1,110	1,280	1,332	1,359
Peru	15,009	13,571	10,346	12,522	13,921	14,492	14,782
Venezuela	2,121	2,425	2,467	3,501	3,721	3,874	3,951
Subtotal South America	62,198	64,728	58,652	70,057	70,796	73,699	75,174
Total Budget Latin America	82,844	90,012	84,140	95,780	98,378	102,412	104,448

Source: DEA response to questions from Ranking Member José Serrano (D-New York), July 2003. On file at the Washington Office on Latin America (WOLA).

Table A2.2   DEA Staffing (Agents and Other Personnel)

Country	1998	1999	2000	2001	2002	2003 est	2004 est
Belize	2	4	6	6	6	4	4
Costa Rica	6	8	8	8	8	8	8
El Salvador	3	4	4	4	4	4	4
Guatemala	10	10	10	10	10	10	10
Honduras	5	5	5	5	5	5	5
Mexico	69	74	74	74	74	77	77
Nicaragua	2	5	6	6	6	5	5
Panama	7	8	11	11	11	11	11
Subtotal Central America & Mexico	104	118	124	124	124	124	124
Argentina	7	7	9	9	9	9	9
Bolivia	65	67	67	67	67	61	61
Brazil	13	17	20	20	20	19	19
Chile	3	4	6	6	6	6	4
Colombia	64	66	66	66	66	79	79
Ecuador	10	13	13	13	13	13	13
Paraguay	3	5	5	5	5	5	5
Peru	41	43	45	45	45	38	38
Venezuela	10	10	14	14	14	12	10
Subtotal South America	216	232	245	245	245	242	238
Puerto Rico						142	142
Other						61	61
Subtotal Caribbean						203	203
Total Staffing Latin America and Caribbean (2003 and 2004 only)						569	565

Source: Data in this appendix are based on DEA responses to questions from Ranking Member José Serrano (D-New York), July 2003. On file at WOLA.

Abbreviations and Acronyms

ACI	Andean Counternarcotics Initiative
ACS	Association of Caribbean States
AFTA	Andean Free Trade Agreement
AI	Amnesty International
AOJ	administration of justice
AOR	area of responsibility
ARI	Andean Regional Initiative
ATF	Bureau of Alcohol, Tobacco, and Firearms
ATPA	Andean Trade Preference Act
ATPDEA	Andean Trade Promotion and Drug Eradication Act
AUC	United Self-Defense Forces of Colombia
CAFTA	Central American Free Trade Agreement
Caricom	Caribbean Community
CBRN	Caribbean Basin Radar Network
CIA	Central Intelligence Agency
CICAD	Inter-American Drug Abuse Control Commission
CSL	cooperative security location (formerly FOL)
DEA	Drug Enforcement Administration
DIA	Defense Intelligence Agency
DOD	Department of Defense
ELN	National Liberation Army (Colombia)
ESF	Economic Support Funds
EU	European Union
FAA	Foreign Assistance Act
FARC	Revolutionary Armed Forces of Colombia
FATF	Financial Action Task Force
FBI	Federal Bureau of Investigation
FMF	Foreign Military Financing
FOL	forward operating location
FTAA	Free Trade Area of the Americas

GAO	General Accounting Office (now Government Accountability Office)
GTZ	German government's development agency
HIDTA	High Intensity Drug-Trafficking Area
IACHR	Inter-American Commission on Human Rights
ICC	International Criminal Court
ICITAP	International Criminal Investigative Assistance Training Program
ILEA	International Law Enforcement Academy
IMET	International Military Education and Training
INC	International Narcotics Control
INCSR	International Narcotics Control Strategy Report
INL	Bureau for International Narcotics and Law Enforcement Affairs
JCET	Joint Combined Exchange Training
JIATF	Joint Interagency Task Force
JTF	Joint Task Force
LEDET	Law Enforcement Detachment
LEGAT	legal attaché
MEM	Multilateral Evaluation Mechanism
Milgroup	U.S. Military Group
NAFTA	North American Free Trade Agreement
NAS	Narcotics Affairs Section
NGO	nongovernmental organization
NSA	National Security Agency
OAS	Organization of American States
ONDCP	Office of National Drug Control Policy
ROL	rule of law
ROTHR	Relocatable Over-the-Horizon Radar
SIU	Sensitive Investigative Unit
Southcom	U.S. Southern Command
UN	United Nations
UNDCP	United Nations International Drug Control Program
UNDP	United Nations Development Programme
UNHCHR	UN High Commissioner for Human Rights
UNHCR	UN High Commissioner for Refugees
UNODC	UN Office on Drugs and Crime
USAID	U.S. Agency for International Development
WOLA	Washington Office on Latin America

Selected Bibliography

Abya-Yala. *Fuerzas Armadas: Desarrollo y Democracia*. CELA, Academia de Guerra de la Fuerza Terrestre. Quito: ILDIS, 1995.

Acción Ecológica et al. Misión de Verificación, *Impactos en Ecuador de las Fumigaciones Realizadas en el Putumayo dentro del Plan Colombia*. Report. October 2002.

Aguayo Quezada, Sergio. "Los Usos, Abusos, y Retos de la Seguridad Nacional Mexicana, 1946–1990." In *En Busca de la Seguridad Perdida: Aproximaciones a la Seguridad Nacional Mexicana*. Mexico City: Siglo XXI Editores, 1990.

Albro, Robert. "A New Evo-lution? Prospects for Bolivia's Popular Movement." Draft submitted to *Hemisphere: A Magazine of the Americas*. July 2003.

Amnesty International, *Amnesty International Report 2002*.

Andean Information Network, "Análisis Jurídico: Alberto Coca, Agustín Gutiérrez, y el Tribunal Militar." 3 December 2001.

Anderson, Martin Edwin. "Civil-Military Relations and Internal Security in Mexico: The Undone Reform." In *The Challenge of Institutional Reform in Mexico*. Ed. Riordan Roett. Boulder: Lynne Rienner Publishers, 1995.

Andreas, Peter. "U.S.-Mexico Drug Control in the Age of Free Trade." *Borderlines* 8, no. 4 (April 2000).

Arzt, Sigrid. "La Militarización de la Procuraduría General de la República: Riesgos para la Democracia Mexicana." Paper commissioned by the Center for U.S.-Mexican Studies Project on Reforming the Administration of Justice in Mexico, Berkeley, Calif., 15 May 2003.

Astorga, Luis. "Drug Trafficking in Mexico: A First General Assessment." Management of Social Transformations (MOST) Discussion Paper no. 36. Paris: UNESCO, 1999.

Bagley, Bruce, and Adrian Bonilla, eds. *La Economía Política del Narcotráfico: El Caso Ecuatoriano*. Quito: North-South Center, University of Miami and Flacso/Ecuador, 1991.

Bagley, Bruce M., and William O. Walker III, eds. *Drug Trafficking in the Americas*. Coral Gables, Fla.: University of Miami, North–South Center; New Brunswick, N.J., 1994.

Bayley, David H. "What's in a Uniform? A Comparative View of Police-Military Relations in Latin America." Paper prepared for the Conference on Police and Civil-Military Relations in Latin America, Washington, D.C., October 1993.

Benítez Manaut, Raúl. "México: Doctrina, Historia, y Relaciones Cívico-Militares a

Inicios del Siglo XXI." In *Democracias Frágiles: Las Relaciones Civiles-Militares en el Mundo Iberoamericano*. Madrid: Instituto Universitario General Gutiérrez Mellado, 2004.

Bertram, Eva, et al. *Drug War Politics: The Price of Denial*. Berkeley: University of California Press, 1996.

Bonilla, Adrián. "Política Internacional y Narcotráfico: Acercamiento al Caso Ecuatoriano." In *Narcotráfico y Deuda Externa: Las Plagas de América*. Quito: CAAP, CECCA, CERG, Ciudad, 1990.

Bowden, Mark. *Killing Pablo*. London: Atlantic Books, 2001.

Buvinic, Mayra, and Andrew Morrison. "Living in a More Violent World." *Foreign Policy* (Spring 2000).

Call, Charles T. "Institutional Learning Within ICITAP." In *Policing the New World Disorder: Peace Operations and Public Security*. Ed. Robert B. Oakley et al. Washington, D.C.: National Defense University, 1999.

———. "War Transitions and the New Civilian Security in Latin America." *Comparative Politics* 35, no. 1 (October 2002).

Camp, Roderic Ai. *Generals in the Palacio: The Military in Modern Mexico*. New York: Oxford University Press, 1992.

———. "Mexico's Armed Forces, Marching to a Democratic Tune?" In *Dilemmas of Political Change in Mexico*. Ed. Kevin Middlebrook. London: Institute of Latin American Studies, University of London, forthcoming, 2004.

Carothers, Thomas. *Aiding Democracy Abroad: The Learning Curve*. Washington, D.C.: Carnegie Endowment for International Peace, 1999.

Chevigny, Paul. *Edge of the Knife: Police Violence in the Americas*. New York: The New Press, 1995.

Coca, Oscar, et al. *Cifras y Datos del Desarrollo Alternativo en Bolivia*. Cochabamba: CEDIB, 1999.

Comisión Andina de Juristas. *Coca, Cocaína, y Narcotráfico: Laberinto en los Andes*. Lima: CAJ, 1989.

Cuesta, Salomón. *Putumayo, la Frontera de las Fronteras*. Quito: Fundación de Investigaciones Andino Amazónicas [FIAAM], Abya Yala, 1998.

Davis, Diane E. "Law Enforcement in Mexico City: Not Yet Under Control." *NACLA Report on the Americas* 37, no. 2 (September/October 2003).

Degregori, Carlos I., et al., eds. *Las Rondas Campesinas y la Derrota de Sendero Luminoso*. Lima: Instituto de Estudios Peruanos, 1996.

den Boer, M. G. W. "Internationalization: A Challenge to Police Organization in Europe." In *Policing Across the World*. Ed. R. I. Mawby. London: UCL Press, 1999.

Farthing, Linda. "Social Impacts Associated with Antidrug Law 1008." In *Coca, Cocaine, and the Bolivian Reality*. Ed. Madeline Barbara Léons and Harry Sanabria. New York: SUNY Press, 1997.

Farthing, Linda, and Ben Kohl. "The Price of Success: Bolivia's War Against Drugs and the Poor." *NACLA Report on the Americas* (July–August 2001).

Freeman, Laurie. *Troubling Patterns: The Mexican Military and the War on Drugs*. Washington, D.C.: Latin America Working Group, September 2002.

Gamarra, Eduardo. *Entre la Droga y la Democracia*. La Paz: Ildis, 1994.

Government of Mexico. *Drug Control in Mexico, National Program 1989–1994: Progress and Results*. Mexico City: Procuraduría General de la República, 1992.

———. Chapter 1 in *IV Informe de Gobierno del presidente Ernesto Zedillo Ponce de León*. Mexico City: Presidencia de la República, December 1998.

————. *Orden General de Operaciones FTA 2000 del 33 Batallón de Infantería del Ejército.* Mexico City: Secretaría de la Defensa Nacional, 21 February 2000.

————. *Cuatro años en la Procuraduría General de la República.* Mexico City: Procuraduría General de la República, November 2000.

————. *Primer Informe de Labores.* Mexico City: Procuraduría General de la República, 1 September 2001.

————. *Recomendación 12/2002 a la Procuraduría General de la República Sobre el Caso del Homicidio del señor Guillermo Vélez Mendoza.* Mexico City: National Human Rights Commission, 14 May 2002.

————. *Estadísticas Judiciales en Materia Penal.* Cuaderno no. 10. Mexico City: Instituto Nacional de Estadística, Geografía, e Informática, 2003.

————. *Recomendación 15/2003 a la Procuraduría General de Justicia Militar Sobre el Caso del señor Juan Jesús Guerrero Chapa.* Mexico City: National Human Rights Commission, 8 April 2003.

————. *Recomendación 16/2003 a la Procuraduría General de Justicia Militar Sobre el Caso de los Integrantes del 65o. Batallón de Infantería en Guamuchil, Sinaloa.* Mexico City: National Human Rights Commission, 22 April 2003.

————. *Tercer Informe de Gobierno del C. Presidente Vicente Fox Quesada.* Mexico City: Office of the President of Mexico, 1 September 2003.

Hargreaves, Clare. *Snowfields: The War on Cocaine in the Andes.* New York: Holmes and Meier, 1992.

Healy, Kevin. "Coca, the State, and the Peasantry in Bolivia, 1982–1988." *Journal of Interamerican Studies and World Affairs* 30 (Summer–Fall 1988).

————. "The Coca-Cocaine Issue in Bolivia: A Political Resource for All Seasons." In *Coca, Cocaine, and the Bolivian Reality.* Ed. Madeline Barbara Léons and Harry Sanabria. New York: SUNY, 1997.

————. "Ascent of Bolivia's Peasant Coca Leaf Producers." *Journal of Interamerican Studies and World Affairs* (Spring 2001).

Huggins, Martha K. *Political Policing: The United States and Latin America.* Durham, N.C., and London: Duke University Press, 1998.

Human Rights Watch. *Human Rights Watch World Report 1989.*

————. *Human Rights in Mexico: A Policy of Impunity.* Report. New York: Human Rights Watch, 1 June 1990.

————. *State of War: Political Violence and Counterinsurgency in Colombia.* New York: Human Rights Watch, December 1993.

————. *Human Rights Violations and the War on Drugs—Bolivia.* New York: July 1995.

————. *Systemic Injustice: Torture, "Disappearance," and Extrajudicial Execution in Mexico.* Report. New York: Human Rights Watch, 1999.

————. *Military Injustice: Mexico's Failure to Punish Army Abuses.* Report. New York: Human Rights Watch, December 2001.

Instituto Nacional de Estadísticas y Censos (INEC). *VI Censo de Población y Vivienda.* Quito, November 2001.

Interagency Working Group (IAWG) on U.S. Government-Sponsored International Exchanges and Training. *FY1999 Annual Report, Inventory of Department of Justice Programs.* See IAWG website, IAWG Reports, Inventory of Programs, Department of Justice, 1999.

Inter-American Commission on Human Rights. *Report on the Situation of Human Rights in Mexico.* Washington, D.C.: Organization of American States, 1998.

International Consortium of Investigative Journalists. "U.S.-Trained Forces Linked to Human Rights Abuses." Special Report. Washington, D.C.: Center for Public Integrity, 12 July 2001.

Isacson, Adam, and Joy Olson. *Just the Facts: A Civilian's Guide to U.S. Defense and Security Assistance to Latin America and the Caribbean.* Washington, D.C.: Latin America Working Group and the Center for International Policy, 1999.

Jannol, Rebecca, Deborah Meyers, and Maia Jachimowicz. "U.S.-Canada-Mexico Fact Sheet on Trade and Migration." Migration Policy Institute, Washington, D.C., 2003.

Kawell, JoAnn. "Going to the Source: A History of the U.S. War on Cocaine." Unpublished draft manuscript.

Laserna, Roberto. *Las Drogas y el Ajuste en Bolivia: Economía Clandestina y Políticas Públicas.* La Paz: Cedla, 1993.

Laserna, Roberto, Gonzalo Vargas, and Juan Torrico. "La Estructura Industrial del Narcotráfico en Cochabamba." Cochabamba, Bolivia: UNDCP-PNUD, unpublished manuscript, 1995.

Lawyers Committee for Human Rights and Miguel Agustín Pro Juárez Human Rights Center. *Legalized Injustice: Mexican Criminal Procedure and Human Rights.* New York: Lawyers Committee for Human Rights, 2001. (LCHR is now Human Rights First.)

Ledebur, Kathryn. "Coca and Conflict in the Chapare." *Drug War Monitor.* Washington Office on Latin America, July 2002.

Leóns, Madeline Barbara, and Harry Sanabria. *Coca, Cocaine, and the Bolivian Reality.* Albany: State University of New York Press, 1997.

Lobe, Thomas. "The Rise and Demise of the Office of Public Safety." *Armed Forces and Society* 9, no. 2 (Winter 1983).

Loveman, Brian. *Por la Patria: Politics and the Armed Forces in Latin America.* Wilmington, Del.: Scholarly Resources, 1999.

Lumpe, Lora. "U.S. Law Enforcement Involvement in Counternarcotics Operations in Latin America." Appendix Bolivia. June 2002, p. 1. Available on WOLA website, www.wola.org/ddhr_documents.htm.

Marshall, Jonathan. "CIA Assets and the Rise of the Guadalajara Connection." In *War on Drugs: Studies in the Failure of U.S. Narcotics Policy.* Eds. Alfred W. McCoy and Alan A. Block. Boulder: Westview, 1992.

McClintock, Cynthia, and Fabian Vallas. *Cooperation at a Cost: The United States and Peru.* New York: Routledge, 2003.

Menzel, Sewall. *Fire in the Andes: U.S. Foreign Policy and Cocaine Politics in Peru and Bolivia.* New York: University Press of America, 1996.

Montúfar, Cesar, and T. Whitfield, eds. *Turbulencia en los Andes y Plan Colombia.* Quito: Universidad Andina Simón Bolívar, Corporación Editora Nacional, 2003.

Nadelman, Ethan A. *Cops Across Borders: The Internationalization of U.S. Criminal Law Enforcement.* University Park: Pennsylvania State University Press, 1993.

Olson, Eric L. *The Evolving Role of Mexico's Military in Public Security and Antinarcotics Programs.* Washington, D.C.: Washington Office on Latin America, June 1996.

Organization of American States (OAS), Interamerican Drug Abuse Control Commission (CICAD). *Progress Report in Drug Control, Multilateral Evaluation Mechanism (MEM).* 1999, 2000, 2001, and 2002.

Painter, James. *Bolivia and Coca: A Study in Dependency.* Boulder: Lynne Rienner Publishers, 1994.

Palmieri, Gustavo. "Themes and Debates in Public Security; Criminal Investigations." Washington Office on Latin America, July 2000.

Palomeque, Edison. *Diagnóstico Sobre Seguridad Ciudadana en Ecuador.* Quito: FLACSO/Ecuador–PAHO/WHO, 2002.

Pinheiro, Paulo Sergio. "Democracies Without Citizenship." *Report on the Americas.* New York: NACLA, September/October 1996.

Ritter, Martha, ed. *Children of Law 1008.* Andean Information Network, 1998.

Rojas, Isaías. "The Adventure of Zero Coca: Drug Control Policy and the Democratic Transition in Peru." *Drug War Monitor* briefing series. Washington Office on Latin America, February 2003.

Roncken, Theo, et al., eds. *The Drug War in the Skies: The U.S. Air Bridge Denial Strategy.* Cochabamba: Transnational Institute, 1999.

Rospigliosi, Fernando. *Montesinos y las Fuerzas Armadas: Cómo Controló Durante una Década las Instituciones Militares.* Lima: IEP, 2000.

Sarles, Margaret J. "USAID's Support of Justice Reform in Latin America." In *Rule of Law in Latin America: The International Promotion of Judicial Reform.* Ed. Pilar Domingo and Rachel Sieder. London: Institute of Latin American Studies, University of London, 2001.

Stone, Christopher, and Heather Ward. "Democratic Policing; A Framework for Action." *Policing and Society* 10, no. 1, 2000.

Storrs, K. Larry. *Mexican Drug Certification Issues: U.S. Congressional Action, 1986–2001.* Washington, D.C.: Congressional Research Service, 8 January 2002.

Tanaka, Martín, ed. *Las Fuerzas Armadas en la Región Andina. ¿No Deliberantes o Actores Políticos?* Lima: Comisión Andina de Juristas (CAJ) y la Embajada de Finlandia, 2001.

Transnational Institute et al. *Democracy, Human Rights, and Militarism in the War on Drugs in Latin America.* Guatemala: TNI, Cedib and Inforpress Centroamericana, April 1997.

Transparency International. *Corruption Perceptions Index 2003.* Berlin: 7 October 2003.

Truth and Reconciliation Commission. *Report of the Truth and Reconciliation Commission.* Lima, 28 August 2003.

U.S. Agency for International Development. *1999 Annual Report, January 1–December 31, 1999: Bolivia Administration of Justice Project.* Project No. 511-0626, Supplement.

———. *Congressional Budget Justification, FY2002, FY2004.*

U.S. Coast Guard. *Coast Guard Publication 1: U.S. Coast Guard—America's Maritime Guardian.* 1 January 2002.

U.S. Congress. 22 USC 2291j-1. *Foreign Relations Authorization Act 2002–2003 (PL 107-228).* Sec. 706. International Drug Control Certification Procedures. 30 September 2002.

U.S. Defense Department and State Department. *Foreign Military Training and DoD Engagement Activities of Interest in Fiscal Years 1999 and 2000: A Report to Congress.* Washington, D.C.: March 2000.

———. *Foreign Military Training and DoD Engagement Activities of Interest in Fiscal Years 2000 and 2001. Volume I.* Washington, D.C.: March 2001.

———. *Foreign Military Training and DoD Engagement Activities of Interest in Fiscal Years 2001 and 2001: A Report to Congress.* Washington, D.C.: March 2002.

————. *Foreign Military Training and DoD Engagement Activities of Interest in Fiscal Years 2002 and 2003: Joint Report to Congress*. Washington, D.C.: March 2003.

U.S. General Accounting Office (GAO). *The Drug War: Counternarcotics Programs in Colombia and Peru*. GAO/T-NSIAD-92-9. Washington, D.C.: February 1992.

————. *Foreign Aid: Police Training and Assistance*. GAO/NSIAD-92-118. 5 March 1992.

————. *Drug Control—Status of Counternarcotics Efforts in Mexico*. GAO/T-NSIAD-98-129. 1998.

————. *Drug Control: U.S. Counternarcotics Efforts in Colombia Face Continuing Challenges*. GAO/NSIAD-98-60. 1998.

————. *Foreign Assistance; Rule of Law Funding Worldwide for Fiscal Years 1993–1998*. GAO/NSIAD-99-158. 30 June 1999.

————. *Drug Control: DEA's Strategies and Operations in the 1990s*. GAO/GGD-99-108. July 1999.

————. *Drug Control: Efforts to Develop Alternatives to Cultivating Illicit Crops in Colombia Have Made Little Progress and Face Serious Obstacles*. GAO 02-291. February 2002.

————. *U.S. Democracy Programs in Six Latin American Countries Have Yielded Modest Results*. GAO-03-358. March 2003.

U.S. House of Representatives. *Congressional Record*. Vol. 142. "Mexico Must Get Serious About Stopping Drug Trafficking." Washington, D.C., 1 February 1996.

————. *Congressional Record*. Vol. 142. "Mexico Not Cooperating to Stop Drug Trafficking." Washington, D.C., 28 February 1996.

————. *Congressional Record*. Vol. 143. "Disapproval of Determination of President Regarding Mexico." HJ Res 58. Washington, D.C., 13 March 1997.

U.S. Information Agency. *Briefing Paper*. No. B–82–97. Washington, D.C.: USIA, 20 October 1997.

U.S. Justice Department, Drug Enforcement Administration. *A Tradition of Excellence: The History of the DEA from 1973 to 1998*. "The Murder of DEA Special Agent Enrique Camarena." Washington, D.C., April 1999.

————. *Mexico Country Profile for 2003*. Washington, D.C., November 2003.

U.S. Office of Management and Budget. Performance and Management Assessments, FY2004.

U.S. Senate. *Congressional Record*. "Mexico Foreign Aid Disapproval Resolution." SJ Res. 42. Washington, D.C., 26 March 1998.

U.S. State Department. *Defense Trade News* 5, no. 3 (July and October 1994).

————. *Report to Congress on Plan Colombia and Related Program*. Washington, D.C.: State Department, July 2000.

————. *FY2004 Congressional Budget Justification for Foreign Operations*. Washington, D.C.: U.S. State Department, February 2003.

U.S. State Department. Bureau of International Narcotics and Law Enforcement Affairs (INL). *International Narcotics Control Strategy Report (1995)*. Washington, D.C.: INL/U.S. State Department. Released March 1996.

————. *International Narcotics Control Strategy Report (1996)*. Washington, D.C.: INL/U.S. State Department. Released March 1997.

————. *International Narcotics Control Strategy Report (1997)*. Washington, D.C.: INL/U.S. State Department. Released March 1998.

———. *International Narcotics Control Strategy Report (2000)*. Washington, D.C.: INL/U.S. State Department. Released 1 March 2001.

———. *International Narcotics Control Strategy Report (2001)*. Washington, D.C.: INL/U.S. State Department. Released 1 March 2002.

———. *International Narcotics Control Strategy Report (2002)*. Washington, D.C.: INL/U.S. State Department. Released 1 March 2003.

———. *International Narcotics Control Strategy Report (2003)*. Washington, D.C.: INL/U.S. State Department. Released 1 March 2004.

U.S. State Department. Bureau of Resource Management. *FY2002 Congressional Budget Justification for Foreign Operations*. Released 2 July 2001.

———. *FY2003 Congressional Budget Justification for Foreign Operations*. Released 15 April 2002.

———. *FY2004 Congressional Budget Justification for Foreign Operations*. Released 13 February 2003.

U.S. State Department. Bureau of Democracy, Human Rights, and Labor. *Country Reports on Human Rights Practices for 2001*. Released March 2002.

———. *Country Reports on Human Rights Practices for 2002*. Released March 2003.

U.S. State Department. Bureau of Western Hemisphere Affairs (WHA). *Country Information*, Bolivia, "Background Notes," November 2003.

U.S. State Department. Counterterrorism Office. *Patterns of Global Terrorism 2002*. "Western Hemisphere Overview." Released April 2003.

U.S. Treasury Department. Bureau of Alcohol, Tobacco, and Firearms (ATF). *ITAR: International Traffic in Arms, Annual Report FY1993*.

U.S. White House. *The National Security Strategy of the United States of America*. September 2002.

U.S. White House, Office of Management and Budget. *2003 Supplemental Appropriations Request to Congress*. Washington, D.C.: White House, 25 March 2003.

U.S. White House, Office of National Drug Control Policy. *Report to Congress, Volume 1: United States and Mexico Counterdrug Cooperation*. Washington, D.C., 1997.

———. *National Drug Control Strategy 2003*. February 2003.

United Nations Committee Against Torture. *Report on Mexico Produced by the Committee Under Article 20 of the Convention, and Reply from the Government of Mexico*. UN Doc. CAT/C/75. 26 May 2003.

United Nations Development Programme. *Human Development Report 2001: Making New Technologies Work for Human Development*. New York and Oxford, UK: Oxford University Press, 2001.

United Nations Development Programme, Colombia. *Human Development Report for Colombia, 2003: El Conflicto, Callejón con Salida*. Bogota: September 2003.

———. *Informe de Desarrollo Humano en Bolivia 2002*. La Paz: PNUD. 2003.

United Nations High Commissioner for Human Rights. *Diagnóstico Sobre la Situación de los Derechos Humanos en México*. Mexico: United Nations, 2003.

United Nations Office on Drugs and Crime, Caribbean Regional Office. *Caribbean Drug Trends 2001–2002*. Bridgetown, Barbados, February 2003.

United Nations Special Rapporteur on Extrajudicial, Summary, or Arbitrary Executions. *Report of Ms. Asma Jahangir, submitted pursuant to Commission on Human Rights resolution 1999/35, Visit to Mexico*. UN Doc. E/CN.4/2000/3/Add.3. 25 November 1999.

United Nations Special Rapporteur on the Independence of Judges and Lawyers. *Civil and Political Rights, Including the Questions of: Independence of the Judiciary, Administration of Justice, Impunity.* UN Doc. E/CN.4/2002/72/Add.1. 24 January 2002.

United Nations Special Rapporteur on Torture. *Question of the Human Rights of All Persons Subjected to Any Form of Detention or Imprisonment, in Particular: Torture and Other Cruel, Inhuman, or Degrading Treatment or Punishment.* UN Doc. E/CN.4/1998/38/Add.2. 14 January 1998.

United Nations Working Group on Arbitrary Detention. *Civil and Political Rights, Including the Question of Torture and Detention: Report of the Working Group on Arbitrary Detention on Its Visit to Mexico, Addendum.* UN Doc. E/CN.4/2003/8/Add.3. 17 December 2002.

Washington Office on Latin America. *Demilitarizing Public Order; International Assistance for Police Reforms in Central America.* November 1994.

———. *Demilitarizing Public Order; The International Community, Police Reform and Human Rights in Central America and Haiti.* November 1995.

———. *Sustaining Police Reform in Central America.* October 2002.

Wiener, Robert. "Colombia's Faceless Courts." *NACLA Report on the Americas* 30, no. 2 (September/October 1996).

Williams, Jacqueline. *Waging the War on Drugs in Bolivia.* Washington, D.C.: Washington Office on Latin America, 1996.

World Health Organization. *World Report on Violence and Health.* Geneva, 2002.

Youngers, Coletta. *Deconstructing Democracy: Peru Under Alberto Fujimori.* Washington, D.C.: WOLA, 2000.

———. *Violencia Politica y Socieded Civil en Perú.* Lima: IEP, 2003.

Zirnite, Peter. "Under Fire: The Drug Enforcement Administration in Latin America." Unpublished monograph, WOLA, 1998.

The Contributors

Gerardo Cordero is a journalist and assistant professor of sociology at the University of Puerto Rico. He holds two master's degrees: one in social sciences and the other in sociology. He is the former vice president of the Puerto Rico Journalism Association (ASPPRO), where he also anchored the radio news forum "Frente al Pueblo" for seven years. He currently writes for the Courts and Police Section of *El Nuevo Día*.

Rut Diamint is a researcher with the Creating Community in the Americas Program of the Woodrow Wilson International Center for Scholars in Washington, D.C. She is also professor at the University of Torcuato Di Tella in Buenos Aires and has served as adviser to the undersecretary of policy and strategy in the Defense Ministry of Argentina (1993–1996). She has been published in books and academic journals on issues of regional and hemispheric security, and is the author of *Democracy and Security in Latin America*.

Laurie Freeman is associate for Mexico and international drug control policy at the Washington Office on Latin America (WOLA). Freeman worked for more than three years in Mexico, first at the Miguel Agustín Pro Juárez Human Rights Center, and later as a researcher for the *Washington Post's* Mexico bureau. While at the *Post*, she contributed to a series of stories on the rule of law in Mexico that won the 2003 Pulitzer Prize for International Reporting.

Adam Isacson has worked since 1995 at the Center for International Policy (CIP), an independent research and advocacy organization in Washington, D.C., where he coordinates a program that monitors security and U.S. military assistance to Latin America and the Caribbean. Since 1997, Isacson's project has focused especially on Colombia, and his study of U.S. policy and Colombia's peace process has taken him to Colombia twenty-four times, visiting eleven of the country's thirty-two departments.

Kathryn Ledebur studied Andean history at FLACSO in Quito, Ecuador. She has collaborated with a series of human rights and drug policy organizations in the United States and Latin America. Since 1997, she has worked at the Andean Information Network—an organization dedicated to investigation, analysis, education, and dialogue on the impacts of U.S.-funded counterdrugs policy—in Cochabamba, Bolivia, and has been AIN's director since 1999.

Rachel Neild is senior fellow at WOLA. She formerly directed WOLA's public security reform program, which dealt with issues of international police assistance and democratic police reforms in Haiti, Central America, and Mexico, with a particular focus on the role of civil society in defining new citizen security debates. She is a consultant for the Open Society Justice Initiative and has also consulted for the Inter-American Development Bank and the OECD.

María Clemencia Ramírez Lemus received her Ph.D. in anthropology from Harvard University. She is currently a researcher for the Colombian Institute of Anthropology and History and teaches at the University of the Andes. Since 1975, she has worked in ethnohistorical and ethnological research with indigenous groups and small farmers in the Putumayo, Colombia's Amazonian region. She is author of *Between the State and the Guerrillas: Identity and Citizenship in the Coca Farmers' Movement in the Putumayo* and *Fluid Borders Between the Andes, the Piedmont, and the Jungle: The Case of the Sibundoy Valley from the 11th to the 13th Centuries*, as well as coauthor of *Cultural Atlas of the Colombian Amazon: The Construction of the Territory in the 20th Century*.

Fredy Rivera Vélez holds a master's degree in the social sciences, with a specialization in social and cultural modernity, granted by the Latin America Faculty of Social Sciences (FLACSO) in Mexico City. Since 1996 he has been editor of *Ecuador Debate*, the magazine of the Andean Center for Popular Action (CAAP). He is currently associate professor and researcher at FLACSO's Ecuador offices in their master's programs in international relations, political studies, and anthropology. His most recent publication is *Minimalist Democracy and Military Phantoms in Modern Ecuador*, published by the Andean Commission of Jurists in Lima, Peru.

Rick Rockwell teaches journalism at American University in Washington, D.C., and has more than two decades of experience in the media as a reporter, producer, and news manager. He has worked for ABC News as a TV and radio producer, The Discovery Channel as a senior producer, and PBS' "News Hour" as a freelance reporter. He covered the last two Mexican presidential elections and the 2001 Nicaraguan elections for various news organizations, including the Associated Press. He is coauthor of *Media Power in Central America*.

Jorge Rodríguez Beruff is dean of the University of Puerto Rico's Social Sciences Department. He holds a doctorate in political science from the University of York in England. His most recent books are *Fronteras en Conflicto, Guerra Contra las Drogas, Militarización y Democracia en el Caribe, Puerto Rico y Vieques*, and *Las Memorias de Leahy*. He is currently working on a study of the relationship between Puerto Rico and the Dominican Republic.

Isaías Rojas served for several years on the steering committee of the Legal Defense Institute (IDL) in Lima, Peru, and the editorial board for IDL's magazine, *ideele*, of which he is a founding member. He has participated with the National Human Rights Coordination of Peru (La Coordinadora) in delegations to the Interamerican Human Rights Commission, the United Nations Human Rights Commission, and the general assembly of the Organization of American States. His research has focused primarily on political violence and human rights in Peru. Currently a doctoral candidate in anthropology at the Johns Hopkins University, he is working on a critical examination of the experience of truth and reconciliation commissions in Latin America.

Jorge Luis Sierra Guzmán is a Mexican journalist specializing in military and national security themes. Since 1990, he has covered drug trafficking, national security, and military affairs. He has worked as a researcher and consultant with several Mexican nongovernmental human rights organizations and served as advisor on security and defense issues for the PRD in the Chamber of Deputies during the 57th congressional period (1998–1999).

Kimberly Stanton, deputy director and director of studies at WOLA, holds a doctorate in political science from the University of Chicago. She worked for several years as a researcher and program officer at the John D. and Catherine T. MacArthur Foundation, focusing on the peace processes in Central America, U.S.-Cuban relations, and international governance and human rights. She subsequently served as human rights program director at the Robert F. Kennedy Memorial Center for Human Rights. She has consulted for several foundations and for the Inter-American Development Bank and is a member of the board of directors of the U.S. Office on Colombia and the advisory board of the Lexington Institute.

John Walsh is senior associate for the Andes and drug policy at WOLA. Before joining WOLA, he served as director of research at Drug Strategies, a policy research group that builds support for more pragmatic and effective approaches to U.S. drug problems. Walsh also worked on the Rethinking Bretton Woods Project at the Center of Concern, an effort to forge consensus on ideas for reforming the World Bank and the IMF in support of equitable and sustainable development. He holds a master's degree in public policy from the Institute for Policy Studies at the Johns Hopkins University.

- **Editors**

   Coletta Youngers studies human rights and political developments in the Andean region of South America as well as U.S. foreign policy toward the Andes. At present a WOLA senior fellow, she was an associate and then senior associate at WOLA from 1987 to 2003. Youngers is author of *Violencia Política y Sociedad Civil en el Perú: Historia de la Coordinadora Nacional de Derechos Humanos,* published by the Instituto de Estudios Peruanos in Lima, Peru, and regularly contributes articles to *NACLA Report on the Americas, Foreign Policy in Focus*, and Lima journals *ideele* and *Que Hacer.* Prior to joining WOLA in 1987, she worked for Catholic Relief Services in Lima, Peru, managing development projects. She holds a master's degree in public affairs from the Woodrow Wilson School of Public and International Affairs at Princeton University.

   Eileen Rosin has worked on social justice issues in Latin America for over twenty years, specializing in the areas of international development and human rights. She lived in El Salvador for seven years, working with health care and rural integrated development NGOs, and spent more than three years with the United Nations Verification Mission in Guatemala evaluating compliance with the Guatemalan peace accords. Rosin has a master's of science in development management from American University.

Index

401

About the Book

A lthough the United States has spent more than $25 billion on international drug control programs, it has failed to reduce the supply of cocaine and heroin entering the country. It has, however, succeeded in generating widespread, often profoundly damaging, consequences, most notably in Latin America and the Caribbean. The authors of *Drugs and Democracy in Latin America* offer a comprehensive review of U.S. drug control policies toward the region and assess the impact of those policies on democracy and human rights. Included are country and regional case studies that illustrate that impact, plus detailed descriptions of U.S. military and police counterdrug assistance programs.

A project of the Washington Office on Latin America (WOLA), this major work is the first systematic, region-wide documentation and analysis of the collateral damage caused by the U.S. war on drugs.

Coletta A. Youngers and **Eileen Rosin** codirected the Drugs, Democracy, and Human Rights project at the Washington Office on Latin America (WOLA).